The Izumi Shikibu Diary

*Harvard–Yenching Institute
Monograph Series · Volume 19*

The Izumi Shikibu Diary

A Romance of the Heian Court

Translated with an Introduction

by

Edwin A. Cranston

Harvard University Press
Cambridge, Massachusetts
1969

© Copyright 1969 by the Harvard-Yenching Institute
All rights reserved
Distributed in Great Britain by Oxford University Press, London
Library of Congress Catalog Card Number 69–13766
SBN 674–46985–2
Printed in the United States of America

To Fumiko

A millennium ago the literate society of Japan was concentrated in the great capital city of Heian, the ancestor of the modern Kyoto, an imperial metropolis spread across a verdant plain enclosed by steep, wooded mountains. It was a city of wooden buildings with roofs of tile or thatch, arranged along straight streets running east and west or north and south, a pattern learned from the capital of T'ang China as orthodox for the seat of an imperial court. "Heian," meaning "Peace and Stability," also designates the period from the founding of the city in 794 to the passing of power into the hands of provincial warriors in 1192. During the Heian Period the city was home, the center of their affections and their civilization, to the men and women whose lives were caught up in the functioning of the imperial institution. It was a beehive of political intrigue behind a symmetrical bureaucratic facade (borrowed, like the street system, from China), covered with a shimmering veil of manners, art, and taste. At its center, in theory the reason for its existence, was a sacerdotal Emperor who reigned but did not rule, exhausting his energies in court ceremonial and the bedchambers of his consorts. His Fujiwara ministers, the real rulers of the capital, kept him supplied with their nubile daughters, and their own rivalries were inextricably involved with the success or failure of the imperial consorts in producing an heir. The minister who could manage to have his grandson appointed Heir Apparent ruled the land. For those too far beneath the handful of men at the top ever to aspire to the seats of power, the court bureaucracy nevertheless provided rank and office and the opportunity for yearly advancement.

The people of Heian lived amidst scenes of lush and vivid natural beauty. The city was bordered by clear running water to the east and west, and was provided with lakes or large ponds suitable for boating. Flowering cherry and plum were planted in profusion, and in autumn the surrounding hills mingled the green of pines with scarlet maple leaves. The myriad grasses and shrubs beloved of the Japanese grew upon the plain, and dense bamboo thickets reached to the foot of the western mountains. Within the city the wealthy nobles built mansions with elaborate gardens complete with lakes and hills in miniature and blossoming trees for each season. Beyond the city were quiet country retreats, and Buddhist temples reared their roofs over the foliage of the nearby peaks and valleys. Sensitivity to natural beauty has always been a hallmark of Japanese taste in literature, art, and life, and the open pavilion-style of Heian architecture kept people in constant close contact with this source of inspiration.

The educated men and women of this court society possessed a centuries-old tradition of poetry, an art to which they were devoted as few other civilizations have been, and which played an important role in their social life. Gradually they began to experiment with prose, both fiction and non-fiction, and during the great age of Heian laid the foundation for the rich, millennial tradition of Japanese literature. Perhaps the greatest triumphs of this literature result from its preoccupation with the never-ceasing flow of time, and its finest moments come when a segment of time is preserved, a scene or an age is caught in amber. In Japanese literature the human heart stands troubled before the transcience of life, and nowhere more so than in the Heian Period, when life was felt to be sweet, for all that it might vanish like a dream. The phenomena of nature become symbols of the passing of time. The spring blossoms and autumn leaves, lovely as they are, mark the process of the years. The snow and the cycles of the moon pile old age on man. Cries of migratory birds are a reminder that yet another season has come and gone, and dewdrops symbolize both tears and the evanescence of human life. But the sweet and sometimes dark melancholy which forms the underlying tone of many of the writings of this period is balanced by the comic spirit which fortunately also makes up part of the Japanese personality, and which crops up again and again in Japanese art and letters. Heian literature contains humorous passages ranging from broad slapstick to urbane comedy, from pratfalls, puns, and practical jokes to deliciously satirical descriptions of lovers' quarrels and monks' pomposity. Wit and verbal dexterity were particularly prized in elegant verse. It is to our own enrichment that, witty or grave, pensive or gay, the men and women of the Heian court still live in the poems, memoirs, and novels of their time.

A few examples of the best of Heian prose literature have become familiar in English translation. The most important of these are Arthur Waley's translations of Murasaki Shikibu's *Tale of Genji* (first published complete by Allen and Unwin, London, 1935, and now available as a Modern Library Giant, Random House, New York, 1960) and selected portions of Sei Shōnagon's *Pillow Book* (London, Allen and Unwin, 1928, and New York, Grove Press, 1960),★ and Edward Seidensticker's *The Gossamer Years* (Tokyo and Rutland, Vt., Tuttle, 1964), a translation of the *Kagerō nikki* (first published in 1955 in *Transactions of the Asiatic Society of Japan*, ser. 3, IV). These three works, discussed in the section on genre, were written during a period of roughly sixty years spanning the late tenth and early eleventh centuries. They are all by women, a unique characteristic of much of the finest Heian writing.

This book is an outgrowth of a doctoral dissertation submitted to Stanford University in December 1965. It contains the first complete, annotated English translation of a minor classic of Japanese literature, the *Izumi Shikibu nikki*. The authorship and date of this work are matters of considerable controversy, but the central character, the poetess Izumi Shikibu, was a contemporary of Murasaki Shikibu and Sei Shōnagon, which is to say that she lived during the late tenth and early eleventh centuries—the high point of Heian civilization. In her own way she is as famous as the other two ladies. The ideals and methods which have guided the preparation of the English version, and of the annotation, are discussed

---

★The complete *Pillow Book* has recently appeared in an annotated English translation by Ivan Morris, *The Pillow Book of Sei Shōnagon*. 2 vols. (New York: Columbia, 1967).

briefly on pages 126, 127 of the Introduction. The latter consists of a short biographical sketch of Izumi Shikibu, a more detailed treatment of several important problems surrounding the work, and a survey of the development of genres in early Japanese literature.

From their inception this study and translation have profited from the guidance of Professor Edward G. Seidensticker, formerly of Stanford University and now of the University of Michigan. It was in a seminar given by Professor Seidensticker at Stanford in the spring of 1963 that I began my study of the *Izumi Shikibu nikki*. I am particularly indebted to him for his tireless efforts over the following two years to rid the translation of infelicities. Professors William H. McCullough and Robert W. Ackerman of Stanford University have also placed me in their debt for their valuable criticisms and guidance, and for their willing expenditure of time. I am deeply obligated to Professor Endō Yoshimoto of Kyoto University for his inexhaustible kindness and generosity, both personal and professional. He has given unstintingly of his time and learning in discussing many difficult points in the translation and study. Fellowship funds supplied by the Ford Foundation and administered by the Foreign Area Fellowship Program made possible a year's writing and research in Kyoto during 1964 and 1965. Another grant, from the East Asian Research Center at Harvard University, supported revision and augmentation of the manuscript in the summer of 1967. I am most grateful for the generosity and helpfulness of all connected with the Fellowship Program and the Research Center. These organizations and their personnel are of course not responsible for the conclusions, opinions, and other statements in this book, which are my own. I further wish to thank my colleagues at Harvard, Professors Howard Hibbett and Donald H. Shively, for examining the revised chapter on genre, and for their help and encouragement over the years I have known them. Finally, it gives me great satisfaction to thank my wife Fumiko, a professional performer of Japanese classical dance and research assistant in Japanese art at Harvard's Fogg Art Museum, for compiling the index, aiding materially in research, and writing all the *kanji* and *kana* in the many manuscript stages of the book. Her total devotion to the work and to the author made the book possible, and it is with gratitude that I dedicate it to her.

Cambridge   Edwin A. Cranston
1968

Contents

Introduction

I. Izumi Shikibu

Izumi Shikibu's life was one long scandal. Or so it must have seemed to her contemporaries. While the extant sources do not provide sufficient information for a complete biography, it is clear that she largely earned the piquant reputation which still clings to her name. She was intimately involved in the lives of several different men. Her affairs with the two imperial princes, Tametaka 爲尊 and Atsumichi 敦道, brothers of the Heir Apparent (concluding with the untimely death of each), elevated her to the status of *femme fatale extraordinaire*, and made her a prime target of court gossip. Her fame as a poet is deeply involved with her reputation as a passionate woman. A standard Japanese reference work appraises her thus: "Her poems are passionate and free, exploding with brilliance; the wealth of her imagination is like heavenly chargers coursing the void; and her freedom of expression is rare. She must be accounted the first poetess of our land."[1]

It is not known when she was born. Various dates have been

suggested, among them 966, 968, 974, 977, and 979.[2] The earliest genealogical note on Izumi Shikibu appears in *Chūko kasen sanjūroku-ninden* 中古歌仙三十六人傳:[3]

> Izumi Shikibu 和泉式部, daughter of Ōe no Masamune 大江雅致, Governor of Echizen 越前. According to another theory, daughter of Provisional Middle Counsellor[4] Lord Kanehira 懷平 . . . Her mother was the daughter of Taira no Yasuhira 平保衡, Governor of Etchū 越中. She [the mother] was wet nurse to Grand Empress Dowager Masako [Shōshi][5] 昌子,[6] and was styled Suke no Naishi 介内侍.[7] Tachibana no Michisada 橘道貞, Governor of Izumi 和泉, made her [the daughter] his wife. Hence she was styled Izumi Shikibu. Her child-name was Omotomaro 御許丸. She was a lady-in-waiting to Jōtōmon'in 上東門院.[8]

The alternate theory here mentioned concerning Izumi's parentage, that she was the daughter of Fujiwara no Kanehira (died in 1017 at 65),[9] is the weaker of the two. Evidence that Izumi was the daughter of Ōe no Masamune is provided by Masamune's close association with her first husband, Michisada, and by a few references in contemporary documents. In the *Akazome Emon shū* 赤染衛門集[10] there is a poem prefaced by the words "Takachika, beginning to pay court to Masamune's daughter," followed by a reply whose author is given as "her elder sister, Izumi Shikibu."[11] Again, Izumi is mentioned in *Midō Kampaku ki* 御堂關白記, the diary of Fujiwara no Michinaga 藤原道長 (966–1027), entry for Kannin 寛仁 2 (1018). 1. 21,[12] as Kō Shikibu 江式部,[13] Kō being an obvious abbreviation of Ōe.[14] And finally, the *Shūishū* 拾遺集, a *waka*[15] anthology compiled by imperial command during Izumi's lifetime, lists her famous "Kuraki yori" poem (see page 6) as by "Masamune's daughter Shikibu."

A few other sources contain brief notes. *Shūgaishō* 拾芥抄[16] repeats the information given in *Chūko kasenden*. *Sompi bummyaku* 尊卑分脈[17] has alternate genealogies, one of which lists Izumi as the daughter of Fujiwara no Suketaka 資高, and the other as the daughter of Kanehira. Appended to the first genealogy is the note: "This was

4

Izumi Shikibu, lady-in-waiting to Jōtōmon'in; poet. Actually the daughter of Ōe no Masamune, Governor of Echizen . . . Her mother was the daughter of Taira no Yasuhira, Governor of Etchū.'' The second is followed by the comments: ''Styled Izumi Shikibu. Some people say the daughter of Ōe no Masamune, Governor of Etchū. Suketō 資任, Governor of Izumi, adopted her.''[18] Finally, *Fusōshūyōshū keizu* 扶桑拾葉集系圖[19] has the note: ''Daughter of Ōe no Masamune, Governor of Etchū. Suketaka adopted her and brought her up.''[20]

Fujiwara no Suketaka was a nephew of the Kanehira mentioned above. Suketō was the son of Yoritō 賴任 (d. 1030), Kanehira's cousin and brother of the poet Kintō 公任 (966–1041). The same arguments used in the case of Kanehira militate against Izumi having been the daughter of Suketaka. In addition, according to *Ouki* 小右記,[21] Suketaka underwent his *gembuku*[22] ceremony on Chōwa 長和 2 (1013).1.26, and hence would hardly have been old enough either to father or adopt Izumi Shikibu.[23] In the case of Suketō his position as Governor of Izumi Province may have been the source of the confusion. There is also an obvious conflict as to whether Ōe no Masamune was Governor of Etchū or of Echizen. *Midō Kampaku ki* corroborates *Chūko kasenden*. The entry of Kankō 寛弘 7 (1010). 3.30 states that he was appointed Governor of Echizen on the death of the incumbent.[24] At the time of his appointment he held the office of Director of the Bureau of Carpentry.[25] Another office he had previously held, and one important to the future of his daughter, was that of Senior Secretary[26] in the household of Grand Empress Dowager Masako, consort of the Retired Emperor Reizei. According to *Chūko kasenden*, his wife, Izumi's mother, was also in the service of Masako. It is natural to assume then that Izumi was brought up at court.

Her two royal lovers, the Princes Tametaka and Atsumichi, were Reizei's children by a secondary consort. Reizei numbered two future Emperors among his sons. The first was Kazan 花山 (968–1008; r. 984–986), whose mother was Fujiwara no Kaneko [Kaishi] 懷子 (945–975). The other was Sanjō 三條 (976–1017; r. 1011–1016).

5

His mother was Yukiko [Chōshi] 超子 (d. 982), Kaneko's first cousin and sister of Michinaga. Unlike Masako, Reizei's Kōgō 皇后 or Empress, Kaneko and Yukiko held the lesser rank of Nyōgo 女御 (see translation, note 373). Tametaka (977–1002) and Atsumichi (981–1007) were Sanjō's younger brothers. After Yukiko's death in 982 the three brothers were brought up at the home of their maternal grandfather, Fujiwara no Kaneie 兼家 (929–990).

As we have seen from the reference to the *Akazome Emon shū*, Izumi Shikibu had a younger sister who was the object of the affections of Akazome's son Takachika. Allusions to "harakaratachi" or "harakaradomo" (brothers and/or sisters) in the prose prefaces to her poems 240 and 748 (723)[27] indicate that she had at least one other brother or sister.

Presumably Izumi was brought up at the court of Masako, and was called Omotomaro when she was a little girl. *Shūishū* 1342 calls her Shikibu 式部, a typical nickname of the sort given young ladies in court service. One may infer that by the time of the compilation of the *Shūishū*[28] Izumi was probably a lady-in-waiting to Masako, and that her father may have held some position in the Shikibushō 式部省, the Ministry of Ceremonial.[29] This poem is probably Izumi's most famous:

Composed and sent to Shōkū Shōnin:

Kuraki yori	From darkness
Kuraki michi ni zo	Into the path of darkness
Irinubeki	Must I enter:
Haruka ni terase	Shine upon me from afar,
Yama no ha no tsuki	O moon above the mountain crest.[30]

The excellence of this poem, Izumi's sole representation in the *Shūishū*, must have been recognized by the compiler. At the time of its composition she was probably a very young woman, perhaps only a girl, and had not yet gained the fame that put sixty-seven of her poems into the next imperial anthology, the *Goshūishū* 後拾遺集 (compiled in 1086). It also shows another side of her nature, her

6

longing for the bliss and peace offered by the Buddhist religion, for an escape from the whirlpool of worldly love in which she was destined to pass her life.[31] Shōkū Shōnin 性空上人[32] (910–1007), born a Tachibana and as such a distant relative of Izumi's first husband, was a renowned cleric of the period. In 966 he founded a temple, the Engyōji 圓教寺, on Shoshazan 書寫山 in Harima 播磨, and lived there until his death. He was a favorite preceptor of Retired Emperors En'yū 圓融 (959–991; r. 969–984) and Kazan, the latter of whom twice paid him the honor of visiting his temple, and of Empress Masako. It is possible that her service with Masako may have given Izumi Shikibu an opportunity to meet him. Evidently Izumi felt religiously drawn to Shōkū, for "Kuraki yori" is not the only poem she sent him (see translation, note 82). He also figures importantly in legends about her.

It is not clear just when Izumi married Tachibana no Michisada. Shimizu Fumio argues that she was still unmarried at the time of the compilation of the *Shūishū* (which he places about 996), since her name appears in that anthology as "Masamune ga musume Shikibu" (Masamune's daughter Shikibu) rather than as "Izumi Shikibu," as is the case in later *chokusenshū* 勅撰集 (anthologies compiled at imperial command).[33] This evidence of course is hardly conclusive, and is rendered even more questionable by uncertainty as to the actual date of the *Shūishū*. Izumi may well have been married to Michisada for some time before he became Governor of Izumi Province, from which circumstance the first component of her appellation undoubtedly stems. According to *Ouki* he was occupying his post in that province in the ninth month of Chōhō 長保 1 (999), and it may be assumed that she had become his wife by that time.[34] Yamagishi Tokuhei speculates that Michisada may have been somewhat over thirty at the time of his marriage, and Izumi eighteen or nineteen.[35] At an undetermined date they had a daughter, Koshikibu 小式部. Apparently Michisada and Izumi's father Masamune were friendly associates, for Michisada held the parallel post of Provisional Senior Secretary (Gondaishin 權大進) in Empress Masako's household, and Masamune occupied Michisada's residence in the capital while the latter was away governing his province.[36] It would seem that Izumi accompanied her husband there, but spent some of her time with her father in the capital.

The marriage of Michisada and Izumi Shikibu was not destined to endure. Late in 999 Grand Empress Dowager Masako, who had been ill for some time, moved into the mansion of Michisada, then occupied by her Senior Secretary, Masamune. Shimizu suggests that this was probably in accordance with the custom of the time whereby one sought a cure by changing one's abode.[37] However this may have been, Masako died in Masamune's house on the first of the twelfth month of Chōhō 1 (10 January 1000 by the Western calendar).[38] It may have been about this time that an intimacy grew up between Izumi and Prince Tametaka. The theory is that Tametaka, paying visits to his ailing stepmother Masako, would have had opportunity to meet her lady-in-waiting Izumi Shikibu, who may have been residing with her father at the time.[39] Although it is not clear when their affair began, by 1002, the year of the Prince's death, it seems to have been common knowledge.

Prince Tametaka, born in 977, was only twenty-six at the time of his death. According to the *Ōkagami* 大鏡, "When a child the loveliness of his features was beyond measure; there seemed to be a veritable radiance about him. The loss of charm resulting from the manhood ceremony must have been pronounced." The same passage describes his nature as being "a little frivolous,"[40] and the *Eiga monogatari* 榮花物語 says he was "extremely addicted to pleasure."[41]

The following passage from the *Eiga monogatari* describes Prince Tametaka's infatuation and death:

> People were uneasy about the danger involved in Danjō no Miya's[42] continual nocturnal escapades, and with sage expressions protested their dismay. The year was one of general turmoil due to an epidemic . . .[43] Though the streets and great avenues were in a frightful state because of corpses lying about, the Prince kept up his reckless night-roving, averting his eyes from the grisly things. Perhaps as a result he fell ill and died.
>
> At this time he was enamored of Shinchūnagon and Izumi Shikibu,

and though his wife[44] was made miserable by his amorous tendencies, over which he kept a shockingly loose rein, she was grieved by his death and mourned for him, becoming a nun on the forty-ninth day after his demise. She had always been of a most devout mind, and having over the years read the *Lotus Sutra* two or three thousand times, she had come to understand the fleeting nature of this world, and now devoted herself more fervently than ever to the practice of religion.

The news of Danjō no Miya's passing came as a faint rumor to the ears of the Retired Emperor Reizei. "He cannot have left us!" he said. "Search carefully—he is sure to be somewhere." Oh pitiable spectacle of parental love![45]

The Heir Apparent[46] was also extremely upset and grieved. Sochi no Miya 帥の宮[47] too must have grieved, overcome with pathos and regret. The late Prince had turned twenty-five that year.[48]

The date of Tametaka's death was the thirteenth of the sixth month of Chōhō 4 (1002).[49] Izumi Shikibu went into mourning. Michisada's reaction to these events can be imagined. His post as Governor of Izumi Province must have kept him absent from the capital during most of this time, but he obviously knew what was happening, because he soon separated from Izumi permanently. It is not known when his relations with her ceased, but on Chōhō 6 (1004).3.18 he left alone to take up his new post as Governor of Mutsu 陸奥.[50] There is a possibility that Izumi had another child by Michisada in addition to Koshikibu. Yamagishi relates the following poem from the *Izumi Shikibu shū* (*Seishū* 797 [772]) to this second child, born after Izumi's separation from Michisada:

A woman who was said to have had relations with many men gave birth to a child. People asked, "Who is the father?" Time passed, and then someone asked, "What was your decision?"

Izumi replied:

Kono yo ni wa	How can one decide
Ikaga sadamemu	Such matters in this life?
Onozukara	Go ask the man
Mukashi o towamu	Whose natural role it is
Hito ni toe kashi	To make investigation of past deeds.[51]

This poem well illustrates the self-assured sauciness that was one component of Izumi's nature. Several poems in her collection indicate that she continued to correspond with Michisada even after becoming the mistress of Prince Atsumichi, and that she retained a feeling of attachment to him.[52] At the time of Michisada's departure for Mutsu, Izumi's friend Akazome Emon sent her the following poem:

Yuku hito mo
Tomaru mo ikaga
Omouran
Wakarete nochi no
Mata no wakare wa

How will they think of it—
He who goes
And she who stays behind—
Having once parted,
Still to part again?[53]

Izumi replied:

Wakarete mo
Onaji miyako ni
Arishikaba
Ito kono tabi no
Kokochi ya wa seshi

Though we had parted,
Since still we lived
In the same capital,
How could I feel such pain
As now this journey brings?[54]

On the occasion of Michisada's departure Izumi wrote (Seishū 838 [811]):

Morotomo ni
Tatamashi mono o
Michinoku no
Koromo no seki o
Yoso ni kiku kana

Side by side
We had departed then,
But now I listen from afar
To talk of Koromo
Barrier in Michinoku.[55]

The following (Zokushū 8 [850]), sent to him after his arrival in his new province, contains the bitter note of recrimination:

10

Takakarishi	With what emotion
Nami ni yosoete	Do you gaze upon that peak,
Sono kuni ni	Fabled in your far land,
Ari chō yama o	Where lash the towering waves
Ika ni miruran	Of lovers' faithlessness?[56]

The reaction of Izumi's parents to her affair with Prince Tametaka was apparently equally strong. Several of her poems imply that she suffered at least a temporary disownment.[57] *Seishū* 717 (692):

Having been abruptly separated from her parents and sisters, she addressed them at their devotions:

Sono naka ni	One of you
Arishi ni mo arazu	I was, but am no more;
Nareru mi o	Would that I could know
Shirabaya nani no	What sin of former lives
Tsumi no mukui to	Has reaped this recompense.[58]

Shimizu suggests that the following (*Zokushū* 470 [1312]) was composed while in disgrace, in the autumn following Prince Tametaka's death:

One day when dew formed on the very charming *hagi* in front of the place where, reluctant to face her parents, she was living in concealment:

Sa wa miredo	Looking upon the dew,
Uchi mo harawade	I brushed no drop from off
Akihagi o	The autumn *hagi*;
Shinobite oreba	But now a secret breaking brings
Sode zo tsuyukeki	Showers to wet my sleeves.[59]

It is in this state—her sleeves wet with tears and her mind burdened with a past of endless regret—that the poetess first appears in the

Izumi Shikibu nikki. But, before the expiration of a year's mourning for the late Tametaka, his younger brother Atsumichi succeeded in arousing in her the flames of a new love. The *Ōkagami* criticizes Prince Atsumichi along with his brother as the possessor of a frivolous and lustful nature.[60] (In the *Izumi Shikibu nikki*, it may be noted, the Prince protests that he is a particularly quiet and sedate person.) At the outset of his affair with Izumi Shikibu he was living with his second formal consort. Concerning his first wife, the third daughter of Fujiwara no Michitaka 道隆 (953–995),[61] the *Ōkagami* says:

> As for the third sister, her father took the fourth son of the Retired Emperor Reizei, the one called Sochi no Miya, as her bridegroom. But her relations with her husband deteriorated rapidly, and she ended her days in most unseemly surroundings in the Ichijō district . . . It has been said that her disposition was extremely restless and that partly for this reason the Prince was cold toward her. Once when guests came she raised high the hanging screen and stood with the breast of her robes open. The Prince's visage reddened, and those who attended him felt the color of their own faces change.[62]

Such conduct was evidently too much for Atsumichi. His second wife was the middle daughter of Fujiwara no Naritoki 濟時 (941–995), and the younger sister of Jōshi 娍子 (sometimes recorded as Shūshi 娍子) (d. 1025), consort of Atsumichi's eldest full brother, Prince Okisada. Of her the *Ōkagami* says: "After her father's death she became of her own volition the wife of the Retired Emperor Reizei's fourth son, Sochi no Miya. But after two or three years the Prince transferred his affections to Izumi Shikibu, and matters went quite contrary to her expectations. Therefore she returned to Koichijō 小一條."[63]

The *Eiga monogatari* has the following account:

> The middle daughter of Koichijō [Naritoki] was the younger sister of Sen'yōden.[64] Her parents died without settling her future, but she herself was determined that it should be by no means inferior to that of her elder sister. She approached Sochi no Miya, the younger brother of the Heir Apparent, and was welcomed by him as his bride into his southern mansion.[65] However, with the passage of time his interest in

her waned. He was engaged in a wild passion for the wife of Michisada, the Governor of Izumi, and excluded Naritoki's daughter from his affections. She, finding her position difficult, returned to the home of her paternal grandmother. Both the Heir Apparent and Sen'yōden said to themselves, "If we had served as go-betweens in this marriage, how ugly the scandal would have been! It is a relief that we knew nothing about it." Fortunately the two sisters were so dissimilar[66] as to seem unrelated. As for Izumi, the late Danjō no Miya had also been sorely stricken with passion for her, a passion which seemingly had been passed on to Sochi no Miya. The latter's previous consort, the third daughter of his Lordship the late Regent [Michitaka], was also at present living in the Ichijō neighborhood in a condition she must have found far from her expectations. And now the middle daughter of Koichijō too—people speculated about these things.[67]

And well they might. Atsumichi's high position as younger brother of the Heir Apparent, the bizarre conduct of his first wife, his open flaunting of the shameless woman associated with the untimely demise of his brother Prince Tametaka, and his second consort's desertion, must have made him, too, a prime subject of court gossip and scandal. Not the least shocking aspect of the infatuation of the two brothers must have been the fact that the lady was the daughter of a mere provincial governor, and the gentlemen sons of an Emperor. Atsumichi made a particularly scandalous impression at the time of the Kamo Festival of 1005, when he placed Izumi in the rear of his carriage, her long skirts trailing out behind, and paraded before the spectators. According to the *Ōkagami* the two of them attracted more interest than the actual procession.[68]

Izumi presumably lived with the Prince until his death, which came quite suddenly after a brief illness, on the second of the tenth month of Kankō 4 (1007).[69] He was twenty-seven; according to the Yamagishi theory Izumi was about twenty-nine. She once again went into mourning. Prince Atsumichi was the great passion of her life, and she lamented his loss in over a hundred poems preserved in her personal collection. The following (*Zokushū* 87 [929]) she wrote at the time of the services held on the forty-ninth day after his death:

Ima mo nao	Even now there is
Tsukisenu mono wa	One thing that does not end:
Namida kana	My tears, alas—
Hachisu no tsuyu ni	Though they may serve to bathe
Nashi wa suredomo	Your lotus petals as with dew.[70]

On the seventh day of the new year, the day traditionally reserved for gathering young herbs, she wrote (*Zokushū* 91 [933]):

Omoiki ya	How could I know
Kyō no wakana mo	That I should disregard
Shirazu shite	Today's young herbs,
Shinobu no kusa o	And only pluck
Tsumamu mono to wa	The grasses of longing?[71]

The following is found among a group of poems on "Twilight Reverie" (*Zokushū* 126 [968]):

Yūgure wa	At dusk the path
Kimi ga kayoiji	You followed when you came to me
Michi mo naku	Is blotted out—
Sugakeru kumo no	All hung with spiderwebs
Ito zo kanashiki	And threaded through with grief.[72]

The remaining events of Izumi Shikibu's life can be grasped only in their larger outlines. At some time subsequent to the death of Prince Atsumichi—presumably after the expiration of a year of mourning—she entered the service of the Empress Akiko [Shōshi], daughter of Michinaga and consort of Emperor Ichijō.[73] Akiko's court was a brilliant one whose talented members already included Murasaki Shikibu (ca. 978–1016?), Akazome Emon, and Ise no Tayū (ca. 987–1063?). The addition of Izumi Shikibu may have taken place in the spring of Kankō 6 (1009).[74] Evidently Izumi's daughter Koshikibu accompanied her mother into Akiko's service. It is interesting to observe that the Empress, whom Murasaki portrays as a straight-laced figure, should have been willing to include the notorious Izumi among her ladies. According to the Yamagishi theory Izumi would at this time have been in her thirty-first year. Akiko was about twenty-nine.

It is uncertain how long Izumi remained at Akiko's court. Apparently while there she became acquainted with and married Fujiwara no Yasumasa 保昌 (958–1036), a retainer of Michinaga. Yasumasa, already in his fifties, was evidently a man of military reputation;[75] his name is associated with that of the famous general Minamoto no Yorimitsu (948–1021).[76] Yasumasa, like Izumi's father and her first husband, belonged to the provincial-governor class, serving at various times as Governor of Higo, Yamato, Tango, and Settsu. It is not known when his marriage to Izumi Shikibu took place, but poems in Izumi's private collection indicate that Yasumasa later served in several provincial posts. His term as Governor of Tango was the occasion for a famous literary incident involving Izumi's daughter Koshikibu. Koshikibu was evidently still in service at court, where she was gaining a poetic reputation of her own. *Kin'yōshū*[77] 586 describes the incident:

> During the time when Izumi Shikibu was in Tango with Yasumasa, a poetry meet was held in the capital, and Koshikibu no Naishi[78] was chosen as a participant. Middle Counsellor Sadayori[79] came to her quarters and teased her, asking, "How will you manage your poem? Perhaps you've sent someone to Tango? Hasn't your messenger returned? How uneasy you must be!" As he stood up to leave, Koshikibu stopped him with the poem:

Ōeyama	Far is the road
Ikuno no michi no	That winds through many a field
Tōkereba	Past Ōe Mount and Ikuno—
Mada fumi mo mizu	No message have I seen,
Amanohashidate	Nor Heavenbridge footfall.[80]

The career of Koshikibu was destined to be a short one, and Izumi was to mourn her own daughter's death. On Kannin 2 (1018).12.24, according to an entry in *Midō Kampaku ki*, Koshikibu bore a son to Norimichi 教通 (997–1075), son of Michinaga.[81] This child, brought up as a monk, was given the Buddhist name Jōen 靜圓. Eventually he attained high ecclesiastical rank and was known as Kobata no Sōjō 木幡僧正.[82] On the occasion of his birth Izumi received a jocular poem (*Seishū* 614 [590]) from the grandfather, Michinaga:

Yome no ko no	And how did it turn out,
Konezumi ikaga	Our young bride's
Narinuramu	Little mouse?
Ana utsukushi to	I'll venture
Omōyuru kana	It's as winsome as can be![83]

Izumi replied (*Seishū* 615 [591]):

Kimi ni kaku	To be acknowledged thus
Yome no ko to dani	But as the child of your
Shirarureba	Own son's young bride—
Kono konezumi no	Light will be the burden of offense
Tsumi karuki kana	This little mouse must bear.[84]

Evidently the relationship with Norimichi was not a lasting one, for the *Eiga monogatari* recounts another, sadder, childbirth:

At about this time [the eleventh month of Manju 2 (1025)] . . . a person called Koshikibu no Naishi, a lady-in-waiting to Empress Akiko—she had already had a child by his Lordship the Great Minister of the Center[85] Norimichi—died bearing the child of the Shigenoi First Secretary, Middle Captain[86] Fujiwara no Kinnari.[87] She was of no such formidable rank, but the manner of her death resembled that of Empress Yoshiko.[88] Empress Akiko was much affected by this event, and having fully realized the transitory nature of this world, determined to hasten the fulfillment of her resolve to enter religion, and urged forward the preparation of the articles necessary to that end.

Koshikibu's mother, Izumi Shikibu, looking at the child, wrote:

Todomeokite	Leaving us behind,
Tare o aware to	Whom will she have pitied more—

16

Omouran	Infant or mother?
Ko wa masarikeri	My child it was for me:
Ko wa masaruran	Her child it must have been.[89]

Izumi's husband Yasumasa died in 1036 while serving as Governor of Settsu. He was in his seventy-ninth year.[90] How long his marriage to Izumi Shikibu lasted is not certain, but a passage in the *Eiga monogatari* reveals that she was still his wife in 1027:

> At this time [the tenth month of Manju 4 (1027)] a message was dispatched to Yasumasa no Ason,[91] Governor of Yamato, commanding him to make an offering of jewels for the decoration of the Buddha figure.[92] Yasumasa directed his residence in the capital to make this offering. Izumi sent a poem along with the jewels:

Kazu naranu	Joining to these
Namida no tsuyu o	Even the numberless
Soete dani	Dewdrops of my tears,
Tama no kazari o	I would augment
Masan to zo omou	The jewelled embellishment.[93]

But there is evidence that their married life did not run smoothly to the end, and that they may eventually have separated. *Shikashū*[94] 311 reads:

> In response to an inquiry from Kanefusa Ason,[95] at the time when she had been forgotten by Yasumasa:

Hito shirezu	Well have I learned
Mono omou koto wa	The lessons of a secret grief
Narainiki	Unguessed by men—
Hana ni wakarenu	No spring but forces
Haru shi nakereba	Parting with the blossoms of its trees.

The date of Izumi's death is not known.

The foregoing sketch does not reveal the full range of Izumi's real or reputed love affairs. Her two husbands and her two princely lovers were by no means the only men in her life. *Shikashū* 239 suggests collateral interests even after her remarriage:

> Sent to the residence of a man who had been secretly courting her, on her departure for Tamba Province with Fujiwara no Yasumasa Ason:

Ware nomi ya	Shall I alone
Omoiokosemu	Send longing thoughts,
Ajikinaku	And all in vain,
Hito wa yukue mo	In a world where no one knows
Shiranu mono yue	What lies at the journey's end?

Possibly to be numbered among Izumi's reputed lovers, based on the *Izumi Shikibu nikki* (see translation, notes 135, 136), are Fujiwara no Takaie (979–1044) and/or Minamoto no Toshikata (960–1027), and Minamoto no Masamichi (d. 1017). The imprecise nature of the prose prefaces to many of her poems preserves the anonymity of her lovers, but leaves the impression that they may have been fairly numerous. The following, *Shikashū* 253, is an example:

> Composed when she heard hail striking the leaves of the bamboo in front of the house, one night while she waited impatiently for a man she had trusted:

Take no ha ni	Nights when hail falls,
Arare furu yo wa	Pattering incessantly
Sara sara ni	On rustling bamboo leaves,
Hitori wa nubeki	I swear I cannot find
Kokochi koso sene	The heart to sleep alone.[96]

Other expressions of Izumi's amorous nature are these poems from her collection:
Seishū 86:

Kurogami no	I fling myself down,
Midare mo shirazu	Heedless of the wild disorder

18

Uchifuseba	Of my long black hair,
Mazu kakiyarishi	And soon I'm yearning once again
Hito zo koishiki	For him who used to stroke it smooth.

Seishū 80:

Itazura ni	Recklessly
Mi o zo sutetsuru	I cast myself away;
Hito omou	Perhaps
Kokoro ya fukaki	A heart in love
Tani to naruramu	Becomes a deep ravine?

Seishū 97:

Yo no naka ni	Though in this world
Koi to iu iro wa	There is no color
Nakeredo mo	Known as love,
Fukaku mi ni shimu	Yet deeply is my person
Mono ni zo arikeru	Stained therewith.

It is always well to avoid identifying an author with his work, and in Japanese poetry in particular the conventional element must be kept in mind. Attitudes as well as vocabulary are apt to be controlled by tradition. But Izumi Shikibu's poetry, being largely of a personal nature, does at least imply certain traits of character and personality. Taken as a whole, her poetry reveals a complex person, by turns brash and humorous, moody and sentimental. "Izumi Shikibu's nature was unbridled and unrestrained," says Ikeda Kikan in *Nihon bungaku daijiten*. "She acted as her passions directed her."[97] Some of the poems quoted above show this side of her; she could also create the lyric tenderness of *Goshūishū* 1164:

Mono omoeba	Forsaken and forlorn,
Sawa no hotaru mo	I watch the fireflies
Waga mi yori	Hovering in the marshland dusk,
Akugareizuru	Like jewelled lights
Tama ka to zo miru	Emitted by the longing of my soul.

She loved greatly, and knew the full range of human affections—for her parents, her sisters, and her child, as well as for the men who were drawn to her. Over the latter she seems to have exercised a remarkable fascination. Her passion however was chastened by grief, and her worldliness by a sense of shame and a longing for religious peace.

Izumi Shikibu belongs as well to that company of women whose glamour has extended beyond their own time. She, like that other paragon of amatory verse, Ono no Komachi 小野小町 (ninth century), has become a figure of Japanese legend. These legends are preserved in various local traditions, medieval tales, nō plays, and temple histories. In them the figure of Izumi Shikibu is often vulgarized, caricatured, or oversimplified, and her biography subjected to curious distortions. Two strands of her personality—her amorousness and her longing for religious renunciation—form the chief themes of these stories.

Izumi Shikibu, an *otogizōshi* 御伽草子[98] dating from the Muromachi Period (1336–1568), purports to describe Izumi's relationship with Dōmyō Azari 道命阿闍梨,[99] son of Fujiwara no Michitsuna 道綱 (955–1020) and grandson of Kaneie and the authoress of the *Kagerō nikki*. The plot is as follows: In the days of the Emperor Ichijō there was a courtesan named Izumi Shikibu who plighted troth with Tachibana no Yasumasa (evidently a combination of Izumi's two husbands) and conceived a child by him. When the baby, a boy, was born, Izumi abandoned it on Gojō Bridge, placing a scabbardless dagger by its side. The boy was rescued and brought up by a townsman, and sent to become a monk on Mt. Hiei. In course of time he became famous far and wide as Dōmei (a variation of Dōmyō) Azari. One day the young Dōmei was summoned to recite sutras in the Palace. There he saw a beautiful court lady, for whom he conceived a passion. Later he returned to the Palace in the guise of a tangerine-seller and sought her out. The lady of course was none other than Izumi Shikibu. She returned his love and yielded herself to him. Then, as they were about to part, she noticed his dagger. A few questions brought out the truth, and with a shock she realized he was her son. She was so appalled at the blindness of human passion that she forsook the worldly life and entered the temple of Shōkū Shōnin on Shoshazan. There, at the age of sixty-one, she wrote the famous "Kuraki yori" poem, which in this version runs:

Kuraki yori	From out the dark
Kuraki yamiji ni	Into the Path of Darkness
Umarekite	Was I born;
Sayaka ni terase	Shine on me clearly,
Yama no ha no tsuki	Moon of the mountain crest.[100]

In *Koshikibu*, another *otogizōshi*, Izumi is the daughter of Murasaki Shikibu. Dōmyō is Izumi's poetry master, and it is Koshikibu, her child by Yasumasa, whom she abandons. Koshikibu, after being brought up by an old couple in the country, is discovered by her mother and returns to the capital, where she gains the favor of the Emperor through her poetry.

In some cases Izumi's name has simply become associated with a popular anecdote. The following is an example: Once Izumi Shikibu was suffering from a boil and prayed for relief to Yakushi Nyorai 藥師如來, the Buddha of healing, at the Hokkegokuji 法華嶽寺 in the Province of Hyūga 日向. Her prayers however were without effect. Incensed at the Buddha's indifference, she composed:

Namu Yakushi	"Hail to Yakushi,
Shobyō shitsujo no	Dispeller of all ills!"
Gan tatete	I raise my prayer;
Mi yori hotoke no	But more than my own pain do I regret
Na koso oshikere	Discredit to the Buddha's name.

Yakushi replied:

Murasame wa	This passing shower
Tada hitotoki no	Is but a momentary thing;
Mono zo kashi	I bid you, take
Onoga mi no kasa	Your rain hat off
Soko ni nugioke	And leave it there behind.[101]

Izumi's difficulty was immediately cleared up.[102] Such stories have a wide geographical distribution, as do alleged birthplaces and grave sites.

An example of the latter may be seen at the Jōshin'in 誠心院,[103] a small Shingon temple off Shinkyōgoku-dōri, one of the chief shopping and amusement centers of Kyoto. According to temple tradition the Jōshin'in is descended from a hermitage, the Komidō 小御堂,[104] built by Fujiwara no Michinaga for Izumi Shikibu when the latter entered the religious life in her old age. The Komidō was originally a part of the Tōbokuin 東北院, a temple founded by Michinaga's daughter Jōtōmon'in (Fujiwara no Akiko). It was named Jōshin'in after Izumi's death, and later rebuilt at Ichijō-Ogawa. A second remove, to its present location, took place during the Tenshō Era (1573–1592).

The temple contains several items having to do with Izumi Shikibu. One of these is a set of thirteen block-printed volumes (two of which are missing) entitled *Izumi Shikibu zenshū*, dated Kōka 5 (1848), the product of a lifetime of research by Jōkyo 靜居, an early nineteenth century abbot of the temple. This work contains, among other things, a biography and genealogy of Izumi Shikibu, a collection of her poems, a temple history, a collection of Izumi legends from the various provinces, and a volume of illustrations. Another of the treasures of the Jōshin'in is the *Izumi Shikibu engi* 緣起, two long illustrated scrolls relating the circumstances of the temple's foundation. The painter is unknown, but the text was written by Kaijuan 戒受庵 (1604–1669)[105] in Kan'ei 20 (1643).[106]

The *Engi* states that Izumi Shikibu became dissatisfied with the worldly life as she approached old age, and went on a pilgrimage to Shoshazan, to the temple of Shōkū Shōnin. After at first refusing to see her, Shōkū instructed her to pray to the Bodhisattva Hachiman. Hachiman advised Izumi to become a nun and worship at the Seiganji 誓願寺, a temple in the capital. It was beside this temple, within the confines of the neighboring Tōbokuin, that Michinaga built the Komidō. There Izumi lived the rest of her days, passing into paradise on Chōwa 3 (1014).3.21, enveloped in purple clouds and strange incense. The Jōshin'in holds a service in her memory every year on March 21; her Buddhist name is Jōshin'in Senni Hōni 専意法尼.

The temple also possesses a hanging-scroll painting of Izumi attributed to Kanō Takanobu (1571–1618), a small wooden statue of her in religious garb (date and sculptor unknown), and a folding screen whose panels tradition claims were made from a garment bestowed on Izumi by Jōtōmon'in. A few steps north from the temple is a large stone monument[107] erected in Shōwa 正和 2 (1313), supposedly to commemorate the three-hundredth anniversary of Izumi's death. It originally stood at her grave, according to temple tradition; the grave itself had been lost however by the time the temple moved to its present site. Beside the monument is a small stone marker on which is inscribed one of Izumi's poems (*Zokushū* 169 [1011]):

Kasumi tatsu	Mist-rising
Haru kinikeri to	Spring has come!
Kono hana o	Blossoms of this plum
Miru ni zo tori no	Proclaim, and unawares
Koe mo mataruru	I wait the first bird's call.

Izumi Shikibu's tomb at the Jōshin'in is mentioned by Nakagawa Kiun 中川喜雲 (1636–1705) among the eighty-seven famous places he describes in *Kyō warabe* 京童, a guide to Kyoto published in 1658. Among Kiun's remarks are the following:

> Here is the ancient tomb of Izumi Shikibu . . . Truly there cannot have been in this world another heart as chaste as hers, and for this reason even now I soak my sleeves with tears. Her name is a familiar

23

word which has not fallen into obscurity, and which will remain to the last generation. Since she is buried in the earth, what kind of phantom might she have become, I wonder, and longingly I think, "If only I could meet her now but once!" The plenteously gathering dews are tears to lament her grave.

Hana o tate   Flowers I offer
Tamukuru Izumi   In honor of Izumi—
Shikimi kana   *Shikimi* flowers![108]

Izumi Shikibu's death-day is the eighteenth of the month.[109]

II. The Izumi Shikibu Nikki

A. Description

The *Izumi Shikibu nikki*[110] is a work in one *kan* purporting to describe the beginning of Izumi's relationship with Prince Atsumichi. It is fairly short, occupying forty-six and one-half pages in the Iwanami *Nihon koten bungaku taikei* edition. It covers a time span of about nine months. The opening scene, when Izumi receives her first message from Prince Atsumichi, takes place shortly after the tenth of the fourth month of Chōhō 5 (1003); the last—the day when the Prince's consort leaves him—is in the first month of the following year. The work, though brief, abounds with *waka* poetry. In the *Sanjōnishibon* version there are $144\frac{1}{2}$ poems; counting each of two *renga*[111] as one complete poem, and another seventeen-syllable utterance of the Prince (see translation, note 227) as one half.

Despite its title, the *Izumi Shikibu nikki* is not what we ordinarily

25

understand as a diary. Questions of authorship and formation will be discussed later, and an attempt will be made to see the work in relation to the trends of early Japanese literature. Here the discussion will be limited to what is obvious on a first reading of the *Nikki*: whoever the author may have been, and regardless of whether or not the work is reliable as a true account, it has characteristics alien to those of a simple journal. The narration is in the third person, and the point of view is not limited to that proper to a diarist. There are simultaneous or almost simultaneous scenes in different places, imagined conversations, and descriptions of the thoughts and feelings of different people. The work is at least partially one of imaginative fiction.

Considering the work as imaginative fiction, it is proper to speak of a plot. The plot of the *Izumi Shikibu nikki* is simple, repetitious, and slow to develop.[112] The story line follows a wave-like pattern of alternate ardor and indifference on the part of the Prince, and timidity and yearning on the part of Izumi. She waits in her house for his visits and his messages. After his storming of the fort has overcome her initial reluctance, she longs for him to come again. He, on his part, his passion somewhat cooled, has second thoughts. At last he comes, but she, vexed by his neglect, ignores him. She goes off to visit a mountain temple, and on her return is too exhausted to hear his knock. After this series of frustrations he finally takes her away in his carriage one night to a deserted gallery of his mansion; thereafter they have other midnight excursions. By this time she seems completely in love with him, but when he presses her to come and live in his palace, her resolution wavers. He protests at the difficulties he encounters going to visit her. Despite, or perhaps because of, his high position, he cannot always do as he pleases. Furthermore, the Prince's feelings for Izumi are unstable. Each new rumor casts new suspicion over his mind, suspicion which vanishes in renewed tenderness whenever he sees her again. Finally, after months of hesitation on both sides, the Prince decides to take matters into his own hands, prepares a place for Izumi to live, and simply takes her away one night without telling her where she is going.

Up to this point the plot has been a series of vacillations, visits, and periods of seemingly endless waiting. Gradually the intimacy of the lovers increases, along with their commitment to each other, but the process is not notable for its momentum. In all, eighteen visits or attempted visits by the Prince to Izumi are described. Their greatest frequency comes in the first two months, and in the two months immediately preceding Izumi's entrance into the Prince's mansion. In between, and throughout, are the long days of forlorn waiting. What should be the climax of the whole work, the Prince's removal of Izumi to his mansion, is passed over in a strangely offhand fashion. The Prince's final resolution is never stated, but is simply assumed at the end of a long compound-complex sentence, the bulk of which is devoted to his despair and contemplation of early death (see translation, note 348). The Prince has promised Izumi that in his mansion she will be subjected to no unpleasantness, but the situation turns out quite differently. Her arrival causes a scandal in the household, culminating in the departure of the Prince's legitimate wife. Peered at, whispered about, and surrounded by sharp-fanged female jealousy, Izumi soon regrets the loss of the lonely but independent life she led in her former residence. Throughout most of its length as static as the existence it depicts, the work achieves an ultimate balance, ending as it began, with a sigh.

The characters of Prince Atsumichi and Izumi Shikibu, which are the only ones treated at any length in the *Nikki*, cannot be said to be of great complexity. But they are far from completely flat. The dominant traits of the lovers are amorousness, wit, melancholy, and indecision; in their frailties they are very human. The Prince, who seems rather adept at night-roving, protests his inexperience and his quiet, retiring nature. Izumi, already tinged with scandal and guilt, struggles to be faithful to the memory of her dead lover, Prince Tametaka. But not for long. She reproaches herself for her infidelity, but it is clear that the new love affair is not unwelcome. The first mention of Prince Atsumichi by the page draws from her the exclamation "Ito yoki koto ni koso anare!" (I'm sure that must be splendid!). It is obvious that her interest is aroused. She tries to

27

tell herself that she will do nothing more than talk with the Prince
for a little while, but it is difficult to believe that she could have been
surprised at the outcome. Their jealousies, suspicions, hesitancies, and
witty exchanges make the two an engaging pair. The characteriza-
tion is not fully rounded because the work is brief and centered solely
on one aspect of their lives. Their other concerns and activities are
mostly ignored, and the background is hazy to the point that they
both seem sometimes to exist almost in a vacuum. Only toward
the end, after Izumi has been introduced into the Prince's mansion,
do we get a glimpse of the workings and intricacies of a slightly
larger world.

The tone of the *Nikki*, as of much of Heian literature, is basically
one of melancholy. Outside her relationship with the Prince, the lady
seems to be always alone—psychologically, if not physically. She is
stirred to long, long thoughts by the rain, by the sight of the growing
grasses, by the moon, the crying of the wild geese, the falling of the
autumn leaves—in short, by nearly every natural phenomenon
which impinges on her consciousness or comes to her knowledge in
the restricted world under the eaves of her dwelling. It is *mono-no-
aware*, the sigh-producing sadness occasioned by a world of poignant
beauty and transient love. The first sentence is the keynote: "Yume
yori mo hakanaki yo no naka o nagekiwabitsutsu . . ." (Frailer than
a dream had been those mortal ties for which she mourned . . . with
sighs of melancholy). At the last Izumi realizes that she is one "whose
melancholy thoughts will never end." It is a world of waiting,
where "gazing" and "long rains" merge into the same word. The
Prince too is subject to fits of melancholia, and seems to have a
prescience of his early death. The tone of subdued sadness is broken
by occasional joys—the receipt of a longed-for letter—and by frequent flashes of wit. But often the lady weeps even when she is with
her lover. Fears oppress her. The gentle melancholy of the surface
conceals an undercurrent of anxiety; for both lovers the dread of
censure and wagging tongues is very real. Their world is small and
compact, and its judgements are inescapable. There is one way,
however—to "abandon the world" and take the refuge offered by

28

the Buddhist temples. Both Izumi and the Prince toy with the idea; it must have had a powerful appeal to people sick of society. But as far as is known, neither of the lovers ever took the step. (Note however the traditions about Izumi Shikibu mentioned in the previous section.)

In its prose style the *Izumi Shikibu nikki* is relatively simple and easy to read, at least as compared to such other Heian classics as the *Genji monogatari* and *Kagerō nikki*. Obscurities and special problems have been taken up in the notes to the translation. In general these are such as obtrude on the notice of the translator rather than of the reader. Sentences tend to be reasonably short and straightforward for a text in classical Japanese prose, and the small number of characters helps to reduce confusion. The prose is soft and mellifluous, and when describing natural scenes of strong emotional content it occasionally rises to lyric intensity. A particularly admirable feature is the skill with which the poetry and prose are interwoven, often through syntactical devices unfortunately not available to the English translator.[113] The poems vary in quality; some are rather trite, but others are successful in matching thought or emotion with expression. A great many, typical of their age, are examples of verbal dexterity, admirable or not according to one's taste.

The prose makes extensive use of honorific verbs, which often distinguish between the two principal characters, as in *obosu* for the Prince and *omou* (both meaning "think") for Izumi. A noticeable characteristic of the style is the abundance of causatives, the vast majority of which are applied to actions of the Prince or other characters of exalted station. They are in fact used mostly as honorifics. The context usually makes clear whether an honorific or a causative function is intended. But in the case of verbs of speech this is not always true. In this connection it may be noted that Izumi and the Prince each has a characteristic verb expressing the idea "to say"—*notamau* for the Prince, and *kikoyu* for Izumi. Forms of the verb *notamau* are used with the Prince as subject seventy-one times. Izumi is the subject of this verb only four times, when the Prince, addressing her, refers to her speech. On the other hand, forms of the verb *kikoyu*, including a few instances of its use as an auxiliary verb, have Izumi as subject eighty-three times, and the Prince only eighteen times, mostly when the Prince refers to his own speech or messages. In most instances the verb *notamau* is used in its causative form *notamawasu*. In over a fourth of the cases the equivalent is true of *kikoyu*.

The question then arises as to whether the speech or communication is to be considered direct or indirect. There is much employment of messengers to carry poems to and fro in the *Nikki*, and it is a well known fact that ladies in the Heian age often sat concealed behind screens. High nobles too might be expected to communicate their wishes through intermediaries. It would be convenient if the causative or noncausative form of verbs of communication reflected the presence or absence of intermediaries, but such is not the case: there seems to be no discernible rationale for their use. In a particular confrontation causative and noncausative forms will be mixed in together, and this is so whether the situation is one in which a third party might conceivably be serving as go-between speaker, or whether it is of such an intimate nature that two people are obviously speaking directly to each other. The same is true of messages—sometimes the text of a poem will be followed by "to kikoetari" or "to notamaeba"; in other instances a causative form such as "to kikoesasetareba" or "to notamawasetari" will be used. There seems to be no reason for the difference. One is forced to the conclusion that simple variety was the effect sought. Since people of exalted station did often communicate through subordinates, the causative form would naturally come to be commonly used in reporting their speech. This habitual association of causatives with the elite might quite naturally evolve in the direction of the use of such forms as honorifics even in the reporting of direct speech.

B.   Textual History

The origin and authorship of the work known as the *Izumi Shikibu nikki*[114] are matters of scholarly debate which will be discussed in the next section. Before examining the evidence which can be brought to bear on those problems, it would be well to take stock of the actual physical variations in which the work itself exists.

Yoshida Kōichi mentions thirty-one manuscripts and five block-printed versions of the *Izumi Shikibu nikki* in his *Izumi Shikibu kenkyū*.[115] These he groups into four textual families: (1) the *Sanjōnishibon* 三條西本 Group; (2) the *Kangembon* 寬元本 Group; (3) the *Ōeibon* 應永本 Group; (4) the *Konseibon* 混成本, or "Hybrid," Group. The first is named for the family in whose archives its sole specimen was formerly preserved; the second and third for the year periods found in the colophons of some of their manuscripts; and the fourth for the nature of its texts. None of these groupings contains a document which physically antedates the fifteenth century, but the *Kangembon* family consists of seventeenth-century copies of a manuscript bearing a colophon dated 1246. This date is the earliest found in any of the manuscripts.

The *Sanjōnishibon* Group consists of a single manuscript in the hand of Sanjōnishi Sanetaka 實隆 (1455–1537).[116] It is unique among hand-written texts in bearing the title *Izumi Shikibu nikki*, a title it shares only with the printed *Gunsho ruijū* version. All other manuscripts and wood block editions (with the exception of the *Fusō-shūyōshūbon;* see below, page 40) are entitled *Izumi Shikibu monogatari*. The *Sanjōnishibon* has no colophon other than a brief genealogy of Princes Tametaka and Atsumichi, and a biographical note on Izumi Shikibu.[117] Although there is no statement identifying the copyist, the accreditation is apparently sure, for Sanetaka's hand is well known. Yoshida states that as a transmitter of old texts he must be ranked next to Fujiwara Teika (1162–1241).[118] Formerly in the library of the Sanjōnishi family, the document is now preserved in the Archives of the Imperial Household (Kunaichō Shoryōbu). Yoshida speculates that it may have been written about 1492.[119]

The *Sanjōnishibon* is generally considered a superior text, perhaps closer than any other to the original; part of the confidence placed in it stems from Sanetaka's reputation. It has also been noted that its text is closer to the *kotobagaki* (prose headnotes to poems) of the *Izumi Shikibu kashū* than is the case with other extant versions. (The problem of the relation of the *Nikki* to the *Kashū* will be dealt with in the next section.) With the exception of a passage near the end, also lacking in the *Kangembon* (see translation, note 358), the *Sanjō-nishibon* contains few obvious errors and omissions, and is apparently free of emendations based on the copyist's personal opinion. Such emendations (inserted between the lines of text) and *misekechi*[120] as do appear are, in Yoshida's opinion, examples of Sanetaka catching his own errors in copying, rather than variant readings taken from another text.[121] Variant readings, drawn from the *Ōeibon*, are given in the case of poems. It seems reasonable to suppose, as Yoshida remarks, that these variants were not inserted by Sanetaka, but were already present in the text he copied, for if he himself had seen a manuscript of the *Ōeibon* Group, he might have been expected to catch the omission mentioned above.[122]

The *Sanjōnishibon* was introduced to the scholarly world by Ikeda Kikan in "Ihon *Izumi Shikibu nikki*," *Bungaku* (November 1931), and was printed for the first time in the same journal in August and November of 1933. A photographic facsimile edition containing a four-page introduction by Yamada Yoshio, was produced in 1937 by the Koten Hozonkai. A second offset facsimile edition was released by Musashino Shoin in 1956. It contains an introduction and collation by Suzuki Tomotarō, but these are missing from the first printing. The ninth printing of this edition appeared in 1964.

The excellence of the *Sanjōnishibon* was quickly recognized, and it has been adopted as the basic text for most recent editions. These include:

(1) *Izumi Shikibu nikki,* ed. Shimizu Fumio, in *Iwanami bunko,* vol. 2750 (Iwanami Shoten, 1941; revised 1957). This edition contains an introduction by Shimizu, a few notes identifying people and poems, and an index of poems.

(2) *Izumi Shikibu nikki,* ed. Suzuki Tomotarō, in *Koten bunko,*

XV (Koten Bunko, 1948). This book also contains the first reproduction of the *Katsuranomiyabon* (see below, under *Ōeibon*).

(3) Yoshida Kōichi, *Izumi Shikibu zenshū: hombunhen* (Koten Bunko, 1959). This valuable work contains, on pages 1–101, a collation of the *Kangembon* with the *Sanjōnishibon* and *Ōeibon;* also, on pages 205–237, a printing of the *Sanjōnishibon*.

(4) Azuma Setsuo, Tsukabara Tetsuo, and Maeda Kingo, *Izumi Shikibu nikki sōsakuin* (Musashino Shoin, 1959). This book contains a parallel printing of the *Sanjōnishibon* and *Ōeibon*, along with a few notes identifying persons, sources for poems, and other information. It also has a complete word index, a *kakekotoba* index, and a poem index.

(5) Endō Yoshimoto, *Shinkō Izumi Shikibu monogatari* (Hanawa Shobō, 1962). This excellent work, a detailed discussion of stylistic and grammatical problems of the *Ōeibon* version, contains, on pages 185–246, a collation of that text with the *Sanjōnishibon*.

Commentaries and thoroughly annotated texts include:

(1) Tamai Kōsuke, *Izumi Shikibu nikki shinchū* (Sekaisha, 1950). This is the first complete commentary on the *Sanjōnishibon*. It also contains a translation into modern Japanese.

(2) Ozaki Tomomitsu, *Izumi Shikibu nikki kōchū* (Bunkyō Shoin, 1954; revised and enlarged, Tōhō Shobō, 1957). This commentary also contains a translation into modern Japanese.

(3) *Izumi Shikibu nikki*, ed. Endō Yoshimoto, in *Nihon koten bungaku taikei*, XX (Iwanami Shoten, 1957, 1962). The volume also contains the *Tosa nikki*, *Kagerō nikki*, and *Sarashina nikki*.

(4) *Izumi Shikibu nikki*, ed. Yamagishi Tokuhei, in *Nihon koten zensho* [no vol. number] (Asahi Shimbunsha, 1959). There is a sixty-eight-page introduction by Yamagishi covering the life of Izumi Shikibu, formation and authorship of the *Nikki*, a critical appraisal, and textual history. Notes are less adequate than in the editions mentioned above. The volume also contains the *Heichū monogatari* and *Takamura monogatari*.

(5) *Izumi Shikibu nikki*, ed. Shimizu Fumio, in *Nihon koten kanshō kōza*, VI [*Ōchō nikki*] (Kadokawa Shoten, 1959). This book contains

only extracts from the *Nikki*. The annotation is sparse, but there is a detailed commentary. The volume contains a similar treatment of the *Tosa nikki, Murasaki Shikibu nikki*, and *Sarashina nikki*.

(6) Suzuki Kazuo and Enchi Fumiko, *Zenkō Izumi Shikibu nikki* (Shibundō, 1965). This is the most recent and thorough commentary, with a translation into modern Japanese.

The *Kangembon* Group consists of three manuscripts, each containing a colophon dated Kangen 4 (1246).[123] The actual manuscripts however are seventeenth-century copies.

(1) The *Asukai Masaaki hippon* 飛鳥井雅章筆本 is a manuscript in the hand of Asukai Masaaki (1611–1679), entitled *Izumi Shikibu monogatari*. Its colophon, the distinguishing feature which has attracted much interest to this group of texts, reads:

書本云

存生之時不見此草子沒後所見及也
老病之後狂事歟以養子之禪尼令書
云々文章詞躰不尋常雖恥披露暫
不破却

前戶部以自筆如此所被書也
寛元第四五月十二依大理典侍御命書寫了

(The manuscript says: "During his lifetime I did not see this booklet; only after his death did I come to see it. A trivial thing written after the illness of his old age? He had his adopted child, the nun, write it down, thus and so. The style and diction are not ordinary. Although it would be embarrassing for the work to become generally known, for the moment I shall not destroy it."

Written thus with his own brush by the former Minister of Revenue.

Copied in full on the twelfth day of the fifth month of Kangen 4 [1246], at the command of Dairi [no] Tenji.)

Since this colophon has a strong bearing on the problem of the authorship of the *Izumi Shikibu nikki*, its meaning and significance will be discussed in the next section. Here it will be sufficient to

34

observe that the "former Minister of Revenue" refers to Fujiwara Teika, and that the first part of the colophon is ostensibly his statement attributing authorship of the *Nikki* to his father Shunzei (1114–1204). Formerly in the possession of the Imperial Palace, and later of the Tokugawa family, the *Masaaki hippon* is now in the personal collection of Yoshida Kōichi.

(2) The *Hōreibon* 寶玲本 is an early Tokugawa manuscript, perhaps dating from the Kan'ei Era (1624–1644), in the hand of an unknown copyist. Its colophon is the same as that in the *Masaaki hippon*. Formerly in the Hōrei Bunko, it too is now in the possession of Yoshida Kōichi.

(3) The *Kurokawabon* 黑川本 is another early Tokugawa manuscript, probably copied in or near Kan'ei. Its copyist is unknown. The text contains a collation with the *Fusōshūyōshūbon* (see below under *Konseibon*), variant readings having been inserted in red ink by Oda Sugao 小田清雄 (1848–1894). A note to this effect by Oda, dated 1881, appears at the end, following the Kangen 4 colophon. The manuscript has been in the possession of the Hino, Oda, and Kurokawa families, and of the Muraguchi Shobō of Tokyo, and is now in the library of Tenri University.

The *Kangembon* texts are apparently descended from a common ancestor which had been collated with the *Ōeibon*, for they all have a series of variants supplied from a text of that group. A considerable number of small differences exist among the three manuscripts. The *Masaaki hippon* is considered by Yoshida to be the most reliable member of the family. This appraisal is again based partly on Masaaki's high reputation as a transmitter of texts. His manuscript is relatively free from the numerous small errors and omissions which are found in the *Hōreibon* and *Kurokawabon*, and evinces a more faithful attitude toward the text. Variations in the use of *kana* (Japanese syllabic writing) and *kanji* (Chinese characters) indicate that the *Hōreibon* and *Kurokawabon* are much more closely related to each other than either is to the *Masaaki hippon*. Perhaps the most serious flaw in the *Kangembon* Group is a misplaced passage of seven lines beginning with the poem "Nagusamuru" and ending im-

35

mediately before the poem "Ware hitori" (see translation, page 179). These lines have mistakenly been placed immediately before the poem "Utsutsu to mo" (translation, page 184). This error is shared only by the *Hōreibon* and *Masaaki hippon* however. The *Kurokawabon* has the passage correctly placed; Yoshida speculates that its copyist made the correction from a version of the *Ōeibon*.[124]

Editions of the *Kangembon* are as yet few in number. The *Kurokawabon* was introduced by Kawase Kazuma in "*Izumi Shikibu nikki* wa Fujiwara Shunzei no saku," *Aoyama Gakuin Joshi Tanki Daigaku kiyō* (September 1953). This article is a discussion of the significance of the famous colophon however rather than a reproduction of the text. The first publication of a *Kangembon* manuscript was that of the *Masaaki hippon* by Yoshida Kōichi in "*Izumi Shikibu monogatari*," *Heian bungaku kenkyū* (November 1953, February 1954, and June 1954). As noted above, Yoshida's *Izumi Shikibu zenshū: hombunhen* contains a collation of the *Kangembon* (*Masaaki hippon*) with the *Sanjōnishibon* and *Ōeibon*. There is also, on pages 103–112, a collation of the *Masaaki hippon* with the *Hōreibon*. A more recent volume by Yoshida, *Izumi Shikibu zenshū: shiryōhen* (1966), contains on pages 1–126 a photographic reproduction of the *Masaaki hippon*. The *Shiryōhen* is mostly devoted to the reproduction of manuscript texts of the Izumi Shikibu poetry collections and to the printing of several minor collections which were not included in the *Hombunhen*. The first annotated edition of the *Kangembon* was a classroom text edited by Kawase: *Izumi Shikibu nikki*, in *Shinchū kokubungaku sōsho* (*gakuseiban*) (Kōdansha, 1956). The first (and, as far as I have been able to ascertain, the only) complete commentary on the *Kangembon* was published by Hōbunsha in the same year: *Izumi Shikibu nikki, Murasaki Shikibu nikki*, ed. Yamagishi Tokuhei and Murakami Osamu, in *Saishin kokubun kaishaku sōsho*.

Ōeibon manuscripts are numerous, and have been divided by Yoshida into three groups: the *Ōei okugakibon* Group, the *Kyōroku okugakibon* Group, and the *Mushikigo* (Colophonless) Group. The

36

Ōei okugakibon Group consists of three manuscripts:

(1) The *Kyōdaibon* 京大本 is a manuscript in the hand of an unknown copyist, probably pre-Genroku (1688–1704), perhaps of the Kambun-Empō Eras (1661–1681). In addition to a collation in black ink, it contains in red ink, in the hand of a later man, *misekechi* and emendations. It has the following colophon:

于時應永廿一年孟春日書之
權大納言從二位爲尹判

(Written on a day early in spring in the twenty-first year of Ōei [1414]. [Signed][125] Acting Major Counsellor Tamemasa of Junior Second Rank.)[126]

This manuscript, then, is a descendant of one copied by Reizei 冷泉 Tamemasa (also pronounced Tametada) (1361–1417) in 1414. Yoshida is of the opinion that the *Kyōdaibon* is probably at two or three removes from Tamemasa's manuscript. The source for the latter may have been a document dating from Teika's time which Tamemasa inherited as a member of the Reizei family of poets descended from Teika, the great litterateur. The *Kyōdaibon* is now in the possession of the Literature Department of Kyoto University.

(2) The *Keidaibon* 慶大本 is a manuscript in the hand of an unknown copyist; it is a late Tokugawa or early Meiji (1868–1912) copy of the *Kyōdaibon*. It has the same colophon as the *Kyōdaibon*, but lacks the red-ink emendations. It is preserved in the library of Keiō University.

(3) The *Kitanishibon* 北西本 is a manuscript in the hand of an unknown copyist, probably late Tokugawa. It is a faithful copy of the *Kyōdaibon*, including the red-ink emendations, and has the same colophon. Formerly in the possession of the Kitanishi family, it is now in the library of Yoshida Kōichi.

Of the nine texts of the *Kyōroku* 享祿 *okugakibon* Group, only the following two need be mentioned. The others are all Tokugawa or later copies, reprints, or otherwise closely related texts.

(1) The *Awa no Kuni Bunkobon* 阿波國文庫本 is a manuscript in

the hand of an unknown mid-Tokugawa copyist. The colophon reads:

此一册借右中辨彙秀本從去月十四日染筆今日終功畢
享祿二年五月朔日右少將藤言繼草名
以後三條左大臣實量公自筆之本一校了

(Concerning this volume: Having borrowed a text of Middle Controller of the Right[127] Kanehide, I began copying on the fourteenth day of last month, and brought the task to completion today.

[Signed][128] Minor Captain of the Right[129] Fuji[wara] Kototsugu, first day of the fifth month of Kyōroku 2 [1529].

Compared with a text in the hand of the Latter Sanjō Great Minister of the Left,[130] Lord Sanekazu.)

Evidently Kototsugu (also read Tokitsugu) (1507–1579) borrowed a manuscript in the hand of (or belonging to) Fujiwara (Hirohashi 廣橋) Kanehide (1506–1567), and copied it. Later either Kototsugu or someone else (Yoshida favors the latter, in that other manuscripts in this group lack the last line of the colophon, and were apparently copied directly from Kototsugu's uncollated manuscript) compared this copy with a text in the hand of Sanjō Sanekazu (1415–1484).[131] Since there are no variants inserted, evidently the texts were identical. Hence it seems likely that the Kanehide manuscript was either a copy of the Sanekazu manuscript, or was otherwise closely related to it. Yoshida theorizes that the text Sanekazu himself copied may have been the Ōei 21 Tamemasa manuscript (the ancestor of the *Kyōdaibon*).[132] Considerable differences however have been found between the *Kyōdaibon* and the *Awa no Kunibon*. The latter manuscript, formerly in the possession of the Awa no Kuni Bunko and Hōrei Bunko, is now in the library of Tenri University.

(2) The *Kambun hampon* 寛文版本 is an illustrated wood-block edition, in three volumes, printed in 1670. After the Kyōroku colophon appears the printer's notice:

寛文十年霜月吉日　八尾清兵衛開板

(First impression made by Yao Seibei on an auspicious day in the Month of Frost [the eleventh month] in the tenth year of Kambun [1670].)

This printed edition, which has several errors and omissions, is based on some manuscript other than the *Awa no Kuni Bunkobon*. There are copies in, among other places, the Osaka Prefectural Library (Ōsaka Furitsu Toshokan 大阪府立圖書館) and the East Asiatic Library of the University of California at Berkeley.

The third subdivision of the *Ōeibon* family is a group of four manuscripts lacking colophons. Only one of them needs to be described here.

The *Katsuranomiyabon* 桂宮本 is a manuscript in an unknown hand, probably copied during the Kambun-Empō 延寶 Eras (1661–1681). It contains, in the same hand, collation, insertions, and corrections of errors found in the Ōei and Kyōroku texts. It follows *Ōeibon* peculiarities of omission, but has a passage found otherwise only in the *Kangembon*. It is hence reasonable to assume that the copyist of the *Katsuranomiyabon* or of one of its ancestors had access to a text of the *Kangembon* lineage. Formerly in the possession of the Katsuranomiya family of imperial princes, the manuscript is now in the Archives of the Imperial Household.

Taken as a whole, the texts of the *Ōeibon* Group have attracted less scholarly interest than those of the other two textual lineages brought to light in recent years. The *Kangembon* has caused considerable debate because of its controversial colophon, and the *Sanjōnishibon* has been recognized as a superior text. The *Ōeibon* however has yet to be published in an annotated edition (but see number four below). The *Kyōdaibon* was first printed and introduced to the scholarly world in 1928, in a facsimile edition mimeographed from a copy traced from the original manuscript. This was published by Ryūkoku Daigaku Kokubun Gakkai as *Ōeibon eisha Izumi Shikibu nikki*, ed. Ogawa Juichi, in *Ryūkoku Daigaku Kokubun Gakkai shuppan sōsho*, III. The facsimile retains the red-ink emendations in the *Kyōdaibon*. A five-page introduction by Ogawa deals with description of the text and other texts then known. Despite the care employed in producing the facsimile, errors crept in. The copy in the possession of Kyoto University has a note indicating it was collated with the original in 1940. The *Ōeibon eisha Izumi Shikibu nikki* was republished by Shumi Kōza Shuppambu (Kyoto) in 1937.

Other publications of *Ōeibon* texts include the following:

(1) *Izumi Shikibu nikki*, ed. Suzuki Tomotarō, in *Koten bunko*, XV (Koten Bunko, 1948). This book contains the first printing of the *Katsuranomiyabon*; it also includes the *Sanjōnishibon*.

(2) Yoshida Kōichi, *Izumi Shikibu zenshū: hombunhen*. As noted above, this work contains, on pages 1–101, a collation of the *Kangembon* with the *Sanjōnishibon* and the *Kyōdaibon*. There is also, on pages 112–114, a rectification of mistaken readings in the *Kyōdaibon*, and, on pages 119–202, a collation of the *Kyōdaibon* with the *Keidaibon*, *Katsuranomiyabon*, *Shimabarabon*, *Sakakibarabon* (two manuscripts of the "Colophonless" Group), Ōei wood-block editions, and texts of the *Konseibon* Group.

(3) Azuma Setsuo, et al., *Izumi Shikibu nikki sōsakuin*. As noted above, this work contains, on pages 1–78, a parallel printing of the *Sanjōnishibon* and *Kyōdaibon*.

(4) Endō Yoshimoto, *Shinkō Izumi Shikibu monogatari*. As noted above, this work contains, on pages 189–246, a collation of the *Kyōdaibon* with *Sanjōnishibon*, as well as a series of essays dealing with problems in the former.

The *Konseibon* Group consists of fourteen items as listed by Yoshida. Only three of these are of enough significance to warrant discussion here. The others are without exception later copies and editions of the first two.

(1) The *Fusōshūyōshū kenjōbon* 扶桑拾葉集獻上本 is in *kan* 28 of a manuscript copy of the anthology of Japanese writings, the *Fusōshūyōshū*, collected and presented by Tokugawa Mitsukuni 徳川光圀 (1628–1700) to the Retired Emperor Gosai 後西 (1637–1685; r. 1656–1663) in 1680. The *Nikki* is entitled *Waga mi no monogatari* 我身の物語 (A Story About Herself). There is no colophon, nor are there any corrections or insertions. This copy of the *Fusōshūyōshū*

is now in the Archives of the Imperial Household.

(2) The *Fusōshūyōshū Genroku ninen hampon* 元禄二年板本 is the only block-print edition of the *Fusōshūyōshū*. It has no printer's notice, but the date Genroku 2 (1689) is given in the preface. The *Nikki*, here entitled *Izumi Shikibu monogatari*, is included in *kan* 5. There are copies of this edition in the Shōkōkan Bunko 彰考館文庫 and the Literature Department of Kyoto University. On the basis of comparative studies, Yoshida concludes that the version of the *Izumi Shikibu nikki* found in the *Fusōshūyōshū* was created by combining texts of two different lineages. The redactor evidently had at hand, and drew upon according to his own preference, a manuscript of the *Kyōroku okugakibon* Group and a copy of the *Masaaki hippon*.

(3) The *Gunsho ruijūbon* 群書類從本 . The *Gunsho ruijū*, a huge collection of Japanese writings classified by category, began publication in 1779 under the editorship of Hanawa Hokiichi 塙保己一 (1746–1821), and was completed in 1819. It comprises 530 *kan*. The *Izumi Shikibu nikki*, so titled, appears in *kan* 320, in the section on *nikki*. The *Gunsho ruijū* text is based on the *Fusōshūyōshūbon*, but incorporates willful changes of *kana* to *kanji*, and corrections of supposed errors. It contains moreover many instances of wrong, missing, or superfluous *kana*, and other errors of its own. Although an inferior text, it became the *rufubon* 流布本 , the most widely available version, because of the wide circulation of the *Gunsho ruijū*. It was the basis for all commentaries prior to the publication of the *Sanjōnishibon*.

The *Gunsho ruijū* was published in Western-style format by Keizai Zasshisha in 1897–1902, under the editorship of Kuroita Katsumi. More recent editions have been published by Naigai Shoseki Kabushiki Kaisha in 1928, 1938, and 1962. The *Izumi Shikibu nikki* is in volume fourteen of the 1938 edition. The *Gunsho ruijū* text is included in *Kōchū Nihon bungaku taikei*, III (Kokumin Tosho Kabushiki Kaisha, 1925; Seibundō, 1931), and in *Yūhōdō bunko*, VIII [*Heian-chō nikkishū*] (Yūhōdō Shoten, 1927). It was also published in *Izumi Shikibu zenshū*, ed. Yosano Hiroshi, Yosano

Akiko, and Masamune Atsuo, in *Nihon koten zenshū*, ser. 2, LXXII (Nihon Koten Zenshū Kankōkai, 1927). This volume also contains the *Izumi Shikibu kashū* 歌集 and an introduction by Yosano Akiko.

The following commentaries have taken the *Gunsho ruijūbon* as their basic text:

(1) Takeno Chōji, *Kōtei Izumi Shikibu nikki shinshaku* (Seibundō, 1930).

(2) Miyata Kazuichirō, *Sarashina, Izumi Shikibu, Murasaki Shikibu nikki kōgi* (Nihon Bungakusha, 1935).

(3) Komuro Yoshizō and Tanaka Eizaburō, *Izumi Shikibu nikki shōkai* (Hakuteisha, 1937, 1957).

(4) Igarashi Tsutomu, *Shōwa kan'yaku Izumi Shikibu nikki* (Hakuhō Shuppansha, 1947).

(5) *Izumi Shikibu nikki*, ed. Kieda Masuichi (Shūbunkan, 1947).

Internal evidence and a comparison with the *Izumi Shikibu kashū* show that all extant versions of the *Izumi Shikibu nikki* have one fault in common (see below, section on Authorship and Formation, and translation, note 178). In an exchange of poems between Izumi and the Prince one morning in the ninth month, one of Izumi's poems has fallen into the prose text. Since it seems highly unlikely that this error could have existed in the *Nikki* as first written, it follows that the extant texts must all be descended from a common ancestor at some remove from the original, an ancestor in which for some reason this garbling first occurred. The *Sanjōnishibon* and *Kangembon* texts are further differentiated from the *Ōeibon* family by the large omission near the end which they share (see above under *Sanjōnishibon*, and translation, note 358), and must also be descended from a common ancestor. The *Ōeibon* Group is divided into three branches: texts having the Ōei 21 colophon, texts having the Kyōroku 2 colophon, and texts having no colophon. The best representatives of these three branches are, respectively, the *Kyōdaibon*, the *Awa no Kuni Bunkobon*, and the *Katsuranomiyabon*. It is possible that both of the first two subdivisions descend from the copy made by Reizei Tamemasa in Ōei 21 (1414). On the basis of its colophon the *Kyōdaibon* may be considered a direct descendant. The *Awa no Kunibon* is a descendant of the copy made by Fujiwara (Yamashina 山科) Kototsugu in Kyōroku 2 (1529). This was copied from a text of Hirohashi Kanehide, and later compared with one in the hand of Sanjō Sanekazu; the lack of emendations indicates that the Sanekazu and Kanehide texts may have been identical, perhaps the latter a copy of the former. As noted previously, it is possible that Sanekazu's manuscript was itself a copy of the Reizei Tamemasa text. The large number of errors and omissions in the *Awa no Kunibon* however makes it unlikely that this manuscript preserves the pure form of its distant ancestors. Texts of the group lacking colophons are evidently based on readings taken from both the Ōei and Kyōroku subdivisions, plus revisions and corrections on the part of the copyist. The latter tendency is especially notable in the case of the *Katsuranomiyabon*.

With the exception of a collation with the poems in the *Ōeibon*, the *Sanjōnishibon* seems to have had little contact with other extant texts. The *Kangembon* and *Ōeibon* groups have influenced each other in various ways, however. Texts of the *Ōeibon* lineage have a lacuna of several words beginning with "nowakidachite" (see translation, page 156, ".... the wind blew fiercely"). The *Katsuranomiyabon* has this passage intact, however, the copyist evidently having supplied it from a manuscript of the *Kangembon* Group. On the other hand, the *Kurokawabon*, a text of the latter lineage, is distinguished from the *Hōreibon* and *Asukai Masaaki hippon* by lacking the displacement referred to previously (see above under *Kangembon*). The correction is presumed to have been made from a text of the *Ōeibon* Group. The most important result of intermingling between the *Kangembon* and *Ōeibon* lineages however was the creation of a new variant of the *Izumi Shikibu nikki*—the *Fusōshūyōshūbon* and its descendant, the *Gunsho ruijūbon*—which was to become the standard version for over a century.

There can be no single, sure answer to the question of why such a variety of textual lineages and idiosyncratic manuscripts should have come into existence. The cause must be assigned to a combination of tendencies and accidents at work over a period of several hundred years. One need not even posit the existence of a single "original." There could have been two or more drafts by the author, some more highly polished than others, which came into the possession of different copyists and were thus transmitted. Unconscious errors in copying must have happened not infrequently. And different copyists could be expected to have different conceptions of their work; the ideal of complete faithfulness to the received text might not prevail in all cases. Indeed the hand of the redactor can be detected at work in some of the instances discussed above. Physical damage to perishable manuscripts and the loss or disordering of sheets must also be taken into account. The original of the *Izumi Shikibu nikki*, whatever that may have been, no longer exists, and it can hardly be expected that its descendants will not have changed with time.

C. Authorship and Formation

It has already been noted that the *Izumi Shikibu nikki* is not a diary, but at least in some measure a work of imaginative fiction. Acceptance of this thesis opens the possibility that, contrary to tradition, it may have been written by some one other than Izumi herself. The question of authorship has received considerable scholarly attention in recent years.

Perhaps the first to question attribution of the *Nikki* to Izumi Shikibu was Ikeda Kikan. It is interesting to note that Ikeda evidently changed his opinion during the course of his career. In his *Kyūtei joryū nikki bungaku* (1927) he voiced a strong assent to the self-authorship theory: "The poems in the work are Shikibu's, and it has an autobiographical flavor although written in the third person. It cannot be considered that it was composed by a later person on the basis of the poems. The style has an antique elegance and is definitely not post-Heian. In the absence of contrary evidence it can be considered the work of Izumi Shikibu."[133] This opinion is reiterated in Ikeda's article on the *Izumi Shikibu nikki* in *Nihon bungaku daijiten*.[134] In 1934 however he listed the *Izumi Shikibu nikki* among a group of works which supposedly developed from private poetry collections put together by someone other than the author of the poems.[135] In 1944 he stated that "the *Izumi Shikibu monogatari*, apparently based on Izumi Shikibu's poetry collection . . . was ✓ written by a third person and not by the heroine herself."[136] He made the same assertion again in 1951.[137]

Imai Takuji attacked along the same lines in 1935, a year after the first publication of Ikeda's objections. In *Heian-chō nikki no kenkyū* he raised the points mentioned previously, that the *Nikki* is written in the third person and contains scenes beyond the knowledge of a single person. He further argued that the utter simplicity of the plot is a point in favor of authorship by someone else—that incidental or extraneous events would have been included by a diarist. And he agreed with Ikeda in suggesting that the materials for the *Nikki* were taken from the *Izumi Shikibu kashū*.[138]

Support for authorship by someone other than Izumi Shikibu took on new and more concrete form with the publication of Kawase Kazuma's article, "*Izumi Shikibu nikki* wa Fujiwara Shunzei no saku," in 1953.[139] Kawase claims, on the basis of the Kangen 4 colophon in the *Kurokawabon*, that the *Izumi Shikibu nikki* must be considered indisputably the work of Fujiwara Shunzei. Yamagishi Tokuhei accepts this thesis in his 1959 introduction to the *Nihon koten zensho* edition of the *Izumi Shikibu nikki*.[140] In this exposition he conducts a six-pronged attack on attribution of the *Nikki* to Izumi Shikibu:

I.   None of the poems in the *Nikki* appears in any private or imperial anthology before the *Senzaishū* (1188), despite the fact that other poems by Izumi were included in such works, as well as poems selected from other *nikki*.

II.   The *Nikki* contains objective criticisms of Izumi's conduct which run counter to the strong denials of misbehavior to be found in her poetry collection.

III.   In contrast to other *nikki*, the work is written in the third person, contains scenes beyond the knowledge of a diarist, and describes the feelings of other people.

45

IV. There are several historical inaccuracies and other peculiarities in the *Nikki* which argue against its composition by Izumi Shikibu:

a. The ceremony of *In no hairai* (see translation, page 189) is described as taking place on New Year's Day, whereas in reality it was performed on the third day of the first month. In the late Heian Period however it was customarily performed on the first.

b. At one point in the *Nikki* Izumi seems to quote one of her own poems (see translation, note 263). This device would be more probable at the hands of someone other than the poet herself.

c. In another place Izumi seems to be referring to a poem by Dōmyō Azari (see translation, note 242). This poem is in the *Goshūi-shū*, and reference to it indicates that the *Nikki* was probably written after the date of the compilation of that anthology (1086).

d. Many poems have different wording in the *Nikki* from that which appears in the *Kashū*. These are probably examples of a later writer (the author of the *Nikki*) making changes to suit the prose situation in the *Nikki*. There is even one poem he has split into a *renga* (see translation, page 183).

e. As pointed out by Ozaki in *Izumi Shikibu nikki kōchū*, the passage "The fifth day of the fifth month came, and still the rain did not stop" (see translation, page 141) does not agree with recorded historical fact. According to *Honchō seiki*,[141] the first half of the fifth month of Chōhō 5 (1003) had clear weather every day except the tenth and sixteenth.[142]

V. The *Izumi Shikibu nikki* is one of a group of works with alternate titles. The others—the *Ise monogatari (Zaigo Chūjō nikki)*, *Tōnomine Shōshō monogatari (Takamitsu nikki)*, *Takamura monogatari (Takamura nikki)*, and *Heichū monogatari (Heichū, or Sadabumi, nikki)*—are all stories or collections of stories written later on the basis of poems by and anecdotes about their chief character. Not one was written by the author of the poems.

VI. On the basis of the *Kangembon* colophon Fujiwara Shunzei can be accepted as the author of the *Nikki*. While he was in the process of compiling the *Senzaishū* he must have come across a collection

46

of Izumi Shikibu's poems, taken an interest in her affair with Prince Atsumichi, and written a work about them. He probably changed the wording of some poems to suit his narrative, and composed others himself.[143]

The objections raised by Yamagishi amount to perhaps the most clearly articulated, powerful, and wide-ranging assault on the traditional attribution yet to be published. They have called forth various rebuttals from holders of opposing views however and cannot be said to represent the preponderance of Japanese scholarly opinion. The more generally accepted view still favors Izumi Shikibu as the author of the work to which her name is attached. A presentation of evidence and some of the more important arguments may be arranged in three categories: (1) external evidence of the *Nikki*'s existence; (2) the problem of the *Kangembon* colophon; and (3) internal evidence bearing on authorship and date.

1. *External Evidence*

Murasaki Shikibu nikki

Yoshida, *Kenkyū*, pages 562–566, argues that a certain passage in the *Murasaki Shikibu nikki*[144] has reference to the *Izumi Shikibu nikki*:

> Izumi Shikibu to iu hito koso, omoshirō kakikawashikeru. Saredo, Izumi wa keshikaranu kata koso are, uchitokete fumi hashirigakitaru ni, sono kata no zae aru hito, hakanai kotoba no nioi mo miehaberumeri. (Izumi Shikibu is one who really did carry on a fascinating correspondence. But Izumi has a far from praiseworthy side also. She writes her compositions in a loose and easy style, and is really quite talented in that direction. Her prose gives an impression of surface sheen.)[145]

It is impossible to decide whether this passage, which goes on to criticize Izumi's abilities as a poet, does indeed refer to the *Izumi Shikibu nikki*. The more usual interpretation is that "omoshirō kakikawashikeru" and "fumi hashirigakitaru" allude to Izumi's correspondence. But since the *Nikki* is composed largely of precisely that, Yoshida's hypothesis cannot be ruled out. Yoshida argues that

Murasaki would have been more likely to have seen Izumi's *Nikki* than her letters, and points out that Murasaki's comments on Sei Shōnagon must similarly have been based on a reading of the *Makura no sōshi*.

Genji monogatari

Yoshida, *Kenkyū*, pages 560–587, further alleges influence exerted by the *Izumi Shikibu nikki* on Murasaki Shikibu in her composition of the *Genji monogatari*.[146] This influence is said to evidence itself in three places—the "Yūgao," the "Kochō," and the ten Uji chapters. In the first instance Genji expresses in the following words his decision to take Yūgao away from her plebeian surroundings: "Iza, tada, kono watari chikaki tokoro ni, kokoro yasukute akasan" (Come! Let us finish the night in a certain place nearby where we can rest with our hearts at ease).[147] There is an obvious resemblance to the Prince's invitation to Izumi on the occasion of their first midnight excursion (see translation, page 143): "Iza tamae. Koyoi bakari. Hito mo minu tokoro ari. Kokoro nodoka ni mono nado kikoen" (Come . . . just for tonight. There is a place where no one will see. We can talk to our hearts' content).

A passage in the "Kochō" chapter containing a description of verdure and an exchange of poems on the *tachibana*[148] (see translation, notes 14, 15, 17) has a certain similarity in phraseology to the opening pages of the *Izumi Shikibu nikki*:

From the *Izumi Shikibu nikki* (see translation, pages 131–132):

Yume yori mo hakanaki yo no naka o nagekiwabitsutsu akashikurasu hodo ni, uzuki tō yo hi ni mo narinureba, ki no shita kuragarimoteyuku. Tsuihiji no ue no kusa aoyaka naru mo, hito wa koto ni me mo todomenu o, aware to nagamuru hodo ni, chikaki suigai no moto ni hito no kehai sureba, tare naran to omou hodo ni, komiya ni saburaishi kotoneri warawa narikeri . . . Tachibana no hana o toriidetareba mukashi no hito no to iwarete . . . Nani ka wa adaadashiku mo mada kikoetamawanu o, hakanaki koto o mo to omoite,

Kaoru ka ni/yosouru yori wa/hototogisu/kikabaya onaji/koe ya shitaru to.

48

(Frailer than a dream had been those mortal ties for which she mourned, passing her days and nights with sighs of melancholy. And now the tenth of the fourth month had come and gone, and the shade beneath the trees grew ever deeper. The fresh green of the grass on the embankment—though most people would hardly have given it a glance—somehow aroused an emotional awareness within her, and as she sat gazing out at it she noticed a movement at the nearby openwork fence. Who could it be, she wondered, only to discover a moment later that it was the young page who used to wait on the late Prince . . .

The page extended a sprig of orange blossom.

"The sleeves of him of old"—the words came to her of themselves . . .

But then, as yet he had no name for scandalous behavior. Should she risk a trifling verse?

> Rather than dwell
> On memories this fragrance breathes,
> O *hototogisu*,
> Sooner would I hear your voice—
> Is it the same as his?)

From the *Genji monogatari*: The first sentence of the "Kochō" chapter:

Yayoi no hatsuka amari no korooi, haru no omae no arisama, tsune yori koto ni tsukushite niou hana no iro, tori no koe, hoka no sato ni wa "mada furinu ni ya" to, mezurashū, miekikoyu. (It was past the twentieth of the third month, but the garden of the spring pavilion still reveled in the radiant hues of its blossoms and the songs of its birds, reaching a peak of perfection beyond that known in years past, so that the inhabitants of the other apartments marveled at how long its splendor lasted without fading.)

The scene in the same chapter in which Genji makes an amorous approach to Tamakazura, comparing her to her mother, his former mistress Yūgao:

Omae no wakakaede, kashiwagi nado no, aoyaka ni shigeriaitaru ga, nan to naku kokochiyoge naru sora o miidashitamaite . . . Tachibana no aru o masagurite,

"Tachibana no/kaorishi sode ni/yosoureba/kawareru mi to mo/
omoenu kana
Yo to tomo no kokoro ni kakete wasuregataki ni, nagusamu koto
nakute sugitsuru toshigoro o, kakute mitatematsuru wa, 'yume ni
ya' to nomi omoinasu o . . ." tote mite o toraetamaereba, onna . . .

Sode no ka o/yosouru kara ni/tachibana no/mi sae hakanaku/nari
mo koso sure.

(He looked out at the fresh, luxuriant green of the young maples and
oaks in the garden, standing together there against the sky, and the scene
brought him an ineffable delight . . .

Toying with an orange [that lay with other fruit in a box-lid], he said:

> Orange-flower
> Fragrant were the sleeves she wore
> Whose memory now returns
> Unaltered in a being
> I cannot think is other than she was.

"And indeed, after bearing in my heart through all these years the
image of an unforgettable love for which time has brought no consola-
tion, to look upon you thus makes me half believe this is only a
dream . . ."
With these words he took her hand. The girl . . .

> Because you turn
> Toward me these memories
> Of fragrant sleeves
> The fruit of the orange tree
> Can hardly last for long.)

Finally, the story of the courting of Ukifune by Kaoru and Niou
in the "Uji jūjō," the last ten chapters of the *Genji*, is alleged to
have drawn its conception and some of its details from the notorious
infatuation of the brothers Tametaka and Atsumichi with Izumi
Shikibu, and from certain passages of the *Nikki*. Among the latter
are the scene in which Prince Atsumichi is reproved by his old
nurse, as Niou is by Yūgiri and the Akashi Princess; and the midnight

escapades of Izumi and the Prince, likened to the passage in which Niou takes Ukifune to the far bank of the Uji.[149]

These parallels to the *Genji*, like the evidence provided by the *Murasaki Shikibu nikki*, are interesting, if not completely convincing. But the question of influence between the *Genji monogatari* and the *Izumi Shikibu nikki*, even if such influence were definitely established, would be difficult to judge because of uncertainty as to the date of composition of both works.[150] It is not impossible that the influence, if any, went in the opposite direction.

Kohon setsuwashū

Probably the first definite trace of the *Izumi Shikibu nikki* is that found in a late Heian *setsuwa*[151] collection, the *Kohon setsuwashū*.[152] The latter contains a story, "Sochi no Miya Izumi Shikibu ni kayoitamau koto," which combines two incidents in the *Nikki* and preserves considerable similarity of text. The same story is also included in two later *setsuwa* collections, the *Yotsugi monogatari*[153] and *Uji Dainagon monogatari*.[154] All three contain the episode of the Prince's visit when he walks about in the garden and hands Izumi a poem on his fan, put directly after the "Matamashi mo" poem passage (see translation, pages 135, 148). Each contains the words "to nikki ni kakitari" (she wrote in her diary). The author and date of the *Kohon setsuwashū* are unknown; Kawaguchi Hisao favors a date close to 1130 for its formation.[155] Although the matter is not definitely established, the work seems generally accepted as belonging to the twelfth century.[156] In the absence of more precise information, this item of evidence can be taken as strongly suggesting—but not proving—that the *Izumi Shikibu nikki* was in existence by the last century of the Heian Period.

Meigetsuki

Probably the next allusion to the *Izumi Shikibu nikki* is in *Meigetsu-ki* 明月記, the diary of Fujiwara Teika. In his entry for Jōei 貞永 2 (1233).3.20 he discusses a scroll with one picture for each month of the year, each a scene from a work of Japanese literature. The caption for the picture for the ninth month is given as 和泉式部帥宮叩門

(Izumi Shikibu: Sochi no Miya knocks at the gate).[157] It is a moot point whether "Izumi Shikibu" refers to the lady herself, or whether Teika meant it as the title of a work—presumably the *Izumi Shikibu nikki*. It seems quite likely however that the reference to knocking at the gate alludes to the episode "past the twentieth of the ninth month" when Prince Atsumichi knocks in vain because Izumi can rouse no one to let him in (see translation, pages 156–160). This likelihood is strengthened by the fact that Teika had included the Prince's poem, "Aki no yo no," in the *Shinkokinshū* 新古今集(number 1169). The allusion could be to the poem alone, but on the other hand this particular poem appears nowhere else than in the *Nikki* and the *Shinkokinshū*. The evidence seems to indicate then that Teika was referring to the *Izumi Shikibu nikki*.

Other Sources

The earliest reference to the latter title is in the thirteenth-century catalog of Japanese books, the *Honchō shojaku mokuroku* 本朝書籍目錄. This work, which was in existence by 1294, lists 和泉式部日記一卷 (*Izumi Shikibu nikki*: one *kan*) in its section on *kana* literature.[158] *Kakaishō* 河海抄, a fourteenth-century commentary on the *Genji monogatari*, also refers to the *Izumi Shikibu nikki*.[159] And *Kachō yosei* 花鳥餘情 (1472), another *Genji* commentary, refers to an "Izumi Shikibu kanaki 假名記."[160] The passage quoted however does not appear in the extant *Nikki*.[161]

Izumi Shikibu kashū

It has been alleged that the *Izumi Shikibu nikki* was written by a later author, using materials (poems and *kotobagaki*) drawn from the *Izumi Shikibu kashū*. Shimizu, Endō, Yoshida, and others have argued however that such a thing could hardly have happened—in fact, that the process was probably just the opposite.[162] The complete canon of Izumi Shikibu's poetry can be found in no single work, being scattered through the *Nikki*, several *chokusenshū* and privately compiled anthologies, and a group of documents which collectively make up the *Izumi Shikibu kashū*. Of these latter the largest and most important are the *Seishū* 正集 and *Zokushū* 續集. These titles have nothing to do with the date of compilation, but are merely convenient names assigned by recent scholars. Many poems appear in both the *Seishū* and *Zokushū*, and the problem of the formation of these two collections is complex.[163] It is certain that the *Seishū* however was in existence in the thirteenth century, for manuscript copies exist with colophons by Fujiwara Teika and his daughter Mimbukyō no Tsubone (1195–?). Both the *Zokushū* and the *Seishū* are thought to have been put together in stages, by different hands.[164] As analyzed by Shimizu, the *Seishū* is composed of five groups of poems, differentiated by theme, source, compiler, or by virtue of constituting clearly defined poetic sequences.[165] Of the 144½ poems in the *Nikki*, 63 (counting the two *renga* "Koto no ha fukaku"—"Shiratsuyu no" and "Naozari no"—"Otsuru namida wa" as one poem each) appear also in the *Seishū*. The *Zokushū* has very few poems from the *Nikki*, and those duplicate ones in the *Seishū*. Consequently the *Zokushū* need not enter into the discussion here.

The *Nikki* poems in the *Seishū* are not scattered evenly throughout the collection, but are arranged in three separate groups. Their placement can best be understood through Yoshida's analysis of the *Seishū*:[166]

Poem Group	Poems numbered:
A	1–97
B	98–267 (contains *Nikki* Poem-Group One: 220–224, 226–231—11 poems)
C	268–310
D	311–391 (311–366)
	Nikki Poem-Group Two: 392–421 (367–397)[167]—30 poems
	E–1: 422–536 (398–512)
E	E–2: 537–615 (513–591)
	E–3: 616–867 (592–819)
	Nikki Poem-Group Three: 868–893 (820–842)[168]—26 poems

The composition of the three *Nikki* poem-groups is as follows, the numbers referring to the order in which the poems appear in the *Nikki*:[169]

Group One: 41, 53, 54★, 55★, 57, 1, 2, 27, 28, 59★, 100
Group Two: 82, 84, 85, 87, 89, 92, 93, 96, 99, 103, 104, 108, 109,
             112, 113, 115, 117, 119, 121, 122, 125, 126, 128,
             129, 130, 131, 138, 140, 142, 143
Group Three: 10, 11, 34, 36, 38, 40, 42, 46, 48, 49, 51, 54★, 55★, 58,
             59★, 61, 63, 65, 65†, 66, 67, 68, 74, 75, 78, 81

It will be noted that there are three duplications (marked by stars) between Groups One and Three. The poem represented by 65† in Group Three is the "Kienubeki" poem which has fallen into the prose text (see translation, note 178) in the *Nikki*, but which here exists in its independent form. Thus the total count is sixty-seven. All of these are Izumi's poems with the exception of numbers 2, 28, 53, and 57 in Group One; and half of 93 (a *renga*) and 130 (also a *renga* in the *Nikki*, but treated as entirely the Prince's poem in the *Seishū*) in Group Two. These five-and-a-half poems are attributed to Prince Atsumichi in the *Nikki*.

From the above data several lines of evidence can be drawn. In the first place, the most striking phenomenon is the numerical imbalance between poems by Izumi and those by the Prince. If the *Nikki* was written by a later author drawing on the *Seishū*, he must either have supplied the Prince's poems from another source or have composed them himself. There is no record of an "Atsumichi shū" ever having existed (but see below, page 68). Even Kawase admits that there probably never was such a collection, for if there had been, poems from it would probably appear in the various *chokusenshū*.[170] But no collection has been found to contain any poem by Atsumichi which is not also in the *Nikki* or the *Izumi Shikibu kashū*. Hence Kawase asserts that the latter alternative was the case—the missing poems were written by Fujiwara Shunzei.[171] This theory will be examined later. In any case it is clear that the *Nikki* could not have been based on the *Seishū* alone.

It will be noticed that the poems of Group Two and Group Three preserve a perfect internal order, but that the two groups seem to be

54

reversed with relation to each other. One possible explanation of the latter phenomenon is that a section of manuscript sheets may at some point have been misplaced. It can be argued that the order was originally the opposite. According to a theory of Konishi Keiko, Groups Two and Three were originally one group, running sequentially from poem 10 through poem 143, and located immediately following Group D in the total *Seishū* structure. Then the first half of the group (poems 10–81) was lost. The pages were recovered by a later copyist who did not know their correct location, and simply added them at the end.[172] This explanation seems plausible. But in any case the internal order is more important in discussing the relation between the *Nikki* and the *Seishū*. This order can be taken to indicate that the compiler of this portion of the *Seishū* worked from the *Nikki*, selecting (in the order in which they appear in the *Nikki*) Izumi's poems and leaving out most of those by Prince Atsumichi—the opposite process from what has been suggested by Ikeda, Imai, Yamagishi, and others.[173] *Nikki* Poem-Group One however does not evince the same impeccable order as the other two and includes a higher proportion of poems by the Prince (four out of eleven). These facts indicate to Yoshida that Group One was selected directly from Izumi's unedited poems by the first compiler of the *Seishū*, and that it has no connection with the *Nikki*. The other two groups were, he argues, selected from the *Nikki* by a later compiler.[174] The existence of three duplications between Groups One and Two-Three also favors separate compilation.

Further evidence can be found in different types of *kotobagaki* employed. *Kotobagaki* in Group One refer to Atsumichi as "hito" (person) only once, as "Sochi no Miya" twice, and as "Miya" (Prince) four times. But in the other two groups he is consistently referred to as "hito." Yoshida concludes from this that the compiler of Group One simply took the *kotobagaki* as he found them when going through Izumi's poems, while the compiler of Groups Two and Three, working from an already formed text (the *Nikki*), uniformly adopted the appellation "hito" in conformity with the general practice throughout Group E.[175] Further, there is a *kotoba-*

gaki for each poem in Group One, and these *kotobagaki* are such that the occasion for each poem and exchange in the group can be understood without reference to the *Nikki*. There is thus no obvious necessity for assuming that Group One was supplied by that work. Groups Two and Three however present a different picture. Several poems have no *kotobagaki* at all; others have a brief notation such as "hito no kaerigoto ni" (in reply). Since these are Izumi's replies to the Prince, and his poems are not given, such a *kotobagaki* is insufficient to explain the occasion for the poem. Groups Two and Three cannot be understood as a whole without reference to the *Nikki*.

The evidence which may be drawn from a comparison of the *Nikki* and *Seishū*, while inconclusive, can be read to indicate that the former was not based on the latter, but that the latter probably drew in part from the former. If a connection is assumed, it seems more likely that the *Nikki*, whose plot explains the internal order of Poem Groups Two and Three, could have supplied material to the *Seishū* than that the opposite process should have occurred. But the *Seishū* could not have drawn from the *Izumi Shikibu nikki* as it exists today. The compiler of Groups Two and Three must have had before him a text in which the "Kienubeki" poem (see above, page 42; translation, note 178) was still in its ungarbled form.[176] Since the common ancestor of all extant versions of the *Nikki* must already have contained this error, the source of the *Seishū* poems—if the *Nikki* supplied them—must have been a still more remote text, or the descendant of such a text. Shimizu envisions a fairly primitive stage in the development of the *Nikki*, a work with little more than the poems and short *kotobagaki*.[177] Yoshida does not agree, but posits the existence of a different text of the *Nikki*, no longer extant. This text and the common ancestor of all extant texts would in turn be the descendants of a common ancestor—a manuscript in which the "Kienubeki" error had not yet occurred.[178]

The *Kashū* provides other extremely interesting, if only suggestive, evidence supporting attribution of the *Nikki* to Izumi Shikibu. This evidence, discussed in Yoshida, *Kenkyū*, pages 533–537, is all drawn from the group of elegiac poems, *Zokushū* 38–159

(880–1001), mourning Prince Atsumichi. The main points are as follows: Poem 40 (882), apparently dating from the forty-ninth day after the Prince's death,[179] refers to materials that may have gone into the *Nikki*:

> When a person belonging to the Prince's mansion sent me some of his stray notes,[180] asking me to look them over:

Nagareyoru	With grief I look at them
Awa to narinade	(I who have not vanished in the foam),
Namidagawa	These fragments of a past
Hayaku no koto o	So swiftly gone, now borne to me
Miru zo kanashiki	Like froth on a river of tears.[181]

Yoshida thinks that the materials mentioned in the *kotobagaki* may have included notes that the Prince had written concerning his affair with Izumi, and that acquisition of them was the immediate stimulus that spurred her to write the *Nikki*. Here also could be the source for the scenes she could not have witnessed.[182]

Other poems and *kotobagaki* dating from the period of Izumi's mourning contain phraseology and imagery similar to that found in the *Nikki*. Among them are:

Zokushū 99 (941):

> On seeing how green were the growing grasses:

Waga kokoro	Although my heart
Natsu no nobe ni mo	Is not a summer field,
Aranaku ni	How choked it is
Shigeku mo koi no	With tangled love
Narimasaru kana	That will not cease its growth!

Zokushū 110 (952):

> Around the second month someone asked for some of the oranges in front [of the house?];[183] on sending one only:

57

Toru mo ushi	Even to pluck is pain,
Mukashi no hito no	When I consider how
Ka ni nitaru	A flowering orange tree,
Hanatachibana ni	Fragrant as the scent he wore,
Naru ya to omoeba	Might grow from out this fruit.[184]

Zokushū 150 (992):

Kouru mi wa	Was my so loving self
Kotomono nare ya	A being in some different life?
Tori no ne ni	When was the time
Odorokasareshi	That I could still be wrenched
Toki wa nanidoki	By cockcrow from my dreams?[185]

There is an obvious similarity between the first poem's *kotobagaki* and the second poem's subject on the one hand, and the opening passage of the *Nikki* with its description of the grasses growing on the embankment and of the Prince's gift of a branch of orange blossom on the other. And it seems quite plausible that the third poem refers to the scene on page 145 of the translation, in which Izumi and the Prince are startled from sleep by the crowing of a cock; especially so since the episode is made the occasion for an exchange of poems. The three *waka* quoted above, and others like them, suggest that Izumi may have been at work on the *Nikki* at the time they were written.

Finally, the following two poems belong to a group which dates from the expiration of the mourning period:

Zokushū 84 (926):

Someone I had known at the Prince's mansion requested the inkstone he had used; on sending it:

Akazarishi	My tears have been
Mukashi no koto o	Water for the ink
Kakitsukuru	Ground on this stone
Suzuri no mizu wa	To write of days now gone
Namida narikeri	We spent in unwearied love.

58

Zokushū 86 (928):

On sending some writings of the Prince to be remade into paper for inscribing sutras:

Yaru fumi ni	Because my thoughts
Waga omou koto shi	Cannot be written now
Kakareneba	Upon this paper which I send,
Omou kokoro no	The time will never come
Tsukuru yo mo nashi	When longing will leave my heart.

These two poems can be taken together to indicate that during her mourning Izumi occupied her time and consoled herself by writing a record of her love, using the Prince's own inkstone and a collection of his correspondence. By the first anniversary of his death (Kankō 5 [1008].10.2), the composition completed, she could part with his inkstone, which had served its purpose, and dedicate the piles of his letters and other miscellaneous writings to be remade into paper for inscribing sutras to be read at memorial services.

The best that can be said of the evidence provided by the elegiac poems in the *Zokushū* is that it is intriguingly suggestive; of course it is too ambiguous to be accepted as proof.

Other Poetry Collections

Yamagishi has pointed out that none of the poems in the *Nikki* appears in any anthology of poetry antedating the *Senzaishū* (compiled in 1188). While this is true, there is a poem by Izumi in the *Goshūishū* (compiled in 1086) which is similar enough to one in the *Nikki* to seem almost a variant of it. This verse, *Goshūishū* 1096, appears also as *Seishū* 173 and *Zokushū* 570 (1412). (It will be noted that it thus falls outside any of the *Nikki* poem-groups in the *Seishū*.) With its *kotobagaki* it reads:

Once a man with whom she was having an affair asked for a poem to send to a certain woman. The poetess first composed the following to express her own feelings:

Kataraeba	Will you not forget,
Nagusamu koto mo	Bemused by this new love,
Aru mono o	The solace that we found
Wasure ya shinamu	When we held each other close
Koi no magire ni	In sweet converse?

A comparison with "Katarawaba," the fifth poem in the *Nikki* (see translation, page 133), reveals obvious parallels in phraseology but also significant differences. The *Nikki* poem is addressed by the Prince to Izumi; it seems to appear nowhere else than in that work. "Kataraeba," on the other hand, is sent by Izumi to an unnamed lover, in circumstances very similar to those in the episode on pages 160–161 of the translation. "Kataraeba" however is not used in the *Nikki*. It is not clear what significance should be attached to these facts, but they can be taken as arguing less for composition of the *Nikki* before the time of the *Goshūishū* than for the possibility that a later writer took from "Kataraeba" a hint for the above-mentioned episode in which the Prince asks Izumi for a poem to send to another woman,[186] as well as for the *Nikki* poem "Katarawaba." But this is no more than a guess. There may be no connection between "Katarawaba" and "Kataraeba."[187]

The *Senzaishū* contains two poems which are recognizably the same as poems found in the *Nikki*. *Senzaishū* 968 is "Kaoru ka ni," Izumi's answer to the Prince's gift of *tachibana* bloom (see translation, page 132). This verse also appears in the *Seishū*, as number 226, and is thus on the face of it no conclusive argument for the existence of the *Nikki*, unless one accepts the theory of the relation between the *Seishū* and *Nikki* proposed by Yoshida and others (see above, pages 52–56). The *kotobagaki* in the *Seishū* reads: "Sochi no Miya tachibana no eda o tamaeritarishi" (When Sochi no Miya presented a branch of the *tachibana*). That attached to *Senzaishū* 968 is fuller: "Danjō no Miya Tametaka no Miko kakurehaberite nochi Dazai no Sotsu Atsumichi no Miko hanatachibana o tsukawashite ikaga miru to iite haberikereba tsukawashikeru" (Sent when Dazai no Sotsu

Prince Atsumichi, after the demise of Danjō no Miya Prince Tame-taka, presented a flowering *tachibana*, saying, "How will she look upon it?"). The *Senzaishū kotobagaki* is obviously much closer to the text of the *Nikki*, containing as it does the words "ikaga miru," and can be taken as arguing that the compiler (Fujiwara Shunzei) drew on the *Nikki* rather than the *Seishū*.

The other *Nikki* poem in the *Senzaishū* is number 843. This poem, the eleventh in the *Nikki* (see translation, note 47), appears also as *Seishū* 869 (821). In both the *Nikki* and the *Seishū* the text reads: "Matamashi mo/Kabakari koso wa/Aramashika/Omoi mo kakenu/Kyō no yūgure." The *Senzaishū* version is different, however, the opening line reading "Matsu tote mo," and the closing "Aki no yūgure." The latter difference is crucial, for "autumn evening" is the wrong season for the *Nikki*, where the scene takes place in summer. The *kotobagaki* reads: "Dazai no Sotsu Atsumichi no Miko naka taehaberikeru koro akitsukata omoiidete monoshite haberikeru ni yomihaberikeru" (Composed in autumn when Dazai no Sotsu Prince Atsumichi remembered and wrote to her after a period in which their relations had lapsed). It would seem likely that in this case Shunzei drew on a source other than either the *Seishū* or the *Nikki*. Again the relationship between *chokusenshū* and the *Izumi Shikibu nikki* seems hard to fathom. The possibility of experimentation by Shunzei with various versions and prose settings for Izumi's poems (see below under "*Kangembon* Colophon") probably cannot be ruled out. Ōhashi, *Kenkyū*, page 139, however suggests that in connected script けふ (*kyō*) could easily have been mistaken for 秋 (*aki*), and that a change of "matamashi mo" to "matsu tote mo," essentially the same in meaning, would have been no great matter. The *Senzaishū* version, in other words, may be a mistranscription of the *Nikki* and *Seishū* version, and the *Senzaishū kotobagaki* an attempt to explain the mistranscribed poem.

The next imperial anthology, the *Shinkokinshū* (1205), contains the first poem for which no other source can be found than the *Izumi Shikibu nikki*. This, number 1169, is the "Aki no yo no" poem referred to above, page 52, in connection with Teika's entry in *Meigetsuki*. It would seem, as a piece of independent evidence, to indicate at least a strong possibility that the *Nikki* was in existence by the time of the compilation of the *Shinkokinshū*, and that Teika had read it. (For a fuller discussion of this problem see below under "*Kangembon* Colophon.") Teika also included four poems from the *Nikki* in the *Shinchokusenshū* (compiled in 1235), three of which have no other extant source. Of even more interest is an undated fragment in Teika's handwriting, the "Teika jihitsu *Izumi Shikibu nikki* utagire."[188] This consists of three poems from the *Nikki*, the twenty-seventh, thirtieth, and thirty-first poems in that work: "Yomosugara"—"Ima wa yomo"—"Yoigoto ni" (see translation, pages 141, 142, 144). The last two are found nowhere else but in the *Nikki*. The order is significant. It seems plausible that Teika extracted these three poems by Izumi from the *Nikki*, leaving out the intervening two by Atsumichi (numbers 28 and 29). Poems from the *Izumi Shikibu nikki* also appear in the *Shokugosenshū* (compiled in 1251), *Shokukokinshū* (1265), *Shokusenzaishū* (1320), *Shinsenzaishū* (1359), *Shinzokukokinshū* (1439), and *Fubokuwakashō* (early fourteenth century).[189]

Evidence concerning the relation of the *Izumi Shikibu nikki* to various poetry collections other than the *Izumi Shikibu kashū* tends to support the contention that the *Nikki* was written late in the Heian Period or at the beginning of the Kamakura Period. It is not clear, however, what interpretation should be placed on some data; the evidence again is suggestive rather than conclusive.

The total effect of the external evidence is to leave one in uncertainty as to the date and authorship of the *Izumi Shikibu nikki*. Intriguing hints are provided by passages in the *Murasaki Shikibu nikki*, *Genji monogatari*, and *Izumi Shikibu kashū*. These can be taken to indicate that Izumi Shikibu was the author of the *Nikki*, and that she wrote it during the year 1008. This evidence is at best tenuous and open to conflicting interpretation however. The relationship between the *Nikki* and the *Seishū* can be taken to indicate, though not to prove, that the *Nikki*, in some form, was in existence before the *Seishū* in its present form. Uncertainty concerning the formation of the latter however again throws the date of the *Nikki* into doubt. The same can be said of the *Kohon setsuwashū*, though the evidence here points, somewhat uncertainly, toward the early twelfth century as the latest possible period for the writing of the *Nikki*. The *Senzaishū* and *Shinkokinshū* indicate, but again do not absolutely prove, that the *Nikki* was in existence by the late twelfth or early thirteenth century. A *Meigetsuki* entry of 1233 seems to refer to the *Nikki*; and in a late thirteenth-century catalogue, the *Honchō shojaku mokuroku*, the full title of the *Nikki* at last appears.

2. *The Kangembon Colophon*

The sole attempt to ascribe authorship of the *Izumi Shikibu nikki* to a specific individual other than Izumi Shikibu herself was that made by Kawase Kazuma in 1953.[190] As stated previously, Kawase's candidate is Fujiwara Shunzei, and his chief evidence the colophon of the *Kangembon*. The significance and reliability of this colophon will now be examined. Its translation, once again, may be given as follows:

> The manuscript says: "During his lifetime I did not see this booklet; only after his death did I come to see it. A trivial thing written after the illness of his old age? He had his adopted child, the nun, write it down, thus and so. The style and diction are not ordinary. Although it would be embarrassing for the work to become generally known, for the moment I shall not destroy it."
> Written thus with his own brush by the former Minister of Revenue.
> Copied in full on the twelfth day of the fifth month of Kangen 4 [1246], at the command of Dairi Tenji.

It is clear that Zenkobu 前戸部, the "former Minister of Revenue," a *tōmyō* 唐名 or "Chinese style" for Mimbukyō 民部卿, the Minister of Popular Affairs, refers to Fujiwara Teika, who held that office during the years 1217–1227, and who used that style in signing manuscripts he copied. The identity of Dairi Tenji, and of

63

the copyist of Kangen 4, is not known.[191] Kawase asserts that the unnamed person during whose lifetime Teika had not seen the manuscript in question was Teika's father Shunzei, who died in 1204 at the age of ninety, and that the *Izumi Shikibu nikki* is thus Shunzei's work.[192] This assertion is made plausible by the fact that Shunzei did have an adopted daughter (actually his granddaughter) who became a nun.[193] It has however been attacked on several grounds.

The most important argument is that a colophon including identical phraseology is attached to another work, the *Kenju Gozen nikki*. This work, a memoir written by Teika's elder sister Kenju Gozen, was completed in 1219.[194] Its first colophon, written by Kenju Gozen herself, gives the date of completion: "I finished writing on the third day of the third month of Kempō 7 [1219]. About noon, a slight breeze blowing along the western front, I gave the manuscript to Shōnagon-dono[195] to read." There follows a series of colophons telling how Teika found the *Kenju Gozen nikki* among his sister's papers after her death and added extra material. First there is the notation, "This is something that she wrote during her lifetime." There follow the words: 存生之時不見此草子沒後所見及也高橋殿南向にて老病之後狂事歟以養子之禪尼令書云々文章詞躰不尋常雖恥披露暫不破却

> (During her lifetime I did not see this booklet; only after her death did I come to see it. A trivial thing which she wrote at the south face of the Takahashi residence[196] after the illness of her old age? She had her adopted child, the nun, write it down, thus and so. The style and diction are not ordinary. Although it would be embarrassing for the work to become generally known, for the moment I shall not destroy it.)

Next comes the sentence "Kore wa mina nochi ni Nyūdō-dono no kakisoesaseowashimashitaru kotodomo o kakitsuku" (These words which I append are all ones which the Lay Monk[197] added later). From the honorifics it is clear that this sentence was inserted by a later copyist. It could refer either to the immediately preceding colophon by Teika, or to the material he added to his sister's *nikki*.

64

Then there follows another passage apparently written by Teika:

> Kore ika wa iseki hogo no naka, jihitsu o mote kakiyoseri. Hajime mo
> hate mo naki itazuragoto o, nani to naku, kakisuteraretarikeru o
> mitsukete, ato naru hito no kakitsukuru nari. Kiregire, sanzan, erabi-
> atsumete kakiutsusu. (What follows I myself wrote down from among
> her miscellaneous posthumous papers. They are idle scribblings without
> a beginning or an end, which she had simply written and cast aside.
> I, her survivor, discovered them and append them here. Scraps of paper
> scattered here and there, I have collected and culled them and copied
> them out.)

After this there are several pages of the material added by Teika.
At one point he comments: 此事殊有憚早々破却 (This passage is of
a particularly sensitive nature; I shall destroy it without delay).[198]
From the detailed nature of the above colophons, and the fact
that they are attached to an acknowledged work of Teika's sister,
it seems likely that they are genuine and do belong to the *Kenju
Gozen nikki*. It will have been noticed however that one of Teika's
colophons is almost identical to that of the *Kangembon*. The question
must now be raised: Is the *Kangembon* colophon genuine? Kawase
thinks it is, contending that Teika wrote both the colophon in the
Kenju Gozen nikki and that in the *Kangembon*. He assumes that
Teika went through the posthumous papers of both his father and
his sister, discovering in the one case the *Izumi Shikibu nikki*, and
in the other the *Kenju Gozen nikki;* he appended colophons using
identical phraseology because the two cases were strikingly similar.[199] Tamai Kōsuke questions this assertion, pointing out that
Shunzei and Kenju Gozen died about twenty years apart. He
thinks one of the colophons must have been inserted by mistake,
and lists four reasons for believing that the *Kangembon* contains the
one erroneously attached:

(1) The detailed notations in the *Kenju Gozen nikki* colophons
concerning Teika's editorship make those colophons seem genuine.

(2) Teika would hardly have included in the *Shinkokinshū* and
Shinchokusenshū poems from the *Izumi Shikibu nikki* and attributed

them to Izumi Shikibu or Prince Atsumichi if he recognized them as fakes written in his father's declining years.

(3) The meaning of the expression 老病之後 (after the illness of old age) is clear in the case of Kenju Gozen, vague in the case of Shunzei. Kenju Gozen suffered a serious illness in 1212, several years before her death.[200] Shunzei in his early sixties was also gravely ill, and took religious vows. But this event occurred in 1176, a full twenty-eight years before his death.[201]

(4) The term "yōshi no zenni" (adopted child, the nun) is appropriate in the case of Kenju Gozen, who adopted a girl in the service of Shunkamon'in 春華門院 (1195–1211, daughter of Emperor Go-Toba 後鳥羽 [1180–1239; r. 1183–1198]). This girl, called Uemon no Suke 右衛門佐 by Teika in *Meigetsuki*,[202] and "daughter" by Kenju Gozen in her *nikki*,[203] motivated by the death of Shunkamon'in in 1211, became a nun in 1212 at the age of twenty-five.[204] Shunzei's adopted daughter, Koshibe no Zenni, however did not take her vows until at least nine years after Shunzei's death.[205]

Tamai's objections would seem to cast serious doubt on the Shunzei-authorship theory. But assuming for the moment that the *Kangembon* colophon does actually belong to the *Izumi Shikibu nikki*, how do we know that it refers to Shunzei and not to Kenju Gozen? The colophon does not state during whose lifetime it was that Teika had not seen the work in question. There is nothing in the original equivalent to the "his" and "her" which I have supplied in the translation. Both Shunzei and Kenju Gozen had an adopted daughter who became a nun. Another source of confusion is the sentence 文章詞躰不尋常, which I have translated as "The style and diction are not ordinary." This translation is deliberately ambiguous, for a question exists as to what "not ordinary" means. Kawase has interpreted it to mean "superior," but I agree with Endō that "inferior" is more likely, especially in view of the statement that follows.[206] And if "inferior" is the correct meaning, it seems more likely that Teika would so criticize his sister than his famous father. In short, Teika could be saying that Kenju Gozen was the author of the *Izumi Shikibu nikki*.

66

If we grant the possibility that Teika, on going through his sister's papers after her death, might have found two works—the *Kenju Gozen nikki* and the *Izumi Shikibu nikki*—and appended similar colophons, two arguments can still be leveled against her authorship of the *Izumi Shikibu nikki*. The first is that Teika would have been no more likely to include in imperial anthologies poems he recognized to be spurious works actually written by his sister than he would have if the fabrication had been done by his father. The other is that Prince Atsumichi's "Aki no yo no" poem was in the *Shinkokinshū* by 1205, whereas Kenju Gozen did not die until 1219 or later.

Ozaki Tomomitsu points out that Atsumichi's poem is noted in the *Shinkokinshū* as having been the choice of Teika and Ietaka[207] among the anthology's six compilers.[208] The group of poems in the *Shinkokinshū* having notations concerning the selector is believed to belong to the selection of the fourth month of Kennin 建仁 3 (1203).[209] But in 1203 Shunzei was still living. Hence Teika and Ietaka must have seen the *Izumi Shikibu nikki* during Shunzei's lifetime, contrary to what is claimed in the *Kangembon* colophon. But even if the poem was not included until 1205, that would be only a few months after Shunzei's death (Genkyū 元久 1 [1204]. 11.30). The selection of poems for the *Shinkokinshū* was a subject of lively debate among poets, including the Retired Emperor Go-Toba; it seems hardly likely that Teika, even had he wished to do so, could have slipped in a poem he himself knew to be spurious on such short notice.[210]

According to the arguments presented above, the essential dilemma faced by those who would accept the *Kangembon* colophon as genuine is this: If Teika "discovered" the *Izumi Shikibu nikki*, he must have done so by 1205 in order to have included Atsumichi's poem in the *Shinkokinshū*. But this is too soon for Shunzei's adopted daughter to be referred to as "yōshi no zenni." If the other *zenni* was meant, then the work becomes Kenju Gozen's. But Kenju Gozen did not die until 1219 or after, too late for Atsumichi's poem to have been included in the *Shinkokinshū*. Indeed, if it was a work written "after her illness," she did not begin writing until after 1212. There is a possible way out of the difficulty: Teika discovered the *Izumi Shikibu nikki* soon after Shunzei's death, included Atsumichi's poem (actually Shunzei's) in the *Shinkokinshū*, but did not write the colophon until years later, after "Shunzei's daughter" had become a nun. In this case the words "for the moment I shall not destroy it" seem curiously out of place. That moment would already have lasted at least nine years. It is a possibility, but a rather forced one.

These arguments against the *Kangembon* colophon can however be circumvented in another way, for they rest on two unproven assumptions—that poems by or believed to be by Prince Atsumichi did not survive in Teika's time outside the *Nikki* and what now constitutes the *Izumi Shikibu kashū*, and that Teika would necessarily consider spurious those poems which he saw for the first time in a work whose prose portions he recognized to have been written by his father. If the first assumption is not granted—if the "Aki no yo no" poem was available to Teika from a source other than the *Izumi Shikibu nikki*—then the evidence provided by the *Shinkokinshū* will not conflict with the statements in the *Kangembon* colophon, and attribution of the *Nikki* to either Shunzei or Kenju Gozen cannot be ruled out. And even if Teika did see the "Aki no yo no" poem for the first time in the *Nikki*, it cannot absolutely be assumed that he would have considered it his father's rather than Prince Atsumichi's work. Therefore, on this second ground, attribution of the *Nikki* to Shunzei (but not to Kenju Gozen, because of her death date) gains slightly in plausibility.

As mentioned previously, on page 54, there is no evidence that an "Atsumichi shū" ever existed, and Japanese scholarly opinion seems to be that there was no independent collection of the Prince's poems. It is of course possible that those poems may have survived in some other way, perhaps attached to some other no longer extant collection. It is simpler and more plausible however to suppose that Teika took the "Aki no yo no" poem from the *Izumi Shikibu nikki*, a work we know could have supplied it along with material for a *kotobagaki*, than to assume the existence of a collection or collections

68

of which there seems to be no trace. And since Teika probably had as broad a knowledge of poetry as any man of his day, it seems likely that he would at least have had his suspicions aroused by a group of previously unseen poems in a work he recognized to be by his father.

A few other points may be noted. Kawase thinks that the two *Nikki* poems in the *Senzaishū* indicate that Shunzei was already taking an interest in Izumi Shikibu, and had perhaps already written the *Izumi Shikibu nikki*.[211] But it would seem odd if Teika had heard nothing about this during his father's lifetime. After all, it would have been a case of the most famous poet of one age writing about (and putting poems into the mouth of) the most famous poet of another. Ōhashi, *Kenkyū*, page 141, also remarks that Shunzei would probably not have included in the *Senzaishū* a *kotobagaki* adapted from a work he himself had written (that to "Kaoru ka ni"—see above, pages 60, 61). And how, he asks, is one to account for the *kotobagaki* of "Matsu tote mo"? Why would Shunzei have changed the wording and the season in the *Senzaishū* but not in the *Nikki*? Finally, Suzuki Tomotarō seeks to put the whole problem to rest by observing that if the ancestor of the present *Kangembon* were really the original of the *Izumi Shikibu nikki*, as would be the case if its colophon were proved genuine, that colophon should appear in all other texts, since it relates to authorship and not to mere copying, and since all other versions would be descended from the manuscript to which Teika first appended it. The colophon does not so appear; hence, it must be spurious.[212] But this leaves out of consideration the possibility that the manuscript had already been copied before Teika found it and attached his colophon.

To view the matter from the other side, how, if the *Kangembon* colophon is assumed not to be genuine, did it become attached to one textual lineage of the *Izumi Shikibu nikki*? Yoshida proposes the following solution: Teika, on going through his sister's post-humous papers, noticed two works of similar length and in the same handwriting (that of Uemon no Suke, Kenju Gozen's adoptive daughter). One was the *Kenju Gozen nikki*, the other the *Izumi*

Shikibu nikki. Without carefully examining the contents of the latter, he assumed it also to be his sister's work, and affixed a similar colophon. According to this hypothesis, the *Izumi Shikibu nikki* was a work that Kenju Gozen had had her daughter copy.[213] This explanation is plausible only if one assumes that Teika first saw the *Izumi Shikibu nikki* after his sister's death, and that he took the "Aki no yo no" poem from another source. For if he had previously seen the *Nikki,* one glance at its opening should have been sufficient to tell him what he was looking at. Ōhashi, *Kenkyū,* page 107, suggests that a later copyist may have found a copy of the *Izumi Shikibu nikki* together (perhaps sewn into one book) with a copy of the *Kenju Gozen nikki,* and thinking the former a work composed under the same circumstances, may have added a part of the same colophon. This is another guess, plausible but not provable. In conclusion, it must be stated that the credibility of the *Kangembon* colophon has not been completely destroyed; it is not impossible that either Shunzei or Kenju Gozen could have written the *Izumi Shikibu nikki.* Serious doubts have been raised however, and the preponderance of scholarly opinion is against such attribution. Either way, the difficulties and uncertainties are such that the *Kangembon* colophon still poses an unsolved problem.

3. Internal Evidence

The Title

It was noted in the section on textual history that of all the old manuscripts only the *Sanjōnishibon* bears the title *Izumi Shikibu nikki.* The others are all entitled *Izumi Shikibu monogatari.* The following list gives in the left-hand column the titles or ways of referring to the *Nikki* found in the works or manuscripts entered opposite in the right-hand column.

Izumi Shikibu	*Meigetsuki*
Nikki	*Kohon setsuwashū, Yotsugi monogatari, Uji Dainagon monogatari*
Izumi Shikibu monogatari	*Kangembon* texts, *Ōeibon* texts

Izumi Shikibu kanaki (?)	*Kachō yosei*
Izumi Shikibu nikki	*Sanjōnishibon, Honchō shojaku moku-roku, Kakaishō, Gunsho ichiran, Gunsho ruijūbon*[214]

It is obvious from the above that some confusion has existed since at least early in the Kamakura Period as to just what sort of work the *Izumi Shikibu nikki* is. It should be noted however that to assert that the *Nikki* is a *monogatari*, a "tale"—apparently the opinion of the originators of the *Ōeibon* and *Kangembon* lineages—is not the same as asserting that Izumi Shikibu did not write it, nor does it tell us when or in what way it was constructed. As pointed out by Yamagishi, the *Izumi Shikibu nikki* is one of a group of works with alternate titles; a discussion of the significance of this fact will be postponed to the section on genre. Here it should be sufficient to observe that the *Izumi Shikibu nikki* is clearly different in structure and narrative technique from the *Ise* and the *Heichū;* all other evidence aside, a simple reading would lead one to suppose it had been composed in a different way. It is the opinion of Ōhashi, Endō, Suzuki Tomotarō, and others that literary works of the Heian Period were for the most part not given definite titles by their authors, but that various appellations were attached later by readers and copyists in order to distinguish one work from another.[215] If this is true, the alternate titles of the *Izumi Shikibu nikki* tell us nothing about how the author viewed his own work—much less about who that author was—but only how later groups of readers thought it appropriate to refer to the work.

The Chronology

Yamagishi and others have asserted that the *Izumi Shikibu nikki* contains anachronisms and inconsistencies of chronology which favor authorship by someone other than Izumi Shikibu. The question of historicity and internal consistency can be approached in two stages. The first is to examine the *Nikki* to discover if the charge is true; the other is to ponder what significance should be attached to the evidence found.

In a previous section a brief synopsis of the plot was given from the viewpoint of the *Nikki* as a work of fiction. Here a more detailed analysis of the time sequence will be undertaken to decide whether the *Nikki* can also be regarded, chronologically at least, as a true record; it will also be of value as an outline of the structure. The following is an episode-by-episode enumeration of the sequence of events. I have followed the order of the *Nikki* itself, in the *Sanjō-nishibon* version. The dates and other notations on the left are taken directly from the *Nikki*, or are based on time lapses indicated in the text.[216] It may be noted in advance however that chronological inconsistencies and downright impossibilities will become apparent in the course of the analysis. The whole question of the chronology has been thoroughly studied by Yoshida Kōichi in his *Izumi Shikibu kenkyū*, I, 291–402. Yoshida attempts, through comparison with historical records, to give the *Nikki* a more precise chronology than can be found in the text itself, and to justify apparent inconsistencies. The latter he does chiefly by alleging mistranscriptions of date by copyists and disordering of events in the mind of the author (Izumi Shikibu) writing some years after the fact. The events themselves, he contends, could all have happened, though in a somewhat different order. The "corrected" chronology proposed by Yoshida will be given in parentheses in the following presentation.

Chōhō 5 (1003)

4.10+? 1. One day "after the tenth of the fourth month" (uzuki tō yo hi) the page comes to visit Izumi. There follows her first exchange of poems with the Prince: "Kaoru ka ni"—"Onaji e ni." (4.12 or 13 according to Yoshida.)

An indefinite interlude of poem–exchanges.

? 2. The Prince makes his first visit. Probably past the middle of the month, judging from the time of the moon's "shining forth." (4.18 according to Yoshida, based on computations of the time of moonrise.)

?+1 3. The next morning (akenureba) the Prince and Izumi exchange poems: "Koi to ieba"—"Yo no tsune no." A further exchange of poems takes place (the same day?): "Matamashi mo"—"Hitaburu ni"—"Kakaredomo." (4.19 according to Yoshida.)

An interlude of several days (higoro ni narinu) without a visit.

4.30 4. On the last day of the month (tsugomori no hi) Izumi sends a poem: "Hototogisu."

5.1 5. The next morning (tsutomete) the Prince reads the poem, and answers: "Shinobine wa."

5.3–5 6. Two or three days later (futsuka mika arite) the Prince makes his second visit, only to be ignored all night. (5.3 according to Yoshida.)

5.4–6 7. The next morning (tsutomete) the Prince sends a poem: "Isa ya mada." (5.4 according to Yoshida.)

5.5–7 8. The next day (mata no hi) the Prince asks when Izumi intends to go on her pilgrimage and return. She answers: "Ori sugite." The poem indicates the day must be the fifth.[217] She goes to the temple. (5.5 according to Yoshida.)

5.7–9 9. Izumi returns after two or three days (futsuka mika bakari arite). She exchanges poems with the Prince: "Sugusu o mo"—"Makuru to mo." The Prince pays a nocturnal call (his third visit), but cannot gain admission because all are asleep. (5.8 according to Yoshida.)

5.8–10 10. The next morning (tsutomete) the Prince and Izumi exchange poems: "Akezarishi"—"Ikade ka wa." (5.9 according to Yoshida.)

"A long interval" (ito haruka nari) passes while the Prince hesitates to make a visit.

?	11. On a day of rain and melancholy the Prince and Izumi exchange poems: "Ōkata ni"—"Shinobu-ran"—"Fureba yo no"—"Nani sen ni." (Yoshida assigns this passage to 5.16 on the basis of historical records. *Honchō seiki* shows rainfall on the six-teenth.)[218]
5.5	12. The fifth of the fifth month comes (satsuki itsuka ni narinu). The rains still go on. (Yoshida assigns this day to 5.19 on the basis of historical records of a flood on the night of the nineteenth. 五日 he takes to be a mistake in copying which evolved from 十九日 written in cursive form.)[219]
5.6	13. Next morning (ito furiakashitaru tsutomete) Izumi and the Prince exchange messages and poems: "Yomosugara"—"Ware mo sazo." About noon the Prince goes to see the flood. More poems: "Ōmizu no"—"Ima wa yomo." The nurse prevents the Prince from making a nocturnal visit. (5.20 according to Yoshida.)

An indefinite interval during which relations be-tween the two lovers drift into uncertainty (obo-tsukanō narinu).

?	14. "At long last" (karōjite) the Prince comes (his fourth visit), and takes Izumi away to a deserted part of his mansion. (Yoshida places this on 6.14, noting that "the moon is very bright," a fact which argues for a date toward the middle of the month. The thirteenth was the first anniversary of Prince Tametaka's death. Prince Atsumichi attended the ceremonies held at Keishin'in 慧心院, Yokawa.[220] Thereafter he would have felt freer, Yoshida speculates, to adopt a more serious attitude toward his late brother's mistress.)[221]
?+1	15. The next morning (akenureba) the Prince

sends Izumi home in the carriage. They exchange poems: "Yoigoto ni"—"Asatsuyu no." That night the Prince comes and takes Izumi away again (his fifth visit). (6.15 according to Yoshida.)

?+2   16. The next morning (akenureba) the Prince sees Izumi home. They exchange poems about the unfortunate cock. (6.16 according to Yoshida.)

?+4–6   17. Two or three days later (futsuka mika bakari arite), on a night of brilliant moonlight, the Prince and Izumi exchange poems: "Waga gotoku"— "Hitoyo mishi." (6.18 according to Yoshida.)

?+5–7   18. The next night (mata no yo) the Prince comes again (his sixth visit), but sees a carriage and goes home thinking Izumi has another visitor. (6.19 according to Yoshida.)

?+6–8   19. The next day (yobe wa mairikitari) the Prince and Izumi exchange reproachful poems: "Matsu-yama ni"—"Kimi o koso." (6.20 according to Yoshida. The day is described as one of rain, which agrees with records for the twentieth.)[222]

An indefinite interval of silence (hisashiku notama-wasede).

?   20. Exchange of poems: "Tsurashi to mo"—"Au koto wa." (About the end of the sixth month according to Yoshida.)

?   21. On a night of bright moonlight Izumi writes to the Prince: "Tsuki o mite." He goes to visit her (his seventh visit), and hands her a poem on his fan. They exchange poems: "Kokoromi ni"—"Ajiki-naku." (Yoshida places this event about 7.15, noting the reference to bright moonlight.)

An indefinite period during which the Prince, having heard rumors about Izumi's lovers, does not write.

? | 22. A visit by the page apprizes Izumi of the reason (the coach seen at the gate) for the Prince's neglect. The lovers exchange reproachful poems: "Yoshi ya yoshi"—"Sode no ura ni." (Yoshida places these events about 6.23–24, thus bringing them closer to the affair of the nocturnal carriage, and prior to the Prince's fan-passing moonlight visit.)

7.7 | 23. On the seventh of the seventh month (fuzuki ni narinu; nanuka) Izumi exchanges poems with the Prince: "Omoiki ya"—"Nagamuran."

late 7 | 24. Near the end of the month (tsugomorigata ni) the lovers exchange poems: "Nezameneba"—"Ogikaze wa." (Yoshida places this event about 7.21–22.)

2 days later | 25. Two days later (futsuka bakari arite) the Prince makes a sudden evening visit (his eighth). Izumi feels embarrassed at being seen. (7.23–24 according to Yoshida.)

Several days (sono nochi higoro) of no communication.

? | 26. Izumi and the Prince exchange poems: "Kuregure to"—"Hito wa isa." (Yoshida places this exchange on 7.29, assuming that during the previous three days the Prince has been attending the annual *sumai* festival.[223] The previous two entries come, then, immediately before this festival.)[224]

8.? | 27. On an unspecified date in the eighth month (hazuki ni narinureba) Izumi departs on a seven-day pilgrimage to Ishiyama. (Yoshida places this event about 8.8.)[225]

?+x | 28. The Prince, thinking to send a message to Izumi, finds she has gone to Ishiyama. He writes a message for the page to deliver the next day. (8.10 according to Yoshida.)

next day   29. The next morning (tsutomete makare . . . yuki-tareba) the page leaves for Ishiyama. Presumably he arrives the same day. He delivers the Prince's message, and Izumi replies: "Ōmiji wa"—"Yama nagara." (8.11 according to Yoshida.)

?   30. The Prince sends the page back to Ishiyama with his replies: "Tazuneyuku"—"Uki ni yori." Izumi answers: "Sekiyama no"—"Kokoromi ni." (8.12 according to Yoshida.)

?   31. Izumi returns (presumably seven days after the time of her departure). She and the Prince exchange poems: "Asamashi ya"—"Yama o idete." (8.15 according to Yoshida.)

late 8   32. Near the end of the month (tsugomorigata ni), on a day of wind and rain, the Prince and Izumi exchange poems: "Nagekitsutsu"—"Akikaze wa." (Yoshida places this on 8.28 on the basis of weather records.)[226]

"The usual interval" (rei no hodo henu).

9.20+?   33. After the twentieth of the ninth month (naga-tsuki hatsuka amari bakari), toward dawn on a night of waning moon, the Prince makes a nocturnal call (his ninth visit), but returns home before Izumi can rouse someone to open the gate. Izumi spends a sleepless night and records her impressions at dawn. A poem comes from the Prince: "Aki no yo no." In reply she sends him her composition. He answers with five poems. (Yoshida assigns this episode to 9.17, rejecting the date 廿日あまりはかり [some-time after the twentieth] found in the *Sanjōnishibon* in favor of the 十よ日 [after the tenth] in *Ōeibon* and *Kangembon* texts, which he assumes to be a scribal error for 十七日 [the seventeenth]. He objects to a date past the twentieth because the moon would not yet be "slanting down in the west" at the early morning hour when Izumi was gazing at it. On the morning of the seventeenth it would have been in the proper position. These contentions he supports with astronomical data.)[227]

late 9

34. Near the end of the month (tsugomorigata ni) the Prince has Izumi compose a poem for a departing lady friend: "Oshimaruru." Izumi and the Prince exchange poems: "Kimi o okite"—"Uchisutete." (9.29 according to Yoshida.)

10.10

35. On the tenth of the tenth month (kaminazuki tōka hodo ni), a night of alternating cold drizzle and moonlight, the Prince visits Izumi (his tenth call). He composes the first "pillow-sleeves" poem.

10.11

36. The next day (aware naritsuru yoru . . . kesa no ma ni) Izumi and the Prince exchange poems: "Kesa no ma ni"—"Yume bakari."

An indefinite period during which the Prince visits Izumi frequently (shibashiba owashimashite).

?

37. On one such visit (ten+x+1) the Prince urges Izumi to come and live with him. She considers his proposal but makes a hesitant reply. (Yoshida assigns this visit to 10.14 on the grounds that the bright moon of the next night must be that of the fifteenth [full moon].)

?+1

38. Late that night ("yo fukaku"—presumably in the early hours of the next morning) the Prince leaves, and in the morning there is a poem-exchange: "Tsuyu musubu"—"Michishiba no." Night falls, and the lovers gaze at the brilliant moon from their separate dwellings. (10.15 according to Yoshida.)

?+2

39. The next morning (tsutomete) the Prince wishes to send a message, but his page is tardy

and Izumi's poem arrives first. The lovers exchange poems about the moon, the advisability of killing the page, and pillow-sleeves. (10.16 according to Yoshida.)[228]

An interval of two or three days during which no word comes from the Prince.

?+4–6

40. Late one night the Prince sends a poem: "Miru ya kimi." Izumi answers: "Fukenuran." (Yoshida assigns this exchange to 9.13 on the grounds that the reference in the Prince's poem to "aki no yo no tsuki" [moon of an autumn night] indicates that the poem could not belong to the tenth month, the first month of winter.[229] Also, the surprise expressed by Izumi on hearing a knock at the gate seems unnatural, since only "two or three days" have gone by since the Prince's last visit, and he has been calling frequently. A third reason is that an impossibly large number of events is crowded into the last twenty days of the tenth month. By placing this exchange on the night of 9.13, one of the famous nights for moon-viewing, Yoshida makes the next two entries come out exactly before his 9.17 date for the night when the Prince knocks at the gate in vain and Izumi writes her long composition.)[230]

?+6–9

41. Two days later (futsuka bakari arite) the Prince comes (visit ten+x+2) in a ladies' coach. Izumi is embarrassed at being seen for the first time by daylight. The two discuss the Prince's proposal (to come and live with him) and exchange a *renga*: "Koto no ha fukaku"—"Shiratsuyu no." Izumi admires his apparel as he leaves. (9.15 according to Yoshida. It must be noted however that the discussion of moving into the Prince's mansion thus

antedates the 10.14 date Yoshida suggests for that proposal. Yoshida counters this difficulty by arguing that the present passage indicates that the Prince has already been urging such a course of action.)[231]

?+7–10   42. The next day (mata no hi) the lovers exchange poems: "Kazuraki no"—"Okonai no." (9.16 according to Yoshida.)

An indefinite interval during which the Prince visits Izumi more frequently than before (arishi yori wa tokidoki owashimashi), and other men send her messages and loiter about her house. She is still unable to make up her mind to accept the Prince's proposal.

?   43. On a morning white with frost Izumi and the Prince exchange poems: "Waga ue wa"—"Tsuki mo mide." At evening he pays a call (visit ten+ x+2+x+1) and invites her to go with him on a foliage trip. (Yoshida places this event about 10.5 on the basis of a comparison with the dates given for foliage-viewing in other Heian texts, the present average date for first frost, and a comparison with a series of poems in the *Izumi Shikibu kashū*. *Zokushū* 613 [1455], dated 10.5 [year not given], describes a frosty morning.)[232]

?+x   44. On the day appointed for the outing (sono hi ni narite) Izumi is unable to make the trip. That night wind and rain strip the leaves from the trees. (About 10.8 according to Yoshida. *Zokushū* 637 [1479], dated 10.8, year unspecified[233] [see translation, note 263], contains the phrase "kaze no mae naru" which Izumi murmurs to herself on this night.)

?+x+1   45. The next morning (tsutomete) the lovers exchange a series of poems about their lost op-

portunity to see the colored leaves. That evening
the Prince comes (visit ten+x+2+x+2) and
quietly leads Izumi away to the residence of his
cousin, where he is spending a forty-five-day
period for astrological reasons (see translation, notes
104, 277). The lovers pass the night in the carriage
house. (Yoshida separates this entry into two.
The poem-exchanges and the Prince's evening
visit take place about 10.9. In order to make the
calculations for the forty-five-day *imitagae* period
come out correctly, he places its beginning on 10.2,
along with the night in the carriage house. According to this interpretation the "leading away"
on the night of the poem-exchanges, and the
night spent in the carriage, are two separate occasions.)[234]

?+x+2   46. The next morning (akenureba) the Prince
escorts Izumi home, returns, and they exchange
poems: "Nenuru yo no"—"Sono yo yori." (10.3
according to Yoshida.)

A period of indefinite duration during which
Izumi turns over in her mind the advantages and
disadvantages of accepting the Prince's proposal,
finally deciding that she will accept. As a result
she refuses to answer the letters sent her by various
gallants. (Yoshida places this passage around 10.20.)

?   47. The Prince sends a curt letter implying that
Izumi has been unfaithful. They exchange notes and
poems: "Ima no ma ni"—"Kimi wa sawa"—
"Utagawaji"—"Uramuramu." Whether all these
are exchanged on the same day is not clear. At
evening the Prince calls (visit ten+x+2+x+3)
and urges Izumi to avoid scandal by coming to
live with him. (About 10.21 according to Yoshida.)

?+1

?

?

?

?

?

48. The next morning (akenureba) the Prince returns home. (About 10.22 according to Yoshida.)

49. One evening after a day of wind and rain Izumi writes to the Prince complaining of his neglect: "Shimogare wa." He replies: "Karehatete." (Yoshida places this event on 11.13, according to historical record a day of violent winds and thunder.[235] It immediately precedes the last few days of *imitagae* [see below], and hence a date in the eleventh month is most likely.)

50. The Prince sends a carriage for Izumi and has her come again to his *imitagae* retreat (visit ten +x+2+x+4). This passage could possibly be placed on the same day as the preceding entry. (11.14 according to Yoshida.)

A period of indefinite duration which the lovers spend together (okifushi).

51. The Prince's *imitagae* ends and the two return to their own homes. They exchange poems: "Tsurezure to"—"Omou koto." (11.16 according to Yoshida's reckoning. He calculates the period of *imitagae* by expanding the forty-five days in both directions from the point, apparently late in the tenth month, when it is first mentioned. He figures the terminal date by counting a reasonable number of days from the day of winds [see above, no. 49], and then counts backward to arrive at the beginning date [10.2].)[236]

An indefinite period of further hesitation on the part of Izumi.

52. One evening after the leaves have all fallen, Izumi and the Prince exchange poems: "Nagusamuru"—"Yūgure wa." (About 10.24 according to

Yoshida, on the assumption that by then the leaves would all have fallen. He proposes an alternate placement in the first part of the eleventh month.)[237]

?+1   53. Early the next morning (mata no hi no mada tsutomete) the lovers exchange poems: "Oki-nagara"—"Ware hitori"—"Kimi wa kimi." (About 10.25 according to Yoshida.)

An indefinite period during which Izumi is ill.

?   54. One day when she has slightly recovered she and the Prince exchange poems: "Taeshi koro"—"Tama no o no." (Around the end of the tenth month according to Yoshida.)

The year is almost over (toshi mo nokori nakereba), and Izumi is thinking of moving to the Prince's mansion in the spring (i.e., in the new year).

App. 11.1   55. On approximately the first of the eleventh month (shimotsuki tsuitachi goro) the lovers exchange poems on a snowy day: "Kamiyo yori"—"Hatsuyuki to."

An indefinite interval during which they occupy themselves with such casual exchanges (yoshinashi-goto ni akashikurasu).

?   56. The Prince writes to say that he is kept away by a Chinese poetry meeting. He and Izumi exchange poems: "Itoma nami"—"Waga yado ni." (Yoshida places this exchange on 11.28 on the historical grounds that a meeting for composing Chinese poetry was held in the Imperial Palace on that date.)[238]

?   57. On a day when the frost is unusually heavy Izumi sends a poem to the Prince: "Sayuru yo no." Perhaps on the same day, she also writes:

83

"Ame mo furi." That night the Prince comes (visit ten+x+2+x+5) and speaks of the possibility of his abandoning the world. The lovers exchange a *renga:* "Naozari no"—"Otsuru namida wa." (Yoshida places this visit about 12.8 by reckoning backward a likely number of days from the beginning of the sutra-reading ceremonies mentioned below.)

?+1

58. The next morning (akenureba) the Prince takes his departure. The lovers exchange poems: "Utsutsu nite"—"Shika bakari"—"Utsutsu to mo"—"Hodo shiranu." (About 12.9 according to Yoshida.)

An indefinite interval during which Izumi sighs and regrets that she has not been more prompt to accept the Prince's proposal.

?

59. One day about noon (hirutsukata) a poem comes from the Prince: "Ana koishi." Izumi replies: "Koishiku wa." Since at this time the Prince is studying the sutras, he brings that fact into his rejoinder: "Au michi wa." Izumi replies: "Ware saraba." (This series of exchanges is placed by Yoshida about 12.15. He takes the reference to learning sutras [onkyō narawase] to be an allusion to the Ki no Midokyō 季御讀經 ceremony, a reading of the *Dai hannya kyō* performed in the Imperial Palace twice a year, an event which the Prince would naturally have attended.[239] In Chōhō 5 it was held from 12.15 through 12.18.)[240]

?

60. On a day of heavy snow the lovers exchange poems: "Yuki fureba"—"Ume wa haya." (Yoshida suspects that these poems were written on separate occasions and linked together later by the author, on the grounds that Izumi's poem, "Ume wa haya,"

appears in the *Zokushū* [475 (1317)] as a New Year's Day poem, and the weather conditions of New Year's Day Chōhō 6 are confirmed by an entry in *Gonki*.[241] The Prince's poem says that spring has not yet come however. Yoshida also notes that the exchange is unique in being solely a description of nature, divorced from the emotional progress of the plot.)[242]

?+1   61. On the morning of the following day (mata no hi, tsutomete) the lovers exchange poems: "Fuyu no yo no"—"Fuyu no yo no." (12.16 or 17 according to Yoshida.)

An indefinite period during which Izumi's melancholy is alleviated by exchanges such as the above.

?   62. The Prince sends Izumi a message indicating he is not long for this world (or perhaps he visits her and speaks his message). They exchange poems (the last in the *Nikki*): "Kuretake no"—"Kuretake no." (Yoshida takes this exchange to have been made on the same day as the following entry. The wording is ambiguous enough to make such an interpretation possible.)

12.18   63. On the night of the eighteenth of the twelfth month (shiwasu jūhachi nichi) the Prince (visit ten +x+2+x+6) secretly conducts Izumi and a servant to quarters he has prepared in his mansion.

12.19   64. The next morning (akenureba) Izumi sends her servant to bring some of her belongings. Presumably on the same day, she and the Prince discuss moving to the northern wing.

12.21–22   65. Two days later (futsuka bakari arite) Izumi is moved to the northern wing. The Prince's consort learns of her presence and becomes indignant. (12.21 according to Yoshida.)

An indefinite period during which the Princess continues indignant and the Prince keeps away from her.

?   66. The Prince and Princess exchange words about Izumi. (Yoshida assigns no date.)

An indefinite period during which Izumi serves the Prince, and the latter sees his consort but infrequently.

Chōhō 6

1.1   67. On New Year's Day (shōgatsu tsuitachi) the Prince attends ceremonies honoring the Retired Emperor.[243] He is escorted home by a crowd of nobles, and an evening of music ensues.

An indefinite period during which Izumi suffers from the gossip of the underlings and the Prince neglects the Princess.

?   68. The Princess receives a letter from her elder sister, the Consort of the Heir Apparent, urging her to leave the Prince and come home. The Princess answers, asking that a carriage be sent for her. She has her quarters cleaned and informs her maids that she will be leaving. They join in criticizing the Prince. The carriage sent by her sister arrives. The Prince is warned of what is happening. Izumi wishes she could leave and avoid such painful scenes, but resigns herself to her fate. The Prince exchanges his last words with the Princess. (It is not clear whether or not all these events happen on the same day. Yoshida assigns no date.)

It will have been seen from the above that the *Izumi Shikibu nikki* as it stands is a chronological impossibility. This is especially noticeable in regard to the large number of events attributed to the tenth month, and in such minor inconsistencies as the doubling back to

86

the fifth of the fifth month and the matter of the Prince's out-of-season poem in praise of the autumnal moon. It is evident that whoever wrote the *Nikki* was careless in such matters. The question remains—was the carelessness Izumi's or that of another writer? Yoshida has attempted, by dint of much research and ingenious rearranging of episodes, to demonstrate that the raw material of the *Nikki* can be made to fall into a plausible chronology, and one which furthermore is in accord with known meteorological, astronomical, and ceremonial data.[244] But his analysis, though extremely ingenious, has its weak points, and may give an impression of being too labored and contrived. Impressive though it is, it will not convince everyone.

A few other problems related to the question of anachronisms must be mentioned. Yamagishi's points IV b and c (see above, page 46), having to do with allusions in Izumi's poetry, are dubious. The first is dealt with in translation, note 263: Izumi was apparently referring to a well known phrase from a Buddhist text. As for the alleged reference to a poem by Dōmyō Azari, even if such an allusion was intended, that fact would not prove that Izumi need have waited until the compilation of the *Goshūishū* in order to see a poem by a contemporary. Another alleged anachronism is the reference to "opening a hole" (ana o ake) in something to peek at Izumi on New Year's Day (see translation, note 370); this has been taken as evidence for composition at the end of the Heian Period. Itō Hiroshi argues that *akari shōji* 明障子 (sliding doors with translucent paper panels such as could easily be punctured with a finger) were not yet in use in the age of Izumi Shikibu.[245] Yoshida quotes similar passages from the *Genji monogatari* however concerning peeping through holes in *shōji*.[246]

But how significant after all is historicity or internal consistency? Historical inaccuracies, which are not lacking in other works (such as the *Kagerō nikki*),[247] whose authorship has not been questioned, can be explained simply as lapses of memory or as stemming from an attitude quite alien to that of the historian or annalist. As has been noted, the *Izumi Shikibu nikki* is an at least partially fictionalized, if not fictional, work. The author, whoever he may have been, was obviously less concerned with chronology than with lyricism. Although it is difficult to justify the *Nikki* as a record of actual event, that fact is not crucial. Even if Izumi Shikibu was the author, she was writing a story; if she could describe imagined scenes, she could also have rain fall and the Retired Emperor congratulated when she wished. But so, of course, could any other writer. Alleged anachronisms do raise doubts, but none of them lacks an explanation or counter-argument. Here too the evidence must be judged inconclusive.

Other Evidence

Other arguments, some of them subjective, have been advanced for or against attribution of the *Nikki* to Izumi Shikibu or a contemporary. Endō, Ozaki, and others have agreed with Ikeda's early opinion (see above, page 44) that the prose of the *Nikki* belongs to the era of literary florescence at the beginning of the eleventh century; Endō states that the work definitely could not have been written by as late a figure as Fujiwara Shunzei.[248] Some scholars claim to "feel" Izumi in the *Nikki*, or allege that the mode of expression is similar to that found in the *Izumi Shikibu kashū*.[249] Yamagishi (see above, page 45) takes the opposite view—that criticisms of Izumi in the *Nikki* argue against her as author. Yet it is true that, while she blames herself for being unfaithful to the memory of Prince Tametaka, and has herself criticized by the old nurse and the wife of the Prince, she also defends her conduct repeatedly against the accusations of her lover and the slanders of society.[250] It is frequently urged by supporters of attribution to Izumi that only she could so successfully have woven the prose and poems together into one unbroken fabric. It is not clear however on exactly what grounds this assertion is made. The first "Kuretake no" poem (see translation, page 186) can be and has been taken as providing a hint that Izumi was already during Prince Atsumichi's lifetime thinking of writing the *Nikki*.[251]

88

And then there is the question of objectivity. It has been noted that the *Izumi Shikibu nikki* is written in the third person; "onna" (the woman) is the only name the heroine is given throughout.[252] The question of "person" is dealt with in more detail in the section on genre. It might be well to keep in mind however that in Japanese —where verbs do not reflect differences in subject, and where pronouns are usually dispensed with—"person" is far less apparent than it is in English. It is the middle of the third page of the *Izumi Shikibu nikki* [*Iwanami text*, page 401] before the first "onna" appears and it becomes plain that the work is not in the first person. (See translation, page 134, "The lady was extremely embarrassed . . . ").

But is the narrative of the *Izumi Shikibu nikki* really objective throughout? Suzuki Tomotarō asserts that Izumi's mask slips from time to time.[253] Attention is preponderantly centered on the lady, and her feelings are described more frequently than those of the Prince.[254] They are also described directly, whereas her lover's are usually—though not always—conjectured. A survey of emotionally charged adjectives and verbs, such as *kanashi* (sad), *omoi-midaru* (to be distraught), *ayashi* (strange, suspicious), *katawara itashi* (discomfiting), *warinashi* (indiscriminate, distressing), *migurushi* (ugly), and *kokorobososhi* (downhearted), shows that the great majority are the lady's utterances or are used to describe her feelings.

Unquestionably it is Izumi's emotional life, more than that of the Prince, which constitutes the *Nikki's* subject. But is this really tantamount to saying that only Izumi could have been the author? Suzuki asserts that there are places in the *Nikki* where the lady's self-conscious reflections could only be based on actual experience.[255] With this I can hardly agree, for surely one of the prime achievements of fiction is the imaginative penetration of personality. According to such an argument any novel must have been written by its central character. The *Izumi Shikibu nikki*, as its title indicates, is about Izumi Shikibu. But the internal evidence is too diffuse, inconclusive, and conflicting to decide whether or not she wrote it herself.

What then can be stated as a general conclusion to the total survey of evidence? Only that no firm conclusion can be reached. Some items of evidence suggest that Izumi Shikibu could have been, or was, the author. Others point toward later composition. Many difficulties surround attribution to Fujiwara Shunzei or Kenju Gozen, but those possibilities have not been completely invalidated. Japanese scholarly opinion, of which only a sample has been presented, is sharply divided; the majority however seems to favor the traditional attribution to Izumi Shikibu. Shunzei apparently has few supporters.

D. The Question of Genre

The foregoing pages have described the uncertainties surrounding the authorship, formation, and date of the *Izumi Shikibu nikki*. It may now be helpful to consider the work against its natural background of early Japanese court literature.

Varieties of Nikki

The term *nikki* 日記,[256] literally "day record," in its earliest Japanese[257] usage refers to official records of events at court rather than to anything that can be identified as literature. Thus *geki nikki* 外記日記 and *naiki nikki* 内記日記 were records kept by the Geki and the Naiki, document-drafting officials of the central bureaucracy.[258] The first reference to such *nikki* dates from 821.[259] Another species of writing classified as *nikki*, though usually not so titled, consists of the privately kept journals of court nobles. These become quite numerous from the Heian Period onward. They are written in true diary form, with a separate entry for each day, and have as one of their main purposes the minute recording of correct ceremonial. Such examples as *Teishinkōki, Ouki, Gonki, Midō Kampaku ki*, and *Sakeiki* are important sources for the history of the Heian court.[260] All these documents, both official and private, are written not in Japanese but in a peculiar Chinese known as *kiroku kambun* 記録漢文 (record Chinese). The authors of the private journals sometimes attempted and achieved a stylistic elegance which nevertheless is

90

not generally considered sufficient in itself to qualify these works as literature.

A third group of writings described as *nikki* is composed of records of poetry competitions[261] held at court or in the homes of the nobles. Such competitions, beginning apparently in the ninth century, became and remained very popular throughout the middle and late Heian and early Kamakura periods.[262] The spirit of rivalry in fact was highly cultivated, especially among the court ladies, and took an extraordinary variety of forms. Not only were poems matched, but fans, shells, paintings, iris roots, chrysanthemums, songbirds, short stories, and a great variety of other living things, inanimate objects, and products of manual and verbal skill. Sei Shōnagon 清少納言 (fl. last decade of the tenth century) listed victory in such contests among the things which gave her pleasure,[263] and readers of the *Tale of Genji* will recall the furious preparations and high excitement occasioned by the picture competition. Contestants were grouped into teams of the left and right, judges were appointed, and records kept of their decisions. Since the writing of verse often accompanied the matching of objects, such a document as "The Shell-Matching Held on the Sixth Day of the Fifth Month of the First Year of Chōkyū [1040] in Honor of the Ise Shrine Virgin Princess Ryōshi"[264] is an item in the history of Japanese poetry. If written in Chinese, the prose portions of such records were called simply *nikki;* if in Japanese, *kana nikki.* These *kana nikki* are often lively and detailed in their descriptions, dwelling on the circumstances leading up to the competition and painting a picture of the setting with its carefully wrought decorations and the contestants in their costumes of various colors. They are written with obvious literary intent.[265]

To Heian court society then the concept of *nikki* was that of a record of actual event, whether public or private, written in Chinese or Japanese, either carefully styled or baldly factual. From the tenth century onwards it came to refer more specifically to a type of personal memoir, a genre now known as *nikki bungaku*—"*nikki* literature"—to which, according to the traditional view, the *Izumi*

Shikibu nikki belongs. These memoirs, examples of which will be discussed below, are expressions of a fundamental and persistent urge motivating the creation of much of Japanese literature. All writing, to begin with, partakes of a felt need to preserve the past, and there is nothing specifically Japanese about this. The early chronicles and songs have their counterparts in other countries. Along with the development of a literary consciousness however there began to appear in Japanese writings an interest in a personal as well as a national past, a tendency for an author to collect and set down certain incidents of his own life which seemed to him worth recording. This bias toward the autobiographical, or in broader terms the factual, forms one current running through the sea of Japanese literature. It is a wide and meandering stream, whose boundaries are ill-defined and whose waters have often mingled with and colored other literary currents. Its origins are involved with the peculiarly fluid nature of Japanese verse.

Lyricism and Prose Contexts

The lyric impulse in Japan, as in other countries, antedates the beginning of literacy; Japanese literature is unusual however for the dominantly lyric tone it preserves throughout its history. Personal writings—journals, jottings, and reflective essays—and the old fictional tales constantly merge into poetry as the author, the hero, or the heroine expresses his or her thoughts in a well turned verse. The plays of the *nō*, the puppet, and the *kabuki* theaters are fabrics of interwoven prose and verse, and are recited, declaimed, or sung in ways which mark them off from ordinary speech. Travel records and the travel scenes in drama are series of lyric evocations of the qualities and associations of places and their names. The lyric tradition continues through the various genres of popular literature of late traditional Japan, and in significant ways into the work of some of the best modern authors.

Why this should be so constitutes one of the most interesting problems in the history of Japanese letters. Japanese poetic forms are short compared to those traditional in the West. Primitive poetry had a concept of long and short lines, but no fixed length or number of lines. With the emergence of consciously literary creativity in the seventh century—a flowering from native roots but nourished by Chinese example—alternate lines of five and seven syllables became the norm, and poems were grouped into types by number of lines. The most prevalent form, the *tanka* 短歌, consists of thirty-one syllables in subdivisions of five, seven, five, seven, and seven. The *chōka* 長歌, the second most common form during the first literary period—roughly, the seventh and eighth centuries—is made up of an indefinite number of alternating five- and seven-syllable lines with an extra seven-syllable line at the end. It was theoretically capable of practically unlimited development, but in fact the *Man'yōshū* contains no *chōka* longer than 149 lines—not very long by Western standards. Despite narrative elements the impulse of the poetry is basically lyrical, and therefore relatively short-winded. There was also a tendency for the *chōka* poets to write in very long syntactic units, or even to make the whole poem one unit. This was a triumph of language, and some of the best effects in Japanese poetry were achieved by means of such long, tightly integrated structures, but there are obvious practical objections to unlimited extension or addition of the prepositional modifying clauses which are a fundamental feature of the syntax. After the eighth century the *chōka* in any case was abandoned as a serious literary vehicle, leaving the *tanka* to dominate poetry for the next several centuries. Eventually an even briefer form developed, the seventeen-syllable *haiku*.[266]

From earliest times then most Japanese poetry was of a length to fit easily into longer prose settings. Of at least equal importance to the evolution of mixed forms was the role of verse in Japanese society. The view of poetry as a lofty and serious art can be traced in its development through the works of gifted poets and critics; but poetry had always been, and remained, something else as well. It was a means of communication, a mode of speech and later of writing. When the primordial creators of the earth, the male and female deities Izanagi 伊弉諾 and Izanami 伊弉冉, met to begin their divine procreation beneath the Floating Bridge of Heaven, they exchanged ritual greetings: "Ana ni yashie otome o! Ana ni yashie otoko o!" (Truly what a fine girl! Truly what a fine man!).[267] These exclamations were treated as the beginning of the Japanese poetic tradition, and Ki no Tsurayuki 紀貫之 (ca. 868–945) could claim in the *Kana Preface* to the *Kokinshū*, "Our poetry has existed from the beginning of heaven and earth." This enshrinement of the poetic exchange reflects a social reality in early Japan. As indicated by the Izanami-Izanagi myth, singing back and forth between young men and maidens may have played a part in ancient courtship practices.[268] In later times, in any case, exchange of poems was the standard procedure in initiating a love affair, and one cannot but be intrigued by a vision of the Heian capital constantly alive with messengers carrying that lightest of burdens, a lover's note. Since poetry was such a common and essential adjunct of polite existence, it was composed by practically everyone of culture—universally, in Tsurayuki's view[269]—and naturally had a highly cultivated occasional aspect. Poetry was part of everyday discourse, and a knowledge of situation is often needed in order to understand what is meant in a given poem. Even formal verses written as deliberate acts of poetic creation and designed to be read by a wide public are usually prefaced by an explanatory headnote or at least an indication of the topic. The celebrated poem by Princess Nukata 額田王 (fl. ca. 660–690) on the relative charms of spring and autumn, for instance, is introduced by the following: "When the Emperor commanded the Great Minister of the Center, Lord Fujiwara, to match the radiance of the myriad blossoms of the spring mountains against the colors of the thousand leaves of the autumn mountains, Princess Nukata decided the question in verse with this poem."[270] Her *chōka* is quite understandable on its own terms, but as much cannot be said of an epistolary poem such as number twenty from the *Izumi Shikibu nikki*:

Makuru to mo   Surrender and come
Mienu mono kara   To me? I see no sign of that,

Tamakazura	And yet I wait,
Tou hitosuji mo	Although the crawling vine sends out
Taemagachi nite	Scarcely one visiting shoot.

Here we need to know that Izumi is replying to a poem from the Prince in which he has said that today he will surrender (makenan) to love, and that she is making a play on this statement by use of the word *makuru* ("surrender," but also "come" and "coil"; see translation, note 69). Izumi's verse is typical of an extremely large class which are more or less hermetic without a context. An English love poem can be expected to stand on its own feet, whether its metres move it straight forward in the direct declaration of "My luve is like a red, red rose," or through the circuitous reasonings of "To His Coy Mistress." But the first poem in the *Ise monogatari*—that elegant guidebook of courtly love—would look this way in a rather literal-minded prose gloss:

Kasugano no	The garment printed with the dye
Wakamurasaki no	of the young *murasaki* plants of
Surigoromo	Kasuga fields—in *Shinobu* pattern
Shinobu no midare	—the distraction of concealed
Kagiri shirarezu	love knows no bounds.

A somewhat freer verse rendering might run:

> The wild pattern of
> This garment stained with purple
> Of the young herbs of Kasuga:
> The turmoil of a secret love
> Can know no boundaries.

But even this more interpretive second version presupposes a knowledge of the incident in which the poem finds its setting: A young nobleman visiting his country estate near the old capital of Nara catches a glimpse of two lovely sisters living in humble surroundings on the fields of Kasuga. Smitten at the sight, he tears off the skirt of his hunting dress and sends it to the maidens with the verse quoted above. The cloth of the garment is, the author tells us, a "*Shinobu* print" (*shinobuzuri* 忍擢)—a product of Shinobu 信夫 district in the province of Mutsu—famous for its wild, haphazard pattern. Hence the pun on *shinobu*, which also means both "to long for" 偲ぶ and "to conceal" 忍ぶ. In the context the young *murasaki* 紫 plants (the gromwell, whose root was the source of a purple dye) growing on the Kasuga fields are a metaphor for the young girls who have aroused in the hero the turmoil of desire (*shinobu no midare*). The episode ends with a comment to the effect that the men of former times were adept at such elegant expressions of tender passion.

It was not only in "former times" however but throughout the history of traditional Japan that poetry flourished in its role of direct personal communication, whether with lovers, family, or friends. As we see them in the romances and memoirs of the Heian court such missive poems are commonly accompanied by a brief message in prose. The ease with which prose and poetry lie together in the same bed provides, along with social function and brevity of form, a third factor favoring development of hybrid genres. This literary symbiosis is perhaps most highly developed in the texts of the *nō* plays, but Heian literature also exemplifies the tendency in striking fashion. A few examples from the *Genji monogatari* may be used as illustrations. In order to emphasize the way in which poems grow out of and blend into the prose text, the translations are not divided into five lines as is the practice elsewhere in this book, but are placed within an extra set of quotation marks and printed otherwise as if they were prose statements. This technique resembles the format of Japanese books, where a *tanka* usually occupies only one vertical line and is marked off from surrounding text only by a slight indentation.

In the first chapter of the *Genji* the mother of the dead Kiritsubo writes to the Emperor about her anxiety over Kiritsubo's infant son: "I am quite overwhelmed with awe at this most gracious condescension. But this message from on high has cast dark confusion over

96

my mind: 'Now that the sheltering tree that held rough winds away has withered and gone, my heart can never rest from fret for the young bush-clover.' " In the original the prose statement does not come to a full grammatical stop, but leads into the poem in a more effortless and natural way than is conveyed in the translation: "Ito mo, kashikoki wa, okidokoro mo haberazu. Kakaru ōsegoto ni tsukete mo, kakikurasu midarigokochi ni namu, 'Araki kaze fusegishi kage no kareshi yori kohagi ga ue zo shizugokoro naki.' "[271]

In the second chapter Genji sends a note to Utsusemi, another man's wife with whom he has spent one fleeting night: " 'Mishi yume o au yo ari ya to nageku ma ni me sae awade zo koro mo henikeru,' nenuru yo nakereba."[272] Here the statement following the poem can be understood, through a very common reversal of syntax, as a grammatical extension of the poem and a comment on it. The translation attempts to convey this carry-over: " 'While I have sighed and wondered if the night would ever come when I could truly meet that dream I dreamt, time has passed and gone, and even my eyelids have not met,' for there has been no night when I could sleep." The same technique is used repeatedly in the *Izumi Shikibu nikki* (see, for instance, translation, notes 52, 62, 66, 296, 334). A further example can be drawn from the fourth chapter of the *Genji*. The hero has just taken Yūgao to the deserted mansion where she is to meet her untimely death. Gazing through a shroud of morning mist at the grim, decaying, vine-covered pile they are about to enter, Genji speaks:

"I never knew what such an experience would be like—it almost makes me lose heart. 'Did men of old wander thus lost on this same path I follow, ignorant of where I go, through the ghostly light of dawn?' But perhaps you are no novice at this?"

Blushing, the girl replied, " 'Unable to guess what lies in store beyond the horizon mountains, the moon may cease to shine while yet it travels through the sky.' Or so I fear."[273]

In the Japanese Genji's poem ends with a noun, "michi" (way), which immediately becomes the object of the following question:

"naraitamaeri ya" (Have you learned this way [of love]?). Similarly, Yūgao's poem ends in a verb followed by a comment, adverbial in form. "Kage ya taenan" ([the moon's] light may cease) can be glossed as modified by "kokorobosoku" (forlornly). However, since the adverbial form is identical with the continuative form of the adjective, "kokorobosoku" is also Yūgao's direct statement of her own emotions—"I feel so helpless."

Thus it can be seen that Japanese prose and verse tend to go well together—indeed, have an affinity for each other. Not only do they blend easily, but some kinds of poetry cry out for a prose context. This is not to deny poetry its place as an independent art in Japan. Poems could and did exist as independent units. And integration, when practiced, was often with other poems rather than with prose.[274] In addition the flowering of linked verse in the fourteenth and fifteenth centuries replaced the long defunct *chōka* with an extended form of serious literary value albeit of far different nature. But, at least partially for the reasons mentioned above, and particularly because of the near universality of versifying by the literate society centered around the imperial court, Japan early came to possess an extensive literature of works which are neither wholly prose nor wholly verse, but a combination of the two.

These works are of several kinds, not always readily distinguishable. The spectrum ranges from undoubted fiction through an uneasy middle ground to writings intended as factual. Four words from the vocabulary of Japanese literary historians—*monogatari*, *zuihitsu*, *nikki*, and *shū*—will cover the larger part of what we know as Heian literature. But these "tales," "miscellanies," "diaries," and "collections" tend to have fuzzy boundaries, and an uncritical use of such designations can perpetuate confusion. As noted by Yamagishi, some works find themselves in more than one category, a fact that bespeaks partly our own ignorance of the circumstances of their composition, and partly the somewhat fluid sense of genre possessed by their authors.

The Rise of Autobiographical Writings

In the beginning were the songs and the stories—the oral traditions and poetry of a pre-literate people. These were collected and copied down during the eighth century in works which still survive—the first two histories, the *Kojiki* 古事記 (712) and *Nihon shoki* 日本書紀 (720); the *fudoki* 風土記, collections of local lore;[275] and the *Man'yō-shū* 萬葉集, the great compendium of Japanese poetry from its beginnings to the year 759. The histories, which are largely collections of myth and legend in their earlier parts, and the local lore contain much poetry placed in the mouth of god, man, and beast, and show that Tsurayuki's vision of the universality of song was founded on the most ancient concepts and practices of his nation. The *Man'yōshū* is a massive anthology of over four thousand poems, and must represent the culmination of several decades of gathering together both the old heritage of song and the works of living poets. Once the composition of poetry passed from the shadowy age of anonymous singers—when verses with names attached are likely to have been attributed arbitrarily to emperors and gods—into the daylight of a literate court, men who valued their status as poets began to make collections of their own works. The emergence of the poet as an individual and self-conscious literary figure is marked in arresting fashion by the career of Kakinomoto no Hitomaro 柿本人麿 during the last two decades of the seventh century. The compilers of the *Man'yōshū* drew upon his private collection and those of his contemporaries and successors, as well as previous anthologies, thus preserving, as the event proved, works and writers which otherwise would not have survived.

Of Hitomaro's life we know essentially what his poems tell us. He had a passionate fealty toward the imperial house, a love of life deepened and enriched by a profound sense of its ironies and tragedies, and a broad feeling of brotherhood or identity with his fellow man. He particularly prized and praised the tender bonds joining man and wife. Of this much we can be sure. For the rest,

99

we know only that he traveled much, presumably on orders from the court, lived for a time in Iwami on the Japan Sea coast and perhaps died there, loved at least two women, and experienced loss through death and parting. It was he who brought the *chōka* to perfection, and he occupies an impregnable position in Japanese letters because of the human significance and technical mastery of his works. But most of his major poems which have come down to us are not marked as having been taken from the "Hitomaro Collection," and there is some uncertainty as to how many of the more numerous but shorter, lesser poems which the *Man'yōshū* compilers did select from that source are actually his own compositions. In short, it is not known in what state of organization Hitomaro left his writings at his death. He is hardly unique in this respect, but there are later poets whose literary remains give clearer evidence of a concern for arrangement which evolved gradually in the direction of a poetic diary or memoir.

The man who is credited with having done the most to shape the *Man'yōshū* as we know it is Ōtomo no Yakamochi 大伴家持 (716–785). Yakamochi was the last great poet of the Man'yō age, a man of many interests and responsibilities, a prolific writer whose copious output dominates the latter part of the collection. Through his poetry we can see him as the amorous gallant corresponding with many women, as the grave official and provincial governor, and as the unhappy bearer of a proud and ancient but now tarnished name.[276] He is regarded as a transitional figure because among the variety of his poetry can be found foreshadowings of a shift in the concerns of Japanese poetry—a turning away from the larger world of nature and human society to the more limited vistas of a garden and the inward questing after the essence of the poet's own sensibilities. That he was a dominant literary figure in his day can be seen from his 453 extant poems—of which 46 are *chōka*—and in even larger measure from his work as final compiler of the *Man'yōshū*. The point of greatest significance to the present discussion however is that the last four of the twenty books of that collection, dominated by his work, constitute a kind of rough poetic journal. In these books are set out in chronological order, and interspersed with prose passages, the poems of Yakamochi and his circle of clansmen, correspondents, and acquaintances written over thirty years, from 730 to 759. Many of the poems are carefully dated.

As a general rule throughout this collection Yakamochi is referred to in the third person, as are the other authors represented in it. Of course it is not known whether or not this section of the *Man'yō-shū* has come down unaltered from Yakamochi's hands; the process of compilation is not understood with that degree of surety. But his personal touch is visible everywhere. When he left the Capital in 746 to take up his duties as governor of Etchū Province his departure brought grief to more than one lady. Among those who expressed her feelings in verse on this occasion was a girl of the Heguri 平群 clan. The twelve heart-stricken poems (*MYS* 3931–3942) she sent to her lover at his distant post are followed by Yakamochi's note: "The above verses came by messenger at different times; they were not sent all at once." He regularly states when he received or heard each poem not of his own composition, once complains that he cannot find his replies,[277] and at the end of *maki* 19 remarks that the poems with no author given are his own. Further, his occasional use of a humble formula, *sechie* 拙懷 ([my] humble feelings),[278] in reference to his own poems is equivalent to employing the first-person singular in English. As will be seen, some inconsistency of person is also to be found in later works which are in a sense autobiographical. Yakamochi's collection contains, in addition to poetry in Japanese, the Chinese poems and correspondence he exchanged with his kinsman Ikenushi 池主 (fl. 738–757). His own poetry is mingled with verses sent him in letters, quoted to him by his friends, or composed at banquets. He was Japan's first great anthologist, and no doubt his habit of noting down every poem coming to his attention, along with information as to date and source, sprang from the same respect for the works of others and desire to preserve them that directed his labors on the *Man'yōshū*. Apparently he was particularly interested in the *sakimori* 防人, the eastlanders conscripted for military service in western Japan, for he made a diligent collection of over eighty of their poems, noting carefully the name, province, and district of each man, as well as writing several poems himself on the theme of their hardships. Parcelled in among Yakamochi the anthologist and literary scholar is Yakamochi the private man and public figure. His lengthy collection is by no means a day-by-day diary, but it enables us to follow many of his doings and the various happenings and occasions that inspired his poetry. Official tours and imperial progresses, drinking parties, the discovery of gold in Michinoku, the loss of his favorite hawk, the death of a friend's mother, his own illness, the songs or stubborn silence of the *hototogisu*—all are topics for his verse. The years of his governorship of Etchū (746–751) are dealt with in particular detail.

Yakamochi was a man of parts, and his four books of the *Man'yō-shū* reflect a wide-ranging curiosity and an intellect of unusual vigor, but the fact that they include poems not of his own composition does not set them apart from later private collections. Unlike the "collected works" of our Western poets, the personal collections—*shikashū* 私家集 or *ie no shū* 家集—of the classical Japanese tradition include not only the poems of the author but some of those he received in the exchanges which were a normal part of everyone's social and private life. From this habit of preserving poetic exchanges arises much of Heian and later Japanese literature, including the autobiographical or factual tendency previously mentioned. A collection of such exchanges, arranged in chronological order and accompanied by the usual explanatory prose, required only slight elaboration to become a *nikki*—a diary or memoir.

In order to visualize the process by which such autobiographical writings came into being we must conjure up a picture of a capital overrun by message-bearers of every description, hurrying up and down the broad avenues, scurrying into narrow alleys, going in and out of palaces, mansions, and monasteries. Along with the billets doux they carry confidences exchanged between court ladies, letters from one family member to another, desperate pleas to a young nobleman not to abandon the world, documents drawn up in Chinese concerned with matters of government and family estate, writings of all sorts dealing with all the romantic or everyday business of life. At their destinations these various messages are carefully inspected and copied into official records, negligently glanced at and tossed aside, or eagerly awaited and immediately answered, according to their contents and the responsibilities and dispositions of their recipients. The arrival of a personal note and poem, written in elegant brushstrokes on a carefully selected paper of appropriate hue, folded into a knot and attached to a flowering branch may cause a hurried repair to the inkstand to indite an equally graceful reply. Before the answer is handed to the waiting messenger the author makes a copy for his or her own personal collection. Or if no copy, then the first draft is kept. The received message joins a growing pile of correspondence. It may in turn be copied, serving as a model for calligraphy practice.

In such ways, over a period of years, an educated aristocrat with a nimble brush would accumulate a considerable volume of miscellaneous writings. Some would be mere scraps—notes from someone dashed off hurriedly. Others might be poems or letters which were the source of particular pride or pleasure. If the collector had serious poetic aspirations, to these would be added more formal verses—on such traditional subjects as the four seasons, love, and parting—or verses written for entry in competitions or in response to requests for poems to decorate screen paintings. And finally, a court lady or gentleman might include in his or her bundle of personal writings some more or less extended prose sketches, mingled with poetry, called forth in response to especially affecting scenes or events. All the above practices are alluded to or implied in Heian literature. When Genji, for instance, writes a poem for the little girl Murasaki, he does so in a simple hand easy for a child to read. Delighted, her attendants exclaim, "Yagate, ontehon ni" (This will go into her copybook at once).[279] Later, when Murasaki has grown up and become Genji's wife, he sends her letters and drawings from his exile at Akashi. She keeps them and puts them to good use at the time of the picture competition. During their separation she also records her thoughts and experiences "in the fashion of a diary" (niki no yō ni).[280] One scene of the *Izumi Shikibu nikki* (translation, pages 156–160) shows the heroine doing the same thing, writing down her impressions of a long, lonely night and misty dawn—a composition she later decides to send to the Prince. Sei Shōnagon's celebrated *Pillow Book* is a long collection of just such jottings. The *Murasaki Shikibu nikki* 紫式部日記 provides another interesting sidelight on the treatment of accumulations of paper. Murasaki is explaining why the record of her thoughts and experiences (what we now call her *nikki*) which she is sending to an unnamed correspondent to read is so illegible and unsightly, and why she has written no more. She has been writing on the backs of old letters, and her supply is now exhausted: "There is still much that I could tell, but recently I have gotten rid of my whole accumulation of old notes and odd scraps of paper, tearing them up and burning them, or using them to build the doll houses I made last spring. Since then I have had no letters. I have deliberately avoided writing on fresh paper, and so this is hardly fit to be seen."[281] Of course the destruction of such a pile of old paper implies that it was first accumulated, and shows the result of years of correspondence.

We have then a picture of a society much given to reading and writing, to scribbling off notes and poems, and to keeping—at least for a time—piles of correspondence and personal memorabilia. Individuals of particularly strong literary ambitions were naturally inclined to shape these formless heaps of paper into something which could help establish a reputation and preserve a name for posterity. The first and most obvious stage was the personal poetry collection—the *shikashū*. These might be organized along the lines of the *chokusenshū*, the imperial anthologies, i.e., categorically by the topic of the poem, or chronologically, or miscellaneously, or in a mixture of all three ways. Such collections were sometimes put together specifically for the purpose of serving as raw material for the imperial anthologies. Inclusion in the latter of course was the highest seal of official immortality.

Also among the collectors of poetry and miscellaneous writings were those who shared in some degree the narrative urge described in the words of Arthur Waley's *Genji*: "An emotion so passionate that he can no longer keep it shut up in his heart. Again and again something in his own life or in that around him will seem to the writer so important that he cannot bear to let it pass into oblivion."[282] Genji is discussing "the art of the novel," but the passion he speaks of—sometimes diluted, sometimes intense—is to be found as a motivating force behind the autobiographical genres as well. In *shikashū* the urge takes the form of long *kotobagaki* or headnotes. Length of headnotes varies greatly from one collection to another, and between different sections of the same collection. Poems of a formal nature written on set topics may have no story behind them and hence no need for a *kotobagaki*. Sequences such as *hyakushuuta* 百首歌[283] and *kunzoku* 訓續[284] also would not be interrupted by explanatory material. The *kotobagaki* was most obviously necessitated by the informal exchange of poems and flourished mightily in this context. In putting together a collection or part of a collection including many such exchanges, the poet with the autobiographical passion might elaborate the *kotobagaki* more and more until the result was a poem-centered story, or group of stories, of his own experiences—in short, something which might as well be called a *nikki*.

As we have seen, the writings of Ōtomo no Yakamochi partake somewhat of this character. The four books of the *Man'yōshū* dominated by his poetry however are still too loosely and fortuitously shaped, with the prose too scattered and subordinate, to be characterized as a true *nikki*. They are a step on the way, no more. It is to the Heian Period that we must look for the full development of the new form. An early example is provided by the *Ise shū* 伊勢集, the private collection of the Lady Ise (fl. ca. 895–935). Of its over five hundred poems the first thirty-three are accompanied by particularly lengthy prose sections put together in such a way as to form a narrative of several years in Ise's life. The first of these begins: "During the reign of a certain Emperor there was, serving in the apartments of his consort, a lady whose father resided in the province of Yamato."[285] There follows the story of Ise's unhappy affair with Fujiwara no Nakahira 仲平 (875–945), the younger brother of her mistress Onshi 溫子 (872–907), one of the consorts of Emperor Uda 宇多 (867–931; r. 887–897). As a result of this affair Ise leaves to stay with her father in Yamato, but later returns to court at Onshi's request. Then come exchanges with would-be lovers Taira no Sadabumi (the hero of the *Heichū monogatari*; see below, page 120) and Nakahira's brother Tokihira 時平 (871–909). After successfully keeping both men at a distance, Ise receives the favor of the Emperor and bears him a son, a prince who dies while yet a young child. The introductory, *nikki*-like, section continues until the death of Onshi in 907, an event which is commemorated by a *chōka* at the end of the collection.

A *shikashū* of similar structure is the *Ichijō Sesshō gyoshū* 一條攝政御集, the personal collection of Fujiwara no Koretada 伊尹 (also read Koremasa) (924–972). It contains over 190 poems in all, of which the first 41 constitute an independent collection. They relate amorous incidents in the life of a lowly young official named Kurahashi no Toyokage 倉橋豊蔭, a fictitious stand-in for Koretada. *Toyokage* is used as an alternative title of the collection. The first sentence may be translated, "Kurahashi no Toyokage, a scribe in the Treasury, though of lamentably low rank, during his younger days made a collection of the verses he sent to women."[286]

Both *Toyokage* and the *Ise shū* are usually listed as *shikashū*, but their earlier sections have developed far beyond mere collections of poems. It will have been noticed that both are written in the third person. This characteristic they share in a measure with some of the works generally designated as *nikki*. The *Izumi Shikibu nikki* is of course one of these. Another is the *Tosa nikki* 土佐日記, traditionally described as the parent of the *nikki* genre and of its variant, the travel record. The *Tosa* is not formally third-person because its narrative is put into the mouth of an anonymous woman by its real author, Ki no Tsurayuki. The technique is slightly different— narration by an individual involved in the action rather than by the author—but the effect of fictionalizing a true story is much the same. The *Tosa nikki* relates the return sea voyage from the province of Tosa in Shikoku to the capital by a provincial governor whose term of office has expired. The governor is Tsurayuki himself, who held the post from 930 through 934. He is never referred to by name, but by such familiar if sometimes vague terms as *aru hito* (a certain person), *chichi* (the father), and *okinabito* (the old man). The opening sentence is a famous one: "Otoko mo su naru niki to iu mono o, onna mo shite min tote suru nari"[287] (They say men keep something they call a "diary"; now a woman will try her hand). The reference to the diaries kept by men is thought to be to the private journals in Chinese mentioned previously; this "woman's diary" is written in Japanese in the native *kana* script. The time-span covered is a little less than two months, from Shōhei 承平 4 (934). 12.21 (28 January 935 by the Western calendar) to Shōhei 5.2.16. The influence of the *kambun* diaries is apparent in the structure, which is in the form of day-by-day entries, rather than the flowing narrative style usual in *nikki bungaku*, in which whatever dates appear are woven into the text. Nevertheless the *Tosa* is unquestionably a literary work, in an elegant style relying heavily on balanced antithetical phraseology, with vivid vignettes and sharp character sketches. It abounds in satire, some of which Tsurayuki directs against himself, and the narrative technique is quite effective in this respect. Written from notes kept and verses composed on the voyage, it was probably completed soon after Tsurayuki's return to the capital. At the time the *Tosa nikki* was the longest prose work yet to appear in *kana*, the previous examples having been limited to more or less extended *kotobagaki*, a few *utaawase nikki*, and Tsurayuki's own *Kana Preface* to the *Kokinshū* in 905.

A less well known work of the travel journal genre is that entitled *Ionushi* 廬主, "The Master of the Hermitage." It was written by a priest whose Buddhist name was Zōki 増基, but whose identity is otherwise unknown. It is not even certain whether he lived in the tenth or the eleventh century. The work actually consists of three parts, an account of a trip to the Kumano shrines (*Kumano kikō* 熊野紀行), a section of miscellaneous poems, and another travel section, the *Tōtomi michi no ki* 遠江道の記. There are 123 poems in all. The author refers to himself as Ionushi, and begins the *Kumano kikō* in this way: "Once—when could it have been—there was a man who, wanting to escape from the world and live as he pleased, set out to visit the various renowned and interesting places of which he had heard, thus fulfilling his desires; he had at the same time the intention of praying at all the holy places in order to eradicate his sins."[288] Ionushi is a good traveling companion, for along with his Buddhist sentiments he shows a light and humorous turn of mind delighting in jokes and puns. The work is supposed to have been written in the author's late years.

Third-person narration is maintained in token form—a gesture as it were—at the beginning of the *Kagerō nikki* かげろふ日記. This work provides an excellent example of the typical process of *nikki* formation. It was begun probably in 971 by a secondary wife of Fujiwara no Kaneie, the grandfather of Princes Tametaka and Atsumichi (see page 6) and one of the dominant figures of his day at the Heian court. The author was herself the daughter of a minor Fujiwara official, but is known only as "the Mother of Michitsuna,"[289] the son she bore to Kaneie. The work deals with twenty-one years (954–974) of her married life, years in which she became increasingly embittered by neglect, and it is slanted to present her side of an unhappy situation. The opening passage all but allows us to see her, seated before an accumulation of poems and letters reaching back to the days before her marriage and pondering what use to make of this mass of damning evidence of a wasted life: "Kaku arishi toki sugite . . ." (The times when things were thus have passed . . .). The sentence as a whole may be translated, "There was a person whose youthful days had passed and whose worldly ties had proven most unstable, but who went on living aimlessly, unable to adopt any certain course."[290] The brief third-person introduction continues with a statement of the author's purpose in writing—to describe the painful, unromantic realities of marriage—and an apology for any lapses of memory. The body of the *nikki* then begins, with a change to first-person narration and a turning back to the beginning, the days of her courtship seventeen years before. It is apparent that the *Kagerō*, sketchy in its early passages but thereafter increasingly detailed, is no longer retrospective from about the time of the author's retreat at Narutaki in 971. The rest was probably written as events occurred. The *Kagerō* is then a combination autobiography-diary, depending on saved letters, poems, and other memorabilia for over four-fifths of the period it covers.

The *Sarashina nikki* 更級日記 is another work looking back over a whole lifetime, and it too preserves a tiny vestige of third-person narration. This is no more than the use of *hito* (person) in the first sentence (the same word used in the *Ionushi, Kagerō,* and *Ise shū*): "How outlandish must a person be who grew up in a place even beyond the end of the Eastern Road. . ."[291] The person who felt herself to be so barbaric was the daughter of Sugawara no Takasue 菅原孝標 (973–?), an official of the provincial governor class. Since her mother was a daughter of Fujiwara no Tomoyasu 倫寧 (d. 977), she was the niece of the author of the *Kagerō*. She was born in 1008, and in 1017 accompanied her father to the province of Kazusa in eastern Japan, where he occupied the post of vice-governor. There she developed a lifelong fondness for tales and legends. The *Sarashina* begins with her journey back to the capital in her father's entourage, a trip which took three months in the fall and winter of 1020. The scenery, the incidents, and the stories told along the way are recounted with something of the naive wonder of a twelve-year-old girl. The rest of the *nikki* relates almost forty years of a rather quiet and uneventful life. The author had a romantic outlook and was given to imagining herself the heroine of some private *Tale of Genji*. In reality however little of an exciting nature ever ruffled the surface of her dreamy calm. Dreams in fact bulk large in her memoirs, eleven different ones being recounted in some detail. She seems to have had a rather naive faith in them, but chides herself at the end for not taking them seriously enough. Shy and introspective, she was content to stay at home with her parents and her books. Eventually, at the age of thirty-two, she entered court service, though due to no desire of her own. Still later she married Tachibana no Toshimichi 俊通, to whom she bore two daughters and a son. Family responsibilities brought more practical interests to the fore, but her husband's death in 1058 at the age of fifty-seven sent her off once again into a land of dreams, this time in the form of religious yearnings and self-reproaches. It is supposed that she wrote the *Sarashina nikki* in her late years on the basis of her memories and a lifetime of the usual kept exchanges, notes, and poems. Four works of fiction have also been attributed to her: *Hamamatsu Chūnagon monogatari* 濱松中納言物語, *Yowa no nezame* 夜半のねざめ, *Asakura* あさくら, and *Mizukara kuyuru* みづからくゆる. The first two are tales in the tradition of the *Genji monogatari*, and have come down to us, but the other two have been lost. *Hamamatsu Chūnagon* at least is generally accepted as her work.

Third-person narration is not employed in a majority of the works making up *nikki bungaku*. The above examples indicate however that it was an available style. Not all *nikki* are dominated by poetry, but the court society as a whole was, to the extent that neither *nikki*, *monogatari*, nor *zuihitsu* was conceivable completely devoid of poems. The social fact was naturally reflected in the literature. In the autobiographical genres, writers with discursive tendencies naturally produced the works which are farthest removed from the private poetry collection. Murasaki Shikibu (ca. 978–1016?) can hardly be considered less than adept and prolific as a poet in view of the hundreds of poems she has left in the *Genji monogatari* and her own private collection, the *Murasaki Shikibu shū*. The latter, like certain sections of the *Izumi Shikibu shū*, is a source of biographical information, and shows the not-quite-*nikki* stage of development noted previously in connection with Ōtomo no Yakamochi. The *Murasaki Shikibu nikki*, on the other hand, contains only a handful of poems, though several of them are tied to rather interesting incidents. It deals with a period of less than two years, from the summer of 1008 to the beginning of 1010, and concentrates on description of events at court, character sketches and critiques of other court ladies, and Murasaki's reflections about her own personality. Murasaki became a lady-in-waiting at the court of the Emperor Ichijō's principal consort, Empress Akiko [Shōshi], probably late in 1007, and was present at the birth of two of her sons, the future emperors

Go-Ichijō 後一條 (1008–1036; r. 1016–1036) and Go-Suzaku 後朱雀 (1009–1045; r. 1036–1045). The birth of Go-Ichijō is treated at the greatest length of any event in this *nikki*. The work dwells in detail on the preparations for Akiko's confinement at her father's residence, the Tsuchimikado Palace, describes the birth, the various ceremonies following, and Akiko's return to the Imperial Palace. Murasaki continues with an account of her own visit to her private residence, her reflections while there, her return to court, and various incidents and ceremonies. The famous remarks on her fellow court ladies follow, along with further self-evaluation. This first division of her *nikki* is concluded with the correspondence section already quoted in part above (page 104). It is known from internal evidence that this letter could not have been written earlier than the fourth month of Kankō 7 (1010).[292] The *Nikki* continues however with material dealing with events of Kankō 6 and the first month of Kankō 7. This includes Michinaga's jocular remarks about the *Genji monogatari*, the scene of his midnight knocking on Murasaki's door, and the ceremonies of the first month of Kankō 7 involving the two infant princes. It is thought that this latter material existed separately and was added later by someone else to the text Murasaki sent to her unnamed correspondent.

The *Murasaki Shikibu nikki* with its various opinions and experiences is not essentially different from the *Makura no sōshi* 枕草子 of Sei Shōnagon (b. ca. 966). The latter is longer and more elaborate, and of course is the product of a quite different personality, but like the *Murasaki Shikibu* is essentially a combination of personal anecdotes and remarks on set subjects. It is the extensive development of the latter element which has caused Sei's work to be classed as *zuihitsu* 隨筆 or informal essay (the first representative of this genre in Japanese literature) rather than *nikki*. But the *Murasaki Shikibu* has more in common with the *Makura no sōshi* than with exemplars of the *nikki*-as-autobiography such as the *Kagerō* and *Sarashina*. This is to say that the notes and various sketches which make up the former two were not put together with the same concern for telling a connected personal story as was the case with the latter two. Sei and Murasaki are not necessarily to be faulted for this lack of long-term narrative interest in their personal writings. Murasaki of course has given us the longest narrative in classical Japanese literature in the *Genji*, and the anecdotal and categorical style of the *Makura no sōshi* seems eminently suited to Sei's personality. The point to consider here is that traditional genre designations do not always make clear where the real similarities and differences lie between one work and another.

Sei's sketchbook deals with a period approximately ten years earlier than Murasaki describes, during the heyday of Akiko's predecessor and rival Sadako [Teishi] 定子 (976–1001), daughter of Michinaga's elder brother Michitaka (953–995). A child of the Kiyowara 清原 family of scholars, Sei was the daughter of Motosuke 元輔 (908–990), one of the compilers of the second imperial anthology of Japanese poetry, the *Gosenshū* (951). She entered Sadako's court probably in 993, and soon began keeping copious notes on everything going on around her. In them she details her opinions on all manner of subjects, illustrates her categories of the pleasant and unpleasant with personal anecdotes, and gives us by far the most vivid and vivacious picture we have of the Heian court. Her manuscript was only partially complete when it was accidentally discovered and made off with by a visitor, Minamoto no Tsunefusa 經房 (969–1023), in 996. Sei insists that she had been keeping it secret and implies dismay at the resultant unintended publication.[293] Apparently she continued to record her memories in the manuscript for several years after leaving court service in 1001 upon Sadako's death.

Even worse disasters befell the writings of Shijōnomiya Shimotsuke 四條宮下野, a lady-in-waiting to the consort of Emperor Go-Reizei 後冷泉 (1025–1068; r. 1045–1068). She states that during the years of her court service (ca. 1051–1068) she had written down her impressions of various amusing incidents, but that her collection was largely destroyed in fires. The remnant she discarded, and was only persuaded to rewrite from memory in her old age.[294] Either something must have been saved, or her memory was prodigious, for her literary remains consist of a chronologically arranged *shikashū*, the *Shijōnomiya Shimotsuke shū*, containing 211 poems with long *kotobagaki*. Eighty of these poems are by someone other than Shimotsuke. Miscellaneous writings could also be gathered and preserved by a posthumous editor of course as is indicated in most vivid fashion by the colophons Fujiwara Teika added to his sister's memoir, the *Kenju Gozen nikki* (see above, pages 64–66; Introduction, note 194).

Works such as the *Kagerō nikki* and *Sarashina nikki* are not really in danger of being mistaken for mere poetry collections; much less are the *Murasaki Shikibu nikki*, *Makura no sōshi*, or *Kenju Gozen nikki*. In all these the prose has assumed a dominant role and the desire to tell a story or express opinions is the guiding force. To this list might be added the *Sanuki no Suke nikki* 讚岐典侍日記,[295] some portions of the *Nakatsukasa Naishi nikki* 中務内侍日記,[296] and the *Towazugatari* 問はず語り,[297] three works which carry the *nikki* tradition on into the late Kamakura Period. All were written by ladies in the personal service of Emperors and are important in various ways for their descriptions of scenes and events at court or for frankness of narration.

It is the other group of personal writings—those in which *shikashū* and *nikki* verge indistinguishably into each other—which is of greater concern here. These include the *Ise shū*, *Toyokage*, *Ionushi*, and *Shijōnomiya Shimotsuke shū* already mentioned. Other examples are provided by the *Jōjin Azari no haha shū*, *Kenreimon'in Ukyō no Daibu shū*, *Ben no Naishi nikki*, and some passages of the *Nakatsukasa Naishi nikki*.

The *Jōjin Azari no haha shū* 成尋阿闍梨母集 is a work unusual in Japanese or any other literature. It was written by an octogenarian mother as an expression of her grief at parting with her son, a man in his sixties. The son was the Tendai cleric Jōjin Azari (1011–1081), who in 1069, in his fifty-ninth year, decided to go to China on a pilgrimage to the monastic centers Wu T'ai Shan 五臺山 and T'ien T'ai Shan 天臺山.[298] This resolve he carried out in 1072. His aged mother, whose one desire had been to spend the rest of her days in the care and company of her son, poured out her feelings in over 170 poems and accompanying prose in a testament of maternal love which she hoped Jōjin would read should he return to Japan after her death. As events turned out however, he never saw what she had written, for he remained in China for the rest of his life. The work begins with events of 1067 and continues into 1073, about a year after Jōjin set sail for China, ending with the author's account of her ill health, feeling of impending death, and hope for rebirth in paradise.

Another poetry collection with prose sections highly enough developed to qualify it for consideration as a *nikki* is the *Kenreimon'in Ukyō no Daibu shū* 建禮門院右京大夫集. Its author was the descendant of a line of famous calligraphers stemming from Fujiwara no Yukinari 行成 (972–1027). In 1173, probably at about the age of eighteen, she entered the service of Taira no Tokuko 平德子 (1155–1213), daughter of the virtual dictator Kiyomori 清盛 (1118–1181) and consort of the reigning Emperor Takakura 高倉 (1161–1181; r. 1168–1180).[299] Her collection begins with the new year, 1174, spans the period which saw the pinnacle of Taira power and glory, the long war with the Minamoto, the downfall of the once proud and mighty Taira, and the establishment of the new military regime in Kamakura. The last poem is from 1213.[300] Ukyō no Daibu withdrew from the Empress' entourage in 1178 and led a private life for the next twenty years, before reentering court service in about 1198. In her youth she was loved by Taira no Sukemori 資盛, a grandson of Kiyomori who died with the last of the Heike warriors at Dan no Ura in 1185. Memories of this love remained with her for the rest of her life, and form the dominant theme of her writings. It is thought that her collection, which comprises two *maki*, was put together at two separate periods, the first *maki* shortly before her return to court service, and the second about twenty years later.[301]

The author of the *Ben no Naishi nikki* 辨内侍日記[302] was very different in personality from the mournful mother of Jōjin and the melancholy Ukyō no Daibu. She was the daughter of Fujiwara no Nobuzane 信實 (1175–?), and counted among her immediate

114

ancestors men with reputations in poetry and painting. Her own
dates are unknown, but she entered the service of the future Emperor
Go-Fukakusa (1243–1304; r. 1246–1259) while he was yet Heir
Apparent, and preserved a poetic diary of several years of his reign.
Her *nikki* begins in the first month of Kangen 4 (1246) with the
abdication of the Emperor Go-Saga 後嵯峨 (1220–1272; r. 1242–
1246) and continues on into late 1252. It is devoted largely to descriptions of court ceremonies, with very little of a personal nature.
The form reverts to that of the *Tosa nikki*, with dated entries,
although there are many gaps between dates. Each entry is centered
around one or more poems. The tone is bright and cheerful; the
author seems to have taken a simple and straightforward pleasure in
everything she saw and to have been untroubled by gloom. The
work contains over three hundred poems, and was probably originally of greater length; the latter sections of all its manuscript copies
are badly worm-eaten. It seems likely that it was written while at
court, close to the time of the events it describes. Together with
certain portions of the *Nakatsukasa Naishi nikki* (see note 296) it
shows how, even after the eclipse of the power of the imperial
court, one of its characteristic literary forms continued to appear—
a form which is at the same time a poetry collection and a diary
or memoir.[303]

The difficulty of distinguishing between *nikki* and *shikashū* is
underlined by the titles of the various works discussed above.
Whether a work was to be titled *shū* or *nikki* must in some cases have
been difficult to decide, and is not always very important. Sometimes the confusion is even more apparent. The *Jōjin Azari no haha
shū* is also referred to as *Jōjin no haha nikki* or *Jōjin Azari no haha
nikki*,[304] and the *Ben no Naishi nikki* has the alternative title *Go-
Fukakusa-in no Ben no Naishi kashū* 後深草院辨内侍家集.[305] The
Sarashina nikki is referred to in one source as a *kashū* 家集,[306] and the
Yoshitaka shū 義孝集, the private collection of Fujiwara no Yoshitaka
(954–974), in another as a *nikki*.[307] Perhaps of greater interest is
the way in which prose and poetry may dominate in different
sections of the same work. There are parts of the *Jōjin Azari* and the

Kenreimon'in Ukyō no Daibu shū, for instance, in which one poem follows another almost without interruption. In these sections the works are truly collections of poetry. Or, as in the case of the *Ise shū* and the *Ichijō Sesshō gyoshū* (*Toyokage*), the *nikki* portion may come first and be followed by poems with shorter headnotes and without the connected story told by the earlier section. The *Kagerō nikki* also has appended to it a collection of fifty-odd poems variously entitled *Fu no Dainagon no haha ue no shū* 傅大納言母上集[308] and *Michitsuna no haha no shū*. The poems do not appear in the *Kagerō*, but are thought to have been culled from the author's posthumous papers shortly after her death.[309] Tamai Kōsuke suggests that if Izumi Shikibu's collected poems had been fewer in number (there are over fifteen hundred in the combined *Seishū* and *Zokushū*) they might have been added to the *Izumi Shikibu nikki*, producing a result similar to the *Ise shū* or *Toyokage*.[310]

Fiction

Autobiographical genres were not the only outgrowth of the peculiarly Japanese mixture of prose and poetry. Perhaps in truly primitive times there was no distinction between fiction and non-fiction, one story being as believable as another and all belonging to a general oral tradition. Or perhaps the clever rabbit who bragged too soon and lost his skin to his dupes the crocodiles was never taken quite as seriously as the sovereign who mounted his palace tower to watch the smoke from his subjects' cooking fires, or even as the hero who fought with a magic sword and changed into a bird after his death, or the god who pretended to eat centipedes combed from the locks of the master of the underworld.[311] One cannot be sure. At any rate all these stories and many more are mixed in together in the *Kojiki* and *Nihon shoki*, and are told with equal grave assurance, not less than that devoted to veritable facts of the reigns of recent emperors. But undoubtedly Yakamochi and the other compilers of the *Man'yōshū* knew a made-up yarn when they heard one, as for instance the story about the old bamboo-cutter and the fairy maidens (*MYS* 3790–3802). This poem-group shows obvious influence from the T'ang story *Yu-hsien-k'u* 遊仙窟.[312] Acquaintance with Chinese fiction must have aided greatly in the development of literary sophistication. Interest in legends as legends is evinced by the whole of *maki* 16, the so-called *yuen* (or *yoshi*) *aru uta* 由緣ある歌, or "poems with a story," a collection of traditions such as that of the girl Cherryblossom who, torn between two lovers, went to the forest and hanged herself from a tree. The lovers' poems follow, commenting on the tragedy with a punning grief: "The cherry blossoms I thought to deck myself withal, alas, are scattered and gone."[313] Each of the little stories either introduces or serves as a footnote to a poem or poems which it explains. The technique is equivalent to that which led to the development of the *nikki*, and had the same potential for evolution into extended prose-poetry genres, this time fictional in nature.

In due time this fiction came. It was at first fanciful and then—partially due to influence from the developing *nikki bungaku*—more realistic. It is all referred to by the general term *monogatari*, "the telling about things." None of the surviving works is likely to antedate the tenth century, but the *Taketori monogatari* 竹取物語, the official "ancestor" of the long fictional tale,[314] is clearly an accretion of various fairy-tales probably of considerable antiquity. The figure of the old bamboo-cutter, as we have seen, was already known to the men of the Man'yō age. The *Genji monogatari*, written during the first decade or two of the eleventh century, is at once the first real achievement of realistic fiction, the high point of Japanese traditional fiction as a whole, and perhaps, as is generally asserted, the pinnacle of the nation's literature. Between it and the *Taketori* there remain only two *monogatari*, both, like the "ancestor," of unknown authorship. One is a very long work entitled *Utsubo monogatari* 宇津保物語; the other, the *Ochikubo monogatari* 落窪物語, is of more modest length. Both suffer in a sense from being the non-missing links between the *Taketori* and the *Genji*, the *Utsubo* suffering perhaps more. The *Taketori* is fantasy delightfully pure and simple, but the *Utsubo*, perhaps not completely the product of one hand, runs from the most fantastic adventures in a faraway country where presumably anything could happen, to a fairly realistic treatment of the dynastic infighting at court. The whole is laced through with a thread of supernatural music, a motif which in more sophisticated hands might have had something of the possibilities of the magic stone in *The Dream of the Red Chamber*. As it is, the *Utsubo* is so jumbled and episodic that it barely holds together. The *Ochikubo* is nothing if not realistic in detail, but in conception it is a Cinderella story deprived of supernatural elements, with a rescuing prince and a happy ending both too good—if we may judge Heian social reality from such works as the *Kagerō*—to be true. All of these, and later *monogatari*, have poems woven into the fabric of plot and dialogue in the most natural way imaginable, a fact already illustrated with examples from the *Genji*. Practically everyone of any consequence in these tales composes poetry as a matter of course. This is so largely for the reasons previously enumerated—the natural affinity of prose and poetry, the fact that the tales sprang from a society where everyone was his own poet, and the brevity of poetic form. Obscurity, whether caused by the inherent vagueness of Japanese or by obvious dependence on a knowledge of situation, made prose contexts inevitable, and brevity made the poems easily acceptable units in a complex whole. This helped lead, as we have seen, to the rise of *nikki bungaku*.

The Poem-Tale

The *monogatari* described above, whether fantastic or realistic, were fiction and recognized as such. But there is another class of writings standing between the autobiographical and the fictional which is the subject of some debate. This in-between literature might be described as semi-fiction, but is usually called *utamonogatari* 歌物語 (poem-tale). It is the product of an in-between sort of motivation, and the degree of fiction present is often difficult to assess and varies from case to case. Its authors are all unknown.

The poem-tale came into existence in a way that paralleled the development of the *nikki*. It was not only the poet himself who was concerned with collecting his poetry and preserving his fame.

The matter of the compilation of private collections is one of many obscure problems in Japanese literature. The question is in need of further study and elucidation, but the process was undoubtedly more complex than has been suggested so far in this discussion. It is known that *shikashū* were sometimes compiled by people other than the author of the poems. This might be done soon after the poet's death by someone closely connected with him. Or such a collection might be assembled at a more remote epoch by someone who admired the poet's work and wished to have at hand a body of his poems to serve as models in composition. Or a poet might leave a collection ordered by his own hand, which after his death would be augmented or rearranged by others. In the cases of the oldest known *shikashū*, those mentioned in the *Man'yōshū*, we do not know to what extent a name like *Kasa no Kanamura kashū* 笠金村歌集 represents the selection of the poet himself.[315] The general opinion is that the so-called *Hitomaro kashū* contains many poems which have nothing to do with Hitomaro but were attributed to him because of his great fame.[316] The collected poems of Izumi Shikibu illustrate very well the complexities of the problem. The *Izumi Shikibu seishū* is the longest of the group of collections comprising her literary remains. As has been mentioned in the discussion of authorship, it is analyzable into several discrete poemgroups. Some of these definitely were arranged by Izumi herself, but the *Seishū* as a whole is thought to have been put together by a later person. The same seems to be true of the *Zokushū*, the second-longest collection. On the other hand, the *Shinkambon* 宸翰本 and *Matsuibon* 松井本 collections of her poems are purely the results of selection and arrangement from various imperial anthologies.[317]

The poems of other poets were subject to varied uses; not only the editorial, but the creative urge found them to be malleable material. As *kotobagaki* might be lengthened at will into *nikki*, so they might be enlarged into little stories by someone other than the poet. Or the stories might be invented to fit poems gleaned from various sources. By some such process the *Ise monogatari* 伊勢物語 came into existence. It contains 125 adventures of an unnamed man, arranged in an order taking him from youth to deathbed. The stories are written simply and with admirable economy, and each reaches its high point with one or more poems, usually an exchange or series of exchanges. About one third of the over two hundred poems were written by Ariwara no Narihira 在原業平 (825–880), and he has always been thought of as the hero. The formation of *utamonogatari* is by no means fully understood even today, and for centuries the *Ise monogatari* was thought the work of Narihira himself. An abundance of other hypotheses, some of which now seem fanciful, has been advanced. It is now generally recognized that a no longer extant collection of Narihira's poems was one of the elements—probably the most important—which went into the composition of the *Ise*. Many of the tales are no doubt elaborations of the *kotobagaki* found in it. Anonymous poems drawn from the *Kokinshū* and perhaps other sources were used as the nuclei of other stories invented by the author or authors. Popular traditions about Narihira and other people were included, and new poems written or old ones changed to fit different contexts. The whole is harmonious in style and subject. The theme is courtly love, and it seems likely that the *Ise* was based most closely on Narihira's life and work because Narihira was not only an excellent poet but a famous lover. Various strands of evidence indicate that the *Ise monogatari* probably dates from about 951 or shortly thereafter, although it is possible that it may be somewhat earlier. Opinion now generally rejects any date before the beginning of the tenth century.[318]

Another poet famous as a lady's man was Taira no Sadabumi 貞文 (also 定文) (d. 923). His collected poems, now lost as a separate work, were apparently taken as the basis of another example of the *utamonogatari* genre, the *Heichū monogatari* 平中物語.[319] The *Heichū* is composed of thirty-eight episodes relating the adventures, mostly amorous, of a character referred to only as "kono otoko" (this man). Though resembling the *Ise* in these respects, the *Heichū* has much more highly developed prose sections, both from the point of view of length of prose without poetry and of actual sentence length. The *Heichū* in this way resembles later Heian fiction. Its hero, understood to be Sadabumi, is less successful as a lover than the passionate Narihira, indeed is rather pathetic, easily turned aside and outwitted by women. He is not yet the figure of fun that Heichū became in later legend however but is a rather appealingly human character.[320] As with other works of this type, the *Heichū* has not been precisely dated, but was perhaps written between 959 and 965.

The *Heichū* and the *Ise* form an obvious pair, dealing as they do with the lives of famous lovers. The *Yamato monogatari* 大和物語 is quite different in that it has no central character, but is a collection of short poem-centered stories about many different people. There are 173 of these stories in the most widely circulated version of the *Yamato*. They were probably adapted from various written collections and from oral traditions circulating at court. It is likely that the whole *Yamato* was put together in gradual stages during a period of 50 or 60 years covering the latter half of the tenth century.[321]

The *Tōnomine Shōshō monogatari* 多武峯少將物語 provides a contrast to all three of the works described above. Like the *Ise* and the *Heichū* it centers on one actual historical figure, Fujiwara no Takamitsu 高光 (d. 994). But instead of the usual concern with romantic love, the central theme is the power of the religious impulse over human affections. Takamitsu was the son of the Great Minister of the Right Morosuke 師輔 (908–960) and Princess Gashi 雅子 (910–954), daughter of Emperor Daigo 醍醐 (885–930; r. 897–930). Among his brothers were the Regents Koretada (the author of *Toyokage*; see above, page 106), Kanemichi 兼道 (925–977), and Kaneie (husband of the author of the *Kagerō nikki* and grandfather of Princes Tametaka and Atsumichi; see above, pages 6, 108). Unlike these politically ambitious elder brothers however Takamitsu had from his youth but one aim—to leave behind the entanglements of the mundane world and seek enlightenment in a monastic order. This desire he fulfilled after his father's death. On Ōwa 應和 1 (961).12.5 (13 January 962 by the Western calendar) he went to Yokawa 横川

on Mt. Hiei 比叡, cut off his topknot with his own hand, and entered the religious life. He was probably about twenty-three at the time. In Ōwa 2 (962).8 he left Yokawa for Tōnomine, a mountain in Yamato Province, where he lived in retirement the rest of his life, thus earning the appellation by which he is known (the Minor Captain of Tōnomine). The *Tōnomine Shōshō monogatari* deals with the six months beginning with his abandonment of the secular life. Despite its title, it ends before his retirement to Tōnomine. Contrary to the practice of the *Ise* and the *Heichū*, Takamitsu is referred to by name, and the work has much more the air of a true record. It consists of thirty short episodes, each with poetic exchanges, and concentrates on the grief of Takamitsu's loved ones, especially his wife and younger sister. Over thirty historical personages appear. The author was someone with detailed information about the events, apparently someone very close to the family. Because of the use of honorific language in referring to all the members of Takamitsu's family, Tamai puts forward the hypothesis that the author may have been a serving woman, perhaps the wet-nurse of Takamitsu's wife.[322] The work makes no reference to Takamitsu's going to Tōnomine, probably because it was finished before that event.

The *Ise*, the *Heichū*, and the *Yamato* have in varying degrees the aspect of semi-fiction—a large element of fact along with traditional and perhaps invented material, with the whole worked up into a series of stories about real people. In the *Ise* and the *Heichū* the anonymity of the hero is preserved by referring to him simply as "a man," but the material is known to be based on the lives of Narihira and Sadabumi. Of these two the *Heichū* has the more highly developed prose, and therefore is in a sense a more highly evolved work, further from a mere *shikashū* with its *kotobagaki*-plus-poems. The *Ise*, on the other hand, is a more fully realized work of art, true to a single theme followed through the life of a man, incorporating material not belonging to the life of any single person but handled with unity of tone and style, thus giving to the whole a significance surpassing the merely biographical. The *Yamato* deals with a large number of individuals, naming them by name. It is disparate, with very short anecdotes consisting of nothing more than a headnote and one poem, and other sections in which the prose extends for two or three pages without a line of verse. All three of these works consist of a series of distinct, separate stories, contrasting in this respect with the *Tōnomine Shōshō monogatari* which, despite its episodic quality, is a connected narrative. The *Tōnomine* is much nearer to *nikki bungaku* in form and style and in evident closeness to the facts of a situation. But all show the variety of narrative uses to which written materials—mostly poems and explanatory prose— could be put.

Here again, emphasizing the vague boundaries between genres, there occurs the phenomenon of alternate titles. As pointed out by Yamagishi in his argument on authorship of the *Izumi Shikibu nikki* (see above, page 46), the *Ise*, the *Heichū*, and the *Tōnomine* are, in some sources, referred to as *nikki*. The *Tōnomine*, of which no pre-Edo manuscripts remain, was transmitted without title. The title by which it is now known and which has been employed in this discussion was popularized by the *Gunsho ruijū*. It is referred to as *Takamitsu nikki* however in the *Honchō shojaku mokuroku* and *Kakaishō*.[323] These two sources also refer to the *Heichū monogatari* as, respectively, *Heichū nikki*[324] and *Sadabumi nikki*.[325] And the *Sagoromo monogatari* 狭衣物語, a work of the eleventh century, alludes to the *Ise* as *Zaigo Chūjō no nikki* 在五中將の日記.[326] The *Yamato* is not referred to as a *nikki*; unlike the other three it is not based on the life and poems of a single individual.

The fourth work mentioned by Yamagishi, the *Takamura mono-gatari* 篁物語, is different from the others in one important respect. Like them it is a story about an historical personage, Ono no Takamura 小野篁 (802–852), but it is apparently not based on his private poetry collection. The poems attributed to him are thought to have been written by the author of the story.[327] There exists a genuine *Takamura shū* which has no poems in common with the *monogatari*, and the latter was not the source of Takamura's poems in the *Kokinshū*. The compilers of subsequent imperial anthologies however seem to have accepted this *monogatari* as genuine, for they used it as a source for the poems they credit to Takamura. The historical Takamura was an important scholar of Chinese in a period when Japan was under its strongest cultural influence from China. He was one of the committee who made the official commentary on the legal code, the *Ryō no gige* 令義解, which was put into effect in 834. He was appointed assistant envoy (*fukushi* 副使) to T'ang China in the same year. The departure of the embassy was delayed until 838, at which time Takamura feigned illness and refused to go because of a disagreement with the chief envoy. For his disobedience he was exiled to the Oki Islands for two years, but was pardoned and allowed to return to the capital in 840, after which he proceeded with his official career. The *Takamura monogatari* deals with none of these facts, but relates a strange story in which Takamura in his youth becomes the tutor and lover of his half-sister. When the girl becomes pregnant her mother treats her so cruelly that she dies and comes back to Takamura as a ghost. Despite her haunting presence he lives down his grief and goes on to marry the daughter of the Great Minister of the Right and embark on a flourishing career. The work is very brief and splits in two between the death of the sister and the subsequent marriage. The hero is called both "otoko" (the man) and "Takamura." For some reason, perhaps because of his independent-mindedness—he wrote a satire on embassies to China at the time of his insubordination—the historical Takamura, like his kinswoman Komachi, and like Heichū, Izumi Shikibu, and many others, became a magnet for all sorts of legendary material. The *Takamura monogatari* seems to belong to this category. It is in any case not the product of the same process which led to the development of *nikki* and *utamonogatari*—the elaboration of preserved writings—but is a piece of fiction. The authors of both *Kakaishō* and *Kachō yosei* nevertheless refer to it as *Takamura nikki*,[328] and one of its manuscripts bears the title *Ono no Takamura shū*.

Early Japanese literature then forms a continuum of genres,

mixing prose and poetry—the poetry collection, the personal memoir, the "poem-tale," and the overtly fictional tale. The first three especially have blurred boundaries. Somewhere among them belongs the *Izumi Shikibu nikki*. Is it essentially an *utamonogatari*, a treatment by an unknown author of an important turning point in the life of a famous poet, using materials at least some of which were actually written by its central figure? It resembles the *Ise* and the *Heichū* in the anonymity of its main character, but is closer to the *Tōnomine* in being a connected narrative dealing with a limited period—less than a year in both cases. Or is it a memoir? Heian writers, like Caesar, sometimes used the third person where one might expect the first, and so the argument from third-person narration cannot be conclusive. On the other hand, there is no other acknowledgedly autobiographical work of comparable length which uses that narrative technique throughout. The existence of imagined scenes and conversations is an important comparative factor. Other *nikki*, such as the *Kagerō*, describe scenes which the author did not witness, but always with the explicit or implicit indication that people informed her of what happened. On the other hand, the *Ise shū*, which in its earlier sections verges on *nikki*, sometimes uses verb inflections which state rather than conjecture the emotions of people other than the poetess herself. Conversely, the *Izumi Shikibu nikki* has passages which surmise rather than state the Prince's thoughts or feelings (see translation, notes 50, 208, 345). If Izumi Shikibu did write the work that bears her name, then her *nikki* is an immensely more developed, imaginative, and polished analogue of the *Ise shū*; if written by someone else, it is most comparable to the *Tōnomine*. In either case, like them, it could not survive without its poems. Aside from its terminal prose section the *Izumi Shikibu nikki* is constructed on the framework of the poem-exchange. It is either a "poem-tale" or a fictionalized "poem-memoir," and until the authorship question is finally settled, it must be left to the reader to decide which.

E. A Note on the Translation

The first translation of the *Izumi Shikibu nikki* into a European language, published in 1885, was a German translation by the Austrian scholar August Pfizmaier.[329] For many years the only English version has been that by Annie Shepley Ōmori and Doi Kōchi included in their *Diaries of Court Ladies of Old Japan*, first published by Houghton Mifflin in 1920 and reissued by Kenkyūsha in 1935 and 1961.

The present translation differs from Ōmori-Doi in at least three important respects: it is based on recent Japanese studies of a superior text; it is complete; and it is provided with detailed annotation. Ōmori and Doi apparently worked from the *Gunsho ruijūbon*, then the only commonly available version. Their English tends to be awkward and quaint, and is frequently inaccurate. Two or three examples must suffice. A style seemingly invented especially for this translation is exemplified by the opening words of Izumi to the page (cf. page 131 of the present translation): "Is your coming not long delayed? To talk over the past was inclined." The page is then made to reply, "Would it not have been presuming?—Forgive me—In mountain temples have been worshipping."[330] The Prince's first suggestion of a meeting appears in the present translation (page 133) as "How would it be if I were to come this evening and talk about the things that lie close to our hearts?" Ōmori and Doi have it, "To talk with you about the departed one; how would it be [for you] to come in the evening unobtrusively?"[331] Near the end (page 188 of the present translation), when the Prince is arguing with his consort, he exclaims, "How can you fail to grasp the reason why I have taken a new girl into my service? Chūjō and the others have taken their cue from your own ill humor, and seem to harbor hateful feelings toward me." This appears in the Ōmori-Doi version as, "I brought her for my maid, and I thought that you would allow it; as you are angry with me the Lieutenant-General [her brother] hates me also."[332]

Brief omissions are too numerous to mention, but there are six which consist of a whole episode, poem-exchange, or series of exchanges. All poems and jests about killing the rooster (page 145 of the present translation) and the page (pages 167, 168) are dropped completely. Two passages with particularly difficult problems of interpretation—the *Ōtori* episode (page 171) and the last three poems dealing with the abortive foliage-viewing trip (pages 173–174)—are similarly left out, as are the exchange of poems in the carriage-shed episode (pages 174, 175) and the poem about the preening snipe (page 182). The annotation is sparse and sporadic.

The present translation, based on the *Sanjōnishibon*, has been guided throughout by the ideal of producing a version both readable as English and faithful to the meaning and spirit of the original.[333] Liberties taken with the text are pointed out in the notes. None of these are of great importance; in most cases the translation has adhered quite closely to the original. The poems have presented a special problem. Adequate translation of lyric poetry is always a challenge, at times an apparent impossibility. Here the high incidence of word play has compounded the difficulties. The method followed has been to present a romanization of the original poem parallel to the translation. In cases of dual significance an attempt has usually been made to work both meanings into the English version. Although the poems have been rendered into five lines, following the subdivisions of the Japanese, there has been no consistent attempt to follow the syllable count of five-seven-five-seven-seven. Rhyme has been eschewed. In most instances the notes provide a more nearly literal translation, as well as an explanation of the prosodic devices employed. The general aim of the annotation has been to discuss difficulties in the text and to identify references to people, poems, customs, and institutions.

The Izumi Shikibu Diary

A Romance of the Heian Court

Frailer than a dream had been those mortal ties[1] for which she mourned, passing her days and nights with sighs of melancholy. And now the tenth of the fourth month[2] had come and gone, and the shade beneath the trees grew ever deeper. The fresh green of the grass[3] on the embankment[4]—though most people would hardly have given it a glance—somehow aroused an emotional awareness[5] within her, and, as she sat gazing out at it, she noticed a movement at the nearby openwork fence.[6] Who could it be, she wondered, only to discover a moment later that it was the young page[7] who used to wait on the late Prince.

As he had come at a time when she was flooded with tender memories,[8] she asked, "Why have you stayed away so long? I think of you as a reminder of the old days, you know—days which keep sinking further into the past."

"Since I had no particular errand to bring me here," he replied, "I thought I might be considered overly familiar. Hence my reluctance. Besides, for some time I have been occupied making visits to a temple in the hills.[9] But since I was feeling quite cut adrift and oppressed with my idleness, I decided, now that his Highness is gone, to take service with[10] his brother Sochi no Miya[11] instead."[12]

"How splendid! He has a reputation for being most distinguished and difficult to approach. He cannot be at all like your former master, I suppose."[13]

"No, but still he is very friendly. He asked if I often went to your residence, and when I replied that I did, he said, 'Take this with you and present it to her, and observe her reaction.' " With these words the page extended a sprig of orange[14] blossom.

"The sleeves of him of old—"[15] The words came to her of themselves.[16]

"I must go back," said the page. "What shall I tell his Highness?"

She felt rather uncomfortable about writing him a letter; but then, as yet he had no name for scandalous behavior. Should she risk a trifling verse?[17]

Kaoru ka ni	"Rather than dwell
Yosouru yori wa	On memories this fragrance breathes,
Hototogisu	O *hototogisu*,
Kikabaya onaji	Sooner would I hear your voice—
Koe ya shitaru to	Is it the same as his?"[18]

The Prince was still waiting at the edge of his veranda[19] when he spied the page, half-hidden by the shrubbery, coming toward him with an excited air.[20]

"Well?" he demanded and took the note which the boy extended to him. He read it and at once wrote his reply:

Onaji e ni	"On the same branch
Nakitsutsu orishi	Together with him sang
Hototogisu	This *hototogisu*,
Koe wa kawaranu	Its voice no different—
Mono to shirazu ya	How can you doubt?"[21]

"Don't breathe a word of this to a soul," he cautioned the lad as he handed him his reply. "It smacks of amorous intrigue."

The Prince went inside and the boy left to deliver his message. Though it brought her a glow of pleasure, the lady felt it would not be wise to enter into a habitual correspondence and left the poem unanswered. But the Prince, now that he had begun, would not let the matter drop and again addressed her:

Uchiide demo	"Well had it been
Arinishi mono o	Had I not thus recklessly
Nakanaka ni	Opened my heart to you
Kurushiki made mo	And brought upon myself this pain
Nageku kyō kana	Wherein I sigh today."[22]

Basically by no means profound in her judgement, and unschooled in endurance of bitter tedium, she let her fancy be intrigued by these trifling attentions and replied:

Kyō no ma no	"But of today indeed,
Kokoro ni kaete	This suffering of yours;
Omoiyare	Imagine then, compare
Nagametsutsu nomi	What one must feel whose days
Sugusu kokoro o	Drag on and on in idle melan-
	choly."[23]

Thus their correspondence continued, he constantly plying her with verses, and she occasionally[24] sending an answer, in this way lightening a little the listless boredom of her existence.

Again a message. After a more than usually intimate expression of his feelings the Prince concluded, "How would it be if I were to come this evening and talk about the things that lie close to our hearts?[25]

Katarawaba	If we talk together
Nagusamu koto mo	Might not there be therein
Ari ya sen	Perhaps some solace?
Iu kai naku wa	I would not have you think
Omowazaranan	I am no use to you."[26]

She replied:

Nagusamu to	"Though when I hear
Kikeba katarama-	You speak of solace
Hoshikeredo	I long to talk with you,
Mi no uki koto zo	My misery is quite beyond
Iu kai mo naki	The power of words to help.[27]

Indeed, what is the use? I can but weep 'ceaselessly as the rustling reeds.' "[28]

Nevertheless, about noon that day the Prince made up his mind that he would go secretly and make a surprise visit. He summoned a lieutenant of the Right Inner Palace Guards[29] whom he had been employing of late to deliver his letters and told him, "I shall be going out tonight—but no one is to know."[30]

"Ahah!"[31] thought the lieutenant. He accompanied the Prince in a rather inelegant carriage,[32] and upon their arrival was sent in to explain who had come.[33] The lady was extremely embarrassed, but could hardly pretend that she was not at home. She had sent the Prince a reply that very day. There she was, and it was simply too inconsiderate to send him home without seeing him. She decided she would talk with him for a while—nothing more than that— and pushed a straw cushion out by the western door[34] opening on the veranda, where she received him. Perhaps it was the effect of what his reputation had led her to expect, but she found him of a courtly refinement[35] quite out of the ordinary. She felt abashed in his presence.

The moon rose[36] while they were talking, and it became very bright.[37]

"Old fashioned and retiring as I am," said the Prince, "I have never become accustomed to being in such an exposed position. I really feel very ill at ease. Won't you let me come and sit inside with you? You need not fear—as you will surely come to realize—that I shall behave in a crudely obvious way."

"How silly! Tonight is surely the only time I contemplate troubling you with my conversation," she replied archly. "When shall I 'come to realize'?"[38]

While they spoke the night wore on. Were they to pass it in this fashion? The Prince recited:

Hakamonaki	"If we waste tonight
Yume o dani mide	In wakefulness, dreaming no dream
Akashite wa	Though but a moment long,
Nani o ka nochi no	What night-tales shall we have
Yogatari ni sen	To tell in times to come?"[39]

She replied:

Yo to tomo ni	"Though with the night
Nuru to wa sode o	I sink in waves of sleep,
Omou mi mo	Only my sleeves are drenched,

134

| Nodoka ni yume o | As plunged in tearful thoughts, |
| Miru yoi zo naki | I find no eve of tranquil dreams.[40] |

Much less the kind of dream you mean,"[41] she added.

"I am not someone who can go out on free and easy escapades[42] whenever he pleases," rejoined the Prince. "I am afraid you may consider me lacking in respect for your feelings, but I am really very nervous out here."[43] And in he crept without a sound. Before he departed at daybreak he had quite bewildered her with his vows.

No sooner had he returned home than he wrote, "How is it with you now? I hardly know how to express my feelings:[44]

Koi to ieba	If now I speak of love,
Yo no tsune no to ya	I fear that you may think
Omouran	It but a worldly commonplace:
Kesa no kokoro wa	My heart this morning
Tagui dani nashi	Admits no parallel."[45]

She replied:

Yo no tsune no	"Never could I think
Koto to mo sara ni	Our love a worldly commonplace
Omōezu	On this morning when
Hajimete mono o	For the first time my heart
Omou ashita wa	Is filled with many thoughts."[46]

But even as she wrote, her mind was a tangle of sad and conflicting emotions. What an incomprehensible person she was! After all the tender vows the late Prince had made— Just then the same page came again. Had he brought a letter? No, apparently not. She felt terribly dejected. And this itself proved how susceptible she was!

She sent the page back with a poem:

| Matamashi mo | "Even had I counted on your coming, |
| Kabakari koso wa | My feelings could have been |

Aramashika	No stronger than they are,
Omoi mo kakenu	This evening filled with longing
Kyō no yūgure	Intense beyond all expectation."[47]

The Prince was moved to pity at these words; nevertheless, he made no attempt to repeat such an escapade. He might not be on a quite normally intimate footing with the Princess, his official consort,[48] but even so she was bound to view with suspicion his going out night after night. And further, he reflected, it was because of his infatuation with this woman that his brother the late Prince had been made the subject of vicious gossip until the day of his death.[49] Such were the cautious considerations that crossed the Prince's mind. Perhaps his dedication to the lady was not quite complete.[50]

His reply came about dark:

Hitaburu ni	"Had you but said
Matsu to mo iwaba	You waited with no other thought,
Yasurawade	Without a moment's hesitation
Yukubeki mono o	Had I then set forth upon
Kimi ga ieji ni	The way to your abode.[51]

I am the one who will be hurt if you think me cold."

"How could I?" she replied. "For my part,[52]

Kakaredomo	Be what may,
Obotsukanaku mo	I feel no shadow
Omōezu	Of uneasiness—
Kore mo mukashi no	Perhaps because we share
E ni koso arurame	A bond with him who is no more.[53]

And yet, 'uncomforted, my life must perish like the dew.' "[54]

While he fully intended to go to her, actually doing so involved so much trouble[55] that he let several days go by.

136

She wrote to him on the last day of the month:[56]

Hototogisu	"When shall I hear
Yo ni kakuretaru	The muted singing
Shinobine o	Of the *hototogisu*,
Itsu ka wa kikan	Still hidden from the world,
Kyō mo suginaba	After today is gone?"[57]

But the Prince was unable to look at her message, for just then his quarters were crowded with people waiting on him. The page presented the poem the next morning, and when the Prince had read it he responded:

Shinobine wa	"Why strain to hear
Kurushiki mono o	That muted singing?
Hototogisu	From this day forth
Kodakaki koe o	Listen to the *hototogisu*
Kyō yori wa kike	High in the treetops sound his lofty note."[58]

Two or three days later he stole out to see her again. But as it happened, the lady had decided to go on retreat to a certain temple,[59] and was in the midst of her preparatory purification.[60] And besides, his neglect showed how little interest he had in her anyway.[61] She therefore made scant effort to talk to him, using her religious observances as an excuse for ignoring him all night.

"What a rare night I have spent!" he wrote to her the next morning:

Isa ya mada	"Never had I known
Kakaru michi o ba	In all my life
Shiranu kana	So strange a way of love:
Aite mo awade	To meet, yet be unmet
Akasu mono to wa	All the night long.[62]

It was outrageous!"

Indeed, how outrageous he must have thought her, she reflected ruefully:

Yo to tomo ni	"Yet she who with the dark
Mono omou hito wa	Forever sinks into love's longing,
Yoru tote mo	Though the night come,
Uchitokete me no	Can never know that sweet repose
Au toki mo nashi	When eyelids close, as lovers join in sleep.[63]

And this is no rare thing for me," she said.

The next day brought another note from him: "Will you then be leaving on your pilgrimage today? When should I expect you to return? Time will drag on more drearily than ever, I fear."

She replied:

Ori sugite	"When the moment passes
Sate mo koso yame	All that has been planned must end;
Samidarete	Amid the pelting rain
Koyoi ayame no	Tonight, though perplexed of mind,
Ne o ya kakemashi	I would 'hang the iris root.'[64]

Such are my intentions, but I shall not be gone long."

It was two or three days later when she returned. She received a message from the Prince: "Since I have been feeling very uneasy, I would like to go and visit you. But that miserable experience of the other night has left me too disheartened and crestfallen. It seems we are destined to drift apart.[65] And yet, though of late,[66]

Sugusu o mo	Thinking that as time passed
Wasure ya suru to	Forgetfulness might come,
Hodo fureba	I let the days slip by,
Ito koishisa ni	Today to my exceeding love
Kyō wa makenan	Must I surrender.[67]

Even you must see that my feelings are not shallow."[68]

138

She replied:

Makuru to mo	"Surrender and come
Mienu mono kara	To me? I see no sign of that,
Tamakazura	And yet I wait,
Tou hitosuji mo	Although the crawling vine sends out
Taemagachi nite	Scarcely one visiting shoot."[69]

The Prince came in his usual secretive fashion. But as the lady had discounted any such possibility and was moreover[70] fatigued by her devotions of the past several days, she had drowsed off to sleep, and no one heard the knocking at the gate. Since he had been listening to various rumors, the Prince thought she must be entertaining another lover, and softly stole away, returning home. The next morning she received the following note:

Akezarishi	"As I stood waiting
Maki no toguchi ni	At the pine-wood[71] gate
Tachinagara	You would not open for me,
Tsuraki kokoro no	The proof of your cold heart
Tameshi to zo mishi	Was there for me to see.

'This, then, is wretchedness,'[72] I thought, bitterly disappointed."

Apparently he had come last night! And she had been so mindless as to be asleep! She replied:

Ikade ka wa	"How could you see,
Maki no toguchi o	When the pine-wood gate
Sashinagara	Was locked and barred,
Tsuraki kokoro no	Whether or not
Ari nashi o min	My heart was cold?

The way you seem to have leaped to false conclusions is what is really wretched. 'Could I but show my heart—' "[73]

Though he wanted to go to her again that night, there were those who prevented him from keeping such trysts. He had to be circumspect. In particular,[74] he felt, it would be indiscreet of him to let his Lordship of the Center[75] or the Heir Apparent[76] hear of his escapade. And so a very long time went by.

The rain poured down day after dreary day, and as the lady gazed out on a world of unbroken clouds she pondered what would become of her relations with the Prince. Despite the fact that she no longer paid the slightest heed to the many gallants who pressed their attentions upon her, it seemed she had become the subject of much scandalous gossip. But she resigned herself to the thought that this was the inevitable consequence of her continued existence in society.[77]

A message came from the Prince: "How are you surviving this tedious rain?

Ōkata ni	Nothing remarkable—
Samidaruru to ya	The same old rain that pelts us
Omouran	Every year, you think?
Kimi koiwataru	These are my tears of love
Kyō no nagame o	Falling in a deluge all day long!"[78]

She was pleased that he had not overlooked this opportunity to send her a seasonal poem, especially now that the rain had aroused in her thoughts of the pathos of life. She wrote:

Shinoburan	"Your tears of yearning?
Mono to mo shirade	Indeed I did not know—
Ono ga tada	But only thought
Mi o shiru ame to	This was 'the rain that knows
Omoikeru kana	The sorrows of my life.'"[79]

Turning over the slip of paper,[80] she added:

Fureba yo no	"The rain pours down,
Itodo usa nomi	And time brings nought but pain:
Shiraruru ni	All that I know of life;
Kyō no nagame ni	Would that with today's deluge
Mizu masaranan	The flood might rise and carry me away.[81]

140

Would there be a shore awaiting me?"[82]

When the Prince had read this he replied immediately:

Nani sen ni	"What do you mean—
Mi o sae suten to	To cast your very life away?
Omouran	Do you alone
Ame no shita ni wa	Drag on from day to day
Kimi nomi ya furu	Beneath a rainy heaven?[83]

It is a bitter world for us all."

The fifth day of the fifth month came,[84] and still the rain did not stop. The Prince had been moved by the more than usually forlorn tone of the lady's recent reply, and the next morning, following a night of continuous torrential downpour, he sent a message: "How frightening was the sound of the rain last night!"

She replied:

Yomosugara	"All the night long
Nanigoto o ka wa	What were the things that I
Omoitsuru	Was thinking of,
Mado utsu ame no	While I lay listening to the sound
Oto o kikitsutsu	Of raindrops beating on my window?[85]

'Sheltered though I was,' my sleeves were strangely wet."[86]

"This woman is by no means unworthy of my regard," reflected the Prince, and responded:

Ware mo sazo	"I too was anxious,
Omoiyaritsuru	For I guessed how hard the sound
Ame no oto o	Of rain must be to bear
Saseru tsuma naki	For one who lay alone beneath
Yado wa ikani to	The scant protection of her eaves."[87]

141

About noon word circulated that the water in the river had risen, and a crowd of people went to take a look.[88] The Prince was among them. "How are you feeling now?" he wrote. "I have gone off to see the flood:

Ōmizu no	The banks are all awash
Kishi tsukitaru ni	With waters of the flood,
Kuraburedo	But still my heart
Fukaki kokoro wa	Is deeper,
Ware zo masareru	Out of all comparison.

I wonder if you have realized that?"

She replied:

Ima wa yomo	"Yet I cannot
Kishi mo seji kashi	Bank upon his coming now,
Ōmizu no	He of the flood-deep heart,
Fukaki kokoro wa	For all he talks of love
Kawa to misetsutsu	In river-metaphor.[89]

Mere words are useless."

He would go to her, he decided, and was having his clothes perfumed with burnt incense[90] when his old wet-nurse, Jijū,[91] approached him.

"Where is your Highness going?" she asked. "I hear people are talking about this affair.[92] That woman is of no such high-and-mighty rank. Anyone you wish to have serve you you should summon here as your servant.[93] These rash excursions create a very bad impression. Besides, her place is frequented by great numbers of men. Something awkward is bound to happen. All this good-for-nothing business was started by that Lieutenant what's-his-name. He's the one who led the late Prince off on *his* escapades, too. Can any good come from going about in the dead of night? The person[94] who accompanies you on your excursions may speak to his Lordship.[95] In this world one can never tell what may

142

happen from one day to the next, so changeable it seems.[96] His Lordship[97] has something in mind, you may be sure. I feel it would be best for you to leave off these excursions until you have made certain which way the wind is blowing."

"And just where am I supposed to be going?" replied the Prince. "Since I have been feeling bored, I thought I would seek a little momentary diversion, that is all. It is nothing for people to make such a great fuss about."

The lady was strangely cold to him, no doubt of that, yet she was by no means a waste of time. Perhaps he should call her and settle her close at hand. But that would give rise to still viler gossip. With his mind in such a tangle, he let their relationship drift off into uncertainty.

At long last he went to her. "Please do not attribute it to negligence on my part," he said earnestly, "that due to no intention of mine our relations should have become so exasperatingly uncertain. I think the fault lies with you. When I heard how many gentlemen there were who found my visits to you inconvenient, I was pained; and while I hesitated out of general principle, time simply went by.[98] Come now, just for tonight. There is a place where no one will see. We can talk to our hearts' content."

He had the carriage drawn up and urgently pressed her to get in, until, hardly aware of what she was doing, she complied. She went obsessed by the thought that someone was sure to hear, but as the night was far advanced no one knew that she had gone.

Softly they drew up beside a deserted gallery,[99] where the Prince alighted. "Come!" he urged, but the moon was very bright, and when she too stepped down it was with obvious distaste.[100]

"You see, not a soul about!" he said. "From now on let us meet in this fashion.[101] It makes me feel constrained to think, 'Tonight perhaps someone is with her.'"

He talked with her tenderly until, at dawn, he had the carriage drawn up and placed her in it. "I really should accompany you," he said, "but it would be light by the time I got back, and I should find it disagreeable if people were to think I had spent the night out." And so he remained behind.

All the way home the lady wondered what people were going to think of so strange an escapade. Recalling how extraordinarily touching[102] a figure he had presented in the early light of dawn, she wrote:

Yoigoto ni	"Even if it means
Kaeshi wa su tomo	I have to turn you back each night,
Ikade nao	Still I must find
Akatsukioki o	A way to save you from this pain
Kimi ni sesaseji	Of rising with the dawn.

It was more than I could bear."

He replied:

Asatsuyu no	"The pangs of rising,
Okuru omoi ni	Parting in the dewy morn,
Kurabureba	Though keenly felt,
Tada ni kaeran	Yet seem as nothing to the pain
Yoi wa masareri	Of blankly going home by night.[103]

I refuse to listen to such ideas; since your home is in a forbidden direction[104] tonight, I shall pick you up and bring you here."

"What a scandalous spectacle!" she thought. "If he should make a habit of this—" But he came, in his usual carriage.[105]

"Quickly! Quickly!" he hastened her as he drew up beside the house.

"Oh, how really unbecoming a performance this is," she thought again and again as she crept out and into the carriage. They talked together at the same place as the night before. The Prince's consort thought he had gone to visit his father, the Retired Sovereign.[106]

The dawn came. " 'Cruel is the cock's cry,' "[107] quoted the Prince, and softly climbed into the carriage. As they rode along he said, "On such occasions we really must arrange things this way."

144

"How can we make a practice of it?" she demurred.

He escorted her home and returned, and shortly afterward his message arrived: "I hated the cock whose crowing startled us out of our sleep this morning and have killed it."[108] The note was attached to a cock's feather. With it was the poem:

Koroshite mo	"Killed, but still
Nao akanu kana	I am not satisfied!
Niwatori no	That wretched rooster
Orifushi shiranu	With its ill-timed
Kesa no hitokoe	Cry this morning!"

She replied:

Ikani to wa	"I am the one
Ware koso omoe	Who has been most offended,
Asana asana	Morn after morn,
Nakikikasetsuru	By the cruel crowing of that cock
Tori no tsurasa wa	I have been forced to hear.[109]

Has it not indeed been hateful to me!"[110]

Two or three days went by, and then there came a night when the moon shone with extraordinary brilliance. The Prince sat gazing at it from his veranda. "How is it with you?" he wrote. "Are you too looking at the moon?[111]

Waga gotoku	Do such thoughts
Omoi wa izu ya	Come to you as now to me,
Yama no ha no	Pretending that my heart
Tsuki ni kaketsutsu	Sighs for the moon which soon must set
Nageku kokoro o	Behind the mountain ridge?"[112]

Not only was she unusually charmed by these sentiments, but the message arrived just when her own memories had been aroused, and she was wondering whether someone might not have seen her in the bright moonlight that night at the Prince's mansion. She replied:

Hitoyo mishi	"When I consider how we saw
Tsuki zo to omoeba	This self-same moon that night,
Nagamuredo	Gaze though I may,
Kokoro mo yukazu	My heart is still bemused,
Me wa sora ni shite	My eyes absorbed in vacancy."[113]

She was still gazing alone when the night drew futilely to its close. He did come the following night, but no one heard him. Different people occupied the various parts of the house, and when the Prince spied the carriage of someone who had come to visit one of the other wings he concluded that his lady was receiving a visitor.[114] He was not happy about the situation, but even so, as he had no intention of breaking off with her, he sent a message: "Perhaps you didn't hear that I came last night? It cuts me to the quick to think you didn't even know:

Matsuyama ni	Though I had seen before
Nami takashi to wa	The waves were high
Miteshikado	Upon Pine Mountain,
Kyō no nagame wa	Today in this long rain
Tada naranu kana	I stare incredulous."[115]

The rain was falling indeed. What a strange, upsetting turn of events! Could he have been listening to someone's gossip? She wrote back:

Kimi o koso	"You are the one whose fickleness,
Sue no matsu to wa	As I have heard it told,
Kikiwatare	Brings waves o'er Sue's pines;
Hitoshinami ni wa	Who can compare with you
Tare ka koyubeki	In breaking seas across that mountaintop?"[116]

146

The Prince remained depressed by what he had seen the other night, and for a long time made no contact with her. Finally he wrote:

Tsurashi to mo	"I think you an unfeeling wretch,
Mata koishi to mo	And then again my heart's desire,
Samazama ni	And this and that and thus and so,
Omou koto koso	Till my poor brain, for turning about,
Hima nakarikere	Can find no time to rest."[117]

It was not that she had no answer, but she was loath that he should think she was making some excuse. She sent:

Au koto wa	"No matter what befalls,
Tomare kōmare	Even if we can never meet again,
Nagekaji o	I shall not grieve:
Urami tae senu	One thing only I cannot bear:
Naka to narinaba	Unending bitterness."[118]

And so they grew even more distant. One night of brilliant moonlight the lady reclined, her gaze held by the scene before her. "How enviously limpid—":[119] the words rose to her lips. She wrote to the Prince:

Tsuki o mite	"Though you do not come,
Aretaru yado ni	Please let me hear from you at least;
Nagamu to wa	Whom would you have me tell
Mi ni konu made mo	Of how I gaze upon the moon
Tare ni tsuge yo to	Here in my desolate dwelling?"[120]

She entrusted the poem to a young chambermaid,[121] telling her to hand it to the Guards lieutenant. The Prince was conversing with several people he had summoned into his presence; after they withdrew, the lieutenant brought him the poem.

"Prepare the carriage as usual," said the Prince, and took his departure.

The lady was still gazing at the moon from her veranda, but as soon as she observed someone come into the grounds she lowered the blind[122] and sat behind it. Again she saw the familiar figure which yet never failed to delight her eyes afresh,[123] and whose charm she found only enhanced by a soft, informal costume[124] which had been worn until not a trace of stiffness remained.

"Since your messenger returned without this—" Without another word he placed a note on his fan and had it handed in to her. As the distance between them was too great for her to speak to him easily, she simply reached out and took the message on her own fan.

The Prince decided he too would go up onto the veranda.[125] Walking about among[126] the delightful plants in the garden, he murmured the familiar line, "My love, like dew upon the grass—"[127] It was enchanting.

"I shall not stay the night this time," he said, coming closer. "Actually, I came to discover who it is that you have been secretly meeting.[128] Since I have announced that tomorrow I am to be in seclusion,[129] I think it would look odd if I were not at home." And with that he started to go.[130]

But she:

Kokoromi ni	"If only it would rain!
Ame mo furanan	For then perhaps the moon,
Yado sugite	Which passes by my house,
Sora yuku tsuki no	Sailing the sky, might stay
Kage ya tomaru to	And shed its light within."[131]

He was touched by her childlike sincerity,[132] which was quite beyond anything for which people gave her credit. "My love!" he exclaimed, and went up into the house for a few moments. As he departed he answered:

| Ajikinaku | "Loath though I am to go, |
| Kumoi no tsuki ni | Drawn by the cloud-dwelling moon, |

Sasowarete	My outward form indeed departs,
Kage koso izure	But not my heart:
Kokoro ya wa yuku	How should it go from you?"[133]

After he left she read the poem he had given her:

Ware yue ni	"You told me that it was
Tsuki o nagamu to	Because of me
Tsugetsureba	You gazed upon the moon,
Makoto ka to mi ni	And I have come
Idete kinikeri	To see if this is true."

What a very delightful person he was after all! If only she could somehow correct the quite grotesque impression of her he had picked up from current gossip—[134]

The Prince too felt that the situation was by no means hopeless: she would serve to lighten the tedium of his days. But soon fresh rumors came: "They say that a certain Minamoto captain[135] has been paying court to her lately. I hear he goes to her even during the day." Or again: "Did you know that the Civil Affairs Minister[136] has been favoring her, too?" Such stories were on everyone's lips. He could only conclude that she was inordinately fickle, and for a long time there were no messages from him.

The Prince's page came one day, and being on familiar terms with the lady's chambermaid, fell to chattering with her about this and that.

"Did you bring a message?" asked the maid.

"No," replied the page. "One night my master came and found a carriage at your mistress' gate. I think that must be the reason why he doesn't write. It seems he has heard that other men are visiting this house."

After the boy left, the maid reported what he had said.

It was a long time now, the lady reflected, since she had last exchanged small, intimate messages[137] with the Prince. And she had certainly never made any particular demands upon him. It was true of course that on those rare occasions when he did remember her[138] she was inspired with hope that their relationship might continue unbroken. But that was out of the question now that this contemptible gossip had led him to think of her in the way he did. Why had it come to this?[139] she sighed despondently. And then a message came.

"What with the suffering caused by the strange disorder which has seized upon me of late, I have been quite unable to write. I have gone to see you more than once recently, but it seems my visits were rather poorly timed, for I have always had to turn around and come back. I feel completely humiliated:

Yoshi ya yoshi	Peace, peace, so let it be,
Ima wa uramiji	I shall no longer in my sore offense
Iso ni idete	Go down to the rocky strand
Kogihanareyuku	And watch the fisher's boat row out,
Ama no obune o	Leaving me forsaken by the shore."[140]

He had been listening to really unspeakable rumors, and she felt ashamed to say anything to him at all. Just this once, however, she would reply:

Sode no ura ni	"I am indeed that fisher girl
Tada waga yaku to	Whose task it is to burn
Shio tarete	The salt on Sode's shore,
Fune nagashitaru	But all I do is wet my briny sleeves,
Ama to koso nare	Now that my boat has drifted far away."[141]

While they were exchanging such messages the seventh month arrived. On the seventh day the lady received from amorous gentlemen many verses written on the theme of the Weaving Maid and the Herdsman,[142] but she did not give them so much as a glance. The Prince had always written to her without fail on such special occasions as this, she reflected, but now he seemed to have forgotten all about her. But just at that moment a note arrived. It consisted simply of this:

Omoiki ya	"How could I know—
Tanabatatsume ni	That I myself
Mi o nashite	Would be the Weaving Maid
Ama no kawara o	And look with longing gaze
Nagamubeshi to wa	Across the Riverbed of Heaven?"[143]

Feeling a glow of pleasure that after all he had not let the occasion slip by, she replied:

Nagamuran	"I cannot even look
Sora o dani mizu	Upon that sky towards which you gaze,
Tanabata ni	
Imaru bakari no	When I consider how
Waga mi to omoeba	I am but such as you do loathe
	And shun at Tanabata time."[144]

After all, he could not bring himself to give her up, the Prince realized as he read her poem.

Toward the end of the month he wrote to her. "We have become very distant with each other. Why do you not send me a note from time to time?[145] I feel as if I meant nothing to you at all."

She replied:

Nezaneneba	"Since nothing breaks your sleep,
Kikanu naruran	I think you do not hear
Ogikaze wa	The wind beckoning among the reeds;
Fukazarame ya wa	
Aki no yona yona	And yet does it not blow,
	Night after autumn night?"[146]

Immediately the Prince responded: "I do not 'waken at night,' my love? True, for I never go to sleep! Remember what the poem says—'When I am filled with longing—'[147] Please do not accuse me of indifference:[148]

Ogikaze wa	If it is true the wind
Fukaba i mo nede	Blows beckoning among the reeds,
Ima yori zo	Sleeplessly henceforth
Odorokasu ka to	I'll listen for your wakeful message,
Kikubekarikeru	Expecting to be startled from my bed."[149]

At dusk about two days later a carriage suddenly pulled into the lady's grounds, and the Prince alighted. She was extremely embarrassed, for as yet he had never seen her;[150] but there was no help for it. He left after some rather inconsequential conversation.

After that so many days went by without word that she became very uneasy:

Kuregure to	"As darkly, darkly,
Aki no higoro no	Filled with anxious thoughts,
Furu mama ni	The autumn days slip by,
Omoishirarenu	I've come to know it well,
Ayashikarishi mo	That questionable heart of yours.[151]

But," she added, " 'truly it is hard for man to turn his back upon the world.' "[152]

The Prince replied, "Though of late our relations have drifted off into uncertainty, even so,

Hito wa isa	However it may be with you,
Ware wa wasurezu	I at least have not forgotten,
Hodo furedo	Though the days slip by,
Aki no yūgure	How you and I did meet
Arishi au koto	One autumn evening."[153]

152

It made her feel miserable to realize that the only consolations her relationship with the Prince provided came in such wretched, fugitive, undependable trivia as this.

In the meantime the eighth month had begun. The lady decided she must do something to relieve the tedium of her existence, and set off on a pilgrimage to Ishiyama, leaving word that she would be gone about seven days. Just at this time the Prince was struck by what a long time had gone by without their seeing each other, and summoned his page to carry a message. The latter, however, informed his master that on a recent visit to the lady's house he had heard that she had gone to Ishiyama on retreat.

"Well then," replied the Prince, "since today it is already dark you shall go there the first thing tomorrow morning." And he wrote a message and gave it to the boy.

The latter proceeded to Ishiyama as directed. The lady, however, was not before the Buddha. On the contrary, her mind was filled with thoughts of home, and she reflected ruefully that such pilgrimages showed how greatly she had changed. The world was a very sad place indeed. Just as she was turning inwardly to the Buddha in earnest prayer,[154] a movement below the railing attracted her attention. Curious, she looked down and saw that it was the Prince's page. It was a happy surprise.[155]

"What brings you here?" she asked, and for reply the page handed over the Prince's message. Opening it more hurriedly than was her wont, she read:

"I am impressed with the fervent faith which you have displayed in going off on this pilgrimage, but why did you not apprise me of your plans? You certainly do not seem to consider *me* any impediment[156] in *your* search for salvation. It was unfeeling of you to go off and leave me behind in this way:

Seki koete	And did you guess
Kyō zo tou to ya	I would inquire for you this very day
Hito wa shiru	Across the Barrier?

153

Omoitae senu	No weariness prevents
Kokorozukai o	The running of my heart to you.[157]

When will you come back from your retreat?"

She was pleased that he should thus have gone to the trouble of writing to her (though when she was close at hand he treated her with indifference) but replied:

Ōmiji wa	"Who is it says that he
Wasurenumeri to	Will ask for me, crossing the Barrier,
Mishi mono o	Although from all appearances
Seki uchikoete	He seems to have forgotten
Tou hito ya tare	The Ōmi Road to lovers' rendez-vous?[158]

You ask when I shall return? My resolution is no light matter:[159]

Yama nagara	Though here among the hills
Uki wa tatsu tomo	Life may be hard to bear,
Miyako e wa	When shall I go back to Miyako,
Itsu ka Uchide no	When shall I see
Hama wa mirubeki	The beach at Uchide?"[160]

"This must be exhausting, but go once again," the Prince instructed his page, entrusting to him his reply: "What do you mean, 'Who is it'? What a revolting expression!

Tazuneyuku	And do you well,
Ōsakayama no	Thus to let me fade away
Kai mo naku	From your forgetful mind,
Obomeku bakari	Making my quest up Meeting Moun-tainside
Wasurubeshi ya wa	A trip to no avail?[161]

Indeed:

Uki ni yori	Though from the trials of life
Hitayagomori to	You thought to hide yourself

154

Omou tomo	In strictest solitude,
Ōmi no umi wa	Come now and see the Sea of Ōmi,
Uchidete o miyo	The beach at Uchide where lovers meet.[162]

You know what the poem says: 'If every time that life is difficult—' "[163]

She replied simply:

Sekiyama no	"I think it is the tears alone
Sekitomerarenu	Of her whom you would meet,
Namida koso	Undammable by any Barrier Mountain,
Ōmi no umi to	
Nagareizurame	That flow out like the Sea of Ōmi,
	A flood of misery."[164]

And to one side she wrote:

Kokoromi ni	"Just for a test
Onoga kokoro mo	I'm tempted to make trial
Kokoromimu	Of my own heart:
Isa Miyako e to	Come! Make the attempt—
Kite sasoimiyo	Tempt me to the Capital!"[165]

The Prince wanted to surprise her by going when she would least expect it, but how could he get away? And just at this juncture she came back to the city.

"Your speed in returning," he wrote to her, "made it impossible to comply with your request that I try my hand at temptation:[166]

Asamashi ya	Oh deed deplorable!
Nori no yamaji ni	To leave the path of piety
Irisashite	That led you off into the hills;
Miyako no kata e	Who can have tempted you
Tare sasoiken	Back to the Capital?"

Her reply consisted simply of this:

Yama o idete	"If I have left my hills
Kuraki michi ni zo	And struggled back along
Tadorikoshi	This dark and worldly way,
Ima hitotabi no	It is because I still desire
Au koto ni yori	To meet you once again."[167]

Toward the end of the month the wind blew fiercely. One day while she sat gazing, more than usually depressed by the autumnal tempest and the rain, a poem came from the Prince. It was written with his customary air of knowing just what sentiments were appropriate to the season, so that in the end she had to forgive him for his long neglect:

Nagekitsutsu	"While I was gazing,
Aki no misora o	Lost in melancholy sighs,
Nagamureba	Upon the autumn sky,
Kumo uchisawagi	The clouds churned wildly,
Kaze zo hageshiki	Blown by the violent wind."[168]

She replied:

Akikaze wa	"The merest stirring
Keshiki fuku dani	Of the autumn wind
Kanashiki ni	Is sad enough,
Kakikumoru hi wa	But a day of leaden clouds
Iu kata zo naki	Beggars description."[169]

Her days must indeed be sad, he thought; nevertheless time drifted by as before without his visiting her.

It was past the twentieth of the ninth month when late one night the Prince was awakened by the shining of the dawn moon.[170] What a terribly long time it had been, he mused, and wondered, touched by the thought, whether she too might not be looking at this same moon. Surely she must, but what if someone were with her? Despite his misgivings on this score he set out, accompanied only by his usual page.

The lady was lying awake, thinking of many things, when she heard the knocking at the gate. Perhaps because the season had infected her with an autumnal melancholy, everything of late seemed more than usually touching in its sadness, and now she was lost in vacant revery. Strange! Who could it be, she wondered and awakened the servant who was sleeping nearby to go and inquire. But the girl was in no hurry to get up, and when at long last she was pulled from under the covers,[171] she went off to wake up a manservant who would not be roused either. The latter, when he was finally made to get up, banged about in the dark and bumped into so many things that by the time he reached the gate the knocking had stopped. Whoever it was apparently had gone home, no doubt thinking she was fairly drugged with sleep,[172] lying there without a care in the world. Who could it be, this person who was kept awake by the same thoughts as hers?

The manservant, whom the maid had finally roused,[173] came back grumbling. "Nobody there. Never let a man get any rest, the ladies in this house. Think they hear something and send a fellow off to stumble around in the middle of the night." And he went back to sleep.

The lady however did not sleep but stayed up until at length the night was over. She gazed at the sky, which was obscured by a dense mist, until it grew light and then set about composing an account of all that she had felt on being awake to see the breaking of the dawn. While she was busy writing, a message came. It consisted simply of this:

Aki no yo no	"I went home empty-handed,
Ariake no tsuki no	For I could not linger there
Iru made ni	And wait the setting of the moon
Yasuraikanete	That shines still in the sky at dawn
Kaerinishi kana	After the long autumnal night."[174]

Indeed, how keenly disappointed he must have been! But at

least he had not forgotten her—that was what mattered. She felt happy at the thought that he too had been looking at that spectacle of sky, so moving in its beauty, and she immediately folded[175] and sent him the composition which she had been writing more or less as an exercise.

He read:

"The sound of the wind: The tempest blew so hard it seemed not a leaf could be left on any tree, making me more than ever aware of life's fleeting sadness. The storm clouds lowered, but a mere sprinkle of rain fell. I was unbearably moved:

Aki no uchi wa	Before the autumn ends
Kuchihatenubeshi	My sleeves must rot away,
Kotowari no	Mouldered by my tears;
Shigure ni tare ga	And when the sure, cold rains
Sode wa karamashi	Of winter come, whose shall I borrow?[176]

But there was none to know of my despondency. Even the grass grew pale before my eyes, and though the winter rains should still be far off, it bent in seeming pain before the wind.[177] As I looked upon this scene I compared myself, apt to vanish at any moment like the dew, to the frail leaves of grass, and in my sadness simply lay down near the veranda without making the effort to go into the inner room.[178] But I was quite unable to sleep,[179] though everyone else lay in a profound slumber. There was no specific reason for my wakefulness; still, I lay there through the listless hours, completely unable to drop off and utterly out of sorts. And then there came the faint cry of a wild goose. Others may not be much affected by such things, but I was moved almost beyond my power to endure:

Madoromade	Untouched by drowsiness,
Aware iku yo ni	How many are the nights, alas,
Narinuran	That I have lain,
Tada kari ga ne o	Nothing for me to do but hear
Kiku waza ni shite	The calling of wild geese?[180]

Thinking that anything would be better than simply lying thus all night, I pushed open the door to the veranda. The moon had slanted down the vast sky into the west, and its light shone clearly in the distance. The voice of the bell and the crowing of the cock blended into one under the mist-veiled sky,[181] and I felt that surely there neither had been nor could ever be another moment such as this. The very tears that fell upon my sleeves seemed tenderly, strangely new.[182]

Ware naranu	Not I alone—
Hito mo sazo mimu	Another surely sees,
Nagatsuki no	And knows the Long Month's
Ariake no tsuki ni	Waning moon at dawn
Shikaji aware wa	Cannot be matched for mournful loveliness.[183]

If now someone should knock at my gate, what would my feelings be?[184] But who else would spend the night in wakefulness as I have done?

Yoso nite mo	Though in another place,
Onaji kokoro ni	Is there yet one who with a heart
Ariake no	The same as mine
Tsuki o miru ya to	Looks on the waning moon at dawn?
Tare ni towamashi	Of whom should I inquire?"[185]

Just as she was wondering if she should send this composition to the Prince, his messenger had come, and she had availed herself of the opportunity of presenting it to him.[186] He was by no means ill pleased by what he read, but decided to dash off a hasty reply in order to catch her while she was still in her pensive mood.

His message was brought to her where she sat gazing off into the distance; she felt somehow disappointed[187] as she opened it:

Aki no uchi wa	"Before the autumn's end
Kuchikeru mono o	My sleeves have rotted quite away;
Hito mo sa wa	And yet a certain

Waga sode to nomi	Person thinks of nothing
Omoikeru kana	But that hers may suffer so.[188]
Kienubeki	Think not your life
Tsuyu no inochi to	A drop of dew
Omowazu wa	About to vanish;
Hisashiki kiku ni	Were it not better to rely upon
Kakari ya wa senu	The long-lived chrysanthemum?[189]
Madoromade	Untouched by drowsiness,
Kumoi no kari no	Listening to the calling of wild geese
Ne o kiku wa	That fly the cloudy vault—
Kokorozukara no	If you have found no other thing to
Waza ni zo arikeru	do,
	Your own heart bears the blame.[190]
Ware naranu	Not I alone—
Hito mo ariake no	Another gazed with rapture
Sora o nomi	On that dawning sky,
Onaji kokoro ni	And saw the moon, and felt
Nagamekeru kana	The feelings that were mine.[191]
Yoso nite mo	Though in another place,
Kimi bakari koso	I thought that you at least
Tsuki mime to	Were looking at the moon,
Omoite yukishi	And went to you this morning—
Kesa zo kuyashiki	What a fool I was![192]

The dawn would not break and the gate would not open—it was too much."[193]

Despite these complaints she was glad that she had written to him.

Toward the end of the month a message came. After apologizing for his long silence the Prince went on, "You may think it a bit odd, but I have a request to make of you.[194] It seems that a certain person whom I have been seeing for quite a long time is going off to a distant place, and I would like to say something to her that she would consider touching. The poems you send me are more touching than any others I have known. Please write one for me now."

"What complacency!"[195] she thought. But still, to decline would seem too impertinent. She kept her remarks brief: "As to this kind request of yours, how can I presume—?[196]

Oshimaruru	Pray leave behind at least your image,
Namida ni kage wa	Mirrored in my regretful tears,
Tomaranan	Though, wearied of my love,
Kokoro mo shirazu	You go away with dying autumn,
Aki wa yuku tomo	Ignorant of my heart.[197]

To pour my emotion into this poem cost me dearer than you know." On the margin she added, "And yet:

Kimi o okite	Leaving you behind,
Izuchi yukuran	Where can she think to go,
Ware dani mo	When even I,
Uki yo no naka ni	Lovesick in a world of pain,
Shiite koso fure	Can clench my teeth and live?"[198]

"I should say your poem is perfect," the Prince replied, "though critical opinions sound a bit conceited[199] coming from me. But aren't you carrying it a little too far with this 'lovesick in a world of pain'?[200]

Uchisutete	She who has abandoned me
Tabiyuku hito wa	To journey far away—
Sa mo araba are	Let her go where she will,
Matanaki mono to	I do not care, as long as you
Kimi shi omowaba	Hold me without rival in your heart.[201]

That is all I ask."

Thus the tenth month[202] arrived. About the tenth day of the month he came to visit her. The inner part of the house being dark and eerie, he lay with her near the veranda and spoke of all the touching sadness of this life. The lady could not fail to be moved. Again and again the moon was obscured by clouds, and a light rain fell. It seemed a night deliberately designed to touch the deepest chords of emotion. The lady's heart was a tangled skein, and she shuddered with the cold. When the Prince looked at her he thought strange indeed those reports of her devious behavior. The very sight of her trembling by his side gave them the lie.[203] Moved to tenderness, he roused her from the jumble of painful thoughts in which she lay as if asleep:

Shigure ni mo	"Tonight we sleep
Tsuyu ni mo atede	Untouched by dew or wintry rain,
Netaru yo o	Yet strangely are they wet,
Ayashiku nururu	These sleeves of mine
Tamakura no sode	Whereon my head lies pillowed."[204]

But the lady said nothing, for she did not feel capable of a reply, being submerged in a myriad inextricable thoughts. When the Prince saw her tears falling silently in the moonlight, his heart went out to her, and he said, "Why do you not compose a reply? I see my worthless poem has displeased you. I am sorry."

"I feel somehow too distraught," she replied. "It is not that I ignored your poem. Wait and see," she said as if to jest, "if I ever forget your 'pillow-sleeves.'"

Perhaps it was the tenor of her talk—she *did* seem utterly without a friend to whom she could turn for support. The next morning, troubled by these thoughts which colored his recollection of that sweetly sad nocturnal scene,[205] the Prince wrote to ask how she was feeling.

She replied:

Kesa no ma ni	"Within a morning's space
Ima wa kenuran	They must have dried—
Yume bakari	Those pillow-sleeves
Nuru to mietsuru	So slightly dampened when we lay
Tamakura no sode	In sleep that seemed a momentary dream."[206]

He recalled with amusement her promise not to forget:

Yume bakari	"Although they may have seemed
Namida ni nuru to	The figment of a dream—
Mitsuramedo	My drenching tears—
Hoshi zo kanetsuru	It has been quite impossible
Tamakura no sode	To dry those pillow-sleeves."[207]

Thereafter the Prince made frequent visits, for apparently his heart had been moved[208] by that touching scene under the night sky, so that he now felt a deep and pained concern for her. The more he studied her, the more he realized that she had never been hardened by the world. He was distressed at the way in which she seemed to be merely floating uncertainly on the surface of life and spoke to her from the depths of his sympathy.

"Why should you go on living in this way,"[209] he asked, "gazing vacantly into the distance with nothing to break the tedium of your days? Though I have reached no final decision concerning us, I urge you to come to me. I have been made the object of much vexing criticism. Perhaps because my visits to you are few and far between, I have never been discovered; yet people are saying most distressing things.[210] And as I make my way home from those fruitless excursions when I have been unable to gain admittance,[211] I feel so miserable and despised that again and again I have thought that I must do something to bring an end to this situation. But perhaps I am a bit old-fashioned, for the prospect of breaking off with you seems unbearably sad. However it is out of the question to go on visiting you in this way. If a certain person should hear of it, my freedom of movement would be gone, and you would be as out of reach as the moon in the sky.[212] If you are as bored and lonely as you have said, will you not come with me? Although *she* is there,[213] I can assure you that you will be subjected to no embarrassment. I am by nature unsuited to these nocturnal excursions, and it has not been my wont to have clandestine meetings in unfrequented places. I am a solitary sort, alone even in the practice of my devotions. It would be a comfort to be able to talk to someone with a sympathetic mind."

But the lady was filled with doubt.[214] She wondered how she would manage should she enter at this point upon so unaccustomed a mode of life. There was too the matter of the Eldest Prince still undecided.[215] Were she to seek the consolations of religion, there was no one to serve as her "guide over the mountains."[216] And yet, to continue as she was would be like living through a night without a dawn.[217] There had been many gentlemen who engaged her in idle banter, and apparently her dubious reputation stemmed from this. No, there was simply no one other than the Prince on whom she could depend. Well then, should she give it a try? Of course his official consort had to be reckoned with, but she had separate living quarters, and it seemed that the old nurse took care of everything for the Prince. There was indeed the possibility that the presence of a new lady in the house would come out into the open and be bruited about, but since she would doubtless be staying in some suitably out-of-the-way part of the mansion, what had she to fear? She would be able at last, in spite of all the talk, to rid herself of the cloak of suspicion which had enveloped her.[218]

"Resigned as I have been to a life where nothing goes as I would wish,"[219] she said, "I have had to content myself with waiting for rare occasions such as this, which have been my sole diversion. But though I should like to do whatever you say, it seems we are already made the target of much indecent talk, even though I am living here by myself. It will be no laughing matter when people look at us and say, 'Ahah! So it was true after all!' "

"It is precisely because you are living here that people are talk-

164

ing,"[220] replied the Prince. "Who will see anything improper in your coming to live with me? I shall arrange your quarters with the utmost privacy," he added reassuringly.

It was late that night when he left. She lay down, alone, by the raised lattice shutters[221] near the veranda but could get no rest, for her thoughts fell into a hopeless tangle as she turned the Prince's proposal over in her mind, wondering what she should do, and whether she would be made the butt of ridicule. While she lay there a message was brought to her:

Tsuyu musubu	"All along the road
Michi no manimani	Where dew lay thick
Asaborake	In the dim light of dawn
Nurete zo kitsuru	My pillow-sleeves were soaked
Tamakura no sode	As I went home."[222]

Though this matter of the sleeves was a mere trifle, she was pleased that he had not forgotten:

Michishiba no	"Because of him
Tsuyu ni okiiru	Who rose to greet the dew
Hito ni yori	That lay upon the roadside grass,
Waga tamakura no	My pillow-sleeves also
Sode mo kawakazu	Refuse to dry."[223]

The moon that night was very bright and clear, and both the lady and the Prince[224] stayed up until dawn gazing at it. In the morning the Prince wanted to send his usual message and asked if his page was yet in attendance. The lady also, startled perhaps by the extreme whiteness of the frost, wrote:

Tamakura no	"Even upon
Sode ni mo shimo wa	My pillow-sleeves the frost
Okitekeri	Had formed, and when I rose,
Kesa uchimireba	Behold, this morning they were
Shirotae ni shite	Sheets of linen-white!"[225]

Extremely put out by the way she had gotten ahead of him, the Prince remarked:[226]

Tsuma kou to	"For it was the frost that comes
Okiakashitsuru	After one has worn the night away
Shimo nareba	In longing for his mate."[227]

And at *this* point the Prince was informed that the page had come. He was in a very bad humor. "Since you did not come quickly when you were called, you can expect a severe dressing down,"[228] the Prince's attendant told the boy as he handed him his master's message. The lad delivered it to the lady's residence, and as he handed it in, said, "His Highness had summoned me before[229] he received your note, but I was late, and now he is scolding me for not coming in time."

"Last night's moon was extraordinary!" said the Prince's message:

Nenuru yo no	"Was she too looking
Tsuki wa miru ya to	At the moon that shone upon
Kesa wa shimo	Our sleep that night,
Okiite matedo	I wondered, and arose and waited
Tou hito mo nashi	In the morning frost, but no one came."[230]

It pleased her to see that he had actually written to her first. She answered:

Madoromade	"You wear the face
Hitoyo nagameshi	Of one who's stayed awake
Tsuki miru to	Amid the frost,
Okinagara shimo	Watching the moon we gazed upon
Akashigao naru	All that sleepless night."[231]

Amused by the page's reference to his scolding, she added on the margin:

Shimo no ue ni	"The morning sun, it seems,
Asahi sasumeri	Is shining on the frost,
Ima wa haya	Which in a moment melts away,
Uchitokenitaru	As I would have you show
Keshiki misenan	Your anger too has melted from your face.[232]

The boy really seems terribly crestfallen."

"I was extremely vexed at the evident satisfaction you took in stealing a march on me this morning,"[233] replied the Prince. "I could kill that page!

Asahikage	The frost may melt away
Sashite kiyubeki	Before the morning sun's warm rays,
Shimo naredo	But not so easily
Uchitokegataki	Will be assuaged
Sora no keshiki zo	The angry countenance of this sky."[234]

The lady expressed a mild surprise at the Prince's ferocity:[235]

Kimi wa kozu	"Although you never come,
Tamatama miyuru	The lad at least appears
Warawa o ba	From time to time;
Ike to mo ima wa	And do you now intend to take his life
Iwaji to omou ka	And let him visit me no more?"[236]

On reading this the Prince laughed and sent back:

Kotowari ya	"Right you are!
Ima wa korosaji	I shall be patient
Kono warawa	And not kill him now, that lad,
Shinobi no tsuma no	Obedient to the words
Iu koto ni yori	My secret spouse has spoken.[237]

By the way, I'll wager you've forgotten all about the 'pillow-sleeves.' "[238]

She replied:

Hito shirezu	"Unknown to anyone
Kokoro ni kakete	I hold them in my heart
Shinoburu o	In cherished memory—
Wasuru to ya omou	Think you that I would forget
Tamakura no sode	Those pillow-sleeves?"[239]

But the Prince had the last word:[240]

Mono iwade	"If I had let
Yaminamashikaba	The matter go with nothing said,
Kakete dani	Hold them where you may,
Omoiidemashi ya	Would you have ever called to mind
Tamakura no sode	Those pillow-sleeves?"[241]

For two or three days after that she received not a word from him. What had become of his firm promises? In her anxiety she was unable to sleep, and one night when she was lying wide awake thinking of how late it must be, there came a knocking at the gate.

"What in the world?" she wondered, and sent someone to find out who it was. A message had come from the Prince. And at such an unexpected hour—she wondered if "her heart had gone to wake him."[242] Touched, she opened the door onto the veranda, and read:

Miru ya kimi	"Do you see it, my beloved?
Sayo uchifukete	The hour is late,
Yama no ha ni	And there above the mountain crest
Kumanaku sumeru	Shines limpid, unobscured,
Aki no yo no tsuki	The moon of an autumn night."[243]

As she gazed[244] out at the moon she was more than usually moved. Thinking the messenger must be getting impatient outside the gate, which had not been opened for him, she replied:

168

Fukenuran to	"Although the hour must
Omou mono kara	Be late indeed, I cannot sleep;
Nerarenedo	And yet since it would
Nakanaka nareba	Only increase my loneliness
Tsuki wa shimo mizu	I do not look upon the moon."[245]

He saw she had turned the tables on him, and again realized that here was a woman by no means to be despised. He resolved somehow to find a way to have her close at hand to amuse him with such delightful improvisations.

About two days later he came unobtrusively, his carriage arranged to look as if it carried women passengers.[246] She felt embarrassed because he had never seen her by day,[247] but of course it would not do for her to put on an offended air and hide herself away in shame. Besides, if matters were to be arranged as he had said, it hardly seemed that she need be on very diffident terms with him, she thought and slipped out from behind her screen to greet him.[248]

After making his apologies for his neglect of the past several days,[249] he lay down for a few moments. "Please hurry and make up your mind to follow my plan," he said. "I always feel awkward about going out like this, but on the other hand if I do not visit you I am very uneasy, and our relationship comes to seem agonizingly uncertain."

"I am willing to do whatever you wish," she replied, "but I am worried that 'familiarity may bring regret.' "[250]

"Very well, try me and see. You will find that, as with the garments worn by the salt-gatherers of Ise, 'familiarity makes dear.' "[251] And with that he took his departure. There was a handsome spindle tree[252] growing by the latticework fence near the front of the house. The Prince directed his servant to break off a branch of slightly reddened leaves and lean it against the veranda railing; he spoke the lines:

Koto no ha fukaku	"The leaves of our words too
Narinikeru kana	Have deepened in their color."[253]

She replied:

Shiratsuyu no	"Even as I watched
Hakanaku oku to	The momentary forming
Mishi hodo ni	Of a drop of silver dew."[254]

Her rejoinder was not lacking in taste, he noted with pleasure. And she in turn found his appearance ravishing. From beneath his soft, voluminous costume with its great, billowing sleeves could be seen the skirt of an incredibly beautiful underrobe.[255] Every detail was as she would have wished, and she felt as if her eyes must be playing her false.

The following day she received a note from him saying, "Yesterday you seemed embarrassed, but all the more poignantly touching for that reason."[256]

She replied:

Kazuraki no	"The god of Kazuraki
Kami mo sa koso wa	Must have felt the same as I,
Omourame	The one who tried
Kumeji ni watasu	So awkwardly to build a bridge
Hashitanaki made	Over the Kume Road.[257]

I could not help feeling terribly distraught."

He immediately sent back:

Okonai no	"If ascetic rites
Shirushi mo araba	Have brought me magic power,
Kazuraki no	Will I leave you there,
Hashitanashi tote	Grumbling of the awkwardness
Sate ya yaminan	Of that Kazuraki bridge"?[258]

Now that he came to visit her more frequently than before the tedium of her days was broken and she felt greatly comforted.

170

But soon those wretched people again began sending her letters and even loitering around her house, leading to baseless rumors.[259] Perhaps she had best go to the Prince's mansion, she thought but timidly hung back from taking the step and could not definitely make up her mind. One morning when the frost was very white she wrote:

Waga ue wa	"Perhaps the plover
Chidori mo tsugeji	Will not tell you of my plight,
Ōtori no	But even on your
Hane ni mo shimo wa	Pinions, O great bird, I doubt
Sa ya wa okikeru	The frost lies thick as on my
	sleeves."[260]

The Prince replied:

Tsuki mo mide	"No frost could form upon
Neniki to iishi	The sleeves of one who said she
Hito no ue ni	slept
Okishi mo seji o	And never saw the moon
Ōtori no goto	Like to that which lies upon
	The wings of this great bird."[261]

He came to visit her as soon as evening fell.

"Imagine how delightful the foliage must be in the mountains at this time of year!" he said. "Shall we go and see?"

"They say it is very fine," she agreed, but when the day arrived she was obliged to stay in seclusion.[262]

"What a disappointment!" exclaimed the Prince. "We definitely must go when the period of your confinement passes."

But that night a cold rain fell with more than usual violence, so that it sounded as if not a leaf would be left on a tree. The lady awoke and murmured to herself, " —like a lamp before the wind."[263] The leaves must all have scattered. What a shame that they had not gone to see them yesterday, she thought and did not sleep the rest of the night.

171

In the morning a message came from the Prince:

Kaminazuki	"October rain—
Yo ni furinitaru	The same old thing, you think?
Shigure to ya	You do not know
Kyō no nagame wa	How drenched my spirits are,
Wakazu fururan	Dully gazing at today's down- pour.[264]

Now I am really disappointed!"

She replied:

Shigure kamo	"The chilly rain?
Nani ni nuretaru	Or is it something else
Tamoto zo to	That makes my sleeves so wet?
Sadamekanete zo	Unable to decide,
Ware mo nagamuru	I too gaze bleakly into space.[265]

Beyond a doubt

Momijiba wa	The colored leaves must all
Yowa no shigure ni	Be gone, stripped off by a night
Araji kashi	Of cold and wintry rain;
Kinō yamabe o	If only we had gone to see
Mitaramashikaba	The mountains yesterday!"[266]

When he had read these lines the Prince wrote back:

Soyo ya soyo	"Indeed, indeed,
Nadote yamabe o	Why did we not go
Mizariken	To see the mountains?
Kesa wa kuyuredo	This morning all regret
Nani no kai nashi	Is purposeless."

And on the margin he added:

Araji to wa	"They must be gone,
Omou mono kara	For the storm has blown them down;

Momijiba no
Chiri ya nokoreru
Iza yukite min

Yet some few leaves
May cling unscattered to the trees—
Come! Let us go and see!"[267]

She replied:

Utsurowanu
Tokiwa no yama mo
Momiji seba
Iza kashi yukite
Tou tou mo min

"If the mountains of
Unchanging evergreens
Were to put on colored leaves,
Then truly might we go a-searching,
Searching everywhere, to see.[268]

Your suggestion is quite absurd."

One day when the Prince had come to visit her she had put him off, saying that something[269] prevented her from seeing him. Later, he recalled,[270] she had written:

Takasebune
Haya kogiide yo
Sawaru koto
Sashikaerinishi
Ashima waketari

"Come quickly rowing
In your river skiff,
For I have made a pathway
Through the obstructing reeds
Which sent you poling home before."[271]

Now the Prince teased her with forgetting her own poem:[272]

Yamabe ni mo
Kuruma ni norite
Yukubeki ni
Takase no fune wa
Ikaga yosubeki

"In that case you should be glad
To go with me aboard my carriage
Up into the mountain country too;
But how could we come near those hills
By sculling in a river skiff?"[273]

She replied:

Momijiba no
Mi ni kuru made mo

"But if the colored leaves
Waited, unscattered, on the trees

173

Chirazaraba   Until one came by coach to see,
Takase no fune no   No need would be to scull a river
Nani ka kogaren   skiff,
                      For no one's heart would burn with
                          longing then.''[274]

When that day too drew to a close he came to her, and as her
house lay in a forbidden direction,[275] quietly took her away with
him.[276] At this time the Prince was spending a forty-five-day
period[277] at the home of a cousin of his, a holder of the Third
Rank,[278] in order to avoid a directional taboo. The lady was
distressed at being led off in this way, particularly to an unaccustomed place, and protested that they would create a scandalous
impression. But the Prince insisted, and they drove in. He left
her ensconced in the carriage, which he caused to be drawn out of
sight into a carriage shed,[279] and went into the house. She was
alone with her fears. When everyone had settled down for the
night he came back and climbed into the carriage, where he talked
with her and vowed a myriad vows. His usual lieutenant and page
stood guard close by, but the men of the watch went their rounds
without an inkling of what was happening. Swept by emotion, the
Prince bitterly regretted that he had let so much time go by for
nothing. It was all very well for him to say so now, she reflected.[280]

He escorted her home at dawn and returned, hurrying to arrive
back before anyone had gotten up. Early that morning he sent a
poem:

Nenuru yo no   "Accustomed as I am
Nezame no yume ni   To early waking from my
Naraite zo   Lonely dreams,
Fushimi no sato o   This morning at Fushimi
Kesa wa okikeru   I rose too soon from that we
                           shared.''[281]

She replied:

174

Sono yo yori	"Ever since that night
Waga mi no ue wa	My fate has been beyond my know–
Shirareneba	ing;
Suzuro ni aranu	Therefore have I slept
Tabine o zo suru	So strange a sleep, so recklessly,
	Upon so strange a bed."[282]

How could she treat with cold-hearted indifference the devotion and undeserved attention he was now lavishing upon her?[283] She decided she would go to him. Surely nothing so terrible would happen.[284] There were those who cautioned her seriously against such a step, but she paid no heed. Since her existence brought her nothing but pain in any case, she would simply trust to fate.[285] And yet she had no fundamental desire to enter his household. What she really wanted was to live "in a cavern deep within the crags."[286] But how would she cope with the melancholy that might come to haunt her?[287] People would say that she had no true calling to such a life. After all it would perhaps be best to go on as she was, with her parents and sisters close by where she could look after them.[288] And she had to see to the upbringing of her child, who so reminded her of her former husband.[289] How distressingly difficult it was to decide![290] If she were indeed to go to the Prince, she wanted, if at all possible, to prevent his hearing any more inconvenient rumors before she went—of course when they were together he would see and understand the truth, she thought—and when her amorous gentlemen sent her letters she simply had the messengers informed that she was not in residence and resolutely refused to reply.

A message came from the Prince: "What a fool I was to go on trusting you in spite of everything!" He had not wasted any words, but simply said, "I don't know what to make of you."[291] She felt crushed and dumbfounded. It was true that extraordinary fabrications had circulated in great numbers, but her attitude toward them had always been one of resignation. What after all could one do about such inventions? But now, judging from the serious tone of the Prince's message, it seemed that the rumormongers had caught wind of her decision.[292] To think that because of their lies she was placed in such a stupid position made her so unhappy that she did not even feel able to write a reply. She wondered what he could have heard. And he on his part interpreted her embarrassed silence as shame over her past deeds.[293]

"Why do you not answer me?" he wrote. "I fear my suspicions must have been justified. How quickly your heart changes! But I cannot really credit these rumors and only meant to say, 'If you but care for me—' "[294]

At this she felt slightly relieved. Desiring to know the true state of his mood,[295] and to learn what it was that he had heard, she wrote, "If it is true that you feel as you have said,

Ima no ma ni	I wish that you
Kimi kimasanan	Would come this very moment:
Koishi tote	However strong my love,
Na mo aru mono o	How can I go to you and brave
Ware yukan ya wa	More scandal flung upon my name?"[296]

He replied:

Kimi wa sa wa	"And so you worry
Na no tatsu koto o	About scandal and your name—
Omoikeri	It seems to me
Hito kara kakaru	That such preoccupations
Kokoro to zo miru	Vary with the man involved.[297]

Now you've really made me angry."

While she saw that he must be merely teasing her and really did know how she was suffering, still this sort of thing was painful. "Your poem wounds me deeply," she wrote. "I would do anything to make you see the truth of my innocence."

176

He wrote:

Utagawaji	"Though I resolve
Nao uramiji to	Never to doubt you
Omou tomo	And still less resent,
Kokoro ni kokoro	My doubting heart will not obey
Kanawazarikeri	My heart that so resolves."[298]

And she:

Uramuramu	"Smoulder on,
Kokoro wa tayu na	Resentful heart!
Kagirinaku	For even I,
Tanomu kimi o zo	Who trust you utterly,
Ware mo utagau	Am not without my doubts."[299]

He came to her at dusk, soon after receiving this reply. "I confess that I wrote that letter to you because of what people were saying," he told her, "though at the same time I felt such rumors could not be true. If you would avoid being talked of in this way, then come to me." He stayed with her until daybreak.

Although he was completely faithful in his correspondence, he found it difficult to get away to visit her. One day the rain fell and the wind blew fiercely, but still he did not call. "He must not realize what the sound of the wind is like in a place where hardly anyone lives," she thought, and toward evening she wrote to him:

Shimogare wa	"Frost-withered,
Wabishikarikeri	Desolate is this forsaken scene;
Akikaze no	Yet while the autumn wind
Fuku ni wa ogi no	Still blew music through the reeds
Otozure mo shiki	You used to come to me."[300]

Later, scanning his reply, she read:
"I was moved by the fearsome howling of the wind and wondered how it must affect you:

Karehatete	Lonely in her
Ware yori hoka ni	Withered solitude, with none
Tou hito mo	Save me to visit her,
Arashi no kaze o	What feelings must be hers,
Ikaga kikuran	Hearing the storm-wind rage?[301]

The very thought of it was more than I could bear."

His words brought her a glow of pleasure.

He came to her as usual in his carriage.[302] Because of having changed his residence temporarily due to the directional taboo, he was now living in a highly secluded place, he said.[303] She went with him, deciding that this time she would simply do whatever he asked of her. They talked together to their hearts' content from morning till night, rising or sleeping as they pleased. She felt relieved of the bitter tedium of her days and wished to go and live with him. But the period of his taboo passed, and she returned to her own home.

Today she felt more than ever overpowered with love and longing, until, unable to endure her emotions any longer, she wrote:

Tsurezure to	"Today in idleness
Kyō kazoureba	I reckoned up the count and found,
Toshitsuki no	Of all the months and years,
Kinō zo mono wa	That yesterday alone I was not
Omowazarikeru	Plunged in melancholy thoughts."[304]

Touched, he replied, "I feel as you:

Omou koto	Those yesterdays
Nakute suginishi	We passed without a thought
Ototoi to	To trouble us—
Kinō to kyō ni	Would indeed I had the art
Naru yoshi mogana	To make them turn into today!

But of course I have not. After all, you must make up your mind to come here."

178

However, she was still very hesitant and could not come to a clear-cut decision but simply went on gazing abstractedly at nothing in particular while the days and nights slipped by.

The autumn leaves in all their varicolored beauty had vanished without a trace. The day had been bright, the sky clear, but now the rays of the gradually sinking sun had a bleak and cheerless look. The lady, as was her custom at such moments, wrote to the Prince:

Nagusamuru	"You are here
Kimi mo ari to wa	To bring me consolation—
Omoedomo	This I know, and yet
Nao yūgure wa	Shadows of the deepening dusk
Mono zo kanashiki	Are sad for all of that."[305]

He replied:

Yūgure wa	"There is no one
Tare mo sa nomi zo	Who does not share your sadness
Omōyuru	At the deepening dusk,
Mazu iu kimi zo	But your swift sensitivity
Hito ni masareru	Surpasses all the world.[306]

And it is precisely this about you that touches me. I wish I could go to you this very moment."

The next morning while it was yet early and the frost was very white she received his message inquiring after her. She replied:

Okinagara	"Only a morning
Akaseru shimo no	When the frost lies thick and white
Ashita koso	In the sleepless dawn
Masareru mono wa	Provides a peerless beauty
Yo ni nakarikere	That surpasses all the world."[307]

They exchanged several verses of this sort. One from the Prince accompanied a letter filled with his usual expressions of tender emotion:

179

Ware hitori	"The thoughts of love
Omou omoi wa	That I think alone
Kai mo nashi	Are all in vain;
Onaji kokoro ni	Would that you were
Kimi mo aranan	Of the same heart as I."

She replied:

Kimi wa kimi	"Since there is no separation
Ware wa ware to mo	Of 'You are you'
Hedateneba	And 'I am I,'
Kokorogokoro ni	How can our hearts
Aramu mono ka wa	Be alien to each other?"[308]

The lady had apparently come down with a cold.[309] It was nothing to become alarmed about, but she did feel ill, and the Prince sent frequently to inquire about her. Once after she had begun to mend he wrote to ask how she was, and she responded:

"I am feeling somewhat better. My desire to live a little longer involves me in deep guilt, and yet:

Taeshi koro	When you broke with me
Taene to omoishi	I thought, 'Then let it snap,
Tama no o no	This thread of my life,'
Kimi ni yori mata	But now because of you
Oshimaruru kana	I would again regret to die."[310]

"You make me very happy," replied the Prince, "more so than I can say:[311]

Tama no o no	How could it ever snap,
Taen mono ka wa	Your thread of life?
Chigiriokishi	Within those bonds we swore
Naka ni kokoro wa	Your very heart
Musubikometeki	Is bound inextricably."[312]

While they exchanged such messages the year drew on until only a brief space remained before its close. She now thought of making the contemplated move in the spring.[313] One day about the first of the eleventh month it snowed heavily, and the Prince wrote:

Kamiyo yori	"From the Age of Gods
Furihatenikeru	The snow has fallen, year by year,
Yuki naredo	As old as the world—
Kyō wa koto ni mo	And yet today how rare,
Mezurashiki kana	How lovely does it seem!"[314]

She replied:

Hatsuyuki to	"But as the winters pass
Izure no fuyu mo	When we exclaim
Miru mama ni	Upon the beauty of first-fallen snow,
Mezurashige naki	I only fall yet further into age
Mi nomi furitsutsu	Without a hint of shining rarity."[315]

And she went on whiling away her time with such fugitive verses.

A message came from the Prince: "I have begun to feel lonesome for you and would like to go and pay you a visit, but it seems there is a Chinese poetry meeting being held."[316]

She sent back:

Itoma nami	"If for lack of time
Kimi kimasazu wa	You cannot come, then I shall go,
Ware yukan	For oh how I desire
Fumi tsukururan	To learn the path of poetry
Michi o shirabaya	Which leads my steps to you."[317]

He was delighted and responded:

Waga yado ni	"Pray come indeed,
Tazunete kimase	Visit me here in my house!

Fumi tsukuru	Not only will I teach
Michi mo oshien	That path of poetry—
Ai mo mirubeku	We'll have the tryst to which it leads!"[318]

One morning when the frost was more than usually white he wrote to ask her what she thought of the spectacle.

She replied:

Sayuru yo no	"Are they then I—
Kazu kaku shigi wa	The snipe that preen and preen
Ware nare ya	On winter nights
Iku asa shimo o	When the sky is cold and clear—
Okite mitsuran	That I greet with sleepless eyes each morning's frost?"[319]

Since they had recently been having severe rainstorms, she continued:

Ame mo furi	"The rain has fallen,
Yuki mo furumeru	And the snow, these many days,
Kono koro o	While I kept vigil
Asashimo to nomi	Vainly through the night: your love
Okiite wa miru	Is shallow as the morning frost."[320]

He went to her that night and spoke again the familiar, fleeting words of love. But something seemed to depress him, for he went on, "If after I have taken you to live with me I should go off somewhere and become a monk, and we could no longer see each other, I suppose you would feel disillusioned?"

What could he be thinking of, she wondered. Was it possible that such a thing could happen? Overcome by a wave of poignant emotion, she wept uncontrollably. Outside[321] the rain was falling softly, mixed with sleet. The Prince did not doze off even for a moment, but filled the night with many tender vows of devotion extending even beyond this life. His bearing was so sympathetic and

182

lacking in any trace of coldness that she longed to go and live with him so that he could know exactly what she felt in her heart. She resolved to take the step.[322] But if he were to do as he had suggested?[323] Then she too could do no other than to fulfill her fundamental desire by abandoning the world.[324] The thought was sad. When he saw how she wept silently on and on, he said:

Naozari no	"We wear the night away
Aramashigoto ni	In needless talk
Yomosugara	Of troubles yet to come—"[325]

And she replied:

| Otsuru namida wa | "—While the tears I weep |
| Ame to koso fure | Fall like the very rain." |

But the Prince went on talking in a way that showed how unusually precarious his mood actually was.[326] He left for home at dawn.

Although it was nothing on which she had pinned any very high hopes, she had thought that going to live in the Prince's mansion would fill the emptiness of her existence. But now what should she do? Her thoughts in a tangle, she wrote:

Utsutsu nite	"Viewed as reality,
Omoeba iwan	The things you said tonight
Kata mo nashi	Are quite unthinkable;
Koyoi no koto o	Therefore would I change
Yume ni nasabaya	Your words into a dream.[327]

But how could that be done?"[328] On the margin she added:

Shika bakari	"Although you made
Chigirishi mono o	So strong a pledge of love,
Sadamenaki	Do you now say to me,
Sa wa yo no tsune ni	'Think this the uncertain
Omoinase to ya	World's accustomed way'?[329]

I am sadly disappointed."

When he had read her message he replied, "I had intended to write to you first myself:

Utsutsu to mo	I would not have you think
Omowazaranan	It was reality,
Nenuru yo no	That painful scene
Yume ni mietsuru	We saw but in a dream
Uki koto zo so wa	One night as we lay sleeping.

Did you indeed try to make reality of it? How easily upset you are![330]

Hodo shiranu	A mere lifetime
Inochi bakari zo	Whose length one cannot know—
Sadamenaki	*This is* uncertainty;
Chigirite kawasu	Rather let us swear our love
Sumiyoshi no matsu	Will last as long as Sumiyoshi's pines.[331]

My darling, I shall never worry you again with talk about what may or may not happen in the future. These are matters I must decide alone—a forlorn prospect."[332]

Thereafter she felt utterly downcast and was completely given over to involuntary sighs. If only she had gone to live with him sooner! Toward noon a message came:

Ana koishi	"Ah, how I long for her!
Ima mo miteshi ga	Would I could see her now once more,
Yamagatsu no	The wildflower of Yamato,
Kakiho ni sakeru	Blooming by the hedge before
Yamato nadeshiko	Her lowly cottage in the hills."[333]

Her reaction was spontaneous: "Ah, lunacy![334]

Koishiku wa	If you are filled with longing,
Kite mo miyo kashi	Come and see me then!
Chihayaburu	The road to where I live

| Kami no isamuru | Is not prohibited |
| Michi naranaku ni | By order of the impetuous gods."[335] |

This retort called forth a smile from the Prince. Since he had lately been studying the sutras,[336] he sent back:

Au michi wa	"Though that Meeting Road
Kami no isame ni	Does not offend against
Sawaranedo	The interdiction of our native gods,
Nori no mushiro ni	I may not rise and leave this mat
Oreba tatanu zo	Where I sit studying the Buddha's Law."[337]

She replied:

Ware saraba	"Then I shall be the one
Susumite yukan	To go along that road to you,
Kimi wa tada	As you are busy sitting on your mat,
Nori no mushiro ni	Absorbed in contemplating how
Hiromu bakari zo	To propagate the holy Buddha's Law."[338]

While they passed their time in such repartee a heavy snowstorm was in progress. The Prince attached a poem to a snow-covered branch and sent it to the lady:

Yuki fureba	"When snow has fallen,
Kigi no konoha mo	The leaves of every tree—
Haru narade	Though spring be far—
Oshinabe ume no	Have blossomed into flowers:
Hana zo sakikeru	A panorama of the plum."[339]

And she:

Ume wa haya	"The plum has early
Sakinikeri tote	Blossomed, so I thought,
Oreba chiru	Breaking a branch—

| Hana to zo yuki no | And snow, like petals scattering, |
| Fureba miekeru | Cascaded to the ground."[340] |

Early next morning he wrote:

Fuyu no yo no	"All the winter's night,
Koishiki koto ni	My eyes wide open, longing
Me mo awade	For my love, I lay,
Koromo katashiki	My cloak spread out without a mate,
Ake zo shinikeru	Alone until the dawn."[341]

She replied: "But as for me,[342]

Fuyu no yo no	All that winter's night
Me sae kōri ni	My eyes indeed were closed—
Tojirarete	But closed with ice!
Akashigataki o	While I wore out the darkness
Akashitsuru kana	To the laggard dawn."[343]

And so time went by, and she went on consoling herself in the tedium of her existence with these customary exchanges. But what would they amount to in the end?[344]

What could be weighing on the Prince's mind?[345] Again he began to talk despondingly: "After all, I am not long for this world."

She responded:

Kuretake no	"Will I alone be left
Yoyo no furugoto	To tell the story of our past—
Omōyuru	Destined to be numbered
Mukashigatari wa	With old tales of painful loves,
Ware nomi ya sen	Many as the nodes of black bamboo?"[346]

And he:

Kuretake no	"Here in this world
Ukifushi shigeki	Where trials grow rank
Yo no naka ni	As brakes of black bamboo
Araji to zo omou	I do not think to live
Shibashi bakari mo	One moment more."[347]

He had selected a place where he could keep her secretly, but since it was not at all the sort of thing to which she was accustomed, she seemed to feel uneasy about going there.[348] Here in the mansion, too, tongues would wag. He decided it would be best to go alone and escort her in.[349] On the eighteenth night of the twelfth month, a period when the moon was very fine, he went to her. He greeted her with his usual "Let us be off!" Thinking it was a matter of that night only, she climbed into the carriage alone.

"Take someone with you," he instructed her. "If possible, I would like for us to spend some time together at our leisure."

This was something out of the ordinary. Could he have decided to take her straight off to his mansion? She took a single attendant and went with him. He led her, not to the usual place, but to quarters evidently arranged with a view to housing someone secretly along with her servants.[350] And so it was true? Well, there was no need to make a grand entrance.[351] On the contrary, let them speculate on just when she had come. When morning arrived she sent her attendant back to fetch her comb box and other necessary items.

Since his servants knew the Prince was in the room, they left the lattice shutters closed. Though the lady was not actually frightened by the darkness, she found it rather oppressive.[352]

"I think I shall soon move you to the northern wing,"[353] said the Prince. "This is too near the front of the house[354] to have a properly secluded atmosphere."

Seeing how, closed in behind the lowered shutters, she was quietly listening to what was going on outside, he went on, "During the day the Retired Sovereign's[355] courtiers[356] gather in attendance here. I wonder, can you put up with the disturbance?[357] But what worries me most is that you may find me a disappointment now that we are together."[358]

"I was afraid you would think the same thing of me!" she replied.

He laughed. "Seriously, though, you must be careful when I am away at night. Impertinent people may come peeking around. A little later you should go over to the serving mistress' quarters.[359] No one is so bold as to force his way in there. Yes, that would be the place."[360]

About two days later the household was astonished to discover that the Prince was taking his lady to the northern wing.[361] The Princess, his official consort, was informed. "Even before it came to this he was acting suspiciously enough," she thought, "but now! This woman of his is no such rare specimen.[362] He must be completely under her sway, or he would not have smuggled her in like this without a word to anyone."[363] She was highly offended and in a more than usually unpleasant mood. The Prince felt that the situation was too difficult for him to handle,[364] and for the time being stopped going into her part of the mansion. As it was also distressing to listen to the talk of the other members of his household, and as he felt very sorry for the new lady, he spent most of his time with her.[365]

"I understand that you have been carrying on a certain affair," the Princess complained to him one day. "Why did you not tell me? I would not have tried to stop you. But now that you have handled things in this way, I am despised and made the object of ridicule. I feel disgraced." And she wept bitterly.

"How can you fail to grasp the reason why I have taken a new girl into my service?"[366] replied the Prince. "Chūjō[367] and the others have taken their cue from your own ill humor, and seem to harbor hateful feelings toward me. They depress me, and so I have brought in someone else to take care of arranging my hair and the like. Please feel free to make use of her for your own needs, too."

The Princess was still very put out, but she did not pursue the subject further.

188

As the days went by the lady became accustomed to her duties. She waited on the Prince even during the day, tending to the combing of his hair and performing at his behest a myriad personal offices. He never let her leave his side, and his visits to the Princess became more and more infrequent. The latter was never finished bemoaning her grievances.

The new year came round again,[368] and on the first day the men of the court went in full force to take part in the ceremonies of obeisance to the Retired Sovereign.[369] The Prince made one of their number, and as the lady watched him take his departure she was struck by how young and handsome he looked, so far superior to the others. She felt quite ashamed of her own appearance. The ladies-in-waiting to the Princess came out to view the proceedings, but instead of watching the spectacle outside, they fell over themselves in their eagerness to see the newcomer, poking holes in the paper panels[370] to peer at her. It was disgraceful. With evening the ceremonies drew to a close, and the Prince returned. He came back escorted by a huge assemblage of the highest court ranks,[371] and the whole company made merry to the sound of flutes and strings.[372] The very gaiety of the occasion immediately brought back memories to the lady of the lonely, empty life she had lived in her old home.

While she thus continued in the Prince's service she was constantly exposed to the unpleasant talk of the underlings, which came to the Prince's ears as well. He was thoroughly offended. After all, there was no necessity for his consort to think or speak so meanly of someone else. It was really too much; his visits to her were few and far between. The new lady, too, felt quite uncomfortable about the situation, but what was she to do? She simply followed the desires of the Prince.

The Princess had an elder sister who was Senior Consort of the Heir Apparent.[373] This sister was at present visiting her childhood home,[374] and one day a letter came from her: "Can they possibly be true," she asked, "these things that people are saying? I feel as if I too had been treated with contempt.[375] Do come home—simply leave under cover of darkness."

The Princess was extremely upset. So now the story was out![376] And to think how even trivial matters were gossiped about. She wrote in reply:

"I have received your letter. My relations with his Highness, which have always left much to be desired, have lately deteriorated to a scandalous degree. I want to go home for a little while where I can see your dear children[377] again. How that would comfort my heart! Please come to take me away. I have no intention of staying here any longer to listen to the comments that are passed about me."[378]

She readied the things that she would need to take with her, and had her quarters thoroughly cleaned, getting rid of anything that might leave an unpleasant impression.

"I am going to my sister for a while," she announced. "It is simply too tiresome to go on in this way. I think his Highness' neglect indicates he too must find the situation painful."

Her maidservants joined in a chorus of vilification:

"It is really more than one can be expected to bear. Everyone is astonished at his conduct."

"When that woman came here, he went to escort her in person."

"The whole affair is too shocking to contemplate!"

"He keeps her in that room, and they say he goes to her three or four times every day—during the day, mind you!"

"Teach him a good lesson! He has gone too far in neglecting you so."

In her heart the Princess found these words hard to bear. Well, let things fall out as they would, she thought, at least she would be away from him.[379] At this point her brothers[380] arrived in response to her request. When they announced their errand she realized that the time had come.[381]

The serving mistress heard the nurse engaged in tidying up her room, and at once hastened to the Prince in consternation:[382]

"Apparently, for whatever reason, her Highness is about to

leave you and return home," she reported. "The Heir Apparent will be sure to hear of it! You should go and stop her!"

The lady[383] was extremely sorry and pained to see what was happening, but as she was in no position to say anything she simply sat and listened. She wished she could leave for a while until this distressing period was over, but that was more than she could ask. She decided simply to go on serving the Prince as before, but she knew that after all she was destined never to be free of sorrows.

When the Prince entered his consort's chambers he found her quite composed.

"Is it true, this I hear about your moving to your sister's residence? Why did you not order the carriage?"

"What need was there? It was arranged that they should come for me." And she declined to discuss the matter further.

It is noted in the manuscript that the style of the Princess' letter and the words of the Consort of the Heir Apparent are quite improbable, and must be the inventions of the author.[384]

BMFJ	*Bulletin de la Maison Franco-Japonaise.*
Chūko kasenden	*Chūko kasen sanjūrokuninden*, in *Shinkō gunsho ruijū*.
Dai Nihon kokiroku	*Dai Nihon kokiroku*, ed. Tōkyō Daigaku Shiryō Hensanjo (Tōkyō: Iwanami Shoten, 1953–1966).
GR	*Shinkō gunsho ruijū*, ed. Kawamata Keiichi (Tōkyō: Naigai Shoseki Kabushiki Kaisha, 1938–1939).
Iwanami text	*Izumi Shikibu nikki*, ed. Endō Yoshimoto, in *Nihon koten bungaku taikei*, XX (Tōkyō: Iwanami Shoten, 1957, 1962), 379–459.
Kōchū	Ozaki Tomomitsu, *Izumi Shikibu nikki kōchū* (Tōkyō: Tōhō Shobō, 1957).
Kōchū kokka taikei	*Kōchū kokka taikei*, ed. Nakatsuka Eijirō (Tōkyō: Kokumin Tosho Kabushiki Kaisha, 1927–1931).
KT	*Shintei zōho kokushi taikei*, ed. Kuroita Katsumi (Yoshikawa Kōbunkan, 1929–).
MYS	*Man'yōshū.*
NKBT	*Nihon koten bungaku taikei* (Tōkyō: Iwanami Shoten).
NKZ	*Izumi Shikibu nikki*, ed. Yamagishi Tokuhei, in *Nihon koten zensho* [no vol. number] (Tōkyō, Ōsaka: Asahi Shimbunsha, 1959), 111–263.
Nihon koten zenshū	*Nihon koten zenshū*, ed. Yosano Hiroshi, Masamune Atsuo, and Yosano Akiko (Tōkyō: Nihon Koten Zenshū Kankōkai, 1925–1931).
Ōchō nikki	*Izumi Shikibu nikki*, ed. Shimizu Fumio, in *Nihon koten kanshō kōza*, VI [*Ōchō nikki*] (Tōkyō: Kadokawa Shoten, 1959).
Ōhashi, *Kenkyū*	Ōhashi Kiyohide, *Izumi Shikibu nikki no kenkyū* (Tōkyō: Hatsune Shobō, 1961).
Shinchū	Tamai Kōsuke, *Izumi Shikibu nikki shinchū* (Tōkyō: Sekaisha, 1950).

Shinkō — Endō Yoshimoto, *Shinkō Izumi Shikibu monogatari* (Tōkyō: Hanawa Shobō, 1962).

Shiryō taisei — *Shiryō taisei*, ed. Kawamata Keiichi (Tōkyō: Naigai Shoseki Kabushiki Kaisha, 1934–1938).

TASJ — *Transactions of the Asiatic Society of Japan.*

Yoshida, *Kenkyū* — Yoshida Kōichi, *Izumi Shikibu kenkyū*, I (Tōkyō: Koten Bunko, 1964).

Yoshida, *Zenshū* — Yoshida Kōichi, *Izumi Shikibu zenshū: hombunhen* (Tōkyō: Koten Bunko, 1959).

Zenkō — Suzuki Kazuo and Enchi Fumiko, *Zenkō Izumi Shikibu nikki* (Tōkyō: Shibundō, 1965).

Zōho shiryō taisei — *Zōho shiryō taisei*, ed. Zōho Shiryō Taisei Kankōkai (Kyōto: Rinsen Shoten, 1965).

I. Notes to the Introduction

1. *Shinsen daijimmei jiten*, ed. Shimonaka Yasaburō, I (1938), 239. The phraseology is typical of old-fashioned Japanese hyperbole. Izumi Shikibu was no poetic revolutionary. Her poems adhere to accepted rules of prosody and seem typical products of their age in their frequent word play and concern with the themes of love and separation.

2. These dates have been proposed in, respectively, Okada Yoshio, "Izumi Shikibu to Fujiwara no Yasumasa," *Rekishi to chiri* (Feb. 1927), p. 266; Ikeda Kikan, *Kyūtei joryū nikki bungaku* (1927), p. 121; Yosano Akiko, "Kaidai," *Izumi Shikibu zenshū*, ed. Yosano Hiroshi, Masamune Atsuo, and Yosano Akiko, in *Nihon koten zenshū*, ed. Yosano Hiroshi, ser. 2, LXXII (1927), vi; *Shinchū*, pl. 28; *NKZ*, pp. 150, 151.

3. Compiler and date unknown, but prior to 1248. The work, in one *kan* (or *maki* 巻, a word which originally meant a scroll; with the development of books composed of paper folded into pages and sewn together along one edge, the term came to refer to a subdivision of variable length, roughly equivalent to a chapter) contains genealogies, notes on offices held, death dates, anecdotes, etc., for thirty-six poets.

4. *Gonchūnagon* 權中納言. The Chūnagon were a group of officials, originally three in number but later augmented by "provisional" appointments, in the Daijōkan 太政官 (Great Council of State), the central bureaucracy of the imperial government. This bureaucracy was established in 701 on the model of the

197

government of the T'ang Dynasty (618–907) in China. It was much too elaborate for the needs of Japan and was predicated on concepts of rule alien to the aristocratic nature of the Japanese state with its strong emphasis on hereditary succession. Consequently the various offices of the central government gradually degenerated into empty—though highly prized—titles, and in some cases into personal names. At the period under consideration—about the beginning of the 11th century—the bureaucratic structure of the Japanese court was highly elaborate. A certain amount of paper-shuffling must have gone on in the *de jure* offices, but the real power was held by the Northern House of the Fujiwara 藤原 family, and was exercised through several *de facto* organs and positions which had grown up outside the constitutional framework. The most important of these were the offices of Sesshō 攝政 and Kampaku 關白, regents for a child and for an adult emperor respectively. These offices were always held by the most powerful Fujiwara, who characteristically dominated the imperial line by marrying his daughters to the monarch and putting his grandsons on the throne. A subsidiary extralegal organ through which the Fujiwara conducted court business was the Kurōdodokoro 藏人所, the "Sovereign's Private Office" (translations of court titles and offices are those given in Robert Karl Reischauer, *Early Japanese History* [1937]).

The duties of the Chūnagon were, like those of their superiors the Dainagon 大納言 or "Major Counsellors," to act as advisors to the Emperor, to examine documents submitted to him, and to transmit his decrees. The prefix *gon* 權 indicates a supernumerary appointment (Sekine Masanao and Katō Sadajirō, *Yūsoku kojitsu jiten* [rev. ed., 1935], pp. 343, 514, 562).

5. In cases of uncertainty as to whether an *on* 音 (Sino-Japanese) or a *kun* 訓 (native Japanese) reading was assigned to a name, the *on* reading is given in brackets.

6. Masako (950–1000) was the eldest daughter of Emperor Suzaku 朱雀 (923–952; r. 930–946), and was Empress to Reizei 冷泉 (950–1011; r. 967–969). She was a devout Buddhist. "Grand Empress Dowager" is a translation of *Taikōtaigō* 太皇太后, a title given the grandmother of an Emperor. In Masako's case the title must have been honorary, for she had no children.

7. It is not known why she was called this. When written with the character 介, *Suke* refers to an "Assistant Governor," the second-ranking provincial official (for an explanation of the *Shitōkan* system, see translation, note 29). *Naishi* refers to the third-ranking official in the Naishi no Tsukasa 内侍司 (Palace Attendants Office), a group of female functionaries in the women's quarters of the Imperial Palace.

8. *Chūko kasen sanjūrokuninden*, GR, III, 716. Jōtōmon'in was the name taken by the Grand Empress Dowager Akiko [Shōshi] 彰子 (988–1074) upon her assumption of retired or *In* 院 status in 1026. She had been Empress to the Emperor Ichijō 一條 (980–1011; r. 986–1011).

9. Ages throughout are quoted in the Japanese fashion, according to which a person's age is calculated as the number of calendar years in which he has lived.

For dates I have relied whenever possible on *Kugyō bunin, KT*, LIII-LVII; *Dokushi biyō*, ed. Tōkyō Teikoku Daigaku Shiryō Hensanjo (1942); and *Nihon rekishi daijiten*, ed. Kawade Takao (1958–1961).

10. The personal poetry collection of Akazome Emon, a poetess contemporary with Izumi Shikibu. She married Ōe no Masahira 匡衡 (952–1012), younger brother (according to a theory of Oka Kazuo in "*Izumi Shikibu nikki no kenkyū*," in *Nihon bungaku kōza*, ed. Yamamoto Sansei, V [*Zuihitsu-nikkihen*] [1934], 185) of Izumi's father, Ōe no Masamune. By Masahira, Emon had a son, Takachika 擧周 (d. 1046), who was the suitor in the passage in question (*Chūko kasenden*, p. 716).

11. *Akazome Emon shū*, in *Kōchū kokka taikei*, ed. Nakatsuka Eijirō, XIII (1929), 394.

12. The old Japanese lunar years correspond only roughly to the solar years of the Gregorian (or Julian) Calendar. In cases of exact date the year is given according to the *nengō* 年號 system of named year periods, with the corresponding year of the Christian era added in parentheses. The notation Kannin 2.1.21 indicates the twenty-first day of the first month of Kannin 2. This system is used throughout.

13. *Midō Kampaku ki* (II), in *Dai Nihon kokiroku*, ed. Tōkyō Daigaku Shiryō Hensanjo [no vol. number] (1954), p. 138.

14. *Kō* is the Sino-Japanese reading of the character 江, pronounced *e* in Ōe 大江.

15. *Waka* 和歌 is a generic term for Japanese poetry. It is also used to refer specifically to the 31-syllable *tanka* 短歌, the dominant form in the period under consideration. The full name of the *Shūishū* is *Shūiwakashū;* I have followed the common practice of omitting the *waka* from the name of this and other imperial anthologies.

16. *Shūgaishō*, in *Shintei zōho kojitsu sōsho*, ed. Kawabata Sanehide, XXII (1952), 310. *Shūgaishō* is a miscellany of information on various subjects, in 3 *kan*, compiled by Tōin Kinkata 洞院公賢 (1291–1360). Tachibana no Michisada's name is given as Tachibana no Michizane 道眞.

17. A compilation by Tōin Kinsada 洞院公定 (1340–1399) of genealogies of the principal aristocratic families, in 14 *kan*.

18. *Sompi bummyaku, KT*, LIX, 4, 9.

19. This is a genealogy occupying the last *kan* of *Fusōshūyōshū*, a collection of old writings in 30 *kan*, compiled by Tokugawa Mitsukuni 德川光圀 (1628–1700) and published in 1689.

20. As cited in Shimizu Fumio, "Izumi Shikibu," in *Nihon kajin kōza*, ed. Hisamatsu Sen'ichi and Sanehide Kiyoshi, II [*Chūko no kajin*] (1960), 217.

21. Also pronounced *Shōyūki*. Diary of Great Minister of the Right Fujiwara no Sanesuke 實資 (957–1046) (see note 260). The diary originally covered the years 978–1032. Extant portions cover 982, 984, 985, 988, 995–997, 999, 1001, 1005, 1011–1021, 1023–1029, 1031, and 1032.

22. *Gembuku* 元服 was a boy's manhood ceremony, performed at some time

after his tenth year. At this time his hair, which had theretofore hung loose, was trimmed and tied into a knot, and a headpiece (*kan* 冠) was fitted onto his head (*Yūsoku kojitsu jiten*, pp. 305, 306).

23. *Ouki*, in *Shiryō taisei*, ed. Kawamata Keiichi, I (1936), 306. Suketaka was 15 at the time.

24. *Midō Kampaku ki* (I), in *Nihon koten zenshū*, ed. Yosano Hiroshi, ser. 1, VI (1926), 209. All other references to *Midō Kampaku ki* are to the *Dai Nihon kokiroku* edition.

25. Moku no Kami 木工頭.

26. Daishin 大進.

27. References to poems in the *Izumi Shikibu kashū* are to the numbering in Yoshida, *Zenshū*. Where this differs from that in *Izumi Shikibu shū—Ono no Komachi shū*, ed. Kubota Utsubo, in *Nihon koten zensho* [no vol. number] (1958), the corresponding number in the latter work is included in parentheses. Yoshida's edition of the *Izumi Shikibu seishū* is based on the *Shōkōkan* 彰考館 text, and is identical in numbering to that in Saeki Umetomo, Murakami Osamu, and Komatsu Tomi, *Izumi Shikibu shū zenshaku* (1959), which is based on the *Sakakibarabon* 榊原本. The total number of *Seishū* poems in both texts is 893. The *Nihon koten zensho* edition, based on the *Gunsho ruijū*, contains 842 *Seishū* poems. Furthermore, Yoshida gives a separate series of numbers to the *Zokushū*, while Kubota has one series running through both *Seishū* and *Zokushū*. For useful comparative tables of the various editions and texts of Izumi Shikibu's collected poems, see Yoshida, *Zenshū*, pp. 3–54 (pages with Arabic numerals in the back of the book). For further discussion of the *Izumi Shikibu seishū, zokushū*, and related matters, see pp. 52–59 of the present work.

28. The date and compiler of the *Shūishū*, the third of the imperial *waka* anthologies, are in doubt. Its compilation is attributed both to Emperor Kazan and to Fujiwara no Kintō. Estimates of its date run from 995 to 1008.

29. One of the eight ministries of the Daijōkan. The others were the Nakatsukasashō 中務省 (Ministry of Central Affairs), Jibushō 治部省 (Ministry of Civil Administration), Mimbushō 民部省 (Ministry of Popular Affairs), Hyōbushō 兵部省 (Ministry of War), Kyōbushō 刑部省 (Ministry of Justice), Ōkurashō 大藏省 (Ministry of the Treasury), and Kunaishō 宮內省 (Ministry of the Imperial Household). It was usual for a lady-in-waiting to have as sobriquet some element from the name of her father's office.

30. *Kōchū kokka taikei*, III (1927), 564. Darkness is symbolic of the ignorance of the mundane world; the moon, of Buddhist enlightenment. Since the "dark path" may be interpreted to mean death, this *waka* is sometimes erroneously considered Izumi's deathbed poem.

31. See translation, note 82.

32. *Shōnin* 上人, a title of a particularly holy monk, roughly equivalent to "saint."

33. *Chūko no kajin*, pp. 221, 222.

34. *Ouki, Shiryō taisei*, I, 152.

35. *NKZ*, p. 153.
36. *Ouki, Shiryō taisei*, I, 152.
37. *Chūko no kajin*, p. 222.
38. *Ouki, Shiryō taisei*, I, 161.
39. *Chūko no kajin*, p. 222.
40. *Ōkagami*, ed. Matsumura Hiroji, *NKBT*, XXI (1960), 173.
41. *Eiga monogatari* (I), ed. Matsumura Hiroji and Yamanaka Yutaka, *NKBT*, LXXV (1964), 136.
42. The Prince held the office of President (Kami 尹) of the Board of Censors (Danjōdai 彈正臺), and hence was referred to as Danjō no Miya (for *miya* see translation, note 11).
43. The following words have been added to round out the meaning of this passage: "due to an epidemic," "because of corpses lying about," "grisly," "amorous," "after his demise," "Lotus."
44. The ninth daughter of Fujiwara no Koremasa, regent 970–972 (see page 106). The identity of Shinchūnagon is unknown.
45. According to *Nihon reikishi daijiten*, XIX, 178, from his youth Reizei showed signs of madness. Reference to Reizei's abnormality is made in the *Ōkagami*, *NKBT*, XXI, 131.
46. Tametaka's elder brother, Prince Okisada 居貞, the future Emperor Sanjō.
47. Tametaka's younger brother, Prince Atsumichi. See translation, note 11.
48. *Eiga monogatari* (I), *NKBT*, LXXV, 234. According to *Gonki* 權記, the diary of Fujiwara no Yukinari 行成 (also pronounced Kōzei) (972–1027), *Shiryō taisei*, XXXV (1939), 262, he was 26 at the time of his death.
49. *Gonki, Shiryō taisei*, XXXV, 262.
50. *Midō Kampaku ki* (I), p. 79.
51. I.e., inquire of Emma Ō 閻魔王, the King of Hell, who questions sinners about the good and evil they have done, and assigns punishments. *NKZ*, pp. 154, 155.
52. *Seishū* 200 and 202, and *Zokushū* 209 (1051) and 210 (1052) evidently refer to Izumi's feelings after separating from Michisada.
53. *Akazome Emon shū, Kōchū kokka taikei*, XIII, 392.
54. *Ibid*. "Tabi" is used in the double sense of "instance" 度 and "journey" 旅.
55. Koromo no Seki 衣の關 was a famous "barrier" or inspection point built by the Abe 安倍 family in their domain in northern Japan. Michinoku 陸奥, "the end of the road," of which Mutsu a corruption, comprised Honshū 本州 north of Kōzuke 上野 and Shimotsuke 下野 provinces and east of Dewa 出羽— i.e., it was the portion of the Tōhoku 東北 district facing the Pacific Ocean.
56. A more nearly literal translation: "I wonder how you look upon the mountain, said to be in your province, which is likened to waves which were high." The reference is to Sue no Matsuyama 末の松山 and its associations of infidelity. See translation, note 115.
57. E.g., *Seishū* 251, 252. See also translation, note 114.

58. "Tsumi" probably has the Buddhist sense of sins committed in former lives which earn retribution in this.

59. A more nearly literal translation: "Although I see the dew thus, without brushing it aside I softly break the autumn *hagi*; since I am filled with longing, my sleeves are dewy." *Hagi* 萩 (bush clover) is a flowering shrub. "Shinobite oreba" is a double *kakekotoba* 掛詞 (a literary pun in which a word, part of a word, or a group of words can be read in two or more senses, serving as a turning point between what precedes and what follows): 忍びて折れば (when I secretly break [the autumn *hagi*])/偲びて居れば (since I am filled with longing). "Dew" is to be taken both in its literal sense and as a metaphor for tears. The pun on "oreba" is partially conveyed by the use of "breaking" with its connotations of "a breaking heart" or "breaking into tears," as well as "breaking a sprig of *hagi*."

60. *Ōkagami*, p. 173.

61. Eldest son of Kaneie.

62. *Ōkagami*, p. 179.

63. *Ibid.*, p. 100. Koichijō was Naritoki's residence, in the northeastern quarter of the city.

64. I.e., Jōshi. Sen'yōden 宣耀殿 was her palace name, taken from the building in the women's quarters in which she lived. See translation, note 373.

65. *Nan'in* 南院. A building of the same name is mentioned in *Honchō seiki*, *KT*, IX, 219, as the scene of a burglary on Chōhō 4 (1002).8.8. *Midō Kampaku ki* (I), p. 172, entry for Kankō 3 (1006).1.3, refers to it as the residence of the Heir Apparent (Prince Okisada, Atsumichi's brother). The same diary (I), p. 195, describes its destruction by fire on Kankō 3.10.5, and refers to it as the residence of the Retired Emperor Reizei. Yoshida, *Kenkyū*, pp. 382, 386, locates it north of Shijō, one of the main east-west thoroughfares of the capital, and west of Mibu, an area in the western part of the city. He does this on the basis of Michinaga's account of seeing the fire southwest of his East Sanjō mansion. If all allusions to a *nan'in* actually refer to the same place, it would seem that the building served as residence for various members of Reizei's family. Reizei's own residence, the Reizei-in from which he takes his appellation, was in a different location however (see translation, note 369).

66. Or perhaps "distant." The original is: "Onsaiwai onaji onharakara to mietamawazu" (Fortunately they did not appear to be sisters).

67. *Eiga monogatari* (I), *NKBT*, LXXV, 293.

68. *Ōkagami*, p. 173. The *Eiga monogatari* places this event on Kankō 2 (1005). 4.20; its description of the festival, however, corresponds more closely to that in the *Midō Kampaku ki* entry for the previous year (Chōhō 6 [1004].4.20). See *Eiga monogatari* (I), *NKBT*, LXXV, 244; *Midō Kampaku ki* (I), pp. 84, 142.

69. *Midō Kampaku ki* (I), p. 234; *Gonki, Shiryō taisei*, XXXVI, 87. The *Eiga monogatari*, which claims he died in Kankō 7 (1010), must be mistaken.

70. The lotus petals on which he would be reborn as a Buddha in paradise.

71. There was a plant known as *shinobugusa*, lit. "the grasses of longing."

72. "Ito" is a *kakekotoba*: 糸 ([spider] thread)/いと (very [sorrowful]).

202

73. See *Zokushū* 28 (870).

74. *Izumi Shikibu nikki*, ed. Shimizu Fumio, in *Iwanami bunko*, MMDCCL (1941, 1964), 105, 106.

75. *Sompi bummyaku*, *KT*, LIX, 423, describes him as "a brave warrior and a master of military strategy." In *Baishōron* (an anonymous work in two *kan* dealing principally with the military exploits of Ashikaga Takauji [1304–1358], and probably dating ca. 1349), *GR*, XVI, 142, following a discussion of the nature of shogunal authority, appears the sentence: "In our own land Tamura, Toshihito, Yorimitsu, and Yasumasa expelled foreign brigands; yet their authority did not extend over the whole country." (The other heroes mentioned are Sakanoue no Tamuramaro [758–811], the famous queller of the northern barbarians; Fujiwara no Toshihito [10th cent.], also famous for exploits in the north; and Minamoto no Yorimitsu [see below, note 76].) Other medieval works, such as the *Heike monogatari* and *Jikkinshō*, also list Yasumasa among famous heroes. In "Fujiwara no Yasumasa Ason nusubito Hakamadare ni aeru koto," a story in the *Konjaku monogatari*, Yasumasa overcomes the fearsome robber Hakamadare by sheer force of personality and calm self-control (see *Konjaku monogatari* [IV], ed. Yamada Yoshio, *et al.*, in *NKBT*, XXV [1962], 382–384). Okada, "Izumi Shikibu to Fujiwara no Yasumasa" (4), *Rekishi to chiri* (June 1927), p. 643, points out however that in contemporary sources, such as *Midō Kampaku ki*, *Gonki*, *Ouki*, etc., no exploits are mentioned which would justify Yasumasa's later reputation. He appears as an ordinary member of the bureaucracy with ordinary promotions and appointments. On the other hand, Yorimitsu, whose legendary reputation is even greater, appears similarly prosaic in these sources. There is an incident recorded in *Midō Kampaku ki* (III), pp. 95, 96, entry for Chōwa 6 (1017). 3.11, in which Yasumasa's men set upon and slay Kiyowara (Kiyohara) no Munenobu 清原致信 (son of Motosuke [908–990], and elder brother of Sei Shōnagon), and another in *Nihon kiryaku* (a chronicle history from earliest times to the reign of Go-Ichijō [1008–1036; r. 1016–1036]) in which they kill a dog and leave its body to pollute the precincts of the Palace (*Nihon kiryaku*, *KT*, XI, 287, entry for Chōgen 7 [1034].11.8). Okada speculates that such outrages could happen because Yasumasa's men trusted in their master's military might to protect them.

76. Yorimitsu 頼光, also known as Raikō, was a member of the provincial-governor class who enjoyed the patronage of powerful Fujiwara, especially of Michinaga. He had a reputation for martial valor and for marksmanship in archery. The most famous feat attributed to him—the conquest of the demons of Ōeyama—is a legend which grew up in the Kamakura Period. According to *Sompi bummyaku*, *KT*, LX (Pt. 1), 185, Yorimitsu and Yasumasa were related. Yasumasa's sister married Yorimitsu's father, Mitsunaka (912–997), and bore Yorimitsu's younger half brother, Yorinobu (968–1048).

77. The fifth of the imperial *waka* anthologies, compiled by Minamoto no Shunrai (1057–1129) in 1124.

78. For Naishi see note 7.

79. Fujiwara no Sadayori 定賴 (995–1045), son of the famous poet Kintō.

80. *Kōchū kokka taikei*, IV, 88. Ōeyama, Ikuno, and Amanohashidate are all famous place names in Tango Province. The poem involves the following word play: *Ikuno* 生野 [the place name]/*iku . . . michi* 行く道 (the road one goes)/*iku no* 幾野 (how many fields); *fumi* 文 (message)/*fumi* 踏み (treading). "Fumi" 踏み and "Amanohashidate" (a long, pine-grown sandbar, whose name I have translated "Heavenbridge") are *engo* (words related in meaning or association: "tread—bridge"; use of such related words strengthens the cohesion of Japanese poems). Koshikibu is saying that she could not so quickly communicate with her mother in far-away Tango.

81. *Midō Kampaku ki* (III), p. 189.

82. *Sōjō* was the highest title of the Buddhist hierarchy, granted to important clerics by the court (*Yūsoku kojitsu jiten*, p. 489).

83. As remarked by Kubota, *Izumi Shikibu shū*, p. 99, note 16, *nezumi* (mice or rats) were sometimes called *yome*, a word ordinarily meaning "bride" or "daughter-in-law." Another Heian example of this custom appears in *Gonchūnagon Sadayori-kyō shū*, GR, X, 687, the personal poetry collection of Fujiwara no Sadayori (see note 79):

On seeing where a mouse had nibbled the nun's lotus-berry prayer beads:

Yome no ko no	The mouse that ate
Hachisu no tama o	These beads of lotus fruit,
Kuikeru wa	What did it have in mind—
Tsumi ushinawamu	To lose the evil
To ya omouramu	Karma of its past?

The custom of referring to rats or mice by substitute names was widespread and evidently still exists in some areas. These names usually incorporate the word *yome*, in such honorific forms as *yomego*, *yomesama*, *yome no kimi*, etc. Information on this custom can be found in *Shokoku hōgen butsurui shōko* 諸國方言物類稱呼, a dialect encyclopedia published in 1775 by Koshigaya Gozan 越谷吾山 (1717–1787; actual family name Aida 會田 ; also styled Kokyūan古馗庵 , Shichikuan 師竹庵) (see Yoshisawa Yoshinori, *Kōhon butsurui shōko shokoku hōgen sakuin* [1933], p. 15). Umegaki Minoru, *Yome ga kimi* (1961), pp. 9–20, lists a great many such names used in various localities. He states that they are survivals of a once numerous class of words, *shōgatsu kotoba* (New Year's words), formerly used at the beginning of the year, especially in agricultural communities, to avoid using the real names of things which might adversely affect the year's prosperity. He quotes the theory, also mentioned by Koshigaya, that the syllable *ne* was avoided at New Year's time because of its presence in *neru* (sleep), and describes the custom of staying up all night on the last night of the year to secure good omens. He rejects this explanation for the avoidance of the word *nezumi* because there was no similar ban on *neko* (cat). However the evidence he presents

204

seems to be conflicting on this point. Umegaki also mentions the custom of using such appellations as *yomesama* and *yomego* as names for the rats which come to steal the silkworms, as well as the belief that a fire would break out if one said "nezumi" at New Year's time.

While it thus seems probable that the word *nezumi* was avoided because of fear of the destructive power of rats and mice, it is not known why variations on *yome* were used as substitutes. Tachibana Shōichi, *Hōgengaku gairon* (1941), p. 311, mentions a belief that daughters-in-law who do bad things are changed into rats. *Sōgō Nihon minzoku goi*, ed. Yanagita Kunio, IV (1956), 1714, states that *yomono*, another substitute term for *nezumi*, popularly interpreted 夜物 "night thing," originally meant *imimono* 忌物 or *imu mono* 忌む物 (a thing to be dreaded or avoided). It is interesting to note that "rat" as the first of the twelve beasts of the Sino-Japanese calendrical cycle is written with the character 子, the same as that used to write the word for "child." Hence it is possible to write the first two lines of Michinaga's poem—"the rat's child's child-rat"—thus: 子の子の子子. Perhaps such play was part of Michinaga's jest; another part was the use of "ana" (an interjection, but also "hole," an *engo* for "nezumi"). Note also that the date of the child's birth was very close to New Year's.

84. The first part of the poem means also, "to be acknowledged thus by you even as but a mouse-child." "Tsumi" carries the idea of disabilities incurred through bad conduct in former lives. The child's moral heredity must be good.

85. *Naidaijin*, the fourth-ranking official of the Daijōkan.

86. *Tō no Chūjō*, a customary doubling in brass: First Secretary (Tō 頭) of the Emperor's Private Secretariat, the Kurōdodokoro, and Middle Captain (Chūjō 中將) of the Inner Palace Guards (see translation, note 29).

87. Kinnari 公成 (999–1043), a second cousin of Norimichi.

88. Yoshiko [Kishi] 嬉子 was the fourth daughter of Michinaga, and consort of future Emperor Go-Suzaku (1009–1045; r. 1036–1045). She died in 1025 after giving birth to the future Emperor Go-Reizei (1025–1068; r. 1045–1068).

89. *Eiga monogatari* (III), ed. Matsumura Hiroji, in *Nihon koten zensho* [no vol. number] (1958), p. 228. The fourth line, "It was more so with the child," refers to Izumi's grief for Koshikibu; the echoing fifth line, "It must have been more so with the child," to that of Koshikibu for her baby. Just as Izumi has suffered more over the loss of her daughter than over any of her other griefs, so Koshikibu's greatest regret must have been to leave behind her child.

90. *Sompi bummyaku*, *KT*, LIX, 423.

91. *Ason* 朝臣 was a hereditary title, the second highest of eight such regularized in 685 (*Yūsoku kojitsu jiten*, p. 16).

92. Made in memory of the Empress Dowager Yoshiko [Kenshi] 妍子, also a daughter of Michinaga, and Empress to Emperor Sanjō. She died on Manju 萬壽 4 (1027).9.14.

93. *Eiga monogatari* (III), *Nihon koten zensho*, p. 300.

94. Sixth imperial *waka* anthology, compiled by Fujiwara no Akisuke 顯輔 (1090–1155) in 1144.

95. Fujiwara no Kanefusa 兼房 (1004–1069), a court poet of some note.

96. A more nearly literal translation: "Nights when hail falls rustle-rustle on the bamboo leaves I do not feel in the least disposed to sleep alone." "Sarasara" is a *kakekotoba*: "rustle-rustle"/"not at all."

97. *Nihon bungaku daijiten*, ed. Fujimura Tsukuru (1963), I, 137.

98. A type of medieval popular tale, often quite earthy and frequently dealing irreverently with historical figures.

99. Dōmyō was famous for the beauty of his sutra-chanting. There are legends that sinful men were saved from hell by listening to his voice. *Azari* 阿闍梨 (also *Ajari*), derived from the Sanskrit *ācārya*, a model or pattern, was a title given in Esoteric Buddhism to the instructor in the esoteric traditions, and was awarded as an academic title to learned monks of the Tendai and Shingon sects.

100. This story is printed in Yoshida, *Zenshū*, pp. 719–737. The same work contains *Izumi Shikibu no monogatari*, an early Muromachi tale (pp. 709–719), *Koshikibu*, the story described below (pp. 738–749), and ten *nō* 能 plays dealing with Izumi Shikibu (pp. 751–784). *Izumi Shikibu* also appears in *Otogizōshi*, ed. Ichiko Teiji, *NKBT*, XXXVIII (1958), 312–318.

101. "Kasa" is a *kakekotoba*: 瘡 (boil)/笠 (rain hat).

102. This story is recounted in Yanagita Kunio, "Josei to minkan denshō," in *Teihon Yanagita Kunio shū*, VIII (1962) 343, 344.

103. This pronunciation (with *jō*, the normal *Go-on* 呉音 Buddhist reading of the character 誠) is given in Matsunaga Shōdō, *Mikkyō daijiten*, II (1932), 1171. The wooden plaque in front of the temple gives the reading Seishin'in, which seems to be the popular pronunciation.

104. Michinaga was known as the Midō Kampaku 御堂關白 (Regent of the August Hall) because of his residence in the Amida-dō 阿彌陀堂 (Amida Hall) of the Hōjōji 法成寺, a temple which he founded. "Komidō" means "Little August Hall."

105. Said to be a style of Ryōjun 良純 (1604–1669), the eighth son of Emperor Go-Yōzei 後陽成 (1571–1617; r. 1586–1611).

106. The colophon at the end of the second scroll indicates that a work of similar if not identical nature had existed earlier. The present *Engi*, whatever its relation to this previous scroll may have been, is based, according to Ōhashi, *Kenkyū*, p. 527, on another temple history, the *Seiganji engi*, and was influenced by the *nō* play *Seiganji*. The *Izumi Shikibu engi* is printed in Ōhashi, *Kenkyū*, pp. 529–541.

107. A *hōkyōintō* 寶篋印塔, an elaborate structure with a square base and middle sections, and a cylindrical spire on top, erected in Buddhist graveyards in memory of the dead.

108. The *shikimi* 樒 (anise flower) is considered appropriate for Buddhist offerings. There is a play on Izumi's name.

109. *Meishoki* (I), in *Kinsei bungei sōsho*, ed. Kokusho Kankōkai, I (1910), 295, 296. It may be noted that the death-day given by Kiun does not agree with

that in the *Izumi Shikibu engi.*

110.   The title is translatable in modern terms as "The Izumi Shikibu Diary." The last section of this study deals with the nature of *nikki* as a literary genre.

111.   A form in which two people compose one poem. The first seventeen syllables of a *waka* would be written by one poet, the last fourteen by another. Or the process might be reversed, with the concluding fourteen syllables being given first, a process which foreshadows the humorous *maekuzuke* 前句付 form of the Tokugawa Period (1600–1867). (See translation, notes 227, 254, and 325.) *Renga* later developed into a long poetic form with elaborate rules in which several poets might take part, adding alternate units of seventeen and fourteen syllables almost without limit. This genre had both its serious and humorous varieties. The former is one of the most important poetic forms of the 14th and 15th centuries.

112.   A detailed analysis of the time sequence of the *Izumi Shikibu nikki* is presented in the section dealing with date, authorship, and formation. Here the discussion is limited to a general synopsis of the plot—the work being for the moment regarded in its fictional aspect—and the relation of structure to authorship and formation is deliberately ignored.

113.   This stylistic phenomenon is discussed in the section dealing with genre.

114.   As noted below, a more frequently used title is *Izumi Shikibu monogatari.* For a discussion of the significance of alternate titles, see the final section, "The Question of Genre."

115.   Yoshida, *Kenkyū*, pp. 18–76. The following discussion of textual lineages is based largely on Yoshida's research.

116.   Ikeda Kikan, *Nihon bungaku daijiten*, I, 139, mentions another manuscript, the so-called *Adachibon* 足立本. This text, said to be in the possession of the Adachi family, is described as belonging, with the *Sanjōnishibon*, to a different lineage from texts such as the *Gunsho ruijūbon.* Yoshida, *Kenkyū*, p. 20, says that location and particulars concerning this manuscript are unknown.

117.   This note reads: "Izumi Shikibu: daughter of Gonchūnagon Kanehira. Her mother was the daughter of Taira no Yasuhira, Governor of Etchū. She [the mother] was wet nurse to Grand Empress Dowager Masako [Shōshi], and was styled Suke no Naishi. Tachibana no Michisada (the father of Koshikibu no Naishi), Governor of Izumi, made her [Izumi Shikibu] his wife; hence she was styled Izumi. She was a lady-in-waiting to Jōtōmon'in, and her child-name was Omotomaro. Another theory claims she was the daughter of Ōe no Masamune, Governor of Echizen" (quoted from *Izumi Shikibu nikki* [facsimile edition], ed. Suzuki Tomotarō [1964], p. 112. The note adds nothing new to the biographical information presented previously).

118.   Yoshida, *Kenkyū*, p. 174.

119.   *Ibid.*, p. 77.

120.   A method of indicating an error by placing dots beside the mistaken word or words.

121.   Yoshida, *Kenkyū*, pp. 78, 79.

122. *Ibid.*, pp. 80, 81.

123. A fourth, the *Tanakakebon* 田中家本 , is mentioned by Kawase Kazuma in "*Izumi Shikibu nikki* wa Fujiwara Shunzei no saku," *Aoyama Gakuin Joshi Tanki Daigaku kiyō*, II (Sept. 1953), pp. 25, 27. He states that the manuscript is of Kan'ei 寛永 (1624–1644) date, and claims it was seen and collated by the scholar Yokoyama Yoshikiyo 横山由清 (1826–1879). Yoshida, *Kenkyū*, p. 26, says that he has not been able to locate such a manuscript, but points out that another manuscript containing the *Kangembon* colophon is in the possession of Tōkyō Kyōiku Daigaku. This is a collation by Yokoyama of the *Fusōshūyōshūbon* with the Kyōho block print edition and the *Gunsho ruijūbon*. The *Kangembon* colophon, in the hand of Kimura Masakoto 木村正辭 (1827–1913), has been pasted in.

124. Yoshida, *Kenkyū*, p. 25.

125. The character *han* 判 indicates that in the original manuscript there was a signature in the form of a cipher (*kaō* 花押) made by a fanciful distortion of the strokes used to write the name.

126. For a discussion of court rank see translation, note 48.

127. *Uchūben* 右中辨, an official of the Ubenkan 右辨官, a subdivision of the Daijōkan which had the function of supervising the four ministries of War (Hyōbushō), Justice (Kyōbushō), Treasury (Ōkurashō), and the Imperial Household (Kunaishō).

128. The word *sōna* 草名 indicates that in the original manuscript there was a signature in cursive writing.

129. *Ushōshō* 右少將. See translation, note 29.

130. *Sadaijin* 左大臣. In the customary absence of a Daijōdaijin 太政大臣 , the highest official in the Daijōkan (*Yūsoku kojitsu jiten*, p. 369).

131. Sanekazu was Great Minister of the Left for several months during 1460. He is referred to as the "Latter" Sanjō Great Minister of the Left in distinction to Sanjō Sanefusa (1147–1225), who held the same office from 1190 to 1196.

132. Yoshida, *Kenkyū*, p. 35.

133. Ikeda Kikan, *Kyūtei joryū nikki bungaku* (1927), pp. 107, 108.

134. *Nihon bungaku daijiten*, I, 139.

135. Ikeda Kikan, "Nikki bungaku to kikō bungaku," in *Nihon bungaku kōza*, ed. Yamamoto Sansei, V [*Zuihitsu-nikkihen*] (1934), 22.

136. Ikeda Kikan, *Heian jidai bungaku gaisetsu* (1944), p. 190.

137. Ikeda Kikan, "Monogatari bungaku," in *Nihon bungaku kyōyō kōza*, VI (Shibundō, 1951), 140.

138. Imai Takuji, *Heian-chō nikki no kenkyū* (1935), pp. 257–275.

139. See note 123.

140. *NKZ*, p. 118.

141. A chronology compiled by Fujiwara no Michinori 通憲 (d. 1159), covering, with many gaps, events at court from 889 to 1153.

142. *Honchō seiki*, *KT*, IX, 240, 241.

143. *NKZ*, pp. 118–128.

208

144.   For a discussion of this work see pp. 110–111.

145.   See *Murasaki Shikibu nikki*, ed. Ikeda Kikan and Akiyama Ken, in *NKBT*, XIX (1958), 495. For a full translation of the passage in question see Arthur Waley, trans., *The Tale of Genji* (Modern Library, G–38, 1960), p. xii.

146.   Yoshida's arguments are largely drawn from Shimazu Hisamoto, *Genji monogatari kōwa* (1949–1951).

147.   *Genji monogatari* (I), ed. Yamagishi Tokuhei, *NKBT*, XIV (1962), 140.

148.   *Ibid.* (II), *NKBT*, XV (1959), 395, 410, 411.

149.   *Ibid.* (IV), *NKBT*, XVII (1962), 423, 433, 434; *ibid.* (V), *NKBT*, XVIII (1963), 236–241.

150.   Murasaki probably started to write the *Genji* after the death of her husband, Fujiwara no Nobutaka 宣孝, in 1001. That at least some portions were in circulation by 1008 is known from references in the *Murasaki Shikibu nikki* (see text in *NKBT*, XIX [1958], 470, 500, 504). It seems plausible that Murasaki may have been selected for service at the court of Empress Akiko because of her reputation as a writer. It is not known when the *Genji* was completed, but a work of such great length (fifty-four chapters, occupying five volumes of the *NKBT*) could well have taken several years to write. Murasaki's death-date is also unknown, but may have been as early as 1016 (see Tamai Kōsuke, *Nikki bungaku no kenkyū* [1965], p. 184). It will be noted (Introduction, p. 59) that Yoshida argues, on the basis of evidence from the *Izumi Shikibu zokushū*, that the *Izumi Shikibu nikki* was completed by Kankō 5 (1008).10.2, the first anniversary of the death of Prince Atsumichi. If Yoshida is correct, in order to have been influenced by the latter work, the portions of the *Genji monogatari* where such influence is alleged must have been written after that date. The earliest reference to the *Genji* in the *Murasaki Shikibu nikki* is in a passage describing a banquet held on Kankō 5.11.1, less than a month after Yoshida's proposed date for completion of the *Izumi Shikibu nikki*. It is known from the *Murasaki Shikibu nikki* reference that at least chapter five of the *Genji*, "Waka-murasaki 若紫," must have been in existence then. The earliest passage of the *Genji* in which Yoshida alleges influence is chapter four, "Yūgao 夕顔." However, according to a widely accepted theory proposed by Ikeda Kikan and others (cf. Hisamatsu Sen'ichi, ed., *Nihon bungakushi: chūko* [1964], pp. 302, 303), "Yūgao" is one of a group of "short story" chapters inserted after completion of the first stage in the composition of the *Genji*, and was actually written later than "Wakamurasaki." Hence Yoshida is not in as difficult a position here as at first appears.

151.   *Setsuwa* 説話 is a term applied rather vaguely to various kinds of stories or anecdotes, especially those incorporating legendary or traditional materials. The stories of the *Konjaku monogatari* and similar collections are considered to belong to this literary type.

152.   A recently discovered untitled *setsuwa* collection, introduced to the scholarly world and given the designation *Kohon setsuwashū* 古本説話集 in 1943. Only one manuscript exists, apparently dating from the early or middle

Kamakura Period, and now in the possession of Umezawa Giichi 梅澤義一 .
See *Kohon setsuwashū*, ed. Kawaguchi Hisao, in *Iwanami bunko*, vol. 5412–5413
(1960); Hisamatsu, ed., *Nihon bungakushi: chūko* (1964), pp. 608, 609.

153.   Not to be confused with the *Eiga monogatari* or *Ōkagami*, both of which
have this alternate title. The *Yotsugi monogatari* 世繼物語 in question is a collection
of *setsuwa* put together by an unknown compiler. The first part, which is based
on material drawn from the *Yamato monogatari, Makura no sōshi, Izumi Shikibu
nikki, Eiga monogatari*, and other works of courtly literature, is considered early
Kamakura. The second part, evidently added later, is based on material from
the *Konjaku monogatari, Uji shūi monogatari* 宇治拾遺物語 , and similar works.
See Nishio Kōichi, "Chūsei setsuwa bungaku," in *Iwanami kōza Nihon bungaku*,
VI (1959), 10; and Hisamatsu, ed., *Nihon bungakushi: chūsei* (1960), pp. 146, 147.

154.   Not to be confused with the *Konjaku monogatari*, which has this alternate
title. The origin of the *Uji Dainagon monogatari* 宇治大納言物語 in question is
obscure, but according to Kobayashi Tadao, "*Yotsugi monogatari, Uji Dainagon
monogatari* no seiritsu ni tsuite," *Kokugo-kokubun* (June 1957), it is based on the
Yotsugi monogatari with additions from the *Jikkinshō* 十訓抄, and probably
dates from before the middle of the Kamakura Period. See also Hisamatsu, ed.,
Nihon bungakushi: chūsei, p. 146.

155.   *Kohon setsuwashū*, p. 207.

156.   Hisamatsu, ed., *Nihon bungakushi: chūko*, pp. 608, 609.

157.   *Meigetsuki*, ed. Kokusho Kankōkai (1912), III, 341. The text reads
町門 (town gate) instead of 叩門 (knocks at the gate). According to Ōhashi,
Kenkyū, p. 46, the character 町 is a mistake stemming from a wood-block edition.
Ōhashi states that he has seen a manuscript with 叩.

158.   *Honchō shojaku mokuroku, GR*, XXI, 553.

159.   *Kakaishō, kan* 10, in *Kokubun chūshaku zensho*, ed. Muromatsu Iwao,
III (1908), 242.

160.   *Kachō yosei, kan* 5, in *Kokubun chūshaku zensho*, III, 65.

161.   The passage in question consists of the words "kaeru hito no ōgi o
torikaete" (exchanging fans with the person who was returning).

162.   Shimizu Fumio, "*Izumi Shikibu nikki kō*," *Kokubungaku shiron*, XXVII
(Dec. 1935); Shimizu, "*Izumi Shikibu nikki* seiritsu ni kan-suru shōkō—iwayuru
'genkashū' o megutte," *Kokubungaku kō* (May 1962); Endō Yoshimoto, *Shinkō
Izumi Shikibu monogatari*, pp. 174–185; Yoshida, *Kenkyū*, pp. 203–241.

163.   See Shimizu, "*Izumi Shikibu seishū* no seiritsu," *Kokubungaku kō*, I
(Nov. 1934); Yanase Kazuo, "Izumi Shikibu no nikki-uta to shū to no kankei
ni tsuite," *Shomotsu tembō*, XIII (April 1943); Fujioka Tadami, "*Izumi Shikibu
shū* no seiritsu," *Kokugo to kokubungaku*, XXVIII (May 1951); "Kaisetsu,"
Izumi Shikibu kashū, ed. Shimizu Fumio, in *Iwanami bunko*, vols. 5542–5544;
Saeki Umetomo, *et al., Izumi Shikibu shū zenshaku* (1959), pp. 659–683.

164.   *Waka bungaku daijiten*, ed. Itō Yoshio, *et al.* (1962), p. 52.

165.   Shimizu, "Kaisetsu," *Izumi Shikibu kashū*, pp. 321–323.

166.   Yoshida, *Kenkyū*, p. 204; based on Shimizu, "Kaisetsu," *Izumi Shikibu*

kashū. The subdivision of Group E is based on Konishi Keiko, "*Izumi Shikibu shū kō,*" *Kokubun* (July 1959). The numbering in Kubota's *Nihon koten zensho* edition has been added in parentheses when it differs from Yoshida's.

167. The apparent discrepancy here is caused by the assignment of separate numbers to the *renga* "Koto no ha fukaku—Shiratsuyu no" in the *Nihon koten zensho* edition. Yoshida, *Zenshū,* assigns the same number to both halves of the *renga.*

168. Three poems—"Ōmiji wa," "Yama nagara," and "Kokoromi ni" (nos. 879, 880, and 882 in Yoshida, *Zenshū*)—do not appear in the *Nihon koten zensho* edition. See note 27.

169. The following discussion of the relation between the *Nikki* and the *Seishū* is based largely on Yoshida, *Kenkyū,* pp. 203–241.

170. Kawase, "*Izumi Shikibu nikki* wa Fujiwara Shunzei no saku," p. 40.

171. *Ibid.,* pp. 40–46. Kawase further alleges similarities between Shunzei's poetic style and that of the *Nikki* poems. These resemblances are said to consist of Shunzei's use of reversed syntax, repetition of similar sounds, and a like "conception" in his poems. Examples are given to illustrate these points, along with a selection of Shunzei's allusive variations on poems by Izumi Shikibu.

172. Konishi, "*Izumi Shikibu shū kō,*" as cited in Yoshida, *Kenkyū,* p. 207.

173. Of the $81\frac{1}{2}$ *Nikki* poems which do not appear in the *Seishū,* $63\frac{1}{2}$ are by the Prince, 16 by Izumi, and 2 are the old poems "Ana koishi" and "Koishiku wa" which the lovers quote to each other (translation, pp. 184–185). Thirteen of Izumi's 16 poems are among the first 31 poems in the *Nikki* (through "Yoigoto ni," translation, p. 144). If the *Nikki* did indeed serve as a source for the compiler of the *Seishū,* he must have skimmed rather lightly through the first few pages. But from poem 32 on he rejected or overlooked only three of Izumi's poems—nos. 94 ("Kazuraki no"), 106 ("Momijiba no"), and 132 ("Shika bakari") (see translation, pp. 170, 173, 174, 183).

174. Yoshida, *Kenkyū,* p. 205.

175. *Ibid.,* pp. 216, 217, 235. Actually, of the 446 poems in Group E which are not also in the *Nikki,* only 191 or approximately 43 percent refer to "hito" in their *kotobagaki.* Of course this "hito" is not always Prince Atsumichi. Seventy-nine poems (approximately 17 percent) from the same group have *kotobagaki* referring to people by designations other than "hito." These include "otoko," "Miya," "oya," "Nyūdō-dono," "hōshi," "Sei Shōnagon," "Kobata no Sōzu," etc. On the other hand, the 380 non-E poems in the *Seishū* (again excluding those which also appear in the *Nikki*) show 41 examples of the use of "hito" in *kotobagaki* (approximately 11 percent of the total).

Yoshida's theory of the relationship between the *Nikki* and the *Seishū* was first published as "*Izumi Shikibu shū* shoin no nikki-uta wa beppon *Izumi Shikibu nikki* ka," *Bungaku ronsō* (June 1960). Ōhashi attacks some aspects of Yoshida's thesis in his *Izumi Shikibu nikki no kenkyū,* pp. 324–361. He objects especially to Yoshida's reasoning on the use of "hito" and the source of Groups Two and Three. (As Yoshida points out, the theory to which Ōhashi objects was first proposed by Shimizu in "*Izumi Shikibu nikki kō*," *Kokubungaku shiron* [Dec. 1935].) Ōhashi's contention is that the source of Groups Two and Three, as well as of Group One, was Izumi's unedited poems, and not the *Nikki*. He thinks it unlikely that a later compiler, selecting poems from the *Nikki*, would have employed the word "hito," an appellation which is not used for the Prince in that work. Rather, he must have taken that term as he found it in the *kotobagaki* of Izumi's poems. Ōhashi notes that "hito" is a term used generally throughout the *kotobagaki* of the *Seishū*.

Yoshida replies to Ōhashi in *Izumi Shikibu kenkyū*, pp. 231–240. He asserts that the use of the *kotobagaki* "hito ni" and "hito no kaerigoto ni" is concentrated exclusively in Group E, and uses this fact to support his argument that the compiler of Groups Two and Three used the word "hito" to conform with the practice of Group E as a whole. While it is true, however, that *kotobagaki* consisting solely of "hito ni" or "hito no kaerigoto ni" are found only in Group E, it has been shown that other ways of referring to people are also common in E, and that "hito" is used occasionally in *kotobagaki* in the non-E sections of the *Seishū*. The evidence to support Yoshida's argument on this point is not as clear-cut as he implies.

176.   Another textual difference between the *Nikki* and *Seishū* involves *Nikki* poem 130, the *renga* "Naozari no—Otsuru namida wa" (see translation, note 325), which appears in the *Seishū* as a single undivided poem (416 [392]). Yoshida thinks that the *Nikki* version is the correct original, mistakenly transcribed by a copyist of the *Seishū* (*Kenkyū*, p. 209). Shimizu originally held the opposite view ("*Izumi Shikibu nikki kō*," p. 122), but has recently come to support Yoshida's theory ("*Izumi Shikibu nikki* seiritsu ni kan-suru shōkō . . ." as cited in Yoshida, *Kenkyū*, p. 209). It should be noted that the words "to notamawasureba," appearing between the two parts of the *renga* in the *Nikki*, have been placed immediately after the poem in the *Seishū*, as part of the *kotobagaki* to the next poem (417 [393]).

177.   Shimizu, "*Izumi Shikibu nikki kō*," p. 122.

178.   Yoshida, *Kenkyū*, pp. 209, 264. Logically, the text that Yoshida posits as the source of *Nikki* Poem Groups Two and Three in the *Seishū*, a text which must have been free of the "Kienubeki" error, could itself have been the ancestor of the manuscript in which the error first occurred, which in turn became the common ancestor of all extant *Nikki texts*. That is, the situation may have been that represented by Chart I rather than Chart II.

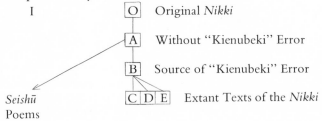

I · O — Original *Nikki*

A — Without "Kienubeki" Error

B — Source of "Kienubeki" Error

Seishū   C D E — Extant Texts of the *Nikki*
Poems

212

II

Seishū
Poems

179. The poem is not dated, but no. 38 (880) was written (according to its *kotobagaki*) on the forty-ninth day after the Prince's death. The *kotobagaki* of no. 39 (881) implies that it was written on the same day. The poems of the group under discussion apparently belong to the year of mourning following the Prince's death.

180. "Tenarai" (calligraphy practice), interpreted by Yoshida, *Kenkyū*, p. 535, as "susabigaki" (idle writings).

181. A more nearly literal translation: "As bubbles floating toward me [I not having become a bubble], swiftly down a river of tears [it is sad to see these early things]." "Awa" (bubble) serves a double syntactical function: "Nagareyoru awa to" (as bubbles floating toward)/"awa to narinade" (not having become a bubble [i.e., still alive]). "Hayaku" is a *kakekotoba*: "Namidagawa hayaku" (swiftly down the river of tears)/"hayaku no koto" (early matters [i.e., matters pertaining to days gone by]).

182. Yoshida, *Kenkyū*, p. 535.

183. Or "before her" (mae naru).

184. See translation, note 15.

185. A more nearly literal translation: "Was the one who loved a different being? What time was the time I was startled awake by the cry of the cock?"

186. It should be noted that the two poems, "Oshimaruru" and "Kimi o okite," which Izumi writes on this occasion in the *Nikki*, are not specifically linked to this event in the *Seishū* (they are nos. 890 [839] and 891 [840]), where they have as *kotobagaki* only "Hito koishiki ni" (Out of love for a certain person).

187. For poems employing similar phraseology see *Zokushū* 447 (1289) and 509 (1351).

188. Printed in Yoshida, *Zenshū*, p. 702.

189. The last is not a *chokusenshū*, but an anthology privately compiled by Fujiwara Nagakiyo 長清 (late 13th–early 14th century).

190. Kawase Kazuma, "*Izumi Shikibu nikki* wa Fujiwara Shunzei no saku," *Aoyama Gakuin Joshi Tanki Daigaku kiyō* (September 1953), pp. 21–52.

191. Dairi (no) Tenji was evidently a woman. Tenji 典侍, also read "suke," was the second-ranking officer in the Naishi no Tsukasa 内侍司 or Palace Attendants Office, a bureau of female functionaries in the women's quarters of the Imperial Palace. The Tenji were usually called by the name of their father's office, as "Dainagon (no) Tenji (Suke)." Hence Dairi 大理 (a "Chinese style"

213

for the head of the police organization, the Kebiishi no Bettō 檢非違使別當) may have been the father of the person who ordered the copying of 1246 (*Yūsoku kojitsu jiten*, pp. 519, 589, 611).

192. Kawase, "Fujiwara Shunzei no saku," pp. 26, 27.

193. She is perhaps best known as "Shunzei-kyō no musume" (Lord Shunzei's daughter). The date of her birth is unknown, but estimates center around 1171. Her mother was Shunzei's daughter Hachijōin Sanjō 八條院三條, and her father Fujiwara no Moriyori 盛賴 (dates unknown); she was however adopted by Shunzei as his own daughter. She married Minamoto no Michitomo 通具 (1171–1227), one of the compilers of the *Shinkokinshū*, probably in the 1190's. She was herself a poet of some consequence, and has left a collection, the *Shunzei-kyō no musume no shū* 俊成卿女集. After bearing Michitomo a son and a daughter she was shunted aside in favor of another woman. In 1202 she became a lady-in-waiting to the Retired Emperor Go-Toba 後鳥羽 (1180–1239; r. 1183–1198). She spent her last years as a nun, living in various places, including Saga 嵯峨 in the western environs of the Capital and Koshibe 越部, an estate in Harima belonging to Shunzei's family. From these latter circumstances she was also known as "Saga no Zenni" (the Saga nun) and "Koshibe no Zenni" (the Koshibe nun). The date of her death is not known. As will be seen, the date on which she became a nun is important in the controversy surrounding the *Kangembon* colophon. Tamai Kōsuke, "Rōbyō no go kyōji ya," *Nihon koten zensho furoku* (an insert supplement to the Asahi edition of *Kenju Gozen nikki*), p. 4, states that she took the tonsure twenty-odd years after Shunzei's death (1204). Yoshida, *Kenkyū*, p. 413, asserts that she came to be called "Zenni" after the death of Michitomo in 1227. Ishida Yoshisada, *Fujiwara Teika no kenkyū* (1957), p. 40, however quotes *Meigetsuki* to the effect that she became a nun on the twentieth of the first month of Kempō 建保 1 (1213) (see *Meigetsuki*, ed. Kokusho Kankōkai, II [1911], p. 248; also *Juntoku-in gyoshū*, in *Kōchū kokka taikei*, X, p. 292). The *Meigetsuki* passage refers to her as "Inokuma no nyōbō" 猪隈女房, evidently after her place of residence. Tamai, "Kaisetsu," *Kenju Gozen nikki*, in *Nihon koten zensho* [no vol. number] (1963), p. 39, also recognizes this as one of her appellations. Tamai and Yoshida do not cite their sources for the date in question. Even 1213 is a sufficiently late date to serve in their argument against the credibility of the *Kangembon* colophon however.

194. Kenju Gozen 健壽御前 , also known as Ken 健 Gozen, Kenshunmon'in Chūnagon 建春門院中納言 and Hachijō-in 八條院 Chūnagon, was born in 1157. Her mother was the daughter of Fujiwara no Chikatada 親忠 (d. 1153); Kenju Gozen was thus Teika's full sister. According to her *nikki*, she entered the service of Kenshunmon'in (1142–1176), the consort of the Retired Emperor Go-Shirakawa 後白河 (1127–1192; r. 1155–1158), in 1168. After Kenshunmon'in's death she retired for a time into private life, but took court service again in 1183 as a lady-in-waiting to Princess Hachijō-in (1136–1211), the daughter of Emperor Toba 鳥羽 (1103–1156; r. 1107–1123). She took religious vows in 1206, but continued in service until Hachijō-in's death. The date of her own death is not

known, but was probably not long after the completion of her memoir (see below, note 200). The *Kenju Gozen nikki* relates incidents and impressions of court life spanning the long period from her first entry into service until her final retirement.

195. Unidentified.

196. The residence of the author during her latter years.

197. Teika.

198. Quoted from the *Nihon koten zensho* edition, pp. 204, 205, 211.

199. Kawase, "Fujiwara Shunzei no saku," p. 29.

200. *Meigetsuki*, Kenryaku 建暦 2 (1212).7.20, *et seq.* In his entry for Kanki 寛喜 2 (1230).9.13, Teika states that of all his brothers and sisters, only Rokkaku no Ama-ue 六角尼上 (known also as Takamatsu-in Shindainagon 高松院新大納言; twelve years Teika's senior, her death date is unknown) passed seventy. Kenju Gozen would have been that age in Karoku 嘉祿 2 (1226). Thus her death must have occurred between 1219 and 1226 (*Meigetsuki*, II, 169 ff; III, 240).

201. Shunzei took the tonsure on Angen 安元 2 (1176).9.28, at the age of 63 (*Kugyō bunin*, KT, LIII, 484).

202. Entry for Kenryaku 1.12.23 (28 January 1212).

203. *Kenju Gozen nikki*, p. 221.

204. *Meigetsuki*, II, 134, entries for Kenryaku 1.12.23, 24.

205. Actually, Tamai claims, about 20 years after; see above, note 193.

206. Iwanami text, p. 390.

207. Fujiwara no Ietaka 家隆 (1158–1237). He was a pupil of Shunzei. The other compilers were Minamoto no Michitomo (the husband of "Shunzei's daughter"), Fujiwara no Ariie 有家 (1155–1216), Asukai Masatsune 飛鳥井雅經 (1170–1221), and Jakuren (d. 1202; lay name Sadanaga 定長, a nephew and temporarily adopted son of Shunzei).

208. *Kōchū*, p. 222.

209. This is given as the most widely accepted theory by Kojima Yoshio in *Shinkokinwakashū no kenkyū* (1944), p. 52. Kojima states, p. 75, that the evidence is inconclusive, but that the above theory is strongly held. The compilation of the *Shinkokinshū* was a complicated process. On Kennin 1 (1201).7.26 the Retired Emperor Go-Toba appointed eleven members to a Poetry Bureau (Waka-dokoro); on 11.3 of the same year he chose six of them (see note 207) to compile the *Shinkokinshū*. Each was to select and present poems representing all periods from ancient times to the present. This presentation was made on Kennin 3 (1203).4.20. Go-Toba himself then culled the poems over. The work of arranging them began, under his direction, on Genkyū 1 (1204).7.22. New poems were selected at the same time. A Chinese preface by Fujiwara no Chikatsune (d. 1210), and a Japanese preface by Fujiwara no Yoshitsune (1169–1206) were added, and a banquet was held on Genkyū 2 (1205).3.26 to celebrate the completion of the committee's labors. But Go-Toba was not satisfied, and work continued intermittently for several years on refining the arrangement of the poems. No great changes were made after about the middle of Jōgen 2 (1208). The

definitive text stems from a copy made by Minamoto no Ienaga (dates unknown) in Kempō 4 (1216). Go-Toba continued to make revisions after his exile to the Oki Islands in 1221, but these did not enter into the accepted text (*Waka bungaku daijiten*, p. 542).

210. *Kōchū*, p. 222.

211. Kawase, "Fujiwara Shunzei no saku," p. 47.

212. Suzuki Tomotarō, "*Izumi Shikibu nikki* ni okeru okugaki no mondai," *Musashino bungaku* (March 1958), as cited in Yoshida, *Kenkyū*, p. 422.

213. Yoshida, *Kenkyū*, pp. 420, 421.

214. Ōhashi, *Kenkyū*, pp. 55–59.

215. Suzuki Tomotarō, ed., *Izumi Shikibu nikki*, p. 10; Ōhashi, *Kenkyū*, p. 60; Endō Yoshimoto, interview, Dec. 23, 1964.

216. As has been the practice throughout, the month is indicated by a number from one through twelve. The day follows, separated from the month by a period. Uncertain dates are indicated by a question mark. A notation such as ?+1 indicates that the event occurs one day after another event whose date is not specified. Where the text states that "two or three days passed" (usually given in the formula "futsuka mika arite"), I have given the results of alternate ways of reckoning the time. The phrase "futsuka mika arite" literally means "there were two or three days." The smallest time lapse feasible would involve counting the first of those days as the same as that on which the previous event occurred. The alternate method would involve no overlapping. Thus, if event A happened on day 1, and then "there were two days," event B would occur on day 3: day 1 (event A), days 1 and 2 (two days), day 3 (event B). If, using the other method, "there were three days," event B would occur on day 5: day 1 (event A); days 2, 3, and 4 (three days); day 5 (event B).

217. See translation, note 64. There is a problem of historical accuracy here since no rain is recorded for the fifth, and since Izumi's poem implies it is raining. Yoshida, *Kenkyū*, p. 302, deals with this difficulty by preferring the *Ōeibon* reading of "samidare no" to the "samidarete" found in other texts. "Samidare" he then interprets as meaning *satsuki*, the fifth month itself, rather than "fifth month rain" (lit., "the disorders of *satsuki*"—i.e., the rainy season), its usual significance. He points out a similar usage in the *Kagerō nikki*, in the passage dealing with the fifth month of Anna 2 (969) (see Kawaguchi Hisao, ed., *Kagerō nikki*, in *NKBT*, XX [1962], 175; Kita Yoshio, *Zenkō kagerō nikki* [1961], pp. 165–167. The passage in question reads: そのまへのさみたれの廿よ日 [after the twentieth of the previous *samidare*]. No manuscript of the *Kagerō* has "satsuki" in place of "samidare," though Kawaguchi suggests that the former may have been the original reading. Kita renders "samidare" as "the fifth month"). Thus interpreted, no rain is necessarily involved. The evidence seems rather slender however. In addition, since "yame" (cease) is an obvious *engo* for "fifth-month rain" (see translation, p. 138), the poem is distorted if the idea of rain is removed.

218. See note 142.

219. Yoshida, *Kenkyū*, p. 304; *Honchō seiki*, *KT*, IX, 241; *Nihon kiryaku*, *KT*,

XI, 202.

220. *Gonki, Shiryō taisei*, XXXV, 289, 290.

221. Yoshida, *Kenkyū*, pp. 312–316.

222. *Honchō seiki, KT*, IX, 243.

223. An annual wrestling meet held at the end of the seventh month. It was held on 7.26, 27, and 28 in Chōhō 5 (*Nihon kiryaku, KT*, XI, 202). While there is no record of Prince Atsumichi attending the festival this year, it was an event that he might normally have been expected to see. It is certain that he did attend the following year (*Ouki, Shiryō taisei*, I, 200).

224. Yoshida, *Kenkyū*, p. 325.

225. Yoshida is quite arbitrary in his reasoning here. He notes, *Kenkyū*, p. 331, that the Prince (see chronology, item 28) feels that a long time has gone by, and that the last time he had written to Izumi was the twenty-ninth of the previous month (Yoshida's "ninth" must be a misprint for "twenty-ninth"). He then simply assumes that "a long time" would bring events to 8.10.

226. *Gonki, Shiryō taisei*, XXXV, 294.

227. Yoshida, *Kenkyū*, pp. 333–340.

228. Yoshida gives a separate date—about 10.17—to the last exchange: "Hito shirezu"—"Mono iwade." This is on the grounds that the Prince's accusation, "You seem to have forgotten about the pillow-sleeves," is inconsistent with Izumi's first poem of the day, which is precisely on that subject. Also the page has already made three trips delivering poems to the lady, and a fourth would be too much for one day (*Kenkyū*, pp. 348, 349).

229. At the end of the "Yūgao" chapter of the *Genji monogatari* appears the following passage (*Genji monogatari* [I], *NKBT*, XIV, 174). Genji, who has recently suffered the loss of Yūgao, has today sent his farewell message to Utsusemi:

Today was the beginning of winter, a fact brought inescapably home by the chilly rain. The overcast sky weighed upon his spirits, and he [Genji] spent the entire day in gloomy ponderings:

Suginishi mo	Both she who is no more
Kyō wakaruru mo	And she from whom I part today
Futamichi ni	Go their separate ways
Yuku kata shiranu	To unknown destinations
Aki no kure kana	Lost in this autumn dusk.

As an out-of-season poem this seems more of a borderline case (see *Zenkō*, p. 436).

230. Yoshida, *Kenkyū*, pp. 352–368.

231. *Ibid.*, p. 359.

232. *Ibid.*, pp. 360–368.

233. It should be noted that this poem appears in a different sequence—i.e.,

belongs to a different year—from that mentioned above.

234.   Yoshida, *Kenkyū*, pp. 367–378. Endō also separates the passage into two episodes (Iwanami text, p. 432). The original reads: "Sono hi mo kurenureba owashimashite, konata no futagareba, shinobite ite owashimasu. Konogoro wa shijūgo nichi no imitagae sesaetamau tote, on'itoko no sammi no ie ni owashimasu. Rei naranu tokoro ni sae areba, 'Migurushi' to kikoyuredo . . ." (see translation, p. 174). To me the flow of the text indicates strongly that the passage is one episode. If it is split before "konogoro," then Izumi suddenly appears at the cousin's home without the aid of a verb to get her there. The mention of directional taboos in the sentences immediately before and after the supposed dividing point provides no evidence one way or the other (see translation, note 277). The word *konogoro* need not be taken as the start of a new episode. A similar usage occurs later in the *Nikki* (Iwanami text, p. 440; translation, p. 185) between two poems in an exchange: "Konogoro wa onkyō narawasetamaikereba" (since he had lately been studying the sutras).

235.   *Nihon kiryaku, KT*, XI, 203.

236.   Yoshida, *Kenkyū*, pp. 370–378.

237.   *Ibid.*, p. 376.

238.   *Gonki, Shiryō taisei*, XXXV, 298. The use of the words "waga yado ni" ("in my house," see translation, note 318) would not necessarily argue against the meeting having been held at the Palace. The Prince would naturally prefer Izumi to come to his house.

239.   The ceremony was usually held once in the spring and once in the fall. Buddhist priests were summoned and took turns reading the six hundred chapters of the *Dai hannya kyō* (more properly, the *Dai hannya haramitta kyō* 大般若波羅密多經, the *Mahāprajñāpāramitā Sūtra*, translated by the Chinese monk Hsüan-tsang 玄奘 [602–664]). The reading took four days, during which the priests were kept supplied with tea.

240.   And from 3.10 through 3.13 (*Nihon kiryaku, KT*, XI, 202, 203).

241.   The word is *kasetsu* 花雪 (flower snow) (*Gonki, Shiryō taisei*, XXXVI, 1).

242.   Yoshida, *Kenkyū*, pp. 394, 395.

243.   See translation, note 369. As noted previously, there is an historical inconsistency involved here. Michinaga states in *Midō Kampaku ki*, Chōhō 6.1.3, that the ceremony was held on the third of the month: "I went to the Reizei-in. The Minister of the Center and all the nobles came. We performed the Ceremony of Obeisance" (*Midō Kampaku ki* [I], p. 64). Other entries in diaries of the period indicate that the day on which New Year's visits were paid to the Retired Emperors (there were five during the lifetime of Izumi Shikibu: Reizei [in retirement 969–1011], En'yū [984–991], Kazan [986–1008], Ichijō [1011], and Sanjō [1016–1017]) varied somewhat from year to year. The third of the first month is the date most frequently mentioned however (see especially *Ōuki*, Eikan 永觀 3 [985].1.1, 2; Kanna 寬和 3 [987].1.2, 4; Shōryaku 4 [993].1.3; *Gonki*, Chōhō 2 [1000].1.3, 4; Chōhō 3.1.1,2,5; Chōhō 4.1.1–5;

Chōhō 6.1.3; Kankō 2 [1005].1.3; Kankō 3.1.4; Kankō 4.1.3; Kankō 5.1.4; Kankō 6.1.3, 4; Kankō 7.1.3; *Midō Kampaku ki*, Chōhō 2.1.3; Chōhō 6.1.3; Kankō 2.1.3; Kankō 4.1.3; Kankō 5.1.4; Chōwa 長和 6 [1017].1.3). Diaries written during the Inseiki—the period beginning with Shirakawa-in (1053–1129; r. 1072–1086) in 1086 and continuing until late in the twelfth century—when the Retired Emperors held a measure of political power, indicate that, weather permitting, the ceremony of In no Hairai 院の拜禮 was always held on the first of the month, before the attendance on the reigning Emperor (see, for instance, entries for the first day of the year in *Gonijō Moromichi ki*, the diary of the Regent Fujiwara no Moromichi [1062–1099], and *Denreki*, the diary of the Regent Fujiwara no Tadazane [1078–1162], both in *Dai Nihon kokiroku*). This combination of facts forms one of the strongest weapons in the arsenal of those who argue for late composition of the *Izumi Shikibu nikki*. Yoshida's answer, *Kenkyū*, pp. 447, 448, is essentially that Atsumichi need not have gone to pay his respects to his father on the same day as Michinaga. To be sure, Michinaga does not mention Atsumichi's presence. But both the *Izumi Shikibu nikki* and the *Midō Kampaku ki* do refer to a crowd of noble attendants (*Gonki, Shiryō taisei*, XXXV, 189, mentions a New Year visit paid by Atsumichi's brother Tametaka to Reizei-in in Chōhō 3 [1001] together with many courtiers. This event took place on the fifth of the first month. The Hairai ceremony in the same year was held on the first.) Since both Michinaga and the *Izumi Shikibu nikki* specifically refer to the Hairai, Yoshida's argument seems a little weak. Another possibility, pointed out to the author by Prof. Endō, is that a copyist of the *Izumi Shikibu nikki*, familiar with the practice of the Inseiki, could have deliberately changed the date as given in the *Nikki* from the third to the first. Such revisionist tendencies were common among Kamakura copyists. If such a change was made, it likely occurred before the rise of divergent texts, for the first of the month is the date given in all versions. If the *Nikki* is viewed as a fictional work, this passage of course need pose no problem. In this connection it is interesting to note that Murasaki Shikibu, in the *Genji monogatari*, also refers to paying respects to the Retired Emperor on the first of the month (see "Aoi," *Genji monogatari* [I], NKBT, XIV, 362).

244. The 68 episodes enumerated above appear in the following order in Yoshida's rearrangement: 1, 2, 3, 4, 5, 6, 7, 8, 9, 10, 11, 12, 13, 14, 15, 16, 17, 18, 19, 22, 20, 23, 21, 24, 25, 26, 27, 28, 29, 30, 31, 32, 40, 41, 42, 33, 34, 45*, 46, 43, 44, 45*, 35, 36, 37, 38, 39, 47, 48, 52, 53, 54, 55, 49, 50, 51, 56, 57, 58, 59, 61, 62–63, 64, 65, 66, 67, 68. The stars indicate the episode, no. 45, which Yoshida splits in two (see note 234). The notation 62–63 refers to two episodes which Yoshida counts as happening on the same day.

245. Itō Hiroshi, "*Izumi Shikibu nikki* no seiritsu jiki o megutte," *Gengo to bungei* (May 1960), p. 37.

246. Yoshida, *Kenkyū*, p. 449. For the passages in question see "Shii ga moto," *Genji monogatari* (IV), NKBT, XVII (1962), 376; "Sawarabi," *Genji monogatari* (V), NKBT, XVIII (1963), 18; "Yadorigi," *Ibid.*, p. 120; "Tenarai," *Ibid.*, p. 400.

247. See pp. 108–109.

248. Endō Yoshimoto, interview, March 15, 1965; *Kōchū*, p. 3.

249. *Shinchū*, p. 20; Fujioka Tadami, trans., *Izumi Shikibu nikki*, in *Gendaigo-yaku Nihon koten bungaku zenshū* [no vol. number] (1954), pp. 353, 354.

250. See translation pp. 139, 140, 146, 147, 149, 150, 164, 171, 175–177.

251. Shimizu Fumio, ed., *Izumi Shikibu nikki*, in *Iwanami bunko*, vol. 2750 (1964), pp. 110, 111.

252. Izumi is also referred to as "onna" in the *kotobagaki* of *Seishū* 617 (592), 743 (718), 794 (769), and 797 (772), and *Zokushū* 393 (1235).

253. Suzuki Tomotarō, ed., *Izumi Shikibu nikki*, in *Koten bunko*, XV (1948), 15–20.

254. Oda Hiroko, "*Izumi Shikibu nikki* no sakusha ni tsuite," *Kokugo-kokubun* (April 1958), pp. 53, 54, points out that of the sixteen uses of *onna* in the *Nikki*, ten are followed by a personal revelation or a "first-person type" of description. *Onna* is also used regularly as grammatical subject; *miya* (Prince) is used in a variety of syntactical positions however.

255. Suzuki, *Izumi Shikibu nikki*, pp. 21, 22.

256. Pronounced *niki* in the Heian Period. The following discussion has been greatly facilitated by reference to Tamai Kōsuke, *Nikki bungaku no kenkyū* (1965).

257. The earliest recorded Chinese use of the character combination 日記 appears in the first century A.D. philosophical and critical text *Lun-heng* 論衡, by the Han scholar Wang Ch'ung 王充 (d. ca. A.D. 97) (*Han-Wei ts'ung-shu*, ts'e 68, 13.2a6). The phrase in which it occurs, 上書日記, is translated by Alfred Forke, *Lun-Hêng*, II (1911, 1962), 88, as "They draw up their daily reports to the throne." Two modern Chinese commentaries however dismiss 日記 as meaningless in context. Huang Hui, *Lun-heng chiao-shih* (1938), I, 582, asserts that 日 is a scribal error for 白 (to relate to a superior that which one has seen), pointing out that the *Lun-heng* passage as quoted in *chüan* 36 of the Li Shan 李善 commentary on the *Wen-hsüan* 文選 reads 上書白記 (*Wen-hsüan*, Commercial Press ed. [1960], II, 800). Liu P'an-sui, *Lun-heng chi-chieh* (1957), p. 266, suggests 日 is a mistake for 占 ("to speak what is in one's mind" [?]; cf. Morohashi Tetsuji, ed., *Daikanwa jiten*). The phrase is also discussed at length by Tamai Kōsuke, *Nikki bungaku gaisetsu* (1945), pp. 10, 11, and Sozawa Takichi, "'Nikki' wa hatashite Chūgoku kara no shakuyōgo ka," *Kokugo-kokubun* (Oct. 1958), p. 98. Neither has taken into account the likelihood that the passage is corrupt however.

258. The Naiki 内記 were attached to the Nakatsukasashō or "Ministry of Central Affairs," one of the eight Ministries subordinate to the Daijōkan (see note 4). Their duties were to draft imperial proclamations and certificates of rank, and keep the records of the imperial palace. The Geki 外記, who were attached directly to the Daijōkan, revised the imperial proclamations drafted by the Naiki, drew up the memorials submitted to the throne by the Daijōkan, and participated as recorders in the annual ceremonies of promotion and assignment to office.

259. An order to the Geki concerning entries in such *nikki* was issued by

Great Minister of the Right Fujiwara no Fuyutsugu 冬嗣 (775–826) in 821, as recorded in *Ruijū fusenshō* 類聚符宣抄, *KT*, XXVII, 125.

260. The titles of these diaries, attached by later copyists, usually are based on elements from the names or offices of their authors. Thus, *Teishinkōki* 貞信公記 incorporates the posthumous honorific name (Chaste and True Lord) of the Regent Fujiwara no Tadahira 忠平 (880–949). *Ouki* 小右記 (also pronounced *Shōyūki*), the diary of Fujiwara no Sanesuke 實資 (957–1046), derives the 小 and the 右 in its title from the fact that Sanesuke was known as "Nochi no Ononomiya Udaijin" 後小野宮右大臣 ("The Latter Great Minister of the Right from Ononomiya"—Ononomiya being the name of the mansion he inherited from his grandfather Saneyori 實賴 [900–970]). *Gonki* 權記 is so called from the office (Gondainagon 權大納言—"Acting Great Counsellor") of its author, Fujiwara no Yukinari (972–1027). *Midō Kampaku ki* 御堂關白記 is the diary of Fujiwara no Michinaga (966–1027), who lived in retirement at the Hōjōji 法成寺 (the Midō or "August Hall" of the title), a temple he founded in 1022. Michinaga never actually held the position of Kampaku however. *Sakeiki* 左經記 takes its title from the fact that its author, Minamoto no Tsuneyori 經賴 (985–1035), wrote the first part of his given name with the character 經, and was Major Controller of the Left (Sadaiben 左大辨).

261. *Utaawase* 歌合.

262. At first they were an elegant game—one of the many amusements of the Heian court—but were taken more and more seriously as time went on, until they became one of the chief arenas for establishing a poetic reputation.

263. *Makura no sōshi*, ed. Ikeda Kikan and Kishigami Shinji, in *NKBT*, XIX (1958), 281.

264. *Chōkyū gannen satsuki muika Saigū Ryōshi Naishinnō kaiawase* 長久元年五月六日齋宮良子内親王貝合. See *Utaawaseshū*, ed. Hagitani Boku and Taniyama Shigeru, *NKBT*, LXXIV (1965), 158–165.

265. The earliest extant record of a poetry competition, the *Zai Mimbukyō no ie no utaawase* 在民部卿家歌合 (The Poetry Match at the House of the Minister of Popular Affairs [Ariwara no Yukihira (818–893)]), dating from about 884–887, shows little development of the prose sections. The *kana nikki* style was set by the *Teiji-in no utaawase* 亭子院歌合 (Poetry Match of the [Retired Sovereign of] Teiji Cloister [Emperor Uda 宇多 (867–931; r. 887–897)]) in 913. The record of this contest is ascribed to the poetess Lady Ise (Ise no Go 伊勢御, fl. ca. 895–935).

266. The *haiku* 俳句 developed from the initial seventeen-syllable link (*hokku* 發句) of "comic" linked verse, *haikai no renga* 俳諧の連歌. The *hokku* began a career as an independent form as early as the time of Yamazaki Sōkan 山崎宗鑑 (1465–1553), one of the founders of the *haikai* tradition. The term *haiku* has been applied to this independent *hokku* in modern times.

267. This is the *Kojiki* version. The *Nihon shoki* records the divine exclamations as 意哉遇可美少女焉 and 意哉遇可美少男焉, which are rendered into Japanese as "Ana ureshie ya, umashi otome ni ainuru koto; ana ureshie ya, umashi otoko ni ainuru koto" (Oh, what joy to have met a lovely girl; Oh, what joy

to have met a handsome man!). In both accounts the goddess originally speaks first, necessitating a repetition of the ceremony in the correct, male-first, order.

268.   The *Hitachi fudoki*常陸風土記, *Kojiki*, and *Nihon shoki* describe a custom called *utagaki* 歌垣 in which youths and maidens gathered in the spring and fall on mountain slopes for a day of feasting and revelry. As the climax of the festivities the men challenged the girls to a poetry contest. The man would speak his verse first, and the girl reply, trying to make her challenger look foolish with a clever, bantering retort. If she could not answer successfully she was his "wife for the night." The custom is considered to have been instrumental in the development of the *tanka* form and the style of later feminine poetry. *Waka bungaku daijiten*, pp. 78, 79.

269.   The opening lines of the *Kana Preface* to the *Kokinshū* proclaim:

"Yamato uta wa hito no kokoro o tane to shite yorozu no kotonoha to zo narerikeru. Yo no naka ni aru hito kotowaza shigeki mono nareba kokoro ni omou koto o miru mono kiku mono ni tsukete iidaseru nari. Hana ni naku uguisu mizu ni sumu kawazu no koe o kikeba iki to shi ikeru mono izure ka uta o yomazarikeru" (The poetry of Yamato has taken as its seed the human heart and burgeoned forth into a myriad leaves of words. It is the utterance, through allusion to things they see and hear, of what people in this world feel in their hearts when faced with life's tangle of event. Listening to the voices of the warbler which sings among the blossoms and the frog which lives in the water, we ask, what of all living things does not make poetry?) (*Kokinwakashū*, NKBT, VIII [1958], 93).

270.   *MYS* 16. The Emperor was Tenji 天智 (626–671; r. 668–671); the Fujiwara minister, Kamatari 鎌足 (614–669). For translations of the poem see Robert H. Brower and Earl Miner, *Japanese Court Poetry* (1961), p. 85; *The Man'yōshū*, tr. Nippon Gakujutsu Shinkōkai (1940, 1965), pp. 10, 11.

271.   *Genji monogatari* (I), NKBT, XIV, 39.

272.   *Ibid.*, p. 101.

273.   *Ibid.*, p. 142.

274.   For a discussion of poetic integration in imperial anthologies see Brower and Miner, *Court Poetry*, pp. 319–329.

275.   In 713 each province was ordered to compile an account of its products, topographical features, local traditions, etc. Only the *Izumo fudoki* 出雲風土記 has been preserved in its entirety. Partially preserved are the *fudoki* of Hitachi 常陸, Harima 播磨, Bungo 豊後, and Hizen 肥前.

276.   The Ōtomo were a traditionally strong military clan who became powerful at court after the overthrow of the Soga 蘇我 domination in the 7th century. In Yakamochi's day rivalry with the rising Fujiwara clan led to decline in the family's fortunes. Yakamochi was never promoted above the office of Middle Counsellor (Chūnagon), although his father and grandfather had been Major Counsellors (Dainagon). In 756 his clansman Kojihi 古慈斐 was slandered

by Fujiwara no Nakamaro 仲麿 (706–764) and demoted to Governor of Tosa. Yakamochi himself was under a cloud and was sent back to the provinces as governor of Inaba 因幡 in 758 and Satsuma 薩摩 in 760. The remainder of his career was marked by many vicissitudes, and even his ashes were sent into exile in the Oki Islands after his death. Yakamochi's concern with the honor of his clan is expressed in several poems, notably *MYS* 4094–7 and 4465–7. See the notes to the footnote following the latter poems, *Man'yōshū* (IV), ed. Takagi Ichinosuke, Gomi Mitsuhide, and Ōno Susumu, *NKBT*, VII (1962), 461, 462.

277. This note follows *MYS* 4131.

278. See *MYS* 4284, 4320, 4360.

279. *Genji monogatari* (I), *NKBT*, XIV, 212.

280. *Genji monogatari* (II), *NKBT*, XV (1959), 86.

281. *Murasaki Shikibu nikki*, in *NKBT*, XIX, 502.

282. Arthur Waley, trans., *The Tale of Genji*, Modern Library G38, p. 501.

283. Hundred-poem sequences.

284. A sequence in which the first syllable of each poem is taken from the Japanese reading of a line of Chinese poetry. Cf. *Izumi Shikibu seishū* 268–310. See translation, note 178.

285. *Ise shū, Kōchū kokka taikei*, XII, 349.

286. Translated from Tamai, *Nikki bungaku no kenkyū*, p. 30.

287. *Tosa no niki*, in *NKBT*, XX, 27.

288. Translated from Tamai, *Nikki bungaku no kenkyū*, p. 240.

289. Michitsuna 道綱 (955–1020), whose highest office was Major Counsellor, had a career of minor importance compared to his half-brothers Michitaka 道隆 (957–995), Michikane 道兼 (961–995), and Michinaga (966–1027), Kaneie's sons by his principal wife, Tokihime 時姫 (d. 980). All three of these elder brothers rose to head the government.

290. *Kagerō no nikki*, in *NKBT*, XX, 109. For a complete translation see Edward G. Seidensticker, trans., *The Gossamer Years* (1964).

291. *Sarashina nikki*, ed. Nishishita Kyōichi, in *NKBT*, XX, 479.

292. In this section of the *Nikki*, Ōe no Masahira (see Introduction, note 10) is referred to as Governor of Tamba, a post he assumed on Kankō 7 (1010). 3.30.

293. *Makura no sōshi*, in *NKBT*, XIX, 331, 332.

294. Tamai, *Nikki bungaku no kenkyū*, p. 264. Shijōnomiya Shimotsuke was the daughter of Minamoto no Masataka 政隆, a Governor of Shimotsuke Province. Her collection covers the years 1051–1071.

295. Sanuki no Suke was the court name of Nagako [Chōshi] 長子, daughter of Fujiwara no Akitsuna 顕綱 (1029–1103). She was born ca. 1079 and entered the service of Emperor Horikawa 堀河 (1079–1107; r. 1086–1107) in 1100. She was a favorite of the Emperor and was present during his final illness, which her *nikki* describes in vivid detail. After his death in 1107 she retired from court service, but was brought back as one of the ladies of the child-Emperor Toba 鳥羽 (1103–1156; r. 1107–1123) in 1108. She remained at court until 1119, when

she retired because of ill health. Her *nikki*, which may be only a fragment of the original, covers one and a half years, from Kajō 嘉承 2 (1107).6.20 to the end of the following year. For the office *suke* 典侍, also read *tenji*, see note 191.

296. The *Nakatsukasa Naishi nikki* deals with the years 1280–1292, and was written by a lady at the court of Emperor Fushimi 伏見 (1265–1317; r. 1287–1298). She is probably to be identified as Tsuneko [Keishi] 經子, a daughter of Fujiwara Nagatsune 永經 (d. 1297). Nagatsune served in the Nakatsukasashō from Kōan 弘安 9 (1286).3.23 to Kōan 10.1.13, a fact which no doubt accounts for his daughter's appellation. Her dates are not known, but she was already in service to Fushimi in 1280, when he was still Heir Apparent. Her *nikki* breaks off abruptly in the third month of Shōō 正應 5 (1292), and nothing is known of her after that. The work describes many court ceremonies, dealing at particular length with those performed on the occasion of the abdication of Emperor Go-Uda 後宇多 (1267–1324; r. 1274–1287) in 1287 and the enthronement of Emperor Fushimi in 1288. The author assisted in the latter ceremony. Her *nikki* contains over 150 poems, and some sections are constructed on the model of the poem-exchange. Others, particularly in the latter portions of the work, consist of lengthy prose descriptions without poetry. The *Nakatsukasa Naishi nikki* was probably put together soon after 1292, based on kept notes and poems. It has been translated by Tamako Niwa in an unpublished doctoral dissertation, *Nakatsukasa Naishi nikki* (Harvard, 1955).

297. *Towazugatari* (the title means "an un-asked-for story"), like the *Sarashina nikki*, covers essentially an entire lifetime, that of Nijō no Tsubone 二條局 (b. 1258), daughter of Minamoto no Masatada 雅忠 (1222–1271?). The author's mother (daughter of Fujiwara no Takachika 隆親 [1202–1279]) had been the first love of Emperor Go-Fukakusa 後深草 (1243–1304; r. 1246–1259) before her marriage, and after she died in 1259 he took her infant daughter into his palace. When the author was fourteen she received Go-Fukakusa's favor, and bore him a son in 1273. The child died the following year, and Nijō no Tsubone lost her chance for a permanent position at court. She was dismissed in 1283. In the meantime however she carried on affairs with three other lovers, in two cases with the permission and urging of Go-Fukakusa. *Towazugatari* contains a frank confession of Nijō's complicated love-life (she bore a total of four children to her lovers while in Go-Fukakusa's service). Its latter portions deal with her life after leaving court. She took the tonsure probably in 1288 or 1289 and set out on a series of pilgrimages which took her over much of the country. Her last years she spent in the environs of the capital, and lived to attend Go-Fukakusa's funeral in 1304. Nijō's death date is not known, but the *Towazugatari* ends in 1306, and was probably written from preserved notes between 1307 and 1324.

298. The mountain Wu T'ai in Shansi Province, named for its five peaks, embraced several temples, notably the Ch'ing-liang-ssu 清涼寺 , So-p'o-ssu 娑婆寺, and Hsien-t'ung-ssu 顯通寺 . Mt. T'ien T'ai in Chekiang Province was the headquarters of the sect of the same name (Japanese, Tendai).

299. Tokuko took the name Kenreimon'in in 1181, after the death of Taka-

kura. From this title comes the first element in the appellation of the author of the *Kenreimon'in Ukyō no Daibu shū*. Ukyō no Daibu (Master of the Office of the Capital, Right Division) was the title of the highest official (Daibu 大夫) of the western (right) division of the formally constituted metropolitan administration of the capital (Ukyōshiki 右京職). Since none of her blood relations held the post, it is not known why the author had the appellation, but Hon'iden Shigemi, *Hyōchū Kenreimon'in Ukyō no Daibu shū zenshaku* (1950), as quoted in Tamai, *Nikki bungaku no kenkyū*, pp. 375, 377, suggests that her mother, the daughter of the famous flutist Ōmiwa (Ōga) Motomasa 大神基政 (1079–1138), may have born a son to Fujiwara Shunzei before her marriage to Sesonji Koreyuki 世尊寺 伊行 (1138?–1175?), the author's father, and that the author may have entered court as Shunzei's foster daughter. Shunzei held the post of Ukyō no Daibu from 1168 to 1175.

300. There is an exchange with Fujiwara Teika at the end, probably dating from shortly before 1232. Teika asks the author for poems to be included in the *Shinchokusenshū*, an imperial anthology he was in the process of compiling. He inquires concerning the name by which she wishes to be known, and she expresses her preference for her old appellation (Kenreimon'in Ukyō no Daibu) over that by which she was called during her second period of court service. Tamai, *Nikki bungaku no kenkyū*, p. 390, thinks that this exchange was appended later to her collection, which had been completed almost 20 years earlier.

301. Tamai, *Nikki bungaku no kenkyū*, p. 390.

302. The "Ben" of the title and the author's appellation indicates a connection with the Benkan 辨官 or "Controlling Board," an office of the central bureaucracy. It is not clear why the author had this appellation.

303. The travel journal also continued to flourish during this period. Descended from the *Tosa nikki*, or even more remotely from the travel sequences of the *Man'yōshū*, and exemplified by works such as *Ionushi* and passages in the *Sarashina nikki*, *Nakatsukasa Naishi nikki*, *Towazugatari*, and other memoirs, it characteristically tied its itinerary together in a string of poems. The process was a more deliberate variant of the usual organizing of poems and notes into a *nikki*. After the establishment of a military government in Kamakura in 1192, the route east from the capital (the Tōkaidō or "Eastern Sea Road") was travelled more frequently than ever before. Several travel accounts of the Kamakura Period describe this route. Most of them are by men and show a transition to a new written Japanese, incorporating words of Chinese origin and employing a terser and more masculine style than that of the predominantly feminine court literature. One however was written by a woman in the old style still used in the court *nikki*. This is the *Izayoi nikki* 十六夜日記, by the nun Abutsu 阿佛 (ca. 1233–1283), widow of the poet Fujiwara no Tameie 為家 (1197–1275), the son of Teika. Only one part of the work is actually a travel account. It begins with a section relating the reason (a lawsuit over some property) which led her to undertake a journey to Kamakura in the tenth month of Kenji 建治 3 (1277). This section also contains poem-exchanges with her children. She goes on to describe

her trip, giving one or more poems for each scene, including her correspondence with friends in the capital after her arrival in Kamakura, and concluding with a *chōka*.

304. The oldest manuscript of this work has, in the hand of Fujiwara Teika or one similar to his, the title 成尋阿闍梨母集. Sasaki Nobutsuna preferred to entitle it 成尋阿闍梨母日記 when he introduced the text in *Shigaku ronsō* in 1930. And Miyata Kazuichirō calls it 成尋母日記 in his *Ōchō sannikki shinshaku* (1956).

305. The title 辨内侍日記 was established as early as the 14th-century work on poetics *Suia gammoku* 水蛙眼目 by Ton'a 頓阿 (1289–1372; lay name Nikaidō Sadamune 二階堂貞宗). The *Wagaku Kōdansho* 和學講談所 and *Komoro* 小諸 mss. have 後深草院辨内侍家集 as their "inner title" (*naidai* 内題), while 辨内侍日記 and 後深草院辨内侍日記 appear as titles on their respective covers. There is another ms., the one in the Naikaku Bunko 内閣文庫, which is entitled *Ben no Naishi Kangenki* 辨内侍寛元記.

306. The *Hachidaishūshō* 八代集抄 commentary of Kitamura Kigin 北村季吟 (1624–1705), in its note on poem 56 of the *Shinkokinshū*. See Yamagishi Tokuhei, ed., *Hachidaishū zenchū* (1960), II, 533.

307. In *Honchō shojaku mokuroku*, GR, XXI, 533.

308. The Fu 傅 was the Head Tutor to the Heir Apparent, an office often filled by a Dainagon, and by Fujiwara no Michitsuna from 1007 to 1011.

309. Tamai, *Nikki bungaku no kenkyū*, p. 112.

310. *Ibid.*, p. 37.

311. The story of the Hare of Inaba (稻羽の素兎) and the adventures of the god Ōkuninushi 大國主 in the underworld are related in *maki* 1 of the *Kojiki*. The exploits of the hero Yamato Takeru no Mikoto 倭建命 are recounted in *maki* 2, and the benevolence of the Emperor Nintoku 仁德 is mentioned in *maki* 3. See *Kojiki*, ed. Kurano Kenji, in *NKBT*, I (1958), 91–93, 95–99, 207–222, 267.

312. The *Yu-hsien-k'u* (Journey to the Cave of Immortals), attributed to the early T'ang literatus Chang Tsu 張鷟 (styled Wen-ch'eng 文成) (ca. 657–730), was probably written late in the seventh century. It is the earliest of the T'ang genre of romantic love stories, but it disappeared in China soon after its composition and survived only in Japan. The Japanese were familiar with it from the eighth century on, and it has been suggested that Yamanoe no Okura 山上憶良 (ca. 660–733) brought it back from China when the embassy which 本 he had accompanied in 701 returned. He mentions it by name and paraphrases from it in a prose passage in *maki* 5 of the *Man'yōshū* dated Tempyō 天平 5 (733).3.1 (*Man'yōshū* [II], NKBT, V [1959], 110). The story tells how a young official on an imperial mission wanders into a remote mountain fastness where he meets two ladies of supernatural beauty if only mortal chastity. He is entertained in their palatial mansion and spends a night of love with one of them. The bamboo-cutter poems in the *Man'yōshū* are not only similar in theme—the meeting of mortal man and fairy maidens—to the *Yu-hsien-k'u*, but have adapted from it some of the phraseology in their prose preface. Howard Levy, *The Dwelling of Playful Goddesses* (1965), discusses the influence exerted on Japanese

literature by the *Yu-hsien-k'u* over more than a millennium and includes an extensive bibliography. See especially pp. 76–79 for a discussion of *Man'yōshū* references to the *Yu-hsien-k'u*.

313. *MYS* 3786, 3787.

314. Referred to as such in the "Picture Competition" chapter of the *Genji*: "monogatari no idekihajime no oya taru Taketori no Okina" (the [Tale of] the Old Bamboo-Cutter, the sire of *monogatari* at its beginnings) (*Genji monogatari* [II], *NKBT*, XV, 179).

315. Kanamura's dates are unknown, but he flourished in the early 8th century.

316. *Waka bungaku daijiten*, pp. 151–153.

317. See Saeki Umetomo, et al., *Izumi Shikibu shū zenshaku*, pp. 659–683.

318. The formation, date, authorship, and other matters relating to the *Ise monogatari* have been thoroughly studied by Frits Vos in *A Study of the Ise-Monogatari with the Text According to the Den-Teika-Hippon and an Annotated Translation*, 2 vols. (1957). My remarks on the *Ise* are largely based on this work.

319. "Heichū" 平中 is an abbreviated appellation for "Taira 平 Middle Captain 中將." See note 320.

320. In later literature, especially *setsuwa* collections such as the *Konjaku monogatarishū*, *Jikkinshō*, and *Yotsugi monogatari*, Heichū is treated as a comic figure. The most famous of the stories about him tells how his pretended grief at parting from a lady-love was exposed as a fraud. According to one version of this anecdote, Heichū always splashed his cheeks with water from the bottle on his mistress' inkstand in order to feign tears of sorrow when leaving her in the morning. She discovered his trick and secretly filled the bottle with ink. When he reached home his wife was confronted with his ink-stained face. The earliest reference to this tale is in the *Genji monogatari*, where it is mentioned twice. In the "Suetsumuhana" chapter Genji puts a red spot on his nose, and when the young Murasaki tries to rub it away he warns her, "Don't add a coloring like Heichū's. I can stand the red." And in the first of the "Wakana" chapters, Genji, talking with his old love Oborozukiyo 朧月夜, sighs over the passage of time. "This was no imitation of Heichū," the author says, "he was truly on the verge of tears." (*Genji monogatari* [I], *NKBT*, XIV, 268; *ibid.* [III], XVI [1961], 261.) Hagitani Boku, *Heichū zenkō* (1959), pp. 244–255, points out that this story is a basic comic type appearing again and again throughout Japanese literature, and usually without reference to Heichū. In discussing the "caricaturization" of Sadabumi, Hagitani puts forward the argument that it was Sadabumi's father Yoshikaze 好風 (fl. 873–913), a noted eccentric and libertine, whose reputation attracted such stories. It was Yoshikaze, rather than his son Sadabumi, who held the office of Middle Captain (Chūjō 中將) and could reasonably have been called Heichū. According to Hagitani, the playboy father and the poet son have become merged in the legends.

321. *Yamato monogatari*, ed. Abe Toshiko and Imai Gen'ei, in *NKBT*, IX (1957), 216–218.

322. Tamai Kōsuke, ed., *Tōnomine Shōshō monogatari* (1960), p. 135. Taka-mitsu married his first cousin, the daughter of his uncle Morouji 師氏 (913–970). Fujioka Sakutarō, *Kokubungaku zenshi: Heian-chō-hen* (1923), p. 312, has sug-gested that the author was one of Takamitsu's attendants, but Iwashimizu Hisashi, in Hisamatsu, ed., *Nihon bungakushi: chūko*, p. 346, alleges a serious historical error in the work which militates against such theories. Tamai, *Tōnomine Shōshō*, pp. 132–136, however demonstrates that the error is not in the *Tōnomine*, but in a note to *Nihon kiryaku*. The point at issue is the death date of Takamitsu's elder sister, the third daughter of Morosuke, and wife of Minamoto no Taka-akira 高明 (914–982). She is one of the dramatis personae of the *Tōnomine*. *Nihon kiryaku*, *KT*, XI, 51, entry for Tenryaku 天暦 I (947).7.8, however mentions a memorial service held on the forty-ninth day after the death of Takaakira's wife. A note identifies the deceased as the third daughter of Morosuke. Tamai shows that the note must be in error; the person who died in 947 was Takaakira's first wife, the daughter of Morosuke's brother Saneyori 實賴 (900–970). Taka-akira later married Morosuke's daughter (Takamitsu's sister), who bore him two sons, Korekata and Toshikata (960–1027) (see *Sompi bummyaku*, *KT*, LXVIII, 58; *Sompi bummyaku* however also gives Takamitsu's younger sister, Aimiya 愛宮, as Takaakira's wife [*ibid.*, p. 59]). If the note in *Nihon kiryaku* were correct, Toshikata would have to have been born after his mother's death. Iwashimizu, *Nihon bungakushi*, p. 290, suggests that the *Tōnomine* was based on a no longer extant collection of Takamitsu's poems. The *rufubon* text of the *Takamitsu shū*, a surviving collection of Takamitsu's poetry, has no poems in common with the *Tōnomine*; another text, the *Nishi Honganjibon*, has eight poems in common.

323. *Honchō shojaku mokuroku*, *GR*, XXI, 534; *Kakaishō*, in *Kokubun chūshaku zensho*, III, 217, 286.

324. *Honchō shojaku mokuroku*, *GR*, XXI, 533.

325. *Kakaishō*, in *Kokubun chūshaku zensho*, III, 68.

326. *Sagoromo monogatari*, *NKBT*, LXXIX (1965), 55. The appellation Zaigo Chūjō 在五中將 (Captain Zai Five) is based on the fact that Narihira was the fifth son of Prince Aho 阿保 (d. 842) and was granted the family name Ariwara 在原 in 826 (hence Zaigo, "the fifth Ariwara," *zai* being the Sino-Japanese reading of 在, the first character in Ariwara). He was appointed Provisional Middle Captain of the Inner Palace Guards, Right Division (Ukonoe Gonchūjō 右近衞權中將) in 877.

327. *Takamura monogatari*, ed. Yamagishi Tokuhei, in *Nihon koten zensho* [no vol. number] (1959), p. 275.

328. *Kakaishō*, in *Kokubun chūshaku zensho*, III, 70, 205; *Kachō yosei*, in *Kokubun chūshaku zensho*, III, 101.

329. August Pfizmaier, "Erklärung des Tagebuches Idzumi-Siki-Bu," *Denkschriften d. Philol.-Hist. Classe d. Kais. Akademie*, Bd. XXXV, 1885.

330. Annie Shepley Omori and Kochi Doi, trans., *Diaries of Court Ladies of Old Japan* (Kenkyūsha, 1961), p. 153.

331. *Ibid.*, p. 155. Brackets are as in quoted translation.

332. *Ibid.*, p. 202. "Lieutenant-General" is a translation of "Chūjō," one of the ranks of the officers of the Inner Palace Guards. Here however it is used as a nickname of one of the Prince's maids.

333. The texts most extensively used have been that edited by Endō Yoshimoto in *Nihon koten bungaku taikei*, Tamai Kōsuke's *Izumi Shikibu nikki shinchū*, Ozaki Tomomitsu's *Izumi Shikibu nikki kōchū*, Yamagishi Tokuhei's edition in *Nihon koten zensho*, Suzuki Kazuo and Enchi Fumiko's *Zenkō Izumi Shikibu nikki*, and Shimizu Fumio's commentary in *Nihon koten kanshō kōza*. Commentators vary in their paragraphing of the text, which in the original manuscript is continuous. I have not followed any particular edition in this matter, but have paragraphed as seemed best, in accordance with the flow of the story. Kenkyūsha Ltd. and Prof. Doi Kōchi have graciously given permission to quote from *Diaries of Court Ladies of Old Japan*.

II. Notes to the Translation

1. "Yume yori mo hakanaki yo no naka." *Yo no naka* means both "human society" and "the relations between a man and woman." Here it refers to Izumi's relations with her lover, the late Prince Tametaka, who died on the thirteenth of the sixth month of the previous year (Chōhō 4 [1002]). For the concept and phraseology of the opening sentence compare the following poems:

Kokinshū 835 (Mibu no Tadamine):

Composed when someone he knew passed away:

Nuru ga uchi ni	Shall we call dreams
Miru o nomi ya wa	Only those that come in sleep?
Yume to iwamu	I do not look upon
Hakanaki yo o mo	This momentary world
Utsutsu to wa mizu	As having more reality than they.

Gosenshū 170 (Mibu no Tadamine):

Yume yori mo	One thing there is
Hakanaki mono wa	More fleeting than a dream:

Natsu no yo no	Parting at dawn
Akatsukigata no	After an evanescent
Wakare narikeri	Summer's night.

Shūishū 733 (Anonymous):

Yume yori mo	One thing there is
Hakanaki mono wa	More fleeting than a dream:
Kagerō no	An all but
Honoka ni mieshi	Indistinguishable
Kage ni zo arikeru	Shimmering of the air.

Izumi Shikibu seishū 268:

Miru hodo wa	Even a dream
Yume mo tanomaru	Can be trusted while it lasts,
Hakanaki wa	But deluded
Aru o aru tote	Is the man who spends his life
Sugusu narikeri	Thinking the real is real.

For a further discussion see *Zenkō*, pp. 365–368.

2. The fourth month of the old calendar was the first month of *natsu* (summer), corresponding roughly to May of our calendar. (Chōhō 5.4.10 is equivalent to May 13, 1003 in the Julian calendar.) Hence the deepening shade cast by the thickening foliage.

3. The image of grass is a recurrent one in Izumi Shikibu's poetry. See pp. 57, 58 and note 177. Cf. also *Seishū* 13:

Harusame no	As the rains of spring
Hi o furu mama ni	Fall, day after day, so I
Waga yado no	Fare on through time
Kakine no kusa wa	While by the fence the grasses grow
Aomi watarinu	And green spreads everywhere.

4. *Tsuihiji* (an evolution in pronunciation from *tsukihiji* [from *tsuku*, "to build by piling up compressed earth and stones"+*hiji*, "mud"]), a wall of pounded earth. In later times the same term was used to refer to a wall made of mud-covered laths stretched between pillars and roofed with tile.

5. I have translated the word *aware*, a key term in the vocabulary of Heian esthetics and sensibility, as "an emotional awareness." *Aware* has a long history, from its origins in an exclamation expressive of admiration, surprise, or delight, to its modern meaning of "misery." In the Heian Period its most characteristic use was to express a feeling of gentle, sorrow-tinged appreciation of transitory

beauty. It could still however be used to express pleasurable surprise (see notes 8, 155). The word is discussed at some length in "The Vocabulary of Japanese Aesthetics (I)," chap. ix of *Sources of the Japanese Tradition*, ed. Ryusaku Tsunoda, *et al.* (1958), pp. 176–184; and in Iwanami text, p. 447, sup. note 4, and p. 450, sup. note 38.

6. *Suigai* (an evolution in pronunciation from *sukigaki* [from *suki*, "opening, gap, interstice"+*kaki*, "fence"]), a board or bamboo fence with interstices.

7. *Kotoneri warawa*, strictly speaking, boys who acted as servants to Chūjō and Shōshō, the second and third-ranking officers of the Konoefu or Inner Palace Guards. Here the term is used loosely in the sense of a page of a member of the nobility.

8. "Aware ni mono no oboyuru hodo ni kitareba." Yamagishi, *NKZ*, p. 183, note 8, gives "aware ni" its meaning of "happily." This interpretation seems questionable to me, since we have had *aware* used in the previous sentence in the sense of "tender emotional awareness," in the clause "aware to nagamuru hodo ni." See, however, note 155; see also *Shinkō*, pp. 12, 13.

9. Perhaps the late Prince Tametaka's burial place (see Iwanami text, p. 447, sup. note 6). *Gonki*, entry for Chōhō 4.6.18, states that Prince Tametaka's funeral took place at the Ungoji, a temple in the Higashiyama district (*Zōho shiryō taisei*, IV, 262). Or the reference may be plural: "mountain temples." In any case it seems appropriate to assume that the "visits" have some connection with services for the late Prince.

10. "Mitatematsuran," more literally, "to look up at with respect."

11. Prince Atsumichi. He held the office (purely honorary) of Governor-General of Dazaifu—Dazai no Sotsu (or Sochi) 太宰帥. Dazaifu was the special military defence headquarters in northern Kyushu. The post of Governor-General was usually held by princes of the blood after 823. The actual duties were delegated to a subordinate. *Miya* (palace) was an honorific term for an Empress, Imperial Prince or Princess, or descendant of an Emperor to the fifth generation.

12. A problem exists in this paragraph, though it has been somewhat ob-scured in the translation. The original runs (punctuated as in Iwanami text): "Sono koto to saburawade wa narenareshiki sama ni ya to tsutsumashū saburau uchi ni, higoro wa yamadera ni makariarikite nan, ito tayorinaku tsurezure ni omoitamaurarureba, onkawari ni mo mitatematsuran tote nan Sochi no Miya ni mairite saburau." The problem revolves about the meaning of "uchi ni," and the proper punctuation of the sentence. Ozaki, Tamai, Yamagishi, and Shimizu all place a period (*kuten* 句點) after "arikite nan." They all interpret "uchi ni" as meaning "besides" or "furthermore" and as connecting with the immediately following clause. My translation has followed this interpretation (the traditional one) as a matter of convenience. Endō however regards "uchi ni" as having a temporal sense and as connecting with "ito tayorinaku." "Higoro wa yamadera ni makariarikite nan" then becomes a parenthetical expression—what he calls a *bummyaku no oremagari*. According to Endō's interpretation the passage could be

translated in some such way as "And while I was hesitating—I'd been going off to a mountain temple lately, too—I began to feel quite cut adrift and oppressed by my idleness." Suzuki Kazuo puts forward still a different interpretation, placing a full stop after both "uchi ni" and "nan," thus dividing the page's speech into three discrete statements. The first, ending in "uchi ni," is elliptical. "Uchi ni," as in Endō's view, is considered temporal. The passage however should be interpreted to mean, "While I was hesitating [I finally let a long time go by without paying my respects to you]. Lately I've been going to a mountain temple. Since I've been feeling very cut adrift . . ." In *Shinkō*, pp. 150–165, Endō examines all examples of the use of *uchi ni* in the *Izumi Shikibu nikki*, and attempts to demonstrate that in each case the proper interpretation is temporal. The matter is further discussed in *Zenkō*, pp. 374–379. For *bummyaku no oremagari* see *Shinkō*, pp. 66–69.

13. "Mukashi no yō ni wa e shimo araji" (He cannot be like [the one of] old, I suppose). For a description of Prince Tametaka see Introduction, pp. 8–9. It should be noted however that the *Ōkagami* gives Prince Atsumichi the same character as his brother. This reputation may have stemmed largely from Atsumichi's affair with Izumi Shikibu, but it is intriguing, as Suzuki remarks in *Zenkō*, p. 76, to consider the possibility that Izumi is aware of the Prince's real reputation but makes this remark in order to draw out the page.

There is a problem concerning the proper punctuation of the sentences I have translated, "He has a reputation for being most distinguished and very difficult to approach. He cannot be at all like your former master, I suppose." The original, punctuated as in Iwanami text and *Ōchō nikki*, runs: "Sono miya wa ito ate ni kekeshū owashimasu naru wa. Mukashi no yō ni wa e shimo araji." Ozaki, Tamai, and Yamagishi have a comma (*tōten* 讀點) instead of a period after "wa." Endō discusses this problem in Iwanami text, p. 447, sup. note 7. He observes that this is a passage of dialogue, and proposes the idea that Izumi deliberately pauses after "wa," and thus invites the page to make some comment on her statement (which the form "owashimasu naru" indicates is hearsay).

14. *Tachibana* 橘 , an ornamental orange tree bearing sour, seedy fruit, *Citrus tachibana;* said to be the only species of citrus native to Japan (*Shokubutsu no jiten*, ed. Ogura Ken [1957, 1959], pp. 440, 441).

15. The present of orange blossom calls to Izumi's mind an anonymous poem, *Kokinshū* 139:

Satsuki matsu	Now that I breathe
Hanatachibana no	The fragrance of the flowering orange,
Ka o kageba	Blossoming at last in June,
Mukashi no hito no	I find in it the fragrance of the sleeves
Sode no ka zo suru	Of someone long ago.

She has of course made the association Prince Atsumichi intended she should make. The poem appears also in section 60 of the *Ise monogatari*, where it is addressed by a man to his former wife. *Satsuki* is the fifth month, roughly corresponding to June of our calendar and translated as such here. My general practice has been to refer to months by their number in the Japanese calendar.

16. "Iwarete." The passive form conveys involuntary action in this case.

17. This paragraph contains several problems. The original runs: "Kotoba nite kikoesasen mo katawara itakute, nani ka wa, adaadashiku mo mada kikoetamawanu o, hakanaki koto o mo to omoite." The first difficulty concerns the meaning of "kotoba," which can be interpreted to mean either "word [of mouth]," i.e., an oral message relayed by the page, or "[prose] words," i.e., a letter in distinction to a poem. Endō, Ozaki, Suzuki, and Shimizu favor the latter interpretation; Tamai and Yamagishi seem to favor the former. A more vexing problem is the relation of "nani ka wa" to the rest of the sentence. Perhaps the most obvious connection would be with "hakanaki koto o mo" plus an understood "mōsan" or some such verb—"How can I send some frivolous message?" This is the interpretation made by Ozaki, *Kōchū*, p. 8; Tamai, *Shinchū*, p. 70; and Yamagishi, *NKZ*, p. 185, note 22. Endō however interprets the passage along the following lines: Izumi is troubled about the need to send a reply (kotoba nite kikoesasen mo katawara itakute). Then she makes up her mind, saying to herself, "nani ka wa," equivalent to "ee, naani": "Well, what [am I worried about]? He has as yet no reputation for scandalous behavior, and so even if I do send him something a little frivolous [what harm can come of it]?" (Iwanami text, p. 448, sup. note 11). Suzuki follows Endō in this interpretation (*Zenkō*, pp. 381, 382).

Another problem concerns the interpretation of "adaadashiku mo mada kikoetamawanu o." Endō, Ozaki, Suzuki, and Shimizu interpret the verb *kikoyu* in the sense of *hyōban* or *uwasa sareru*, i.e., the Prince has not a scandalous reputation. Yamagishi, *NKZ*, p. 185, note 22, thinks that the rumors which do not exist would be specifically those concerning the Prince's relations with Izumi. Tamai, *Shinchū*, pp. 70, 216, interprets "kikoetamawanu" as referring to a message from the Prince—he has not yet said anything scandalous to her—and points out the presence of "mada" (not yet). Thus the author, writing after the fact, remembers that *as yet* she had had no love notes.

The differences of opinion on this passage and the following poem are important because they bear on the question of what sort of person this work portrays Izumi Shikibu to be. I have already given Endō's interpretation of the entire passage. He rejects the obvious interpretation, "How can I send some frivolous message?" because the following poem seems to contain a gentle invitation—i.e., to be in a sense a frivolous message (see Iwanami text, p. 448, sup. note 11). Ozaki on the other hand finds nothing amorous in the poem, but only a feeling of a bond existing because of Prince Atsumichi's relationship to Izumi's late lover. Thus he interprets the passage to mean that Izumi is concerned for the Prince's reputation. According to Ozaki, Izumi, at first attracted because of Atsumichi's connection with Tametaka, gradually falls in love with the younger brother. He cites the similarity of Genji's attraction to Yūgao's child

Tamakazura in the *Genji monogatari*, and notes that the poems exchanged between Genji and Tamakazura are also allusive variations on the "tachibana" poem, and very similar to Izumi's. (See Introduction, p. 50; *Genji monogatari* [II], *NKBT*, XV, 410, 411; *Kōchū*, pp. 10, 11.) Tamai, *Shinchū*, p. 70, has still another opinion on the nature of Izumi's poem. He regards it as extremely meaningful and seductive, and on these grounds to be contrasted with something "hakanaki." Shimizu deals with this passage at length in *"Izumi Shikibu nikki no issetsu—*'hakanaki koto' ni furete," *Kokubungaku kō* (Nov. 1958), pp. 79–82. He concludes that "nani ka wa" is an elliptical expression meaning "How can I send him a prose message?" From a study of the use of *hakanaki* in the *Nikki* he concludes that a "hakanaki koto" probably means a poem, and is to be contrasted with "kotoba." Izumi thinks it would be more acceptable to address the Prince, who has as yet no scandalous reputation, by means of a poem (a conventional trifle), than in a prose message.

The interpretations proposed by Endō and by Shimizu seem equally plausible. I have roughly followed Endō in my translation. In order to follow Shimizu however all that would be necessary would be to change "But then, as yet he had no name . . ." to "How could she, when as yet he had no name . . . ?" Ozaki's ideas are interesting, but I cannot agree that there is no trace of seductive invitation in Izumi's poem. Though still in mourning for one brother, it seems obvious that she is at least intrigued by the other. Otherwise she could have written a poem as conventionally discouraging as hers is conventionally encouraging. It is noteworthy that a few lines farther on she criticizes herself for being easily swayed.

18. This poem is of course an allusive variation on the anonymous *Kokinshū* poem previously quoted. The *hototogisu*, usually translated "cuckoo," was a favorite bird of *waka* poets, associated with summer and the *tachibana* tree and its cries with the pangs of love. Here the *hototogisu* is a metaphor for Prince Atsumichi. Endō, Shimizu, Tamai, and Yamagishi interpret the poem to mean, "Rather than dwell on the associations with the late Prince, your brother, aroused by your gift of orange blossom, I wish I could meet you and discover whether you are the same sort of person as he." Ozaki, *Kōchū*, p. 9, however sees no comparison implied between Prince Tametaka and Prince Atsumichi. Izumi simply wants to meet the latter rather than merely think about him. I find this interpretation unacceptable however for what Izumi would "associate with the fragrance" (ka ni yosouru) of the flowering orange would surely be the memory of "mukashi no hito," her late lover.

A more nearly literal rendering of Izumi's poem would be: "Rather than associate memories of the late Prince with the sweet-smelling fragrance, O *hototogisu*, would I could hear your voice and learn whether it is the same as his voice." The poem appears also as *Seishū* 226 and as *Senzaishū* 968.

19. *Hashi* (the edge); the outermost edge of a Heian house of the *shinden-zukuri* type was a narrow veranda running all the way around the building.

20. My translation of this sentence is an expansion and interpretation of the

original, which runs: "Mada hashi ni owashimashikeru ni, kono warawa kakure no kata ni keshikibamikeru kehai o goran-jitsukete" (Still out on the veranda, he saw this boy, in the hidden direction, with a significant expression). "Kakure no kata" (the hidden direction) I have interpreted along lines suggested by Tamai, *Shinchū*, p. 71. Note that this abrupt change of scene is the first of many obvious departures from the viewpoint proper to a diary or other first-person narrative.

21. A more nearly literal translation: "Do you not know that the *hototogisu* which perched singing on the same branch has a voice which is not different from his?" I.e., we grew up together and are the same sort of person. This poem appears as *Seishū* 227, with "mono to shiranamu" (I would have you know) instead of "mono to shirazu ya" as the last line, and as *Shinsenzaishū* 1739 with a text identical to that in the *Nikki*.

22. This poem appears also as *Shinchokusenshū* 643.

23. More literally: "Instead of this heart of yours of the space of today, consider my heart which passes its time in nothing but continuous idle gazing." This poem appears as *Shinchokusenshū* 644. The final line is "sugusu tsukihi o" (the days and months I have passed).

24. *Tokidoki*. Endō, Iwanami text, p. 401, interprets this as "an answer to each."

25. I have translated "aware naru onmonogatari kikoesase ni," more literally, "to tell tales filled with sad emotion," as "to talk about the things that lie close to our hearts." I have also reversed the order of this sentence and the Prince's poem, which precedes it in the original, because I felt that to do so in this instance improved the sequence of expression. It may be noted that the Prince here uses the honorific *on* 御 for his own speech. This could be an example of the author (Izumi?) unconsciously expressing her respect for the Prince. But it seems analogous to the modern use of honorifics in such locutions as "Chotto otazune shimasu" (May I inquire?). For other examples of self-applied honorifics see notes 42, 348, and 366.

26. A question exists whether "Nagusamu koto mo ari ya sen" refers to solace for Izumi, for Prince Atsumichi, or for both. Grammatically, any of the three alternatives is possible. Endō, Iwanami text, p. 448, sup. note 17, is inclined to favor the second; Ozaki, *Kōchū*, p. 16, the third; Tamai, *Shinchū*, p. 74, Suzuki, *Zenkō*, p. 385, and Yamagishi, *NKZ*, p. 187, note 2, the first. Shimizu, *Ōchō nikki*, p. 157, is as vague as the original. I have also tried to imitate that vagueness, though I feel that the last two lines point to Izumi as the one to be comforted. Suzuki points out that the Prince is still using the memory of his late brother as an entering wedge in his campaign for Izumi's heart, but that behind his words lurks the plea that she not consider him unworthy (iu kai naku) as a lover. See pp. 59–60 for a discussion of the possible bearing of this poem on the question of the authorship of the *Izumi Shikibu nikki*.

27. "Uki koto," which I have rendered "misery," Ozaki, *Kōchū*, p. 16, interprets as "self-disgust."

28. "Oitaru ashi nite, kai naku ya" (Being "the reeds which grow," is it not useless?). Izumi is quoting and referring to a poem (which also serves as one source for her poem above) by Yamabe no Akahito (fl. early 8th century) in the third *maki* of the *Kokinwakarokujō* (*Kōchū kokka taikei*, IX, 369; the *Kokinwakarokujō* is a privately compiled anthology of the early or middle 10th century, variously attributed to Ki no Tsurayuki, to his daughter, and to Prince Kaneakira 兼明 [914–987]):

Nanigoto mo	I could not utter forth
Iwarezarikeri	A single word,
Mi no uki wa	So great my misery,
Oitaru ashi no	But only sounds of sobbing
Ne nomi nakarete	As of rustling reeds
	Grown rooted in the mire.

A more nearly literal rendition would be: "I could not say a single word. As for the misery [mire] of myself: only the sounds [roots] of the reeds which have grown are wept [swept away]." The first two lines are unambiguous. The last three however function on two levels. The primary meaning of the poem is conveyed by the words "Mi no uki wa . . . ne nomi nakarete" (As for my misery, I can but weep). But "uki wa oitaru ashi no ne nomi nagarete" can be read to mean "As for the mire, the very roots of the grown reeds drift away." These lines are built on a triple word play involving *uki* 憂き (miserable) and *uki* 涯 (mire); *ne* 音 (sound) and *ne* 根 (root); and *nakarete* 泣かれて (being wept) and *nagarete* 流れて (drifting away). "Uki" and "ne" are *kakekotoba;* "oitaru ashi no" is a *jokotoba* or "preface," applying only to the secondary level of meaning, and tied into the primary level through the *kakekotoba* "ne." The secondary level contributes the image of the strengthless reeds, an image which expands the poem and intensifies its tone. In my translation I have combined the two levels in interpreting "ashi no ne" as "the rustling of the reeds," and have applied this interpretation to my expanded version of Izumi's allusion, "oitaru ashi nite," as more effectively conveying her meaning and that of the poem she quotes. I have omitted the "nakarete/nagarete" word play, which in any case is not noted by the commentators. "Oitaru" 生ひたる (grown) could also be written 老いたる (grown old), a meaning which would be suitable to the idea of rustling reeds.

29. *Ukon no Jō*. The Konoefu was the senior (in the sense that its officers ranked higher) of the three imperial guard groups, the others being the Emonfu (Gate Guards) and the Hyōefu (Military Guards). The Konoefu (Headquarters of the Inner Palace Guards) was entrusted with guarding the inner compound of the Palace. Its men kept order at court and accompanied the Emperor on his progresses. Like the other guard groups, and the court bureaucratic structure in general, the Konoefu was divided into left and right branches. Each branch was officered by (in descending order): Taishō 大將, Chūjō 中將, Shōshō 少將,

Shōgen 將監 , and Shōsō 將曹 . The Shōgen (lieutenant) is the officer in question here. He is referred to as "Jō" because the officials of each branch and level of the government bureaucracy were grouped into four classes (*Shitōkan* 四等官): (1) Kami 長官 (Head Official); (2) Suke 次官 (Assistant Head Official); (3) Jō 判官 (Secretary); and (4) Sakan 主典 (Clerk). In the case of the Konoefu, the Taishō was in the first class (Kami), the Chūjō and Shōshō in the second class (Suke), the Shōgen in the third class (Jō), and the Shōsō in the fourth class (Sakan). The officers of the Jō class, especially those of the guard groups, were also called "Hōgan" or "Hangan," readings of the characters 判官, arbitrarily read "Jō" in the enumeration of the *Shitōkan*. Thus in the Konoefu, Shōgen=Jō=Hōgan (*Yūsoku kojitsu jiten*, pp. 404, 405).

30. "Shinobite mono e yukan." *Mono* used in this sense was a filler word employed to convey a meaning which would be clear enough to the reader or hearer without being more specific. Such vagueness is typical of this sort of Heian prose (see *Kōchū*, p. 18). "Tonight" has been supplied in translation.

31. "Sanameri" (So it seems).

32. "Onkuruma." The Prince's vehicle is presumably an ox-drawn carriage. As a *kuruma* it is at least a wheeled vehicle of some sort. An unobtrusive (here *ayashiki*, "odd" or "humble") carriage was a common element of disguise used by noble lovers on the way to secret assignations.

33. "To explain who had come" is an expansion and interpretation of " 'kaku namu' to iwasetamaereba" (caused him to say, "Thus").

34. *Tsumado,* double doors which opened on the *sunoko* (or *hashi*—see note 19), a narrow veranda, at each corner of the *shinden-zukuri* type of Heian dwelling.

35. For a discussion of the meaning of *namamekashi*, which I have translated as "a courtly refinement," see Yoshizawa Yoshinori, *Genji monogatari imakagami* (1948), pp. 267–298.

36. Or "shone forth" (sashiidenu). Note that the lady and her lover are on the western side of the house. A position on the southwest corner of the veranda however might enable the Prince to receive the direct light of even a late-rising moon (apparently it is past the middle of the month—see Introduction, pp. 72–73).

37. "Ito akashi" can also be interpreted as part of the following dialogue, and is so taken by Yamagishi.

38. This is a difficult passage. The original, punctuated as in *Kōchū*, p. 18, runs: " 'Sono owasuru tokoro ni suetamae. Yomo sakizaki mitamauran hito no yō ni wa araji' to notamaeba 'Ayashi. Koyoi nomi koso kikoesasuru to omoihabere. Sakizaki wa itsu ka wa.' " The difficulties revolve around the meaning of "sakizaki" and "ran" and the proper punctuation. The traditional and most obvious interpretation of the Prince's part of the dialogue is " 'Surely it would not be as with the men whom I suppose you have been seeing up to now,' he said." This is the interpretation made by Ozaki, Tamai, and Yamagishi. Endō however posits another case of *bummyaku no oremagari*, and punctuates thus: "Yomo, sakizaki mitamauran, hito no yō ni wa araji," which he interprets:

"Surely—as you will see in time to come—I shall not behave as others do" (Iwanami text, p. 401, note 36; pp. 448, 449, sup. note 20). Suzuki, *Zenkō*, pp. 387–390, follows Endō in giving "sakizaki" a future significance, but interprets it as modifying "araji" rather than "mitamauran"—"Yomo sakizaki, mitamauran, hito no yō ni wa araji" (Definitely from this point on—as you no doubt can imagine—I shall not act as the ordinary man would). According to *Dai Nihon kokugo jiten*, ed. Matsui Kanji and Ueda Mannen (1928), II, 699, *sakizaki* has two opposite temporal meanings—time gone by and time yet to come. Examples are given only for the former meaning. The meaning of *sakizaki* is also discussed in *Kōchū*, pp. 20–22, and in Miyake Kiyoshi, " 'Sakizaki' no igi," *Kokugo-kokubun* (April 1955), pp. 48–51. Both Ozaki and Miyake maintain that *sakizaki* must have a past meaning, or be equivalent to "up to the present." Endō agrees that examples from Heian literature indicate that such is usually the case, but maintains that the auxiliary verb *ramu* (often contracted to *ran* in the Heian Period) cannot have a past significance, and hence reinterprets "sakizaki mitamauran" as having a future reference. He asserts, as quoted in *Kōchū*, p. 21, that in order to make a past meaning possible, the verb should be *mitamaikemu* (see also *Shinkō*, pp. 61–86).

Since the function of *ramu* is to express conjecture or supposition about a matter of the present or one in which time is not a factor, and that of *kemu* is similarly to express conjecture about past actions or states, such a view would at first glance seem to be correct (*kemu* is analyzed by Masako Yokoyama, "The Inflections of 8th-Century Japanese," *Language*, vol. XXVI, no. 3, suppl. [July–Sept. 1950], p. 30, as a combination of the perfective morph (*i*)*ke*, plus the presumptive morph *m*, plus the indicative morph *u*. *Kemu* is thus an aggregate of suffix morphs. *Ramu* however is treated in the same work, pp. 21, 22, as a separate verb meaning "seems, is likely"). Miyake, " 'Sakizaki' no igi," p. 51, however asserts that the use of *kemu* would indicate that the matter expressed by it was already a thing of the past—i.e., that Izumi was no longer seeing the gentlemen. *Ramu* furthermore can be used to express conjecture about the past, as for instance in a construction such as *mitamaitsuran hito* (a person I suppose you have seen). The present case however is not one of *mitamaitsuran*, but of *mitamauran*. Miyake deals with this difficulty by proposing that *ramu* can function simply to add an indirect or softening effect to a statement, and by asserting that such is its function in this case. It would simply be too impolite for the Prince to say "mitamau hito."

None of the proposed solutions seems entirely satisfactory. However as Suzuki points out (*Zenkō*, p. 389), it is inappropriate for the Prince at the very outset of his courtship to make a somewhat caustic allusion to other lovers. Nor does "hito no yō ni wa araji" appear to fit as an allusion to Prince Tametaka, derogatory in tone as it is. Since the grammatical issues are confused, I have decided to let the psychological probabilities of the passage be the governing consideration, and have followed Endō in my interpretation.

39. Ozaki, *Kōchū*, p. 23, suggests that "yogatari" has two meanings—世語

(tale of our relationship) as well as 夜語 (night tales).

40. This poem turns on a pun on "nuru," which is both the *rentaikei* of the verb *nu* 寝 (to sleep) and the *shūshikei* of the verb *nuru* 濡る (to become wet). In the previous poem the Prince has suggested that they will be wasting their night unless they sleep (dream) together. Izumi takes him up in her reply, saying, "As for going to sleep at night (yo to tomo ni nuru to wa), all that happens is that my sleeves become wet with my tears (nuru to wa sode o). There is no night when I, longing for him [Prince Tametaka], can tranquilly dream dreams (Omou mi mo/Nodoka ni yume o/Miru yoi zo naki)." "Sode o omou mi" (I who think of my [wet] sleeves) is also a possible reading. In this case "sleeves" serves as a metaphor for "sorrow." Thus Izumi rejects the Prince's suggestion, saying she is still too sadly distraught for "dreams," either of the literal or figurative kind. In order to convey an effect akin to the pun on "nuru," I have introduced the verb "sink" and the noun "waves" to go with the wet sleeves.

41. "Maite" (=*mashite*, "especially"). Endō interprets this one-word remark as meaning that the lady's sleeplessness is even worse now that the first anniversary of the late Prince's death is approaching (Iwanami text, p. 402, note 3). Tamai, *Shinchū*, p. 220, agrees. Ozaki, *Kōchū*, p. 23, however understands the passage to mean that Izumi's sleeplessness—caused by thinking about Prince Tametaka—is made worse by Prince Atsumichi's inconsiderate conduct. I have followed Suzuki, *Zenkō*, p. 92.

42. Only the *Sanjōnishibon* has "on'ariki"; the other texts all lack the honorific. It seems odd that the Prince should employ it concerning his own action (but see notes 25, 348, 366). Shimizu, *Ōchō nikki*, p. 161, note 4, suggests its use may indirectly reflect the author's respect for the Prince.

43. The original reads: "Nasakenaki yō ni wa obosu tomo. Makoto ni monoosoroshiki made koso oboyure." Endō, Iwanami text, p. 449, sup. notes 23, 24, interprets this as consitituting an apology and an excuse for the Prince's action: "Though you may think me lacking in consideration, I really do feel 'monoosoroshiki.'" "Monoosoroshiki" he interprets as a set expression: "This really is a case of 'monoosoroshiki' (being somehow afraid)." He does not believe it means "afraid of the force of my own love," however. Tamai and Shimizu concur, and interpret "monoosoroshiki" as expressing the Prince's putative fear of discovery in so bright a place, previously expressed in his statement, "ito hashitanaki kokochi suru." I have based my translation on this last interpretation. Ozaki, *Kōchū*, pp. 23, 24, has a different view: The Prince is apologizing for future apparent negligence. The Prince's intent may be glossed thus: "Now I am going to come in, and we shall become lovers. But I am a person who cannot go out whenever he pleases. You may think me lacking in feeling (nasakenaki) because of the infrequency of my visits, but in fact I am frightened by the strength of my own love (makoto ni monoosoroshiki made koso oboyure)." This seems perhaps a little too much protestation in advance; Ozaki cites a similar case from the *Genji monogatari* however.

44. This sentence is an expansion and interpretation of "ayashū koso"

(certainly strange).

45. This poem appears as *Shinchokusenshū* 825. It was customary when a gentleman paid a nocturnal visit to his lady to exchange poems as soon as he had returned home the next morning. These messages were known as *kinuginu no fumi* 後朝の文. The expression *kinuginu*, also written 衣衣, literally refers to the clothing (*kinu* 衣) which the lovers donned once more in the morning before parting, and came to have the meaning of "the next morning," and of the parting itself. In these next-morning poems it was naturally customary to speak of love (*koi*); hence the Prince's first line, "Koi to ieba," indicates he fears Izumi may think his feelings are merely conventional. The custom of *kinuginu* is described in *Ōchō nikki*, pp. 165–168.

46. This poem appears as *Shinchokusenshū* 826, with the final line reading "Omou mi nareba" (since I am one who thinks), and as *Seishū* 868 (820).

47. A more nearly literal version: "Even had I waited, this is the very way things would have been: unthought-of, today's dusk." This poem appears as *Seishū* 869 (821), and as *Senzaishū* 843, where the first line is given as "Matsu tote mo," and the fifth as "Aki no yūgure" (see Introduction, p. 61).

48. *Kita no kata* (northern direction) was the term used to designate the official wife of a nobleman. The expression originated in the location of her quarters (*kita no tai*) in the Heian mansion. Prince Atsumichi's *kita no kata* was the daughter of Fujiwara no Naritoki (see Introduction, pp. 12–13). Naritoki was the son of Great Minister of the Left Morotada (920–969) and grandson of the Sesshō and Kampaku Tadahira (880–949). Naritoki rose to Senior Second Rank (see below), and held the offices of Dainagon and Sakonoe Taishō (for the latter, see note 29; for the former, Introduction, note 4). The Heian court aristocracy below the level of Princes of the Blood (Shinnō) was divided into eight numbered ranks (*kurai* or *i* 位). Each rank in turn was divided into a Senior and Junior (*shō* 正 and *ju* 從). From the Fourth Rank on down the ranks were further subdivided into Upper and Lower (*jō* 上 and *ge* 下) levels. Below the numbered ranks was the Initial Rank (*shoi* 初位), divided into Greater (*dai* 大) and Lesser (*shō* 少), and subdivided into Upper and Lower. The system came to a total of thirty rank levels.

49. The *Gunsho ruijūbon* reading of "Komiya no onhate made wa itō soshi-rareji to tsutsumu mo" (His caution in being most careful to avoid criticism until the end of [the period of mourning for] the late Prince) would justify the translation in *Diaries of Court Ladies of Old Japan*, p. 158: "Perhaps he will reserve himself until the mourning for the late Prince is over." The *Sanjōnishibon* reads: "Komiya no hate made soshiraresasetamaishi mo, kore ni yorite zo kashi to oboshitsutsumu mo." The end of the period of mourning would be the first anniversary of Tametaka's death, the thirteenth of the sixth month of Chōhō 5 (1003).

50. Tamai, *Shinchū*, p. 82, interprets "nengoro ni wa obosarenu nameri kashi" as meaning that the Prince, because of his passion, is not fully able to implement his decision to be cautious. Note that this passage is a direct comment

on the Prince from the viewpoint of the author, not of the heroine. This could be an example of "Izumi's mask slipping" (see Introduction, p. 89).

51.　The Prince turns Izumi's own words, "matamashi mo" (even if I had been waiting), against her.

52.　"Koko ni wa." This is an example of the fusing of prose and verse; "koko ni wa" leads directly into the poem and is logically a part of it.

53.　"Mukashi" is interpreted by the commentators to mean "mukashi no hito"—the late Prince. The *Sanjōnishibon* reads "saki" in place of "e ni" in the last line. Endō, Ozaki, Tamai, and Shimizu have adopted the "e ni" 縁に reading found in the *Kangembon* and *Ōeibon* texts. Yamagishi preserves "saki."

54.　"Nagusamezu wa [or nagusamezuba] tsuyu" (to be uncomforted [is to be like] the dew), apparently an allusion to *Gosenshū* 1032:

Nagusamuru	My dew-like life
Koto no ha ni dani	Which has no single word
Kakarazu wa	To comfort it
Ima mo kienubeki	Must perish in a moment like the dew
Tsuyu no inochi o	Without a leaf to cling to.

The pun is on "koto no ha" ("word," but also *ha* [leaf]). Ozaki, *Kōchū*, p. 30, also quotes *Shōwa kan'yaku Izumi Shikibu nikki* as suggesting an allusion to a poem by Ariwara no Shigeharu 滋春 (dates unknown), *Kokinshū* 451:

Inochi tote	Since it is difficult
Tsuyu o tanomu ni	To depend on dew
Katakereba	To sustain one's life,
Monowabishira ni	They cry in misery,
Naku nobe no mushi	The insects of the fields.

This is an example of a *butsumeika* 物名歌 , a type of poem in which the name of something is concealed in the verse. In this case the "thing" is *nigatake* 苦竹 (bitter bamboo), a kind of bamboo so named for the bitter taste of its sprouts. "Nigatake" will be found concealed in the words "tanomu ni katakereba."

55.　I have followed Ozaki, *Kōchū*, pp. 30, 31, in interpreting "uiuishū" as "troublesome" or "annoying." The other commentators give it its usual meaning of "unaccustomed" or "i　　　　　 d." To me it seems unlikely that it is inexperience on the Prince's pa　　 events him from making a second visit. Ozaki quotes several examples 　　the *Genji* to support his interpretation.

56.　*Tsugomori no hi*: "the day　when the moon goes into seclusion [*tsuki komoru* 月籠る]." Under a lunar calendar the month of course extends from new moon to new moon. The day referred to in this case is the last of the fourth month.

57.　The *hototogisu* sang softly and in the shade of the trees throughout the fourth month, but loud and clear from the treetops or the open sky thereafter. The *hototogisu* is of course Prince Atsumichi (cf. Izumi's first poem), and Izumi is asking for another clandestine visit.

58. I.e., from today on I shall go to you openly.

59. "Mono e mairan tote" (thinking to go respectfully somewhere).

60. Sōji or shōjin 精進, a meditation on religious matters and avoidance of defiling influences, including relations with the opposite sex.

61. Another example of the use of uchi ni (see note 12). The original here reads: "Onna wa mono e mairan tote sōji shitaru uchi ni, ito madō naru mo kokorozashi naki nameri to omoeba, koto ni mono nado mo kikoede." I have followed Ozaki and Tamai in this case. Yamagishi, Suzuki, and Endō favor a temporal interpretation.

62. A more nearly literal rendering: "Indeed, not yet had I known such a way: although one has met [one's lover], to stay up all night without meeting [intimately]." In the original the following comment, "asamashiku," is logically and grammatically part of the poem.

63. Izumi takes the verb au (to meet) from the Prince's poem, and says that not even her eye[lids] meet—i.e., that she cannot sleep because of the way he has neglected her. "Me no au toki mo nashi" also means "There is no time when [you] meet [your] mate (me 妻)."

64. This poem and the following sentence pose difficult problems. The poem is obviously in reply to the Prince's message, which contains two questions: "Are you going to the temple today?" and "When will you come back?" It presumably in some way answers one of these questions.

A more nearly literal prose rendering would be: "When the moment is past, then indeed [x] end[s]—fifth-month-raining, tonight I would, perhaps, hang up the iris root." The reference to iris root (ayame no ne) is clearly an allusion to the festival day tango 端午, also known as ayame no sekku 菖蒲の節句, which fell on the fifth of the fifth month. Various customs having to do with iris (ayame or shōbu) became associated with this day. The iris was valued for its medicinal qualities; it was thought to purge evils and prolong life. Hence one of the tango customs practiced at court was to drink sake in which iris root had been steeped. Another was to bathe in water in which sōji roots and leaves had been placed. Iris was also placed beneath the pillow and plaited into garlands worn on the head. And it was the practice of all, both aristocrats and commoners, to cover the eaves of their houses with iris on the night of the fourth. The present reference is evidently to kusudama 薬玉, iris and other flowers bound together with threads of five colors into a circular decoration which was hung on curtains, pillars, and the sleeves of garments. (See Kokon yōrankō, ed. Kokusho Kankōkai, I [1905], 766–805; Nihon rekishi daijiten, XII, 239; Daihyakkajiten, ed. Shimonaka Yasaburō, XVI [1935], 603; Izumi Shikibu seishū 731—734 [706–709].)

On one level at least, Izumi's poem seems to mean, "Since when their proper day (tango, the fifth of the fifth month) is past, the irises I have prepared will be of no use, I would like to hang them up on this rainy night." (There is an expression, muika no ayame [the iris of the sixth], which is used to describe something whose time has passed, and which is now of no use.) "Samidarete" (falling of fifth-month rains) sets the season and adds to the tone. The *samidare* are the drenching rains of early summer.

What we have then so far is a poem written on the fifth, in which Izumi says that she wants or intends (*mashi* can mean either) to put on (or up) her iris decorations that night before it is too late. But how does this answer the Prince's questions? The solution lies in the fact that "ne" here functions in the double meaning of "root" 根 and "sound" 音, and "ne o kaku" 音を掛く is an idiom for "to visit." Thus the hidden meaning of Izumi's poem begins to emerge: she wishes to make a visit before the acceptable time is past. The usual interpretation, followed by Endō, Suzuki, and Yamagishi, is that Izumi is answering the Prince's question, "Are you going to the temple today?" by replying, "Yes, I am going tonight before I lose my chance." Tamai, *Shinchū*, p. 87, however has a more ingenious idea. He bases it on the words following the poem, which in the *Sanjōnishibon* read "to koso omoitamaubekarinubekere," and which he interprets to mean, "This [what I have said in my poem] is the way you should think." In other words, Izumi has written a poem telling the Prince what she wishes he would say. The poem itself Tamai glosses to the effect that if time keeps slipping by, the relationship of Izumi and the Prince will come to an end. Since they cannot go on in this way, he will visit her tonight like the falling of the fifth-month rains. I think this is, grammatically at least, a feasible as well as an interesting interpretation, though it does not answer the Prince's questions.

Ozaki sees the poem as an answer to the question, "When are you coming back?" If it is possible to come back on this rainy night of the fifth to hang the iris roots to her sleeves (to meet the Prince), she would like to do so, but she cannot give him a definite reply. This interpretation he supports by rejecting the rather eccentric *Sanjōnishibon* reading of "to koso omoitamaubekarinubekere" in favor of the reading found in *Ōeibon* texts: "to koso omoitamae kaerinubekere" (just so I think and should return). This version has its grammatical problems too (see *Zenkō*, p. 397; *Kōchū*, pp. 36, 37; Iwanami text, p. 450, sup. note 32). Suzuki has also adopted the *Ōeibon* reading. I have followed him in my rather free translation of it, as well as in my interpretation of the poem, which is essentially as follows (*Zenkō*, pp. 393–397): If Izumi does not go to the temple (if the moment passes), all her abstentions will have been a waste of time. Hence, although she is reluctant to go (*samidarete* contains the verb *midarete* with its additional meaning of emotional conflict or confusion) now that the Prince has complained of how lonely he will be, she still does intend to make her pilgrimage to the temple (hang up the iris roots) tonight. For a discussion of the matter of rainfall on this date, and its relation to the question of authorship, see Introduction, note 217.

65. "Ito oroka naru ni koso narinubekeredo." Tamai, *Shinchū*, pp. 87, 88, takes this to mean "I myself feel I have become a great fool, but . . . ."

66. This is another example of the blending of prose and poetry. In the original "higoro wa" leads directly into the poem and is both grammatically and logically a part of it.

67. Tamai, *Shinchū*, p. 88, interprets "wasure ya suru to" as "Will you not forget me?" Endō, Iwanami text, p. 450, sup. note 33, takes "makenan" (will lose) to be an *engo* with the "ayame" in Izumi's poem, an allusion to the game of root-matching (*neawase* 根合) played on the day of the *tango* festival, the object of which was to have the iris with the longest root.

68. An expansion and interpretation of "asakaranu kokoro no hodo o, saritomo" (the extent of my unshallow heart, even so . . .).

69. "Makuru" in this poem serves three functions. First, it refers to "makenan" in the Prince's poem: "Makuru to mo mienu" (You do not seem to have given in [to love]). Second, it contains the verb *kuru* 繰る (to reel or coil). In this sense it goes with "tamakazura," a decorative term for "vine." Third, *kuru* 來る means "to come": "Kuru to mo mienu" (You don't seem to be coming). "Kuru" 來る and "tou" (visit) are *engo*, as are "kuru" 繰る, "tamakazura," "taemagachi" (tending to break off), and "hitosuji" (one tendril). The poem can best be understood if the order is reversed to read: "Tamakazura tou hitosuji mo taemagachi nite, makuru to mo mienu mono kara" (Even one visiting tendril of vine is becoming rare [you hardly ever visit me at all any more], and therefore it does not seem to be coiling/coming [you do not seem to be coming/you do not seem to have given in to love], but still . . .). "Mono kara" carries the adversative meaning of "it is the case, but . . ." I have interpreted the "but" as "but still I wait," as has Endō, Iwanami text, p. 405, note 20. Yamagishi, *NKZ*, p. 194, note 17, and Tamai, *Shinchū*, p. 88, interpret it to mean "but still I rely on you." Ozaki, *Kōchū*, p. 37, however, favors "but still you say you've given in to love."

70. "Uchi ni." Endō as usual interprets this phrase temporally (see note 12). I have followed Ozaki and Tamai.

71. *Maki* 眞木, which I have translated as "pine-wood," was a decorative term for woods used in building, such as *hinoki* 檜 (cypress), *sugi* 杉 (cryptomeria), what is now called *maki* 槇 (Chinese black pine), etc., according to Tamai, *Shinchū*, p. 89.

72. "Uki wa kore ni ya" (Does misery consist of this?). Yamagishi, *NKZ*, pp. 194, 195, note 4, suggests a reference to *Gosenshū* 1046 (Anonymous):

Majikakute	Bitter though it is
Tsuraki o miru wa	To find how cold you are
Ukeredomo	When we are close,
Uki wa mono ka wa	What matters misery
Koishiki yori wa	Beside the love I feel?

According to its headnote, the poem was written to someone who, though friendly, would not make love. The poem's conclusion does not seem to match the Prince's feelings as I have interpreted them; the reference seems rather doubtful.

73. "Misetaraba," a reference to an anonymous poem, *Shūishū* 672:

Hito shirenu	If only I could show
Kokoro no uchi o	What lies within my heart
Misetaraba	That none can see!
Ima made tsuraki	There is no person cold
Hito wa araji na	As you have said I am.

Tamai, *Shinchū*, p. 90, suggests that "misetaraba" means also, "If I had shown you the inside of my house, you would have understood."

74. "Uchi ni." The same comment applies as in note 70.

75. *Uchi no Otodo* 内大殿, another name for the Naidaijin 内大臣 (Great Minister of the Center), the fourth-ranking official of the Daijōkan (see Introduction, note 4). The holders of this office were nobles of the Second Rank. The Naidaijin referred to here is Fujiwara no Kinsue 公季 (957–1029), the paternal uncle of Yukiko, the consort of Reizei and mother of Princes Tametaka and Atsumichi. Kinsue served as Naidaijin from 997 to 1017, at which time he was promoted to Udaijin 右大臣 (Great Minister of the Right). He was Atsumichi's great uncle.

76. *Togū* 春宮 ("Spring Palace," also written 東宮, "Eastern Palace") was a term for the Heir Apparent, or for his residence. Various explanations are given. In Chinese geomantic relationships, east was the direction of spring, and spring has the connotation of new growth. Further—according to the ancient Chinese book of divination, the *I-ching* 易經—east is the direction of the trigram *chen* 震, written ☳, which symbolizes among other things the eldest son. And finally, in China the palace of the Heir Apparent was historically to the east of that of the Emperor (*Kōchū*, pp. 40, 41; *Yūsoku kojitsu jiten*, p. 593; *Nihon rekishi daijiten*, XIII, 211). The Heir Apparent in this case was Prince Okisada 居貞, the brother of Atsumichi, and future Emperor Sanjō. One of his consorts was Jōshi, elder sister of Atsumichi's wife (see Introduction, p. 12; translation, note 373).

77. An expansion and interpretation of "mi no areba koso to omoite sugusu," which is an allusion to *Shūishū* 930 (Anonymous):

Izukata ni	Whither shall I go
Yukikakurenamu	To hide myself?
Yo no naka ni	As long as I
Mi no areba koso	Am living in this world
Hito mo tsurakere	People will be cruel.

78. A closer translation: "Do you think, I wonder, it is falling as the usual fifth-month rain, this long rain [gazing] of today which loves you without end?" This poem and the next manage to convey the conceit of tears of longing falling in the form of rain without using the word for "tears," a feat I have been unable to duplicate in translation.

79. A closer translation: "I did not know it was something seemingly love-

longing; I merely thought it was rain which knew my own self." There is evidently an allusion to a poem by Ariwara no Narihira, *Kokinshū* 705. The poem, which appears also in the *Ise monogatari*, episode 107, is supposed to have been written by Narihira to Fujiwara no Toshiyuki 敏行 (d. 901). The latter, who was wooing a girl in Narihira's household, wrote saying he would go to her immediately if it were not for the rain. Narihira replied in the girl's stead:

Kazukazu ni	Because I cannot easily inquire
Omoi omowazu	Whether you think many loving thoughts,
Toigatami	Or whether you do not,
Mi o shiru ame wa	This rain that knows my own heart's woe
Furi zo masareru	Falls faster than the other.

"Mi o shiru ame," in short, is a metaphor for "tears," and Narihira is saying that the girl weeps harder than the rain rains. Among other poems by Izumi Shikibu using the same metaphor is the following, *Seishū* 633 (608):

Mishi hito ni	Dwelling forgotten
Wasurarete furu	By the man I once did see,
Sode ni koso	I find the rain that knows
Mi o shiru ame no	My heart of hearts
Itsu mo oyamane	Forever falls upon my sleeves.

80. "Kami no hitoe o hikikaeshite." Or perhaps not on the back of the same sheet, but on the reverse of the *raishi* 禮紙, one or more sheets of ordinarily blank paper folded around the outside of the message (see *Zenkō*, pp. 397–399; *Nihon bungaku daijiten*, VII, 324).

81. A closer translation: "Whereas, since it is raining [since I am passing time], all that can be known is the exceeding unpleasantness of this world, I would that with today's long rain the water might increase." "Fureba" is the usual *kakekotoba: furu* 降る (to rain)/*fu* 經 (to pass time). This poem appears also in *maki* 19 of the *Fubokuwakashō* 夫木和歌抄 (see *Fubokuwakashō*, ed. Ichijima Kenkichi [1906], p. 546).

82. "Machitoru kishi ya." Ozaki, *Kōchū*, p. 44, suggests that Izumi may be referring to *higan* 彼岸, the "Further Shore" of Buddhism, i.e., rebirth into paradise. As an example of Izumi's concern with such thoughts he cites *Zokushū* 174 (1016):

Haruka naru	Although I surely see
Kishi o koso mire	That distant shore,
Amabune ni	I cannot row to it
Nori ni idezuba	Unless I get on board
Kogiidezaramashi	The fishing vessel of the Law.

248

This poem turns on two *kakekotoba*: *ama* 蜑 (fisherman)/*ama* 尼 (nun); and *nori* 乘り (get on board)/*nori* 法 (Buddhist Law). In other words, the poet says she cannot hope to reach the "Further Shore" unless she becomes a nun and devotes her life to religion.

Another example cited by Ozaki is *Seishū* 835 (808), addressed to the "Sage of Harima" (Shōkū Shōnin):

Fune yosemu	Because I know no mark
Kishi no shirube mo	To guide me to that shore
Shirazu shite	Whither I would steer my ship,
E mo kogiyoranu	I cannot reach, for all my rowing,
Harimagata kana	The strand of Harima.

83. "Ame no shita" is both 天の下 ("the under-heaven," i.e., the world) and 雨の下 (beneath the rain). "Furu" is the usual *kakekotoba* on 降る and 經る (see note 81).

84. For a proposed solution to the problem of this date see Introduction, p. 74. A flashback seems out of the question because, aside from the historical fact of no rain on the fifth, Izumi is described as absent on a temple visit for a few days starting on that date. Also, the context indicates no break from the immediately preceding passage.

85. This poem appears also as *Seishū* 228.

86. "Kage ni inagara ayashiki made nan" (Though I am under shelter, to an extent to be wondered at . . .). The allusion is to a poem by Ki no Tsurayuki, *Shūishū* 958:

Furu ame ni	Though I went out
Idete mo nurenu	Into the falling rain
Waga sode no	My sleeves would not be wet,
Kage ni inagara	Yet here within this sheltered place
Hijimasaru kana	How sodden they become!

87. This poem hinges on the *kakekotoba* "tsuma." The most important sense of the word here is its meaning of "husband" 夫. It also has an architectural meaning, usually interpreted as *nokiba* 軒端 (the eaves), from *tsuma* 端 (edge). *Tsuma*, written 妻, also has a technical meaning in architecture, referring to the triangular wall under a peaked roof (*kirizuma yane* 切妻屋根), and in *shinden-zukuri* architecture specifically to that wall of the central gate corridor (*chūmon no rō* 中門の廊). The note in the *Nihon koten zensho* edition of *Izumi Shikibu shū*, p. 51, interprets "tsuma" as meaning the ridgepole (*mune* 棟). Tamai, *Shinchū*, p. 95, who prefers "eaves," believes that "saseru" also functions doubly, meaning not only "dependable," but also "locked" (鎖せる). Presumably he must be referring to the *shitomi* 蔀, a grating under the eaves, whose upper half could be hooked up to the roof, and whose lower half could be removed. It

separated the inner part of the house from the veranda (*sunoko* 簀の子). I have chosen the meaning of "eaves" as most appropriate to the situation of the poem. While I believe my translation renders the poem's intent, the grammar of the original presents problems because of its fragmentation. A plausible prose rearrangement might run: "Ware mo saseru tsuma naki yado wa ikani to omoi-yaritsuru ame no oto o sazo [kokoromotonaku obosuran to omoeri]" (I too [thought how uneasy you must feel because of] the sound of rain which made me anxiously wonder how fared a house with no husband/eaves worthy of the name). The same poem appears as *Seishū* 229, with the reading "yomosugara" (all night long) in place of "ame no oto o."

88. A flood of the Kamo 賀茂 River is recorded in *Nihon kiryaku* as having occurred on Chōhō 5 (1003).5.19 (see Introduction, p. 74).

89. The poem depends for its effect on two *kakekotoba*: *kishi* 岸 (bank), taken from the Prince's poem and used also in the meaning of *kishi* 來し (come); and *kawa*, both 川 (river) and 彼は (he). By using the same words and images, Izumi adroitly deflates the Prince's protestations. My use of the pun "bank" is of course an attempt to render the *kakekotoba* "kishi." A more nearly literal translation: "Now surely he will *not* come [bank], for all he shows the deep heart of the flood to be his own [a river]." "Kishi" 岸 and "kawa" 川 are *engo*. The pun on 川/彼は was a conventional one, as is seen in *Kokinshū* 659 (Anonymous):

Omoedo mo	Though deep in love,
Hitome tsutsumi no	I would avoid the eyes of men:
Takakereba	Those dikes of dread are high,
Kawa to minagara	And though I see her there beyond,
E koso watarane	I cannot cross the river.

Here the *kakekotoba* are "kawa" and "tsutsumi" (慎み [avoidance, hiding, dread]/堤 [embankment]). The *engo* are "hitome"—"minagara" and "tsutsumi" 堤—"kawa"川—"watarane." A more nearly literal rendering might be: "Although I think of my beloved, my avoidance of men's eyes [the embankment] is high, and so, while I see her as the one for me [while I see the river], I cannot go to her [I cannot get across] at all."

90. This was done by spreading the garment over an open-work basket placed above a censer.

91. *Jijū* 侍従, strictly speaking, was the title of a minor official (Chamberlain) in the Nakatsukasashō. It was customary for ladies at court to adopt such titles as nicknames, usually because of some connection through a husband or male relative, as in the case of Izumi Shikibu herself. Judging from Heian literature, the wet nurse seems to have had a privileged position vis-à-vis her grown-up master. Cf. p. 164.

92. "Kono koto hitobito mōsu naru wa." Endō, Iwanami text, p. 407, note 27, and Ozaki, *Kōchū*, p. 49, interpret "wa" as exclamatory in effect. Tamai, *Shinchū*, p. 98, renders it as equivalent to *tokoro dewa*: "Seken no hitobito no

mōsu tokoro dewa" (according to what people are saying), thus forming part of a clause subordinate to the following sentence.

93. I.e., to serve him as his concubine.

94. Or "these persons."

95. "Ōtono" 大殿 (the term is an honorific for "Great Ministers") is perhaps the Naidaijin Kinsue mentioned in note 75. More probably the reference is to Fujiwara no Michinaga, Atsumichi's maternal uncle. Michinaga, who held the post of Sadaijin (Great Minister of the Left) from 996 to 1017, was then the dominant figure at court. A third, more remote, possibility is Michinaga's first cousin Akimitsu 顕光 (944–1021), Udaijin (Great Minister of the Right) from 996 to 1017.

96. The death of the Kampaku Fujiwara no Michitaka in 995 ushered in a period of political turmoil at court. Michitaka was succeeded by his brother Michikane, who died a few days later, thus becoming known to history as the "Seven-Day Kampaku." Michitaka's son Korechika 伊周 (973–1010), the Great Minister of the Center, who had expected to succeed his father, was thwarted by his aunt, Akiko [Senshi] 詮子 (962–1002), the mother of the reigning Emperor Ichijō. After the death of Michikane she influenced her son to bestow upon her favorite brother, Michinaga, the authority of Nairan 内覧 (i.e., the authority to inspect imperial decrees before issuance), customarily reserved for Sesshō or Kampaku. Michinaga dominated the court from that moment until his death. In 996 he disposed of his discontented rival, his nephew Korechika. Early in that year Korechika and his brother Takaie 隆家 (979–1044) were accused of making an attack on the person of the Retired Emperor Kazan, as well as other crimes, and were sent into exile a few months later.

As a result of the disgrace, Korechika's sister Sadako [Teishi] 定子 (976–1001), the most favored of Ichijō's consorts, withdrew from the court and cut off her hair as a symbol of her intention to abandon the world and enter the religious life. She later returned to court however and bore Ichijō two more children, one of whom was his first male child, Prince Atsuyasu 敦康 (999–1019). The birth of a son strengthened the position of Sadako and Korechika, who had meanwhile been recalled from exile, and weakened that of Michinaga. On Chōhō 1 (999).11. 1, just before the birth of Sadako's son, Michinaga gave his own daughter, Akiko [Shōshi] to Ichijō as a secondary consort. In the following year she was promoted to Chūgū and Sadako to Kōgō (the second highest and highest ranks of Empress, respectively), and the stage seemed set for a prolonged rivalry with control of the imperial succession at stake. However on Chōhō 2.12.16 (13 Jan. 1001) Sadako died after bearing another child, a daughter. The danger to Michinaga's position was alleviated, but not completely removed until the birth of Akiko's own son, Prince Atsuhira 敦成, the later Emperor Go-Ichijō (r. 1016–1036), in 1008.

Other events contributing to the turmoil of the times were the deaths of Grand Empress Dowager Masako in 1000, and of Michinaga's mother Senshi and Prince Tametaka in 1002. In addition, epidemics had recurrently plagued the country for several years past, and the imperial palace had burned in 999 and again in 1001. Cf. *Ouki, Shiryō taisei*, I, 111, 114; *Nihon kiryaku, KT*, XI, 184, 185, 193, 196, 217, 192, 198, 199; *Gonki* (I), *Zōho shiryō taisei*, pp. 83, 181, 182; *Midō Kampaku ki* (I), p. 268.

97. "Tono." It is not clear whether the same person is intended as in the reference to "Ōtono." I have assumed with Endō, Iwanami text, p. 451, sup. note 46, that the same person is meant. Tamai, *Shinchū*, p. 99, and Ozaki, *Kōchū*, p. 51, interpret the sentence to mean that "his Lordship" is thinking of making Prince Atsumichi the Heir Apparent. Michinaga would be the only person in a position to make such a decision.

98. "Kaku mairikuru koto bin ashi to omou hitobito amata aru yō ni kikeba, itōshiku nan, ōkata mo tsutsumashiki uchi ni, itodo hodo henuru." "Ōkata mo tsutumashiki uchi ni" (while I was being generally [i.e., without connection to the specific circumstances of the gentlemen's attitude] circumspect) is a parenthetical expression (*bummyaku no oremagari*). This sentence is discussed in detail by Endō, *Shinkō*, pp. 150–165.

99. *Rō* 廊, covered passageways connecting the various buildings composing the Heian mansion.

100. The original runs: "Tsuki mo ito akakereba, 'Orine,' to shiite nota-maeba, asamashiki yō nite orinu." I have followed Endō, Iwanami text, p. 409, note 21; p. 451, sup. note 50, in limiting the Prince's speech to "Orine," and interpreting " 'Orine,' to shiite notamaeba" as a *bummyaku no oremagari*. Tamai, *Shinchū*, p. 101, and Yamagishi, *NKZ*, p. 201, take "Tsuki mo ito akakereba orine" in its entirety as the Prince's speech. Ozaki, *Kōchū*, p. 54, limits the speech to "Orine," but interprets "tsuki mo ito akakereba" as subordinate to "nota-maeba" rather than to "asamashiki yō nite orinu." He also interprets "shiite" to mean "in a low voice." The *Ōeibon* reading of "shinobite" (in place of "shiite") would seem to lend itself more easily to such an interpretation.

101. More literally, "Let us talk in this fashion" (Kayō nite o kikoen).

102. "Nabete narazu" (not the ordinary). Tamai, *Shinchū*, p. 103, interprets this as "extraordinarily sad"; Endō, Iwanami text, p. 409, note 29, as "splendid."

103. A closer translation: "When I compare it to what I feel when I arise on a morning when the dew is settling, an evening when I should simply go home were even beyond that." "Okuru" is a *kakekotoba:* "Asatsuyu no oku" (the settling of the morning dew)/ "okuru omoi" (the thoughts one thinks upon getting up).

104. "Kata futagaritari" (The direction is blocked up). A highly elaborate system of directional superstitions, based on Chinese astrology, was prevalent in the Heian Period. One branch of this system concerned itself with the movements of astral or seasonal deities from heaven to earth and around the points of the compass. These movements were conceived of as invisible, and distinct from observable celestial phenomena. Four such deities were especially dreaded by the court society of Izumi Shikibu's age. Each had a distinct cycle.

Ten'ichi 天一, conceived of as a minor star which had anciently been polar, accomplished his round within the sixty-day cycle of Sino-Japanese chronology.

Descending from heaven to earth on the *tsuchinoto-tori* 己酉 day, he took up his station in the northeast quarter, remaining there six days. Thence he moved to the eastern quarter, staying five days, and so on around the compass, spending five days in each of the cardinal directions, and six days in each of the intermediate ones. On the *mizunoto-mi* 癸巳 day he ascended once more to heaven, where he stayed the remaining 16 days of the cycle. Ten'ichi also had a Japanese name, written 奈加加美 in the *Wamyōruijushō* 倭名類聚抄. The characters can be read either *Nakagami* (or *-kami*) 中神 (Central Deity), or *Nagakami* 長神 (Long Deity). The correct reading is in dispute. The second reading could be justified by this deity's relatively leisurely progress as compared to that of Taihaku.

Taihaku 太白 was conceived of as the planet Venus. He accomplished his cycle three times in every lunation, i.e., once every ten days, stopping one day in each of the cardinal and intermediate directions, entering into the earth at the Center on the ninth day, and ascending to heaven on the tenth.

Daishōgun 大將軍 (the Great General) was thought to be the spirit (*sei* 精) of the same planet Venus. His cycle—around the cardinal points of the compass—took twelve years to accomplish, three years to each point. Due to a secondary cycle however he actually occupied these positions only five days out of every every sixty-day cycle.

Ōsō 王相 or 旺相 was an annual seasonal deity who spent the spring in the east, the summer in the south, the autumn in the west, and the winter in the north. Its shining however affected all directions, and its position was not the same during the first and second part of each season.

The superstitions surrounding these and other similar astral powers had extremely complex ramifications. Essentially however each time one of the above deities installed himself in one of his stations he set up a temporary directional taboo, a *katafutagari* 方塞. The most common of these interdictions, and the one at issue in the present passage, was that against lodging for the night in a place which lay in a forbidden direction in relation to the point of departure, or staying all night in such a place if one had gone there during the day. This was apparently the only prohibition imposed by Ten'ichi and Taihaku. Daishōgun, Ōsō, and other deities however also made inauspicious any construction or disturbance of the earth in the closed direction. In the case of Daishōgun the forbidden activities included taking a son-in-law, giving birth to a child, making Buddhist offerings, and building a tomb (see Bernard Frank, "*Kata-imi* et *kata-tagae*: étude sur les interdits de direction à l'époque Heian," *BMFJ*, Nouvelle Série, V [1958]).

105. "Rei no kuruma nite owashitari." Ozaki, *Kōchū*, p. 56, interprets this as "He came as usual in his carriage," rather than "He came in his usual carriage."

106. The original reads: "Ue wa In no onkata ni watarasetamau to obosu." The commentators agree in interpreting "ue" 上 as the Prince's consort. *In* 院, a large enclosed building, came to be the word used in referring to abdicated Emperors and Empresses, from their residences. Yoshida, *Kenkyū*, p. 313, takes this sentence to mean that the Prince thought his consort had left the house.

107. The reference is to a poem in *maki* 5 of the *Kokinrokujō* (*Kōchū kokka taikei*, IX, 463):

Koikoite	Unending our love,
Mare ni au yo no	But seldom the nights we meet—
Akatsuki wa	A cruel thing
Tori no ne tsuraki	Is the cock's cry
Mono ni zarikeru	In the dawn.

108. The commentators are of the opinion that the Prince is joking.

109. Tamai, *Shinchū*, p. 106, and Shimizu, *Ōchō nikki*, p. 177, make a quite different interpretation of this poem. They think that Izumi is expressing sorrow over the death of the bird, taking "tsurasa" to mean "pitifulness" rather than "unfeelingness." My translation agrees with the interpretations of Endō, Ozaki, and Yamagishi. This poem appears also as *Seishū* 870 (822), in a form more susceptible to the sort of interpretation made by Tamai and Shimizu:

Ikaga to wa	What did it feel, that cock,
Ware koso omoe	That still we heard its cry
Asana asana	Morn after morn,
Nao kikasetsuru	I am the one who wonders,
Tori o koroseba	Now that it is slain.

But this version of the poem can also be glossed to mean "I wonder what will happen to me (who also cry each morning) now that you have killed the cock for crying," as pointed out by Ozaki, *Kōchū*, p. 58.

110. "To omoitamauru mo nikukaranu ni ya." Tamai, *Shinchū*, p. 106, and Shimizu, *Ōchō nikki*, p. 177, are obliged to interpret this, somewhat forcedly, I think, as "I feel I cannot hate it."

111. Ozaki, *Kōchū*, p. 60, interprets "Ika ni zo tsuki wa mitamau ya" as a question concerning how the moon looks to Izumi, instead of punctuating after "zo."

112. I.e., do you, as I, remember how we watched the moon together that night, and sigh that tonight we are apart?

113. This poem appears as *Seishū* 871 (823), with the following variant readings: "omoedo" for "omoeba," "nagamureba" for "nagamuredo," and "kokoro wa yukazu" for "kokoro mo yukazu."

114. More literally, "He thought, 'There is a carriage! Someone has surely come'" (Kuruma haberi. Hito no kitarikeru ni koso). Both Ozaki, *Kōchū*, p. 61, and Tamai, *Shinchū*, p. 109, suggest that Izumi is living with a younger sister, basing this supposition on the headnote to *Seishū* 748 (723): "Oya nado iu koto arikereba, shinobite harakaradomo nado, mukashi arishi yō nite monogatari suru, aware ni oboyureba" (One time when, having been censured by her parents, she secretly talked with her sisters, just as in the old times, being overcome

254

by a sense of the sadness of things). Tamai interprets this reference to parental displeasure as alluding to Izumi's separation from her husband Michisada. Ozaki and Tamai further suggest that the carriage seen by the Prince is one belonging to Ōe no Takachika, the lover of Izumi's sister (see Introduction, pp. 4, 6). Tamai would have "hitobito katagata ni sumu tokoro narikereba" refer only to Izumi and her sister.

115.   The last two lines could more literally be translated, "Today's long rain [gazing] is no ordinary thing." The reference is to *Kokinshū* 1093 (Anonymous):

Kimi o okite	Sooner than I,
Adashigokoro o	Perfidious-hearted,
Waga motaba	Shall forsake you,
Sue no matsuyama	Waves will pour across
Nami mo koenamu	The pine-clad peak of Sue.

The meaning of the Prince's poem therefore may be stated thus: "Although I have known of your faithlessness all along, last night's proof of it leaves me stunned, listlessly staring through today's long rain." "Nagame" is a *kakekotoba*: *nagame* 眺め (gaze)/*naga-ame* 長雨 (long rain).

116.   A more nearly literal translation: "As for 'the pines of Sue,' you are the one that I have been hearing about; who can go over, equal, in the same wave with you?" *Hitoshinami* 等し並 (equal to) is a *kakekotoba* containing the word *nami* 波 (wave). The poem appears as *Seishū* 872 (824), with "omoishika" (I thought) instead of "kikiwatare" (I heard) as the third line.

117.   A prose rendering: "I have had no leisure time, what with thinking of you in various ways, now as unfeeling, again as lovable."

118.   A more nearly literal translation: "As for our meeting, be it this way or that, I shall not sigh—but if our relationship should become one of undying resentment—" This poem appears also as *Seishū* 873 (825).

119.   A reference to a poem by Fujiwara no Takamitsu (see Introduction, pp. 121, 122), *Shūishū* 435. written when Takamitsu was thinking of abandoning the world:

Kaku bakari	In this our world
Hegataku miyuru	That seems so difficult
Yo no naka ni	A place to live,
Urayamashiku mo	How enviously limpid
Sumeru tsuki kana	Dwells the moon!

120.   A more nearly literal translation: "Whom would you have me tell— even if you do not come to see me—that I am looking at the moon, gazing in my desolate dwelling?" "Mi ni konu made mo" (even if you do not come to see me) is an elliptical parenthetical expression which I have, following Endō,

Iwanami text, p. 412, note 2, taken to imply "at least send me a letter."

121.   *Hisumashi warawa* 樋洗童 were young girls whose chore was cleaning chamber pots and privies.

122.   *Sudare* 簾, a screen made of reed or finely split bamboo which could be rolled up or lowered by means of strings. *Sudare* were hung (among other places) behind the *shitomi* (see note 87), between the veranda and the main part of the house, and could be lowered to provide concealment for someone sitting inside looking out.

123.   "Rei no tabigoto ni menarete mo aranu onsugata" (the usual figure which never grew stale no matter how many times she saw it).

124.   *Nōshi* 直衣, a voluminous, large-sleeved gown which was the ordinary wear of high aristocrats. It contrasted with more formal court costumes such as *sokutai* 束帯. For pictures see Ema Tsutomu, *Kokubun kojitsu fūzokugo shūshaku: yōgi fukushokuhen* (1935), pp. 358, 359; Edward Seidensticker, trans., *The Gossamer Years*, plate 4.

125.   After this sentence the following one appears to be a *non sequitur*.

126.   *Ōeibon* texts have "senzai no okashiki naka o" (*through* the pleasant garden) instead of "naka ni" (about in). If the Prince were walking *through* the garden directly toward the house, the previously noted *non sequitur* could be avoided.

127.   "Hito wa kusaba no tsuyu nare ya" (Is it because that person is dew on leaves of grass?), a reference to *Shūishū* 761 (Anonymous):

Waga omou	Is it because
Hito wa kusaba no	The one for whom I long
Tsuyu nare ya	Is dew on blades of grass
Kakureba sode no	That thoughts of love
Mazu shioruran	Should make my sleeves so limp?

"Kakureba" serves a double function: "[sonata no koto o kokoro ni] kakureba" (when I think of you)/"[tsuyu no] kakureba" (when the dew falls on my sleeves).

128.   "Tare ni shinobitsuru zo to miarawasan tote nan." This sentence is variously interpreted by the different commentators. Ozaki, *Kōchū*, p. 69, renders it, "to find out whom you are longing for," interpreting *shinobu* as 偲ぶ (to long for) rather than 忍ぶ (to keep secret). Tamai's opinion, *Shinchū*, p. 114, is similar: "tare ni . . . nan" is essentially a prose statement of the poem "Ware yue ni" which the Prince has handed to Izumi. Endō, Iwanami text, p. 412, note 24; p. 452, sup. note 63, however points out that were the verb in question 偲ぶ, the text should read "tare o shinobitsuru" instead of "tare ni . . . ." I have adopted this approach, but have rejected Endō's further opinion that "tare" refers to the man or men who are presumably visiting the woman or women in the other wing or wings (cf. the affair of the parked carriage; see note 114). I have instead followed Yamagishi, *NKZ*, p. 208, note 8, assuming that the subject of "shinobitsuru" is Izumi herself. The effective difference between

Endō and Yamagishi is very slight however for the essence of the former's interpretation is that the Prince says he has come to find out whom the man or men have really been meeting—Izumi or someone else.

129.   *Monoimi* 物忌, literally, the fear or religious avoidance of things; not necessarily the fear of direction (*kataimi*, see note 104), though Endō, Iwanami text, p. 412, note 15, interprets it in this light. The term evidently also had a more general meaning, designating a period of seclusion during which a person fasted, avoided activity and polluting influences, and in general purified himself. Bad dreams were often the occasion for such measures (*Yūsoku kojitsu jiten*, pp. 799, 800). The other commentators favor the more general meaning of *monoimi*.

130.   "Started to" is an interpretation demanded by the context. The original is simply "kaerasetamaeba" (as he went home).

131.   The moon is of course a metaphor for the Prince. A more nearly literal translation: "As an attempt, would that even the rain might fall, so that the moon's light [form], which goes beyond my house across the sky, might stop within." "Kage" in this instance could mean either "light" or "form" (sugata). Tamai, *Shinchū*, p. 115, suggests it means the moon itself. This poem appears as *Seishū* 874 (826).

132.   I have followed Endō, Ozaki, Tamai, and Yamagishi in adopting the reading "komekite" (being childlike), found in the *Kangembon* and *Fusōshūyō-shūbon*, in place of the "umekite" (groaning) of the *Sanjōnishibon* and *Ōeibon*.

133.   A closer translation: "Unpleasantly lured by the moon-of-the-dwelling-place-of-clouds, it is my form which departs; would my heart go?" *Kumoi*, written 雲居 (cloud-dwelling) or 雲井 (cloud-well), was a poetic name for the sky. "Kage" here is used in the sense of "outward form," contrasted with "kokoro."

134.   "Ikade ito ayashiki mono ni kikoshimeshitaru o, kikoshimeshinaosare-nishi gana to omou" (punctuated as in Iwanami text, p. 413). There are several variant readings of this sentence to be found among the various texts, but the crucial question is whether かな is to be read as the desiderative *gana* or the exclamatory *kana*. *Shinkō gunsho ruijū*, XIV, 460, lacks the *nigori* (sonant mark). Such a reading would justify the translation in *Diaries of Court Ladies of Old Japan*, p. 169, "He seemed to have been thinking her a worthless woman, but he had changed his mind, she thought." Yosano Akiko makes the same interpretation in her translation into modern Japanese (*Heian-chō joryū nikki*, trans. Yosano Akiko, in *Gendaigoyaku kokubungaku zenshū*, IX [1938], 310, 311). The more recent commentators and translators, including Endō, Ozaki, Tamai, Yamagishi, and Enchi Fumiko, make the interpretation necessitated by the reading "gana," as have I.

135.   *Shōshō* (Minor Captain) was the third-ranking position in the Konoefu (see note 29). It is not clear to whom reference is made here, but Ozaki, *Kōchū*, p. 71; Yamagishi, *NKZ*, p. 209, note 16; and Endō, Iwanami text, p. 413, note 23, suggest Minamoto no Masamichi 雅通 (d. 1017). *Gonki, Shiryō taisei*, XXXV, 289, entry for Chōhō 5 (1003).6.5, refers to Masamichi as Ukon Shōshō 右近少将

(Minor Captain of the Inner Palace Guards of the Right).

136. *Jibukyō* (see Introduction, note 29). The Jibukyō at this time was Mina-
mono no Toshikata 俊賢 (960–1027). Texts of the *Ōeibon* group read "Hyōbukyō" (Minister of War) instead of "Jibukyō." The Hyōbukyō at this time was
Fujiwara no Takaie (979–1044) (see note 96).

137. More literally, "She had not said one thing and another for a very long
time" (Ito hisashū nani yo ka yo to kikoesasuru koto mo naku).

138. "Tokidoki mo kaku oboshiiden hodo wa." My translation fails to
account for the "kaku." It seems odd that Izumi should say "remembers me thus,"
when this is precisely a point when the Prince is neglecting her. Perhaps her
reference is to his late abortive visit, of which she has just heard. The page apparently comes for his own purposes, and it seems doubtful that the lady could
have interpreted his call as an example of the Prince's thoughtfulness.

139. "Nazo mo kaku" (Why thus?). Ozaki, *Kōchū*, p. 73, suggests this may
be an allusion to one of two poems:

Kokinshū 934 (Anonymous):

Iku yo shi mo	Few are the years
Araji waga mi o	I now can hope to see—
Nazo mo kaku	Why then are my thoughts
Ama no karu mo ni	Thus seaweed-tangled
Omoimidaruru	In the net of vain desire?

Kokinshū 529 (Anonymous):

Kagaribi ni	How can it be that I,
Aranu waga mi no	Who am no boat-torch
Nazo mo kaku	Such as the fishers use,
Namida no kawa ni	Yet float in flames
Ukite moyuramu	Upon the river of my tears?

I should think either poem a possible reference, though the emotional situation
of neither exactly corresponds to Izumi's. I see no reason why there need be any
allusion at all, and have translated as if there were none.

140. "Uramiji" is a *kakekotoba*: 恨みじ /浦見じ—"I shall not resent"/ "I
shall not look at the shore." The imagery and action of the rest of the poem
spring from this pun, but also apply metaphorically to Izumi. "Ura" (bay),
"iso" (strand), "kogi" (row), "ama" (fisherwoman), and "obune" (little boat)
are all *engo*.

141. This poem is complicated by several puns. "Sode no ura" is a *kakekotoba*:
Sodenoura 袖浦 ("Sleeve Bay," an *utamakura* 歌枕 or famous place name frequently used in poetry)/*sode no ura* 袖の裏 (lining of my sleeves). "Yaku" also
has two meanings: 役 (duty) and 燒く (burn). And "shio tarete" has both its

literal meaning of "dripping brine" and its metaphorical one of "shedding tears." A prose gloss might run: "I am indeed that *ama* [海士, 蜑, etc., a person who makes his living from the sea, by fishing, gathering shellfish, making salt, etc.] whose function is simply to carry [pails of] brine at Sode Bay [in order to make salt by] burning [or: whose only function is to shed tears on the lining of her sleeves], and who has let her boat drift away." Though complicated in explanation, the poem is a cleverly effective reply to that of the Prince. Izumi has taken the "ama" and the boat from the Prince's poem, but has changed their significance. She is indeed the *ama* referred to by him, but far from rowing off and deserting him, she has lost her own boat, that is, been herself deserted by him. The poem appears as *Seishū* 875 (827).

142. "Tanabata-hikoboshi." According to a Chinese legend familiar in Japan, on the seventh night of the seventh month two celestial lovers, the Weaving Maid (Shokujosei or Tanabata 織女星, i.e., the star Vega) and the Herdsman (Kengyūsei 牽牛星 or Hikoboshi 彦星, the star Altair), separated all year by the Milky Way, have their annual rendezvous. On that night the Weaving Maid is enabled to cross the "River of Heaven" (*amanogawa*, the Milky Way) to her lover on a bridge made of the outstretched wings of magpies. The term *tanabata*, literally "shelf-loom" 棚機, refers to the occupation of the Weaving Maid, who is called in full Tanabatatsume 棚機津女 (the girl of the loom). It is also by extension applied to the day of the lovers' meeting, in which case it is written 七夕. That day was the occasion for a festival, Tanabata no Matsuri or Kikōden 吃巧奠, which was one of the group of five annual festivals known as the Go Sekku 五節句. Because of the romantic associations of the legend it was the occasion for exchange of love-notes and the writing of poems on five-colored strips of paper, left tied to branches of bamboo. It was also the time when girls prayed to the Weaving Maid for skill in sewing. Tables were set up in front of houses, and in front of the Seiryōden 清涼殿 at the Palace, with offerings and burnt incense (*Yūsoku kojitsu jiten*, pp. 221, 222, 535).

143. It is grammatically possible that the Prince may mean the poem to refer to Izumi. Endō, Iwanami text, p. 414, note 13, interprets thus. I have followed Tamai, *Shinchū*, p. 120, and Ozaki, *Kōchū*, p. 76.

144. Ozaki, *Kōchū*, pp. 76, 77, interprets "Tanabata ni imaru" as "shunned by Tanabata [the star, i.e., the Prince]," instead of "shunned at Tanabata [time]." The poem appears also as *Seishū* 876 (828), with "amaru" in place of "imaru." Perhaps "amaru" might be interpreted "left over," i.e., "unessential": "When I consider how I am left out of things at Tanabata time . . ."

145. The original reads simply "Nado ka tokidoki wa" (Why, from time to time?).

146. "Ogikaze" is a *kakekotoba*: 荻風 (wind among the reeds)/招ぎ風 (beckoning wind). The sense of Izumi's poem is: "Since you sleep soundly, undisturbed by heartsore longing, you cannot hear the wind of my desire which beckons you. And yet does it not blow for you, night after autumn night?" The poem appears as *Seishū* 877 (829), in the following variant form:

Nezameneba	Since nothing breaks your sleep,
Kikanu naruramu	You do not hear, I think,
Ogikaze ni	My message borne upon the wind,
Fukuramu mono o	Blown through the beckoning reeds
Aki no yogoto ni	On every autumn night.

147. "Mono omou toki wa to zo," a reference to Ki no Tsurayuki's poem:

Hito shirezu	When I am filled with longing
Mono omou toki wa	In my lonely solitude,
Naniwagata	How can I know the momentary sleep
Ashi no sorane mo	Even of the windblown reeds
Serare ya wa suru	Along the shore at Naniwa?

148. "Oroka ni" (indifferently). This could equally well be rendered "I am not indifferent," or "I am far from indifferent."

149. A closer version: "If the reed [beckoning] wind blows, from now on it behooves me to listen, sleepless, and hear whether my beloved, sleepless, will rouse me up." "Ogikaze" is the same pun mentioned in note 146. "I mo nede" is also a *kakekotoba*: *i mo nede* 寝も寝で (not sleeping a sleep)/*imo nede* 妹寝で (my little sister [i.e., mistress] not sleeping). It is possible to take "ima yori zo" as going with "odorokasu ka to," rather than with "kikubekarikeru," and the poem is so interpreted by Endō, Iwanami text, p. 415, note 24, and p. 453, sup. note 73; and by Yamagishi, *NKZ*, p. 212, note 12. In this case "keru" has a past rather than a purely emotional significance, and the last three lines are to be translated: "I should have listened to hear whether your beckoning wind would wake me up at any moment." I have followed Ozaki, *Kōchū*, p. 78.

150. I.e., he had not seen her other than dimly by moonlight or at dawn. See note 247.

151. This poem appears as *Seishū* 878 (830), with the fourth line reading "Omoishigurenu" (My thoughts have been a cold drizzle).

152. An expansion of the original, "Mube hito wa" (men, to be sure). This is a reference to a poem by Ōnakatomi no Yoshinobu 大中臣能宣 (921–991), *Shūishū* 1104:

Kaerinishi	Again the voices
Kari zo naku naru	Of wild geese, back from the north,
Mube hito wa	Fall upon our ears:
Uki yo no naka o	Surely man cannot forsake
Somukikanuramu	The bonds of this bitter world.

Or, more literally, "The geese which had returned are crying; it seems natural that men cannot forsake this trying world." The wild geese migrate south to Japan in the fall and return north in the spring. Japan, to which they have returned to winter, is likened to this world of pain and illusion which men (and Izumi Shikibu) find so hard to give up. Endō, Iwanami text, p. 453, sup. note 76, interprets the reference to mean something closer to "We find it hard to accept our fates."

153.   Possibly a reference to the night the Prince handed Izumi a poem on his fan, or to one of the nights he took her to his mansion. The visit immediately preceding was described as "inconsequential."

154.   There is a question as to the meaning of "kakaru ariki mo hikikaetaru mi no arisama to omou ni" (thinking that such expeditions showed how greatly she had changed). Endō, Iwanami text, p. 416, note 12, and Yamagishi, *NKZ*, p. 214, note 6, take "ariki" to refer to Izumi's not being before the Buddha. I have preferred to assume that she is sighing over how greatly she has changed from the old, happy days when she had no griefs to send her off on pilgrimages. The interpretation is doubtful however.

155.   "Aware ni omoigakenu hodo ni kitareba." Here I have chosen to translate "aware ni" as "happily." For a similar construction and a different interpretation see note 8.

156.   *Hodashi* 絆, a hobble, tether, fetter, and hence earthly ties impeding religious dedication. The Prince is alluding to a poem by Mononobe no Yoshina 物部良名, *Kokinshū* 955:

Yo no ukime	Though I would enter
Mienu yamaji e	The mountain path where this world
Iramu ni wa	And its pain must fade,
Omou hito koso	The thought of one I love
Hodashi narikere	It is that keeps me fettered here.

This is an *onaji moji naki uta*, a poem which deliberately avoids use of any vowel or consonant-vowel combination more than once.

157.   A more nearly literal translation: "Did a person know I would inquire today, crossing the Barrier? The ceaseless concern I feel for you!" The Barrier referred to is Ausaka (Ōsaka) no Seki 逢坂の關, an ancient inspection point east of the capital, long since fallen into ruin (it went out of use in 795), but which remained a favorite place name in poetry because of its pun on "meet" (*au* 逢ふ). My interpretation of the poem follows Endō, Iwanami text, p. 417, note 19. Tamai, *Shinchū*, p. 128, points out that "kokorozukai" may be a *kakekotoba* meaning "heart messenger" (心使) as well as "anxious thoughts" (心遣). The "inquiring" and "crossing the Barrier" are to be understood as "by letter." The "o" ending the last line may be taken either as indicating exclamation (as in my translation), or that "omoitae senu kokorozukai" is also the object of "shiru." The poem appears as *Seishū* 221.

158.   "Ōmiji" is a *kakekotoba*: Ōmiji 近江路 (the Ōmi Road)/*au michi* 逢ふ道 (meeting road). The Prince has said that he would cross the Meeting Barrier on the Ōmi Road to Ishiyama 石山 Temple (in Ōmi Province near Lake Biwa),

but Izumi replies that he seems to have forgotten that Meeting Road. This poem appears as *Seishū* 222.

159. "Oboroke ni omoitamaeirinishi kamo." "Oboroke" here has the opposite of its usual meaning of "vague." Endō, Iwanami text, p. 453, sup. note 78, considers that "kamo" poses a problem, since its usual use in Heian writing is to express doubt or questioning rather than exclamation as in pre-Heian Japanese. Since it would seem unlikely that Izumi is here questioning her own statement, the reading "oboroke ni omoitamaete irinishikaba" found in *Ōeibon* texts is to be considered preferable.

160. The implied answer is "never." "Uchide" is a *kakekotoba*: uchide 打出 (going out)/*Uchide no Hama* 打出濱 (the Beach of Uchide [at Ōtsu on Lake Biwa]). Yamagishi, *NKZ*, p. 215, note 14, regards "uki" as a *kakekotoba* as well: 泥土 (mire), as well as 憂き (frustrating, painful, melancholy, miserable). If such is the case, the first two lines should be rendered, "If, though living in the mountains, my life should fall into the mire." "Uki" 泥土 might be an *engo* of "hama" (beach).

161. A closer version: "Is it right that you have forgotten me, lost in mere vagueness, so that there is no use [valley] for my visiting journey up Meeting-Slope Mountain?" "Ōsakayama" contains the pun on *au* (meet) previously mentioned. "Kai" is also a *kakekotoba*: 峽 (mountain valley)/ 甲斐 (result). In this poem the Prince tosses back at Izumi her accusation of forgetfulness.

162. "Ōmi no umi" 近江の海 ("the Sea of Ōmi," i.e., Lake Biwa) and "Uchide" contain the puns already explained in notes 158 and 160. Essentially the Prince is saying, "Come back and meet me." This poem appears as *Seishū* 224.

163. An allusion to an anonymous poem, *Kokinshū* 1061:

Yo no naka no	If every time
Uki tabigoto ni	That life is difficult
Mi o nageba	Men cast themselves away,
Fukaki tani koso	Even the deepest valley
Asaku nariname	Would be too shallow for them all.

164. There is a play on *seki* 關 (barrier) and *seki* 堰き (dam up). I have interpreted "Ōmi no umi" as a double *kakekotoba*: 近江の海 (the Sea of Ōmi)/ 逢ふ身 の憂み (the misery of one who would meet you [or "whom you would meet"]).

165. A closer version: "As a test I would make trial even of my own heart; come and see if you can tempt me, saying, 'Let us go to Miyako.'" The poem's cleverness and charm lie in the word play of "kokoromi"—"kokoro"—"kokoromimu" (trial—heart—I'd make trial). It appears as *Seishū* 230, with the reading "kimi ga kokoro mo" (make trial of *your* heart) instead of "onoga kokoro mo."

166. An expansion of the original, "Sasoimiyo to arishi o, isogiidetamainikereba nan" (As for your "Try to tempt me," since you hurriedly came out of the mountains . . .).

262

167.   A closer version: "I have left the mountains and made my way back along the road of darkness for the sake of meeting you now once more." The "kuraki michi" is the way of worldly desire. The poem appears as *Seishū* 883 (832), with the variant readings ". . . michi ni o/Tazunekoshi" (came seeking you along the road).

168.   The Prince implies that the heavens reflect his own emotional state (which is not to say that his sighs literally blow up a storm!).

169.   This poem appears as *Seishū* 884 (833).

170.   *Ariake no tsuki* 有明の月 , the waning moon, which, because of its late rising, remains shining in the sky at dawn.

171.   A somewhat free handling of "karōjite okoshitemo" (though at length she made her get up). I have at this point inserted a sentence from the *Kangembon*— "Karōjite odorokashite mata hito okosedo mo okizu"—which I have rendered as indicated in the translation. This sentence makes clear what is implied later in the grumbling comments about the "ladies [i.e., ladies-in-waiting, *omoto* 御許] in this house"—that another servant, presumably a man, has been wakened by the person whom the lady has roused.

172.   "Igitanashi" (soiled with sleep).

173.   Simply "karōjite okite" (finally getting up) in the Japanese.

174.   This poem appears as *Shinkokinshū* 1169 (for a discussion of its role in the controversy over authorship and date of the *Izumi shikibu nikki* see Introduction, pp. 51–52, 61–62, 67–69).

175.   "Hikimusubite," folded it lengthwise into a narrow strip and then bent it into a knot: *musubibumi* 結文.

176.   A closer version: "Within the period of autumn they are going to rot away; whose sleeves shall I borrow for the inevitable winter rains?" *Shigure* 時雨 are the cold rains of early winter; Izumi says that her sleeves will be rotted away with tears before the rains even begin. The poem appears as *Seishū* 885 (834).

177.   "Kusa no iro sae mishi ni mo arazu nariyukeba, shiguren hodo no hisashisa mo madaki ni oboyuru, kaze ni kokorogurushige ni uchinabikitaru ni wa" (As even the color of the grasses became ever more different from the way it had looked, though the distance of the time when the *shigure* would fall seemed not yet, [the grasses] bent with apparent heartsoreness before the wind). I have followed Ozaki, *Kōchū*, p. 79, in taking "hisashisa" to mean "distance" rather than "length," though with "madaki" it becomes redundant. For other examples of Izumi's reactions to the grasses growing about her house see pp. 57, 58, 131, and note 3.

178.   The original: "Tadaima mo, kienubeki tsuyu no waga mi zo ayauku kusaba ni tsukete kanashiki mama ni, oku e mo irade, yagate hashi ni fushitareba." The part from "kienubeki" through "kanashiki" is evidently a garbled poem which has fallen into the prose text (see Introduction, note 178, and pp. 42, 54, 56). That this is likely to be the case can be deduced from the fact that, whereas Izumi's composition contains only four poems, the Prince sends her five replies.

Each reply starts with the same words as one of her poems, but there is nothing to correspond to the Prince's "Kienubeki/Tsuyu no inochi to." A further item of evidence is provided by the fact that this sequence of Izumi's poems—all five of them—is present in the *Seishū* as nos. 885–889 (834–838). The second one reads:

Kienubeki	My life, a drop of dew
Tsuyu no waga mi wa	About to vanish,
Mono nomi zo	Frail as leaves of grass,
Ayauku sawa ni	Can never know tranquility
Kanashikarikeru	Among its multitude of woes.

The fourth line involves a *kakekotoba*: . . . *waga mi wa* . . . *ayauku, sawa ni kanashikeru* (My life is in danger, and many are the things that I am sad about)/ *ayaukusa* 危草 (dangerous [or endangered] grass). In the translation I have followed the *Nikki* text as it exists.

The poem contains an allusion to two lines of Chinese verse in the *Wakan rōeishū* 和漢朗詠集 (an anthology of often-recited Chinese and Japanese poetry, compiled by Fujiwara no Kintō; see *Wakan rōeishū*, ed. Kawaguchi Hisao, *NKBT*, LXXIII [1965], 254). These lines, *Wakan rōeishū* 790, are attributed to one Lo Wei 羅維. However Kakimura Shigematsu, *Wakan rōeishū kōshō* (1926), p. 368, states that this name must be a mistake for Yen Wei 嚴維, an 8th-century T'ang poet. The lines read:

観身岸額離根草

論命江頭不繋舟

(Look upon yourself—grass whose roots have parted from the brow of a bank [or cliff];
Consider your life—a boat loosed from its moorings on the river.)

Kawaguchi, *Wakan rōeishū*, p. 254, quotes a Buddhist parable from the *Wakan rōeishū shichū* 私注, a 12th-century commentary of doubtful authorship (perhaps attributable to Shakushin'a 釋信阿 [dates unknown]; or to Kakumyō 覺明 [1157–1241]): A man, chased by a tiger, flees along a thousand-fathom precipice. In order to escape he hangs over the edge by a single strand of grass. In the abyss below is an openmouthed crocodile; above, a black and a white rat are gnawing at the grass. The crocodile symbolizes hell; the rats, the sun and moon (or days and months—i.e., time?); the grass, evil passions. A similar story appears in a commentary by the Chinese monk Seng Chao 僧肇 (ca. 374–414) on the *Vimalakirtih Sūtra: Chū Yuimakitsu kyō* 注維摩詰經 , *kan* 2, *Taishō shinshū daizōkyō*, ed. Takakusu Junjirō, XXXVIII (1926), 343. In this version a man flees because of an offense he has committed against his king. The king has him pursued by a maddened elephant; in desperation the man leaps into an abandoned well, where he hangs on by a tuft of decaying grass. From below an evil dragon spits

264

venom at him; five poisonous snakes are ready to bite him; two rats gnaw at the grass; the elephant glowers down from above. But honey from a tree beside the well drips into the man's mouth, causing him to forget his terror and his peril. Thus the pleasures of this world delude men into forgetting the true nature of the human condition. For the second line of the *Wakan rōeishū* poem Kawaguchi suggests a source in the *Chuang-tzu* 莊子, *chüan* 10, "Lieh Yü-k'ou" 列御寇: 汎若不繋之舟虛而遨遊者也 (He [the man without abilities] drifts like an unmoored boat; he rambles and roams in vacancy) (*Kambun taikei*, ed. Hattori Unokichi, IX [1911], 9).

Izumi Shikibu's interest in the *Wakan rōeishū* lines is attested by a sequence of 43 poems in the *Seishū* (268–310); each of these *waka* begins with a syllable taken, in sequential order, from the Japanese reading of the Chinese verses: "Mi o kan-zureba kishi no hitai ni ne o hanaretaru kusa/ Inochi o ron-zureba e no hotori ni tsunagazaru fune." The figure of the "dangerous grass" is also referred to by Sei Shōnagon: "Ayaugusa wa, kishi no hitai ni ouran mo, ge ni tanomoshikarazu" ("Dangerous grass" growing on the brow of a bank would certainly be undependable) (*Makura no sōshi*, in *NKBT*, XIX, 104).

179. "Tsuyu nerubeku mo arazu" (I was not to sleep so much as "dew").

180. A more nearly literal translation: "I wonder, alas, how many nights it has been that I have not dozed off—simply making my occupation listening to the cries of wild geese." This poem appears as *Seishū* 887 (836), with the reading "ikuka" (how many days) in place of "iku yo" (how many nights). It also appears as *Zokushū* 397 (1239), with the reading "iku yo."

181. The clearness of the moonlight seems inconsistent with the mistiness of the sky; it is possible that the sky is intended to be understood as only partially misty. This passage is discussed in detail by Endō, *Shinkō*, pp. 166–173. He concludes that *sumu* 澄む in the Heian Period did not have its modern meaning of "is clear," but was applied to any material or scene presenting an even appearance free of foreign admixtures. It could have the sense of *kusumu* (to be of a subdued color of low brilliance). Hence there need be no contradiction between the verbs *sumu* and *kiru* (to be misty): the moon is shining through an even veil of mist.

182. Endō, who stresses the lady's unhappiness throughout this passage, states that "mezuraka nari," which I have translated as "strangely new," means "ill-omened" (fukitsu) in the present context.

183. A closer version: "Even a person not myself will surely see: as for *aware*, nothing can be rated equal to the Long Month's still-up-at-dawn moon." *Aware*, the sentiment and the word which dominate this passage, and which I have translated variously according to the context, is that sad and tender sensibility discussed in note 5. The poem appears as *Seishū* 888 (837), and as no. 438 in the *Shokugosenshū*.

184. "Tadaima, kono kado o uchitatakasuru hito aran, ika ni oboenan." The implication is that she would be extremely moved. Endō comments that the lady has entered a new emotional state since opening her door and looking

at the moon. The force of the "tadaima" is that (although someone knocked before) if *now* someone were to knock she would be completely overcome with emotion. (I have taken the new emotional state to be one in which the lady's depression and irritability are replaced by awe and tenderness inspired by the spectacle of moon and mist. Hence I have preferred my translation of "mezuraka nari" to the one suggested by Endō [see above, note 182].)

185. This poem appears as *Seishū* 889 (838), and as no. 1423 in the *Shokusen-zaishū*.

186. I have supplied the words "His messenger had come, and she had availed herself of the opportunity." The original reads simply: "Miya watari ni ya kikoe-mashi to omou ni. Tatematsuritareba" (As she was thinking she should send it to the Prince. Having presented it . . .). The *Sanjōnishibon* lacks a clause present in the other texts after "omou ni": "Owashimashitarikeru koto o omou ['yo to omou' in *Ōeibon* texts] mama ni" (thinking of how he had come to visit her). It should be noted that in any case the sentence represents an overlapping in narration with the passage immediately before the text of Izumi's composition.

187. "Aenaki kokochi." Because the reply had come too quickly, indicating lack of thought (*Ōchō nikki*, p. 183, note 30)?

188. A closer version: "Although within an autumn my sleeves have rotted, a person thinks of nothing else but 'My sleeves are thus.' "

189. The chrysanthemum was associated with longevity and with the ninth month (*Shinchū*, p. 141).

190. A more nearly literal translation: "To listen, without dozing off, to the cries of wild geese that fly the *kumoi* is an occupation that comes from your own heart." For *kumoi*, here translated "cloudy vault," see note 133. Yamagishi, *NKZ*, p. 221, note 30, suggests that by "kokorozukara no waza" the Prince means that Izumi's fickleness gives her much to think about.

191. A closer version: "A person not myself was also gazing, with the same heart, solely at the sky where the moon was still up at dawn." This poem appears as *Shokukokinshū* 1181.

192. A closer version: "I thought that you at least, though in another place, would be the very one to be looking at the moon, but this morning when I went to you I was chagrined."

193. A very free rendering of "Ito akegatakaritsuru o koso" (It was in partic-ular the way it was very hard to open). "Akegatakaritsuru" is a *kakekotoba*, referring both to the gate and the dawn (Yo ga akegatakaritsuru).

194. I have inserted the words "I have a request to make of you," which are not represented in the original.

195. "Ana shitarigao." Ozaki, *Kōchū*, p. 106, and Endō, Iwanami text, p. 422, note 1, interpret this as meaning "How can I complacently write such a poem for you?"

196. "Notamawasetaru koto wa ikade ka" (As for what you say, how—?). I have followed Yamagishi, *NKZ*, p. 223, note 4. Tamai, *Shinchū*, p. 142, inter-prets "how" as meaning "How can I compose the kind of poem you request?"

197. A closer version: "Would that your image would remain in my regretful tears, even though autumn [satiety] goes, not knowing my heart." "Aki" is a *kakekotoba*: 秋 (autumn)/ 飽き (satiety). In the latter sense the last line means "... even if you become tired of me and go away." The poem appears as *Seishū* 890 (839), in the following form:

Oshimarenu	For the tears I shed
Namida ni kakete	And never stint their number
Tomaranamu	I would have you stay,
Kokoro mo yukanu	Though this stagnant-hearted
Aki wa yuku tomo	Autumn of our passion goes.

198. A more nearly literal translation: "I wonder where she might go, leaving you. Even I am making the effort to live in this miserable world." "Yo no naka" has the secondary meaning of "the relations between a man and woman" here. The poem appears as *Seishū* 891 (840).

199. "Mishirigao" (know-it-all face).

200. A free rendering of "Amari zo oshihakarisuguitamau, uki yo no naka to haberu wa" (As for this "uki yo no naka," you are engaging in too much guesswork).

201. A closer version: "As for the person who abandons me and goes on a journey—if it be thus, so let it be, if you but think of me as a person second to none."

202. The *Sanjōnishibon* has 一月; all other texts have 十月, which I have adopted.

203. A rather free handling of "Koko ni kakute aru yo nado obosu" (He thought, "Here she is, thus!").

204. "Tamakura no sode," sleeves of the arm on which one rests one's head. The phrase is picked up and exchanged in several succeeding poems. The Prince is saying that his sleeves are wet with tears he has shed in sympathy with Izumi's suffering.

205. "Aware naritsuru yoru no keshiki mo, kaku nomi iu hodo ni ya, tanomoshiki hito mo naki nameri kashi to kokorogurushiku oboshite" (He felt pained at heart even about the night scene which had been *aware*, thinking, perhaps because she spoke only thus, that she seemed indeed without a person to rely on). I have here translated "aware" as "sweetly sad," and have introduced the words "the next morning."

206. A closer version: "Within the space of this morning I suppose they have now dried—the sleeves of the arm-pillow which looked as if they had been wet [we had slept] only as much as a dream." "Nuru" is a *kakekotoba*: 寝る (slept)/ 濡る (wet). The poem appears as *Seishū* 892 (841).

207. A closer version: "Though you may have seen them as being wet by only a 'dream' of tears, it has been impossible to dry them, the sleeves of my arm-pillow." The *Kangembon* and *Sanjōnishibon* have "fushi" (lying down) in place

of "hoshi" (drying), and "wazurau" (be a trouble) instead of "kanetsuru" (be impossible). I have preferred the *Ōeibon* version. The other must mean "I cried so much that I felt quite uncomfortable lying there." Shimizu, *Ōchō nikki*, p. 199, mixes the two versions: "Hoshi zo wazurau."

208. "Kokoro kara ni ya." Another instance in which the Prince's feelings are conjectured (see Introduction, pp. 89, 125).

209. I have supplied the words "Why should you go on living in this way?" The original is "Ito kaku tsurezure ni nagametamauran o" (While you seem thus to be gazing in utter tedium).

210. This and the previous sentence are a translation of: "Yo no naka no hito mo binage ni iu nari. Tokidoki maireba ni ya, miyuru koto mo nakeredo, sore mo, hito no ito kikinikuku iu ni." Tamai, *Shinchū*, p. 151, takes this to be a reference to the rumored visits of other men to Izumi, none of whom the Prince has yet seen (miyuru koto nakeredo). Endō, Iwanami text, p. 424, note 3, understands the same phrase to mean that it is Izumi whom the Prince has not seen. I have preferred to follow Ozaki, *Kōchū*, p. 114.

211. I have inserted "from those fruitless excursions when I have been unable to gain admittance," following Endō, Iwanami text, p. 424, note 5, in this interpretation. The original is simply "mata tabitabi kaeru hodo no" (again, on the frequent occasions when I am returning home).

212. "Makoto ni kiku koto no arite sei-suru koto nado araba, sora yuku tsuki ni mo aran" (Truly, if it were heard of and I were restrained, it would be a case of the "sky-traveling moon"). I have limited the "hearing" in translation to a "certain person," perhaps the Prince's official consort, or one of the lords warned about by the nurse (see notes 95, 97). "Sora yuku tsuki" is evidently an allusion to a poem by Tachibana no Naomoto 直幹 (mid-10th century), *Shūishū* 470:

Wasuru na yo	Do not forget—
Hodo wa kumoi ni	Though between us be the distance
Narinu tomo	To the cloudy vault—
Sora yuku tsuki no	Until the moon that goes across the sky
Meguriau made	Shall circle back again.

Ozaki, *Kōchū*, p. 114; Tamai, *Shinchū*, p. 152; and Endō, Iwanami text, p. 455, sup. note 92, attribute this poem to Naomoto. Shimizu, *Ōchō nikki*, p. 202, note 15, and *Hachidaishū zenchū*, I, 488, however, attribute it to Tachibana no Tadamoto 忠幹 (also mid-10th century). The poem also appears in *Ise monogatari*, episode 11. Considering the fact that the poem was written to a girl (see *Hachidaishū zenchū*, I, 488), "I would be as out of reach as the moon in the sky," or "You would be in the position of waiting 'till the moon came circling round,'" might be better translations; especially so, in that there is probably also reference to the exchange of poems in which Izumi likens the Prince to the wandering moon (see notes 131, 133). There is also a possibility that "sora yuku tsuki," whether or not derived from Tadamoto's (or Naomoto's) poem, was a customary phrase used to express separation (see Iwanami text, p. 455, sup. note 92; *Kōchū*, p. 114; *Shinchū*, p. 152; *NKZ*, p. 226, note 8; *Ōchō nikki*, p. 202, note 15).

213. "Hito nado mo aredo." It seems clear in this case that "hito" refers to the Prince's legal spouse.

214. I have inserted this sentence.

215. "Ichinomiya no koto mo kikoekirite aru o." Presumably a reference to an invitation to become a lady-in-waiting to the Retired Emperor Kazan, the eldest son of Reizei, and half-brother of Princes Atsumichi, Tametaka, and Okisada.

216. "Sari tote, yama no anata ni shirube suru hito mo naki o," apparently a reference to *Kokinshū* 950 (Anonymous):

Miyoshino no	Would that I had
Yama no anata ni	A dwelling far beyond
Yado mogana	The mountains of fair Yoshino—
Yo no uki toki no	For when the world goes ill
Kakurega ni semu	I'd make of it my hidden refuge.

217. Perhaps a reference to a poem by Fujiwara no Kiyotada 清正 (d. 958):

Hito shirenu	Unbeknownst to men
Oto ya tae suru	Its note may die away,
Hototogisu	The *hototogisu*,
Tada akenu yo no	Feeling itself living
Kokochi nomi shite	In a night that has no dawn.

218. "Kono nureginu wa, saritomo kiyaminan" (As for this wet garment, despite it all she would cease to wear it). *Nureginu* (wet garments) is a name for an undeserved bad reputation, in this case a reference to the Prince's recurrent accusations of unfaithfulness. If she goes to live in his mansion he will no longer be prone to the suspicions that her solitary life provokes.

219. "Nanigoto mo tada ware yori hoka no to nomi omoitamaetsutsu sugushihaberu." Endō, Iwanami text, p. 425, note 28, suggests that the phrase "ware yori hoka no" was drawn from a poem, but says the source is not clear.

220. This sentence and the previous two read in the original: "'Yoso nite mo migurushiki koto ni kikoesasuran. Mashite makoto narikeri to mihaberan namu katawara itaku' to kikoyureba, 'Sore wa koko ni koso to mo kaku mo iwareme.'" Because of lack of personal pronouns a problem exists in deciding who is being criticized. I have assumed that both Izumi and the Prince are referred to. Ozaki, *Kōchū*, p. 118, favors the interpretation that both Izumi and the Prince are referring to the Prince and takes "koko ni" to refer to Izumi's house. Tamai, *Shinchū*, p. 154, follows this same line, but interprets "Sore wa koko ni koso to mo kaku mo iwareme" to mean "Yes, I no doubt will be talked about

in various ways." Yamagishi, *NKZ*, p. 228, notes 21, 22, thinks that Izumi is concerned with criticism of herself. Shimizu, *Ōchō nikki*, pp. 204, 205, thinks she is worried about the Prince's reputation, but interprets "koko ni" as the Prince's way of referring to himself, not to Izumi's abode. Endō, Iwanami text, p. 425, notes 30–32, and p. 455, sup. note 95, also treats "koko ni" as a reference to the Prince, and applies the criticism to both.

221. "Kōshi" 格子, presumably the *shitomi* (see note 87).

222. We are to understand that his sleeves are soaked with tears as well as dew.

223. A closer version: "Because of a man who is up and about with the dew on the roadside grass, the sleeves of my arm-pillow have not dried either." "Oki-" is a *kakekotoba*: 起き (get up)/置き (settle). In the latter meaning it is not functional, but only an *engo* for "dew."

224. "Koko ni mo kashiko ni mo" (both here and there), i.e., each in his own residence.

225. "Okitekeri" is the same *kakekotoba* noted above—"formed"/"rose." *Shirotae* 白栲 or 白妙 was a white cloth made from the bark of the paper mulberry (*kaji no ki* 梶の木). The word served as a *makurakotoba* with names of several articles of clothing, as well as with *kumo* (cloud), *yuki* (snow), etc. "Linen-white" is of course only an equivalent. The poem appears, with the reading "okikeru o," as *Seishū* 392 (367).

226. "Notamawasetaru." Tamai, *Shinchū*, p. 158; Ozaki, *Kōchū*, p. 121; and Endō, Iwanami text, p. 426, note 5, all interpret this as something the Prince says to himself on reading the lady's poem. Ozaki considers the use of the *rentaikei* exclamatory, Endō posits an understood *ni*, and Tamai has "notamawasetaru" modifying the next sentence.

227. "Oki-" is the usual *kakekotoba*. The Prince takes Izumi's last two lines (Kesa uchimireba/ Shirotae ni shite) as the point of departure for this example of *renga* (see Introduction, note 111).

228. "Towasetareba, toku mairade, imijū sainamumeri" (When he asked for you, you did not come quickly, and it seems he is railing at you). The presence of an "attendant" is implied by the context, the use of the causative, and the auxiliary verb *meri* (seems). If "towasetareba" is not regarded as part of the attendant's speech, the view taken by Yamagishi, *NKZ*, p. 229, note 5, the sentence could be translated "The Prince had his attendant question [or 'call'] the page. The attendant said, 'It seems he is heaping abuse on you because you did not come quickly.' "

229. I have followed Endō, Tamai, Yamagishi, and Ozaki in rejecting the *Sanjōnishibon* reading of "mata" (again) in favor of the "mada" (not yet) found in other texts.

230. A closer version: "Thinking perhaps you were looking at the moon of the night when we slept, this morning I arose [frost formed] and waited, but there was no one who called." "Oki-" is the *kakekotoba* noted previously, and "shimo" doubles as the emphatic particle and "frost." I have followed Endō, Iwanami

text, p. 426, note 10, in interpreting "nenuru yo" as "the night we slept together," presumably the night the Prince sees the lady's tears falling in the moonlight. Tamai, *Shinchū*, p. 159, takes it to mean "tonight when you actually were fast asleep."

231. "But I doubt that you actually did" is implied. There is the usual play on "oki-" and "shimo." There is a question concerning to whom "madoromade" refers. Ozaki, *Kōchū*, p. 123, would have it that "madoromade" refers to the action of the Prince. Tamai, *Shinchū*, p. 159, makes it refer to Izumi: "You say you've stayed up all night looking at the moon that I gazed at without sleeping all one night." I have followed Endō, Iwanami text, p. 426, note 12, and Suzuki, *Zenkō*, p. 227. The poem appears as *Seishū* 393 (368) in the following variant form:

Madoromade	When I look upon the moon
Hitori nagameshi	That I have watched,
Tsuki mireba	Alone and sleepless,
Okinagara shimo	Its countenance seems to say,
Akashigao nari	"I've stayed up all this frosty night."

In this case the moon is a metaphor for the Prince. (This interpretation is based on Kubota's note in the *Nihon koten zensho* edition of *Izumi Shikibu shū*, p. 67, note 14. A similar interpretation might be feasible in the case of the *Nikki* poem.)

232. "Uchitokenitaru" has both its literal and figurative meanings of "melted." The poem appears as *Seishū* 394 (369).

233. "Kesa shitarigao ni oboshitaritsuru mo ito netashi." It seems unlikely that the "shitarigao" (self-satisfied expression) refers to the "akashigao" (stayed-up-all-night expression) with which Izumi has branded the Prince in her poem (note 231). The context shows that the Prince is angry about the page's tardiness.

234. A closer version: "Although it is frost which must melt when the morning sun strikes it, there is a condition of sky hard to melt away." The "sora no keshiki" (condition of the sky) of course refers to the Prince's anger. "Sora" is an *engo* of "asahi" (morning sun).

235. A very free treatment of "Korosasetamaubekannaru koso tote" ("That you should kill him, well—" she said).

236. A more nearly literal translation: "Do you now intend not to say 'live!' [go!] to the lad, who appears at infrequent intervals when you do not come?" "Ike" is a *kakekotoba*: 生け (live!)/行け (go!). This poem appears as *Seishū* 395 (370).

237. "Shinobi" is a *kakekotoba*: "Kono warawa shinobi" (Endure this lad)/ "shinobi no tsuma" (hidden spouse).

238. This accusation seems rather odd, as Izumi has begun this exchange with a "pillow-sleeves" poem, while the Prince has not mentioned the subject. From the point of view of the *Nikki* as a story, this inconsistency casts an interesting sidelight on the Prince's reactions here, as he rather too abruptly changes the

subject after his somewhat absurd remarks about killing the page. As suggested by Suzuki, *Zenkō*, pp. 431–435, however this sort of minor discrepancy may also be regarded as an indication of the process by which the *Nikki* was written— amalgamation of a collection of poems, letters, jottings, etc., pieced out with memory, imagination, and literary skill but with some rough edges still showing.

239. This poem appears as *Seishū* 396 (371).

240. I have inserted this sentence.

241. A more nearly literal translation: "If the matter had ended without my saying anything, would you have called them to mind at all, those pillow-sleeves?" The poem, a rhetorical question implying a negative answer, contains a play on "kakete." Izumi's poem uses the expression "kokoro ni kakete" (hung in my heart, i.e., cherished). In the Prince's reply "kakete dani" means "not in the least," but also "even if you have hung them in your heart."

242. Perhaps an allusion to a poem by Dōmyō Azari (see Introduction, note 99, and pp. 20, 21, 46, 87), *Goshūishū* 785:

Yona yona wa	Night after night
Me nomi sametsutsu	I lie in wakefulness,
Omoiyaru	Sending my thoughts to you—
Kokoro ya yukite	I wonder if my heart will go
Odorokasuran	And startle you from sleep.

There is some doubt about this allusion however because of the late date of the author.

243. See Introduction, p. 79 and note 229, for a discussion of the relationship of this poem to the problem of the authorship of the *Izumi Shikibu nikki*.

244. "Uchinagamerarete." The passive indicates spontaneity. Tamai, *Shinchū*, p. 161, thinks that the object of the gazing is the Prince's poem, not the moon. Ozaki, *Kōchū*, p. 128, takes the verb to be 詠む (to recite a poem) rather than 眺む (to gaze).

245. A more nearly literal translation: "Although I think it must be late, I cannot sleep; but since it would be *nakanaka*, I do *not* look at the moon." "Nakanaka" means *kaette* (contrary to what one would expect); looking at the moon, normally a pleasant experience, would make things worse than before. This poem appears as *Seishū* 397 (372).

246. "Onnaguruma," a carriage decorated in the fashion used by women, with colorful curtains of damask silk hung within the *sudare* screening the openings and allowed to trail out beneath, as were the long sleeves of the passengers.

247. An apparent conflict with the statement on p. 152. See note 150.

248. I have expanded the original, which is simply "Izariidenu" (She crept out on her knees), supplying the words "from behind her screen to greet him."

249. "Higoro no obotsukanasa nado katarawasetamaite." This could equally well be rendered: "Speaking of his [or their] impatient restlessness of the past

several days."

250. "Mite mo nageku." This may be an allusion to *Kokinshū* 752 (Anonymous):

Mite mo mata	See my love once? I must again!
Mata mo mimaku no	Again? Oh let me see her still!
Hoshikereba	So my desire grows;
Naruru o hito wa	And this must be the very reason why
Itoubera nari	She so detests familiarity.

I have followed the interpretation given to this poem in *Kokinwakashū hyōshaku*, ed. Kubota Utsubo (1960), II, 474. Kubota's gloss is essentially this: The more I meet my love, the more our mutual desire grows. But she fears to give way to passion entirely, because she does not trust me. Hence she detests over-familiarity. Tamai, *Shinchū*, pp. 163, 164, takes the poem to be the woman's guess at the reason why her lover has forsaken her—he cannot endure their ever-increasing desire to see each other. Ozaki, *Kōchū*, p. 131, has still another view: When the two lovers live apart and see each other only occasionally, their meetings have real zest. Hence dull familiarity is to be avoided. This last interpretation is closest to the significance which must lie in Izumi's "mite mo nageku"—a fear of indifference coming from over-familiarity—but seems least likely as an explanation of the poem. It is doubtful that Izumi's remark can be assigned a source in this poem, whose sense is uncertain and which lacks the word "nageku."

251. "Shioyakigoromo nite zo aran" (It will be a case of the salt-burning garments). This is an allusion to a poem in the *Kokinrokujō*:

Ise no ama no	Even the rustic garb
Shioyakigoromo	The girls of Ise wear when burning salt
Narete koso	Familiarity makes dear—
Hito no koishiki	And it alone enables one to judge
Koto mo shirarure	How precious the beloved.

"Burning salt" refers to the process of extracting salt by boiling sea water or burning seaweed saturated with brine. Not only does familiarity not breed contempt, the Prince asserts, answering Izumi's allusion with one of his own, but exactly the opposite is true. In the above poem the first two lines constitute a *jo* 序 (preface), related to the basic statement of the poem—only when one has come to know someone thoroughly can one know how much he loves her—as a specific illustration, and also related through "narete koso," which functions grammatically with both the first two and last two lines.

252. *Mayumi* 檀 or 眞弓 (true bow), so called because its wood was used in the making of bows: a small deciduous tree.

253. I.e., our love has deepened. These lines appear as *Seishū* 398 (373), with the reading "Kotoha fukaku mo."

254. The "dew" is a metaphor for the Prince's affection, just a momentary touch of which has deepened the color of her leaves (i.e., has deepened into love). This is another example of linked verse, Izumi in this case supplying the first three lines to cap the Prince's last two. They appear as *Seishū* 398 (374).

255. I have chosen to amplify this sentence in order to give the reader some idea of the sight that so pleases the lady. The original runs: "Onnōshi ni, enaranu onzo, idashiuchigi ni shitamaeru" (With his *nōshi* he wore an unbelievable [lit., 'impossible'] garment as an *idashiuchigi*). For *nōshi*, which I have described in the translation, see note 124. The *uchigi* 袿 was an undergarment, a long robe worn beneath the *hakama* 袴 (a sort of bifurcated skirt). When worn so that its lower edge showed below the *hakama* it was called *idashiuchigi* 出袿 (*Shinchū*, p. 164).

256. "Kinō no mikeshiki no asamashū oboitarishi koso kokorouki mono no, aware narishika" (The very fact that your appearance yesterday showed you felt put out was, although distressing, yet at the same time touching). The reference is to the lady's embarrassment at being seen by day. Ozaki, *Kōchū*, p. 135, interprets "aware" as "happy"—"I was happy to be able to see you." Tamai, *Shinchū*, p. 165, reads おほひたりし without the *nigori* as "ōitarishi" 覆ひたりし (covered)— "... the way you ... hid yourself behind fans and curtains." I have interpreted the verb "izariidenu" (see note 248) as meaning she has emerged from behind such protections.

257. A closer version: "The god of Kazuraki, too, must have thought the very same way indeed—that the bridge to be put across along the Kume Road was an awkward thing." "Hashitanaki" is a *kakekotoba*: "Kumeji ni watasu hashi" (the bridge to be built across at [i.e., along the line of] the Kume Road)/ "hashitanaki made" (to the point of being awkward). This is a reference to the story of En no Ozuno 役小角 and the god Hitokotonushi no Kami 一言主神. En no Ozuno, also known as En no Gyōja 行者 (late 7th-early 8th cent.) was a Buddhist magician, the reputed founder of the mountain ascetics. Once he wanted to build a stone bridge from Kazuraki (now pronounced Katsuragi) 葛城 to Kimbusen 金峰山, two mountains in Yamato Province which were connected by the Kume Road, and he ordered the gods of Mt. Kazuraki to perform the task. One of them however, Hitokotonushi no Kami, also known as Kazuraki no Kami, would work only at night because he was ashamed of his ugliness. Hence the bridge was never completed, and En no Gyōja put a curse on the recalcitrant deity, binding him with a spell in a deep valley. (For another version of this story, see *Ōgishō* 奥義抄, in *Nihon kagaku taikei*, ed. Sasaki Nobu-tsuna, I [1957], 277.) In this poem Izumi is likening herself to the god of Kazuraki because of her reluctance to be seen by day.

258. A closer version: "If I have effective power from religious practices, will I end things just like that, with you saying, 'Kazuraki's bridge is awkward'?" "Hashitanashi" is the same *kakekotoba* explained above. The Prince is in turn likening himself to En no Gyōja and saying that if he has that man's magic power he will not leave Izumi where she is. "Araba ... yaminan" could per-haps more properly be translated, "If I had ... would I ... ?" The Prince is

not claiming he actually does possess such powers. However, *araba* does not imply as strong a negation as *ariseba* (if I had), but stands midway between that inflected form and *areba* (since I have), a definite assertion of possession. Hence I have chosen the translation "if I have," which is intended to be ambiguous.

259.   "Yoshi naki koto" ("things without any reason, meaning, connection"; also, "contemptible things"). Endō, Iwanami text, p. 430, note 2, interprets the phrase to mean "incomprehensible things."

260.   A closer version: "What is upon me even the plover will probably not report; has the frost formed also on the wings of the great bird in this same way?" I have followed Suzuki, *Zenkō*, p. 250, in my interpretation. The poem is an allusion to a folk song entitled "Ōtori" 大鳥. This verse, which exists in more than one version, is one of a group known as *fūzoku-uta* 風俗歌, apparently of very ancient date, collected in the Heian Period (see *Nihon bungaku daijiten*, VI, 213–215; *Kodai kayōshū*, ed. Tsuchihashi Yutaka and Konishi Jin'ichi, *NKBT*, III [1957], 277–281). The *Fūzokufu* 風俗譜 now extant, consisting of 26 of these songs, is attributed to the compilation of Minamoto no Masanobu 雅信 (920–993). It is to be found in *Nihon kayō shūsei*, ed. Takano Tatsuyuki, vol. II (1928); *Kōchū kokka taikei*, vol. I (1929); *Kamo no Mabuchi zenshū*, ed. Kokugakuin Henshūbu, vol. II (1903); and in *Kodai kayōshū*.

The version of "Ōtori" given by Konishi, *Kodai kayōshū*, p. 438, reads:

Ōtori no hane ni	Upon the great bird's wings—
Yarena	*Yarena*!
Shimo fureri	The frost has fallen—
Yarena	*Yarena*!
Tare ka sa iu	Who says so?
Chidori zo sa iu	The plover says so!
Kayaguki zo sa iu	The *kayaguki* says so!
Mitosagi zo	The blue heron
Kyō yori kite sa iu	Comes from the capital and says so!

Konishi tentatively identifies the "great bird" as the stork (*kōnotori* 鸛), though he says it could equally well refer to the eagle (*washi* 鷲), crane (*tsuru* 鶴), swan (*kugui* 鵠), or similar large birds. "Yarena" is a *hayashikotoba* 囃子詞, a meaningless word put in for the sake of rhythm. The *kayaguki* 鶸, now called *kayakuguri* 茅潜 (the plunger in miscanthus), is a small songbird frequenting mountains at low elevations, sometimes kept in a cage as a pet. The *mitosagi* 蒼鷺 is described in the *Wamyōshō* as being a type of small heron, bluish-black in color.

Yamagishi, *NKZ*, p. 236, note 4, quotes another version of "Ōtori," which reads:

Ōtori no hane ni	Upon the great bird's wings—
Yarenamu	*Yarenamu*!
Shimo fureri	The frost has fallen—

Yarenamu	*Yarenamu!*
Tare ka sa iu	Who says so?
Chidori zo sa iu	The plover says so!
Kayaguki zo sa iu	The *kayaguki* says so!
Araji araji	Not so! Not so!
Chidori mo iwajimu	The plover would not say so;
Kayaguki mo iwajimu	The *kayaguki* would not say so;
Mitosagi mo	The blue heron, too,
Kyō yori kite sa iwaji	Would not come from the capital to say so.

I have not resolved the question of the meaning of *-mu* in "iwajimu." A reading of *iwashimu* does not seem feasible, since the causative does not fit the context, either in its basic or its honorific function. Besides, "iwaji(mu)" clearly parallels "araji" and the last "iwaji." It will be noticed that in this version of "Ōtori" the *hayashikotoba* is "yarenamu" instead of "yarena." It may perhaps be assumed that in both cases the *-mu* is without meaning, simply a preference for a final *-mu* or *-n* sound. The songs of the *Fūzokufu* were familiar to the court society of the time through their use at entertainments and as part of the *Kagura* 神樂 performances (for similar poems alluding to "Ōtori" see *Utsubo monogatari* [II], ed. Kōno Tama, *NKBT*, XI [1961], 161).

What Izumi is saying in her poem, then, is this: The plover, for all his fame as a frost-reporter, may not tell you how white are my sleeves with frost, but let me assure you they are, for I have been up all night, unable to sleep because of my loneliness. I doubt that the wings of the great bird [the Prince], which the song says are covered with frost, are anything like as deeply encrusted with it. (I doubt you ever stay up thinking of me.)

Endō, Iwanami text, p. 430; Tamai, *Shinchū*, p. 167; and Ozaki, *Kōchū*, p. 136, prefer a reading of "tsukeji" in place of "tsugeji." In this case the first part of the poem has to be understood to mean "The plover leaves no track on me." Ozaki takes this as a protestation of innocence on the part of the lady. The interpretation is plausible, but "tsugeji" seems a much,more probable reading in the light of the reference to "Ōtori."

The poem appears also as *Seishū* 399 (375), in the following version:

Waga ue wa	Even the plover
Chidori wa tsugeji	Will not tell you of my plight,
Ōtori no	Though on the great bird's wings
Hane ni shimo nao	Such frost has not yet formed
Saru wa okanedo	As lies upon my sleeves.

261. A closer version: "Upon a person who said she slept without seeing the moon it did not—the frost—form as on the great bird." "Okishi mo seji" contains a *kakekotoba: okishi mo seji* 置きしもせじ (it did not form)/*okishimo seji* 置き霜せじ (there was no frosting). "Shimo" can also be taken as the empha-

tic particle. "Oki-" and "shimo" 霜 are *engo*. I have again followed Suzuki's interpretation—"I am the one who has been up all night." The reference to not seeing the moon is an allusion to Izumi's poem "Fukenuran" (see note 245).

262.　Because of *monoimi* (see note 129).

263.　"Kaze no mae naru." Perhaps a reference to a passage in the *Kusharon* 倶舎論 (*Abhidharma-kośa-śāstra*): 壽命猶如風前燈燭 (One's life is like a lamp before the wind). Izumi uses the same phrase in two of her poems:

Zokushū 134 (976):

Itoedomo	Wretched is my life
Kienu mi zo uki	That will not flicker out,
Urayamashi	Detest it as I may,
Kaze no mae naru	And enviable
Yoi no tomoshibi	The evening lamp before the wind.

Zokushū 637 (1479):

Hi o hetsutsu	What thoughts would be mine,
Ware nanigoto o	Who now must struggle through
Omowamashi	Each weary day,
Kaze no mae naru	If I were but a leaf
Konoha nariseba	Before the wind?

264.　A closer version: "Thinking perhaps it is the chilly shower which has fallen [grown old] in the world in the Godless Month, today's long rain [gazing] falls [passes the time], I imagine, without making distinction." The poem has three *kakekotoba: furinitaru* 降りにたる (fallen)/*furinitaru* 古りにたる (grown old); *nagame* 長雨 (long rain)/*nagame* 眺め (gaze); *fururan* 降るらん (presumably falls)/*fururan* 經るらん (presumably passes the time). *Kaminazuki* 神無月 (the Godless Month), so called because all the gods of Japan were believed to assemble at the Grand Shrine of Izumo during that period, leaving the rest of the country "godless," was the name for the tenth month. Other explanations for the name are "Thunderless Month" (*Kaminarinashizuki* 雷無月) and "Month of Fermentation" (*Kaminashizuki* 醸成月). In this poem the Prince is accusing both Izumi and the rain of being indifferent to his desire to see the autumn foliage.

265.　This poem appears as *Seishū* 400 (376), with the reading "shimogare wa" ([in the season of] frost-withering) in place of "shigure kamo."

266.　"Araji" is a *kakekotoba: araji* 在らじ (Probably do not exist)/*arashi* 嵐 (storm). The poem appears as *Seishū* 231.

267.　"Araji" may or may not be intended as a *kakekotoba* in this case; I have translated as if it were.

268.　"But since such is not the case, I see no point in a mountain trip" is implied. The poem appears as *Seishū* 401 (377), with the last two lines having the obscure reading "Ikaga yukite no/Kotogoto ni mimu."

269. "Sawaru koto" (a hindrance), perhaps *monoimi*, Buddhist purification (*sōji*, see note 60), or the onset of the menstrual period. In this passage, covering the next three poems, I have followed Endō, Iwanami text, p. 431, notes 17–20, and pp. 456, 457, sup. note 109. The entire passage, punctuated as in Iwanami text, p. 431, runs:

Hitohi owashimashitarishi ni, "Sawaru koto arite kikoesasenu zo" to mōshishi o oboshiidete
[Izumi] Takasebune haya kogiide yo sawaru koto sashikaerinishi ashima waketari
to kikoetaru o, "Oboshiwasuretaru ni ya
[Prince] Yamabe ni mo kuruma ni norite yukubeki ni takase no fune wa ikaga yosubeki
to areba
[Izumi] Momijiba no mi ni kuru made mo chirazaraba takase no fune no nani ka kogaren
tote.

270. "Oboshiidete." This verb poses a problem if the "remembering" is to be assigned to Izumi, as is done by Yamagishi, *NKZ*, p. 239, note 17. The verb *obosu* is usually reserved for the thoughts of the Prince, and Ozaki, *Kōchū*, p. 143, and Endō, Iwanami text, p. 431, note 17, assign it to him here. Tamai, who assigns it to Izumi, conjectures, *Shinchū*, p. 171, that it is either a mistake in copying for "omoiidete," or an example of Izumi absently slipping in a little respect language while writing about herself in the third person. The fact that the following poem is by Izumi would seem to indicate that she is the subject of "oboshi-idete," but the sense of the entire passage makes a doubling back in the sequence here seem preferable as an interpretation. The Prince "recalls" what Izumi had said, *and* her next poem as well, and then goes on with "Oboshiwasuretaru ni ya" (Have you forgotten it?), which I have freely rendered, "Now the Prince teased her with forgetting her own poem."

271. A closer version: "Shallows boat, quickly come rowing out; the obstruction—the reeds because of which you poled back home—I have parted." In this poem Izumi uses "sawaru koto" in its concrete sense of "an obstruction." Ozaki, *Kōchū*, p. 143, quotes *Wamyōshō* to the effect that a *takasebune* 高瀬舟, lit., "shallows boat," was a small, deep boat. Later boats designated by this name were large and with a shallow draft more appropriate to navigating shallows. My translation, "river skiff," is no doubt only an approximation. "Skiff" in one of its meanings is "a light rowboat." "Sashi" in "sashikaerinishi" refers to punting after getting stuck in the reeds. This poem appears as *Seishū* 402 (378).

272. "Oboshiwasuretaru ni ya" (see note 270). I have followed Endō in considering this a question from the Prince to Izumi. The other commentators assume it to be a part of the narrative—"Perhaps he had forgotten it." Endō

contends that this is unlikely because the Prince proceeds to make a reference to the *takasebune* in his own poem. Tamai, *Shinchū*, p. 171, gets around this difficulty by assuming that what the Prince has forgotten is not Izumi's poem, but the incident out of which it grew—when she told the Prince she could not see him—and that therefore he does not understand the poem's significance, thinking that it must have reference to his invitation to go foliage-viewing. This is a feasible interpretation, though it somewhat strains the order of the Japanese, "to kikoe-taru o, oboshiwasuretaru ni ya," which comes immediately after Izumi's poem, and should refer to it (see note 269). It also depends on taking the poem as something written "now," and not as a past incident.

273. A closer version: "To the mountain country too, getting into a carriage, one should go; as for the boat of the shallows, how could it approach?" The significance of this poem is the subject of much dispute. It seems obviously a reference both to the Prince's invitation to go to see the foliage in the mountains, and to Izumi's "Takasebune" poem. Both Yamagishi, *NKZ*, p. 239, note 19, and Tamai, *Shinchū*, p. 171, take "kuruma" to be a *kakekotoba*: 車 (carriage)/ 暮る間 (the time of darkness). They assert that the Prince is replying to Izumi's request that he come "quickly" (haya)—he cannot come until it is dark. Ozaki, *Kōchū*, pp. 143, 144, has a completely different interpretation: "We can get into our carriage and go foliage-viewing even in that difficult mountain country, but how can I row to a meeting (*ause* 逢瀬) with you in my shallows boat when you have ended such meetings, saying that a hindrance prevented you?" Endō's explanation runs approximately as follows: "You wrote to me some time ago, saying you were waiting for a visit from me. Therefore it would be only natural to assume that you would be glad to get into my carriage and go foliage-viewing with me (and so why this refusal?). But as for going by boat, we obviously could not reach our destination."

274. A closer version: "If the colored leaves did not scatter until one came (by carriage) to see, why would anyone [burn with longing] row the boat of the shallows?" "Kuru made" contains a *kakekotoba*: mi ni kuru made mo 見に來る までも (until one comes to see)/*kuruma de* 車で (by carriage). "Kogaren" is another *kakekotoba*: 漕がれん (would row)/焦がれん (would burn with longing). Endō, Iwanami text, p. 457, sup. note 109, takes the poem's sense to be: "If the leaves did not fall until people came to see them, no one would be anxious to go. It is precisely because they do fall that people burn with longing to see them; after they have fallen there is no point in going (and so I am not going to go with you)." The "takase no fune" is brought in for word play, as a reference to the Prince's poem, and as a way of expressing metaphorical refusal of his invitation. Ozaki, *Kōchū*, p. 144, gives the following explanation: "Your heart is as undependable as the leaves which fall before people can go to see them. If it were not so, why would I wait with burning longing the coming of your 'shallows boat'? It is because you are fickle that I am anxious." He also suggests that "se" in "takase" in this series of poems carries the additional meaning of "man" or "husband," *se* 夫.

275. "Konata no futagareba" (since this direction was blocked up). See note 104.

276. The commentators seem unanimous in making a break at this point. To me the sense of the passage indicates continuity; for a discussion see Introduction, note 234.

277. "Shijūgo nichi no imitagae." The directional superstitions discussed in note 104 necessitated a method by which their penalties could be avoided. A system of such methods was developed, referred to by various names, including *katatagae* 方違へ (conversion of the direction) and *imitagae* 忌違へ (conversion of the interdiction [translations after Frank, "*Kata-imi*"]). The system is but imperfectly understood. One of its aspects however was a means by which one could proceed to a desired destination even if it lay in a "blocked" direction. In order to accomplish this one first went to a house in a different direction, stayed there at least until midnight, and then proceeded safely to one's original destination.

This procedure of making a detour constitutes the most common form of *katatagae*. It is not however the form applicable to the present passage. As remarked in note 104, Daishōgun and Ōsō prohibited not only movement but a large number of other activities. In order to be free to carry on any of these activities in a "closed" direction, a system of "preventive *katatagae*" was evolved. The essence of this system was that one had to leave one's own dwelling and go to lodge in a different location several times a year. The annual point of departure for these changes of residence was the night of spring *setsubun* 節分, the end of the solar year as calculated in the old Sino-Japanese calendar. (Actually, there were two calendars—a lunar and a solar [in addition to the cyclical system of the "ten stems and twelve branches"]. The lunar was divided into twelve months of either 29 or 30 days, plus an intercalary month added about once every three years. The solar was divided into 24 named periods of 15 days each. The first of these periods, *risshun* 立春 [Spring Begins], theoretically fell midway between the winter solstice and the vernal equinox. But since $15 \times 24 = 360$, over five days less than the actual number of days in the solar year, frequent adjustments had to be made in the length of some of the solar periods, and the date of *risshun* would vary slightly from year to year. In terms of the lunar calendar its variation of course was great; it fell within the lunar "old year" about once every three years. *Setsubun* was the day before *risshun* and the corresponding turning-points of the other seasons.) On the night of *setsubun* it was imperative to go and lodge elsewhere for the purpose of *katatagae*. Thereafter the necessity recurred at fixed intervals, depending on which deity was involved and on whether one were living in one's "principal place" (*honjo* 本所) or elsewhere. If someone was occupying his *honjo*, his customary residence, and wished to undertake forbidden activities in a direction blocked by Daishōgun, he was obliged to go elsewhere every night for a period of 45 days. In the case of Ōsō the period was 15 days. If however one was occupying someone else's house, or a building not one's customary residence, one *katatagae* within a period of 45 or 15 days would suffice. Places other than the *honjo* were called *tabisho* 旅所 (travel places). Because interdictions attached much more readily to the *honjo* than to the *tabisho*, the custom arose during the 12th century of having a *honjo* in name only, and actually living in the *tabisho*. If one neglected to make a *katatagae* within the 45-day period, one could transfer the interdiction thereby incurred to the *honjo* by simply going and lodging there for one night. At the time of Izumi Shikibu this convenient procedure had not yet been developed however. The *setsubun* of the other seasons were also, less importantly, points of departure for such series of preventive *katatagae*. These *katatagae* of course imposed themselves not on everyone, but only on those who had a need to circumvent specific interdictions. Interestingly, the place resorted to on such occasions was often the very place in which was planned some "violation of the earth."

Such essentially is the system as pieced together by Frank. It is apparently nowhere stated in historical records however that the "daily" *katatagae* imposed on those occupying their *honjo* actually extended for a period of 45 (or 15) days. Frank makes this assumption on the basis of correspondence to the rule of "once every 45 days" for occupants of a *tabisho*. References, such as the present one in the *Izumi Shikibu nikki*, to a "forty-five-day *imitagae* [or *katatagae*]" can then be explained in precisely this way: it would certainly be simpler to move in with a friend for the period than to commute back and forth for 45 days, leaving one's house every night.

One may perhaps assume then that Prince Atsumichi is circumventing a prohibition by Daishōgun against some activity such as erecting a building. As far as can be seen there would be no connection between this *imitagae* and the *katafutagari* mentioned in the previous sentence. The way to Izumi's residence could be blocked by any one of a number of deities, and either in relation to the Prince's own house or to the site of his *katatagae*. Hence there is here no evidence either pro or con as to whether the passage should be split in two (see Introduction, note 234). As has been pointed out (Introduction, p. 81), Yoshida assigns the beginning of the Prince's *imitagae* to Chōhō 5 (1003).10.2. This date corresponds to 30 October 1003, in the Julian calendar, and according to Frank, "*Kata-imi*," p. 225, winter *setsubun* falls on either 29 or 30 October (varying according to the year, again in terms of the Julian calendar). And the *setsubun* were the points of departure for such *imitagae*. Yoshida, *Kenkyū*, pp. 378–383, apparently not taking into account Frank's researches, theorizes that it is the direction of Ōsō which the Prince is avoiding.

278. See note 48. A cousin of Prince Atsumichi holding this rank in 1003 was Fujiwara no Kanetaka 兼隆 (985–1053), son of Atsumichi's uncle Michikane, the elder brother of Yukiko.

279. "Kuruma yadori." This was a building outside the "central gate" (*chūmon*) of the *shinden-zukuri* type of mansion, used for housing the ox-drawn carriages and other conveyances of both the owner and his guests (*Yūsoku kojitsu jiten*, p. 266). Tsunoda Bun'ei, *Jōkyōden no nyōgo* (1963), p. 93, points out that *kuruma yadori* attached to the homes of Buddhist priests were not mere

garages, but lavish guest-houses where one could live in as much comfort as in the main house. Frank, "*Kata-imi*," pp. 115, 116, mentions a method of *katatagae* performed by staying all night in a carriage parked at the gate of a building. It is unlikely that such a *katatagae* is intended here, for it is Izumi who never descends from the carriage; and besides, a 45-day rather than a one-night *katatagae* is being performed.

280. "Anagachi nari" ([The Prince's regrets] were forced). The commentators interpret "anagachi" as meaning "quite convenient for him," and I have followed this gloss. "Anagachi nari" can also be regarded as a direct comment by the author.

281. A closer version: "Accustomed to wakeful dreams on nights when I would sleep [side by side], in the village of Fushimi [lying down and seeing (a dream)] this morning I arose." "Naraite" is a *kakekotoba: naraite* 慣らひて (accustomed)/*narabite* 並びて (aligned). "Fushimi" is another *kakekotoba: Fushimi no sato* 伏見の里 (village of Fushimi [south of the Capital])/*fushimi* 伏見 (lying down and seeing [i.e., having a dream]). "Mi" and "yume" are *engo*. Yoshida, *Kenkyū*, pp. 382, 383, concludes from this poem that the residence of the Prince's cousin is in Fushimi, south of the Capital, and that the Prince has gone there to avoid the direction of Ōsō (the north in winter).

282. A closer version: "Since from that night matters concerning my own self have been unknowable, I have gone and slept perversely in unheard-of [lit., 'non-existent'] places away from home." "That night" is indefinite. Ozaki, *Kōchū*, p. 148, assumes it to be the night of their first meeting, and interprets "aranu tabine" in the plural. "Tabine" (sleeping on a journey) he further gives a psychological significance, extending over the lovers' nocturnal trysts at Izumi's home as well as in other places. This poem appears as *Seishū* 403 (379), in the following version:

Sono yo yori	From that first night,
Waga toko no ue wa	Although I have not wept
Shigurenedo	Cold, rainy tears upon my bed,
Suzuro ni aranu	Yet I have recklessly
Tabine o zo suru	Slept in strange places and strange ways.

283. "Kabakari nengoro ni katajikenaki onkokorozashi o, mizu shirazu, kokorokowaki sama ni motenasubeki." Evidently an interrogative "ni ya" is to be understood after "motenasubeki" (should treat).

284. "Kotogoto wa, sa shimo arazu." I have followed the interpretation of Ozaki, *Kōchū*, p. 148. Endō, Iwanami text, p. 432, note 14, and Yamagishi, *NKZ*, p. 241, note 1, understand the sentence to mean "I shan't act coldly toward him in one way and another." The key point seems to be whether "kotogoto" is to be taken as 異事, "strange things," or 事事, "various things." I have reversed the order of this and the previous sentence.

285. *Sukuse* 宿世, predetermination by actions in a former life.

282

286. An allusion to *Kokinshū* 952 (Anonymous):

Ika naramu	In what sort of cavern
Iwao no naka ni	Deep within the crags
Sumaba ka wa	Should I have to live
Yo no uki koto no	In order not to hear
Kikoekozaramu	The painful tidings of this world?

Such a life would be that of a mountain ascetic, and Izumi is saying metaphorically that she wishes to abandon the world for the consolations of religion.

287. "Mata uki koto mo araba ikaga sen." Ozaki, *Kōchū*, p. 150, interprets this sentence as having to do with possible unpleasantness at the Prince's mansion.

288. "Nao kakute ya suginamashi. Chikakute oya harakara no on'arisama mo mikikoe." I have followed Ozaki, *Kōchū*, pp. 150, 151, here. Endō, Iwanami text, p. 433, notes 22, 23, and p. 457, sup. notes 112–114, takes "kakute" (thus) to refer to Izumi's resolution to go to live with the Prince. In that case "chikakute" would also refer to proximity to the Prince.

289. "Mata mukashi no yō ni mo miyuru hito no ue o misadamen to omoi-tachinitareba" (As she decided she should see to the future of the person who reminded her of the past . . .). Presumably Koshikibu, whom she bore to her first husband, Tachibana no Michisada, is the person referred to.

290. "Ainashi" (disagreeable). My interpretation follows Ozaki, *Kōchū*, p. 150. Endō, Iwanami text, p. 433, note 25, and p. 457, sup. note 114, contends that the word is a critical comment by Izumi Shikibu as author on her own way of thinking—a disapproval of her caution in avoiding scandal because of her desire to care for her family.

291. "Isa shirazu." My interpretation follows Ozaki, *Kōchū*, p. 152. Yama-gishi, *NKZ*, p. 242, note 8, glosses: "From now on I shall say I do not know any such woman," and suggests the possibility of an allusion to a poem by Ōtsubune, daughter of Ariwara no Munahari (d. 898), *Gosenshū* 635:

Hito wa isa	I do not know what others feel,
Ware wa naki na no	But as for me, an undeserved bad name
Oshikereba	Is something that I should regret,
Mukashi mo ima mo	And so I shall reply
Shirazu to o iwamu	I never knew you either then or now.

The poem, which appears also as *Kokinshū* 630, attributed to Ōtsubune's brother Motokata (888–953), was written in reply to a man who threatened to defame her by saying she was his ex-wife.

292. In the original, this and the first part of the next sentence read: "Kore wa mameyaka ni notamawasetareba, omoitatsu koto sae honokikitsuru hito mo abekameritsuru o, oko naru me o mo mirubekameru kana to" (Since he had said this earnestly, it seemed there must be someone who had gotten some

glimmering of her decision. Hence she must face such a stupid situation). This passage can be interpreted in either of two ways: (1) Evil-minded people have gotten wind of Izumi's plans and have deliberately spread rumors to make the Prince break off with her. (2) Her friends have heard of her decision, and now she will lose face if it turns out that, because of the new rumors, she does not go to the Prince's mansion after all. The two possibilities are discussed by Ozaki, *Kōchū*, p. 155. He favors the latter, I the former.

293. "Aritsuru koto" (things which had been). Perhaps the Prince's accusations?

294. "Omowamashikaba," an allusion to a poem by Ise in the *Kokinrokujō*, kan 4 (*Kōchū kokka taikei*, IX, 405):

Hitokoto wa	Though strangers' tattle
Ama no karu mo ni	Should grow thick
Shigeku tomo	As seaweed that the *ama* cut,
Omowamashikaba	If you but care for me,
Yoshi ya yo no naka	I'll let the world say what it will.

295. I have followed Ozaki, *Kōchū*, p. 153, and Endō, Iwanami text, p. 434, in eliminating the word "kaeri" (reply) found in the *Sanjōnishibon* and *Kangembon* texts before "keshiki," in favor of the reading found in the *Ōeibon*.

296. A closer version: "Would that you would come within this moment; how can I go to you, saying, 'I love you,' even though I have a reputation?" Note that the preceding sentence is grammatically joined to the poem. This poem appears as *Seishū* 404 (380).

297. A closer version: "In this way you have been thinking about rumors arising; I see that such concerns depend on the man." Ozaki, *Kōchū*, p. 153, suggests that "hito kara" be read "hitogara" (your nature)—"It is your [negative] nature to worry about such things."

298. A closer version: "Although I think, 'I shall not doubt; even less shall I resent,' my heart does not fit in with my heart." The poem loses its point unless both "hearts" are taken to belong to the Prince.

299. A closer version: "Let not the heart die out you say resents me; I also doubt—even you, upon whom I am utterly dependent." Doubting is a sign of emotional involvement. Ozaki, *Kōchū*, pp. 156, 157, remarks of this and the previous poem that their use of paradox accurately expresses the psychology of a young man and woman caught in the toils of love. Endō, Iwanami text, p. 434, note 11, takes "tanomu kimi" to mean "you who trust what people say." This poem appears as *Seishū* 405 (381), in the following version:

Uramuramu	Let not that heart die out
Kokoro wa tayu na	You say resents me—
Kagirinaku	I also doubt,
Tanomu yo o uku	Sick with disappointment at our bonds
Ware mo utagau	Of love, wherein I trusted without bound.

284

300.   A closer version: "Frost-withering [separation] is desolate; in the blowing of the autumn wind reeds rustled [you visited me]." "-Gare" is a *kakekotoba: shimogare* 霜枯れ (frost-withering)/*kare* 離れ (separation). "Otozure" is another *kakekotoba:* 音摩れ (sound-chafing)/訪れ (visit). Izumi complains that now that winter has come the Prince no longer visits her as he did in autumn. The poem appears as *Seishū* 406 (382).

301.   "Kare-" is the same *kakekotoba* as in the previous poem. "Arashi" is another: *araji* 有らじ (probably are not)/*arashi* 嵐 (storm).

302.   Or sent the usual carriage for her: "Rei no kuruma areba" (as there was the usual carriage).

303.   "Shinobitaru tokoro ni owashimasu tote." This could also be rendered: "was going to a secluded place." Presumably this is to be understood as the cousin's house previously mentioned (see note 278). Evidently this time the lovers have a better rendezvous than the carriage shed.

304.   A closer version: "When today I idly counted up, I realized that, of all the years and months, yesterday was the only time when I had not thought of mournful things." The poem appears as *Seishū* 407 (383).

305.   A more nearly literal version: "Although I do think that there is you who comfort me, still the dusk of evening is somehow sad." This poem appears as *Seishū* 408 (384).

306.   A more nearly literal version: "As for the evening dusk, everyone feels that way only; but you, who speak first, are superior to others." I.e., she is more sensitive than they.

307.   A more nearly literal version: "It is a frosty morning after one has stayed up all night that truly has nothing in the world to surpass it." With its use of the verb *masaru* (surpass), this poem is a reply to that of the Prince. The last two lines might be interpreted, "There is nothing so touching in the world." "Oki-" is the usual pun on "rise" and "settle." The poem appears as *Seishū* 409 (385).

308.   This poem appears as *Seishū* 410 (386).

309.   Or a nervous ailment accompanied by headache, bodily pains, chills, etc.? *Kaze* in the Heian Period apparently sometimes referred to a disease involving such symptoms, and in grave cases even partial paralysis. For a discussion see *Zenkō,* pp. 301, 302.

310.   Enchi Fumiko in her translation into modern Japanese in *Ōchō nikki shū* (1960), p. 179, interprets "taeshi koro" as having reference to the death of the late Prince Tametaka, which event made Izumi too wish to die. The poem appears as *Seishū* 411 (387).

311.   "Imijiki koto kana. Kaesugaesu mo" (What an extraordinary thing! Emphatically so!).

312.   "Tama no o" 玉の緒 (thread of life), "taen" (break), and "musubi" (bind) are *engo.*

313. I have followed Endō, Iwanami text, p. 437, note 17, and p. 458, sup. note 124, in this translation. The original, punctuated as in Iwanami text, p. 437, runs: "Kaku iu hodo ni, toshi mo nokori nakereba, harutsukata to omou. Shimotsuki tsuitachi goro" (While they were saying such things, since there was nothing left of the year, she thought, "Spring or thereabouts." Around the first of the eleventh month . . .). Ozaki, *Kōchū*, pp. 167, 168, places no punctuation after "omou," and argues that "harutsukata" (toward spring), which seems inconsistent with the month specified unless one accepts a solution similar to Endō's, is a mistake in copying for "hatetsukata" (toward the end [of the year]).

314. A closer version: "Although it is snow which has fallen [grown completely old] from the Age of Gods, today in particular it is rare!" "Furi-" is a *kakekotoba*: 降り (fall)/ 古り (grow old). In the latter meaning it is an *engo* with "kamiyo" (Age of the Gods). I have chosen the reading "naredo" (although it is), found in all other texts, in preference to the "nareba" (since it is) of the *Sanjōnishibon*.

315. A closer version: "As each winter I look and say, 'The first snow!', I get older and older with no feeling of rarity." "Furi-" is the same *kakekotoba* noted in the previous poem. Only in the sense of "aging" is it functional; in the sense of "falling" it merely serves as an *engo* for "hatsuyuki" (first snow). This poem appears as *Seishū* 412 (388).

316. "Hitobito fumi tsukurumereba" (since it seems people are making writings). The commentators interpret "fumi tsukuru" as I have indicated in the translation.

317. A closer version: "Since, having no leisure, you will not come, I shall go; I would like to learn the way in which I might make writings [steps to you]." "Fumi" is a *kakekotoba*: 文 (writings)/ 踏み (treading). "Michi" is also used in both its literal sense of "road" and its metaphorical one of "way [of doing something]." This poem appears as *Seishū* 413 (389).

318. A closer version: "Come to my dwelling to visit me; I will teach you the way of making writings [steps], that we should see a meeting." "Fumi" and "michi" involve the same word play explained above.

319. A closer version: "The many-times-preening snipe of cold-clear nights—are they I? How many mornings has the frost formed [have I stayed up and looked at it]?" "Okite" is a *kakekotoba*, the usual pun on 置く and 起く. This poem contains an allusion to *Kokinshū* 761 (Anonymous):

Akatsuki no	At dawn I hear the snipe
Shigi no hanegaki	Preening their feathers—
Momo hagaki	Preening a hundred times;
Kimi ga konu yo wa	I toss and turn more restlessly than they
Ware zo kazu kaku	On nights you do not come.

Kubota Utsubo, *Kokinwakashū hyōshaku*, II, 483, quotes *Kokinshū seigi* 正義 (1832), a commentary by Kagawa Kageki 香川景樹 (1768–1843), to the effect that snipe really do not preen their feathers, but only stick their bills into the mud and make a *gishi-gishi* sound. The author of the poem, according to this theory, mistook the sound for preening (*hanegaki*). The last line is subject to various interpretations. The author, presumably a woman, tosses and turns while she lies waiting for her lover. Either her restless movements or the sounds she makes are likened to those of the snipe. Kageki however takes "ware zo kazu kaku" to mean "I count the nights you do not come." The poem appears as *Seishū* 414 (390).

320. A closer version: "During this period, when it seems rain falls and snow falls also, just like the settling of the morning frost [thinking only how shallow is your affection], I stay up all night and look." "Asashimo" is a *kake-kotoba: asashimo* 朝霜 (morning frost)/*asashi mo* 淺しも (shallow). "Oki-" is the usual pun on 置き and 起き. Izumi is again complaining of the Prince's neglect. This poem appears as *Seishū* 415 (391), in the following form:

Yuki mo furi	Through the falling snow,
Ame mo furinuru	The falling rain, this winter
Kono fuyu wa	I lie wakeful through the night
Asashimo to nomi	Because of your hard heart,
Okiite wa miru	And watch the light of frosty morning break.

321. I have supplied this word.

322. "Aware ni, nanigoto mo kikoshimeshiutomanu on'arisama nareba, kokoro no hodo mo goranzeraren tote koso omoi mo tate." I have followed Endō, Iwanami text, p. 439, note 12, in my interpretation of "omoi mo tate" (She made up her mind). The other commentators are in agreement. Tamai, *Shinchū*, p. 189, asserts that "aware ni" modifies "kikoshimeshiutomanu" (listened in a manner not distant), and has the meaning of "jitsu ni" (really). I have preferred to follow Endō in assigning it to "on'arisama nareba" (gave the appearance), with its usual meaning of "full of emotional awareness," although strictly speaking it should take the form "aware naru" in order to modify "on'arisama." On the other hand, I have followed Tamai, and Ozaki, *Kōchū*, p. 172, in treating "kikoshimeshi" as an honorific prefix, rather than having it mean "hearing," as Endō does.

323. An expansion of "kakute wa" (being thus). I have followed Tamai, *Shinchū*, p. 189.

324. "Hoi no mama ni mo narinu bakari kashi." The commentators agree on this interpretation of Izumi's *hoi* 本意 (original purpose).

325. A closer version: "In transient might-be's all the night long—" These lines and Izumi's reply are combined into one poem, no. 416 (392), in the *Seishū*.

326. "Mikeshiki no, rei yori mo ukabitaru kotodomo o notamawasete." I have followed Ozaki, *Kōchū*, p. 174, Yamagishi, *NKZ*, p. 251, note 9, and Endō, Iwanami text, p. 439, note 16, in interpreting "ukabitaru" as "uncertain" or "undependable." Tamai, *Shinchū*, p. 281, takes it to mean "in good spirits."

327.   A closer version: "When I think of it as reality there is no way to speak of it; I would like to turn the matter of tonight into a dream." "Koyoi" (tonight) is used in the sense of "this night [just past]." This poem appears as *Seishū* 417 (393).

328.   "Ikaga wa" (How?). I have followed Yamagishi, *NKZ*, p. 252, note 3, in this interpretation. Ozaki, *Kōchū*, p. 175, suggests the passage should be taken to mean "I wonder what you think of this."

329.   A closer version: "Although you vowed to this extent, do you say, 'Think that such is the commonplace of the uncertain world'?"

330.   "Omoinasan to. Kokoro mijika ya" (Deliberately to think. Your heart is short!). I have followed Endō, Iwanami text, p. 440, note 2, in my interpretation. Ozaki, *Kōchū*, p. 175, suggests that these words should be read as one sentence: "Omoinasan to kokoromishika ya" (Did you attempt to [resign yourself to] thinking, ['Such is the way of the world']? [Not likely]).

331.   A closer version: "A mere life whose extent is unknown is uncertain; vowing, exchange: the pines of Sumiyoshi." This poem contains an allusion to *Kokinshū* 905 (Anonymous):

Ware mite mo	Even the time I saw them
Hisashiku narinu	Is now long past;
Suminoe no	How many ages have they known,
Kishi no himematsu	The pines that grow
Iku yo henuran	On Suminoe's shore?

Sumiyoshi 住吉 and Suminoe 墨江 (or 住吉) are the same place—a site in Settsu Province, within the present city of Osaka, where there was a shrine to the god of Sumiyoshi. *Himematsu* 姫松, properly a small, young pine tree, is here used as a word connoting familiarity, according to Kubota, *Kokinwakashū hyōshaku*, III, 82. Endō, Iwanami text, p. 458, sup. note 131, suggests that "kawasu" in the Prince's poem is a *kakekotoba* meaning both "exchange vows" and "mingle branches."

332.   "Hito yarinaranu monowabishi." I have rather freely followed Suzuki, *Zenkō*, pp. 316, 318, 319, in interpreting this sentence. Tamai, *Shinchū*, p. 192, takes "hito yarinaranu" to mean "uncontrollably" or "unbearably."

333.   This is an anonymous poem, *Kokinshū* 695. Yamagatsu was a term for the poor peasants living in the mountains, woodcutters and the like. The *nadeshiko* 撫子 is a wild pink, *Dianthus superbus*. Yamato nadeshiko is a variety native to Japan, as distinguished from *kara nadeshiko*, introduced from China. The term has connotations of pure, unspoiled beauty and serves as a metaphor for "Japanese girl."

334.   "'Ana monoguruoshi' to iwarete." It should be noted that "ana monoguruoshi" parallels, and is apparently a parody of, "Ana koishi" (Ah, beloved!), the first line of the poem quoted by the Prince. "Iwarete" is the passive expressing spontaneous action.

335. A closer version: "If·you are in love with me, then come and see me! [Why do you hesitate,] when it is not a road the swift-acting gods forbid?" *Chihayaburu* 千早振 is a *makurakotoba* for *kami* (deity), *yashiro* (shrine), *hito* (person), and Uji [a place name]. It is derived from the verb *ichihayabu* 逸速ぶ (to act violently), which is in turn composed of the prefix *ichi* (most, extremely) plus the verb *hayabu* (to act swiftly). This poem is taken from the *Ise monogatari*, episode 71, where it is given as a certain man's answer to a woman's amorous proposal. Thus, Izumi has replied in kind to the Prince by also quoting an old poem.

336. See Introduction, p. 84.

337. Here the Prince cleverly turns the tables on Izumi by asserting the superior claims of Buddhism as against the native deities. Ozaki, *Kōchū*, p. 179, asserts that "au michi" 逢ふ道 contains a *kakekotoba: au mi* 逢ふ身 (met person)/*Ōmi* 近江 (Ōmi [Province]). I cannot see the relevance of the provincial name in this case however and have given "au michi" the obvious translation of "Meeting Road." Ozaki further suggests that "oreba" (since I am sitting) is an *engo* of "mushiro" (mat), because of its homonymity with *oreba* 折れば (since I have folded).

338. A closer version: "If that is so, I shall proceed to go; you are doing nothing but 'extending' on the mat of the Law." "Hiromu" (to widen) is used in the sense of extending or propagating the Buddhist faith; in its literal sense of "to spread" it is an *engo* with "mushiro." Yamagishi, *NKZ*, p. 254, note 5, interprets "hiromu" as meaning also that Izumi wishes the Prince to spread out a mat for her, too. This poem appears as *Seishū* 418 (394) with the reading "nori no kokoro o" (the heart of the Law) in place of "nori no mushiro ni."

339. A more nearly literal translation: "When the snow falls, even the leaves of the trees, though it is not spring, have blossomed everywhere into plum blossoms." For a comment on this and the following poem see Introduction, pp. 84–85.

340. A closer version: "When, thinking the plum trees had already blossomed, I broke a branch, the snow in falling from it looked like scattering blossoms." Izumi's poem is an admirably constructed syntactical unit. Feigned confusion between snow and plum blossoms was a conventional attitude, dating back at least to the *Man'yōshū*. The poem appears as *Seishū* 419 (395). It also appears as *Zokushū* 475 (1317), in the following version:

Mume wa haya	The plum has early
Sakinikeri tote	Blossomed, so I thought,
Oreba chiru	Breaking a branch,
Hana koso yuki no	Whose petals scattered
Furu to miekere	Exactly like the falling of the snow.

341. A closer version: "The winter night's dawn came with me one-side-spreading my garment and lying, not meeting my girl [my eyelids not meeting],

in my love-longing." "Me" is a *kakekotoba*: 目 (eyes)/女 (girl). "Koromo kata-shiki" refers to the custom of sleeping on spread-out garments. When two lovers slept together they placed their robes side by side with the sleeves over-lapping, but when separated they had perforce to sleep on only one garment. This is the meaning of *katashiku*, a verb which comes to mean "to sleep alone," with all that that implies of loneliness and deprivation.

342. I have inserted these words in the place of "ideya," an interjection which serves to emphasize the point made in the lady's poem.

343. A closer version: "On this winter night even my eyes were closed by ice; though they were hard to open [though it was hard to stay up], I stayed up all night." The reason the lady's eyes were closed with ice would be that her tears had frozen. "Akashi-" is a *kakekotoba*: 開かし (make [eyes] open)/明し (brighten [the night]—i.e., stay up until dawn). The poem is a clever reply to the Prince's protest about his sleeplessness. It appears as *Seishū* 420 (396).

344. "Ito hakanaki ya" (It [this mode of life] was very aimless).

345. "Ika ni obosaruru ni ka aran." Another indication that the Prince's feelings are sometimes conjectured by the author (see Introduction, pp. 89, 125).

346. A closer version: "Shall I alone tell tales of the past which make one think of old matters of many ages of Kure bamboo?" "Kuretake" (Kure bamboo) is a kind of black bamboo, *Phyllostachys puberula*, with fine leaves and many joints, presumably a native of the Chinese state of Wu 吳 (Jap. Kure). With *no* it forms a *makurakotoba* for *yo* 節 (segment of bamboo) and *fushi* 節 (joint). By virtue of word play it also serves as *makurakotoba* for the homonyms *yo* 代 (age), as in the poem under consideration; *yo* 夜 (night); *ukifushi* 憂節 (painful cir-cumstance), as in the Prince's reply; etc. This poem appears as *Seishū* 421 (397), with the last line reading "Kimi nomi zo sen" (You alone will [tell the tale]). Kubota, *Izumi Shikibu shū*, p. 71, note 16, asserts that "yoyo" refers to Izumi's two lovers, the brothers Prince Tametaka and Prince Atsumichi, and "kuretake" to the bamboo garden of the imperial palace.

347. A closer version: "I think I shall not exist even for a brief space in this world where painful occurrences [joints of Kure bamboo] are rank." "Kuretake" and "ukifushi" have been explained above in note 346. "Yo no naka" is probably intended to convey its secondary meaning of "the relations between a man and woman" as well as its primary one of "the world" or "society." "Araji to zo omou" (will not be, I think) can be interpreted as either supposition or desire/intent.

348. This passage is the source of much difficulty. It reads in the original, with no punctuation marks inserted: "Hito shirezu suesasetamaubeki tokoro nado okite narawade aru tokoro nareba hashitanaku omoumeri koko ni mo kikinikuku zo iwan tada ware yukite ite inan to oboshite." The first fact to be noted is that the narrative has now reached its major turning point, for Izumi is at last to be taken into the Prince's mansion. This important development is introduced abruptly, immediately after—indeed grammatically in the same sentence with—a despairing poem which seems to say that the day will never

come for the two lovers to be united. And the passage involves problems in interpretation. The principal difficulties revolve around "okite"—whether it is used as a noun or a verb. The verb in question, belonging to the *shimo nidan* conjugation, is *okitsu* 掟つ (to decide, settle, fix). The corresponding noun, *okite* 掟, has several usages: (1) "determination, decision"; (2) "regulations, law, rules"; (3) "disposal, settlement, management, plan"; (4) "disposition, nature, temperament"; (5) "custom, conventional practice" (*Dai Nihon kokugo jiten*, I, 533, 535). The most natural way to construe "okite" is as a verb: "Hito shirezu suesase-tamaubeki tokoro okite" (He settled on a place where he could put her without anyone knowing). I have followed this interpretation. The Japanese commentators however feel that the simple *ren'yōkei* ending of "okite" is unnatural—that as a verb in this position it should read "okitete," i.e., *okite* plus the *te* form of the suffix *tsu*, or that it should be combined with an honorific such as *tamaite*. For a discussion see Iwanami text, p. 459, sup. note 137. Tamai, *Shinchū*, p. 196, who does treat the word as a verb, has evidently substituted "okitete" for the "okite" found in all texts. Ozaki, *Kōchū*, p. 182; Yamagishi, *NKZ*, p. 255; Shimizu, *Ōchō nikki*, p. 209; and Endō, Iwanami text, p. 441, place a *tōten* (comma) before "okite" and interpret it as a noun. Doing so leads them into various difficulties. The first of these is how to take "okite" if indeed it is a noun. "Okite narawade aru tokoro" may be interpreted as "a place not set up for hiding a woman" (Ozaki), or "a place to whose customs the lady was not yet accustomed" (Shimizu, Endō). "Narawade" without "okite" would mean essentially the same thing however. A more serious problem is what to do with "tokoro nado" if it is deprived of its verb. Ozaki suggests supplying a *wa*—"As for a place where he could put her . . ." Everything down to "oboshite" then comes to depend on that verb, and the passage must be read to mean, not that the Prince has selected a place (which it soon becomes clear he has), but that he is merely thinking of the unsuitability of a certain kind of place. But Ozaki points out a difficulty in his own interpretation: If "hito shirezu suesasetamaubeki tokoro nado" is to be considered the Prince's own thought, the honorific *tamau* should be altered to the humble verb *tatematsuru*. He suggests that narrative and mental monologue have somehow become fused. Endō, Iwanami text, p. 441, note 20, and p. 459, sup. note 137, avoids this difficulty by assuming that the Prince's thought begins with "hashitanaku omoumeri" instead of "hito shirezu." I have chosen to regard "okite" as a verb and translate accordingly.

349. It is not clear what relation the Prince's decision to go alone to escort the lady to his mansion has to the immediately preceding statements of her hesitancy and the probable reaction at home. I have assumed that it may be twofold—to overcome her fears by going himself (and we see further on that he does not do more than hint to her what is about to happen), and to avoid arousing comment by keeping the matter as secret as possible. This explanation is in accord with Tamai's interpretation, *Shinchū*, p. 285.

350. "Shinobite hito nado iyo to seraretari" (It was set up as if to say, "Lead in your people secretly"). My interpretation follows Endō, Iwanami text, p.

442, note 5. Yamagishi, *NKZ*, p. 256, note 10, understands "iyo" as the imperative of *iru* 居る (to be) rather than of *iru* 率る (to lead). There is very little practical difference, but 居よ could be taken to mean that attendants have been assigned.

351. "Nani ka wa wazatodachite mo mairamashi" (Why should I make a big, deliberate show of coming?). I have followed the various commentators in rejecting the *Sanjōnishibon* reading of "hito" (nani ka hito) in favor of the "wa" found in all other texts.

352. I have inserted the words "his servants" and "by the darkness."

353. The part of the Heian mansion occupied by the principal or legal wife, *kita no kata* (see note 48). Such a move would naturally be viewed with alarm and repugnance by the wife.

354. "Koko ni wa chikakereba" (Since it is near to here). I have followed Shimizu, *Ōchō nikki*, p. 210, in interpreting this as "near to the front."

355. "In," Atsumichi's father, Reizei (see note 106).

356. *Tenjōbito* 殿上人. These were men holding the Fifth Rank (see note 48) and above (in the case of members of the Kurōdodokoro, the Emperor's powerful private secretariat, the Sixth Rank and above). They were permitted to enter the Tenjō no Ma 殿上の間, the audience room on the south side of the Sovereign's Palace, the Seiryōden.

357. Or "prying eyes"?: "Kakute wa arinubeshi ya" (Can things be this way?).

358. I have followed Shimizu, *Ōchō nikki*, p. 210; Ozaki, *Kōchū*, p. 186; Tamai, *Shinchū*, p. 198; and Yamagishi, *NKZ*, p. 257, in inserting this paragraph from the *Ōeibon*. Endō omits it but quotes it in Iwanami text, p. 459, sup. note 139. It is found in all *Ōeibon* texts, but is missing from the *Kangembon* and *Sanjōnishibon*. The passage in question (here set off by stars from the immediately preceding and following words, and punctuated as in *NKZ*, p. 257) is: ". . . to notamawasureba, ★ oroshikomete misoka ni kikeba, 'Hiru wa hitobito, In no tenjōbito nado mairiatsumarite, ika ni zo, kakute wa arinubeshi ya, chikaotori ika ni sen to omou koso kurushikere' to notamawasureba, ★'Sore o nan omoitamauru'." If the passage is omitted, Izumi's remark, "That's what I was thinking," becomes an answer to the Prince's suggestion that her present quarters are unsuitable.

359. *Senji* 宣旨, which I have rendered "serving mistress," was originally a type of document "announcing 宣 the [Imperial] Intent 旨"; it was used also for a female official who transmitted the Sovereign's words. Later it came to be generally used for female servants of very high rank (*Yūsoku kojitsu jiten*, p. 483). Ozaki, *Kōchū*, p. 187, says that the first *owasu* in "owashite owase" is used as the verb "to go"; the second in a purely honorific function. The Prince seems to be saying, "After you have gotten a little better acquainted, go over to the Senji's quarters when I cannot be with you." Texts other than the *Sanjōnishibon* have "Ima shibashi ni narinaba hiru nado mo ano Senji no aru kata" (A little later you should go over to the Senji's quarters during the day). Without these

extra words it would seem more likely that the Prince is advising her to go at night, about whose dangers he has just warned her.

360. "Soko ni mo" (in there too). I have followed Endō, Iwanami text, p. 442, note 18, in my interpretation. A more natural one might be to take these words as going with the preceding sentence: "No one would be so bold as to loiter around that place—not there."

361. "Futsuka bakari arite, kita no tai ni watarasetamaubekereba, hitobito odorokite." Ozaki, *Kōchū*, p. 187, points out that this passage can also be interpreted to mean that the Prince has already installed his lady in the northern wing, and that two days later he is himself discovered going (watarasetamau) to her there.

362. "Nani no kataki hito ni mo arazu" (She is no such difficult [i.e., demanding special treatment] person). "Kataki" may be a scribal error for "takaki" (highborn).

363. "Kaku to notamawasede, waza to oboseba koso, shinobite ite owashi-tarame" (It was because he thought of it as a special matter that he brought her in secretly without saying "Thus" [i.e., without giving an explanation]). I have followed Shimizu, *Ōchō nikki*, p. 210, and Tamai, *Shinchū*, p. 199, in taking "kaku" as going with what follows rather than what precedes it. Ozaki, *Kōchū*, p. 186; Yamagishi, *NKZ*, p. 258; and Endō, Iwanami text, p. 443, place it as an afterthought following "arazu" (see note 362): "She is no such high-and-mighty person that he should treat her thus." They also break the train of the Princess' thought at this point, closing quotes after "kaku," and reading "nota-mawasete" (she said) instead of "notamawasede" (not saying).

364. "Itōshikute." I have followed Endō, Iwanami text, p. 443, note 24, and Ozaki, *Kōchū*, p. 189, in understanding this word to mean something like "baffled," "at a loss," or "in an unpleasant situation," rather than "sorry for." If it is given the latter interpretation it is not clear whether the person the Prince is sorry for is Izumi (who would suffer from his wife's anger) or his spouse herself. Yamagishi takes the former view, *NKZ*, p. 258, note 12.

365. "Hito no iu koto mo kikinikushi, hito no keshiki mo itōshute, konata ni owashimasu." I have followed Shimizu, *Ōchō nikki*, p. 210, note 27, in interpreting the first "hito" as the people in the Prince's mansion, the second as Izumi. Yamagishi, *NKZ*, p. 258, notes 13, 14, takes them both as the former. In this case I have understood "itōshute" to mean "sorry for." Yamagishi however takes it as "hard to bear."

366. "Hito tsukawan kara ni on'oboe no nakarubeki koto ka wa" (Should you be lacking in *oboe* because I would employ a person?). There are several possible ways of interpreting this sentence. I have followed Endō, Iwanami text, p. 443, note 30, in taking "oboe" to mean "something one gets the point of." An equally plausible interpretation would be to understand "oboe" in its common Heian meaning of "favor" or "kind regard," and translate: "Just because I have taken someone into my service, is that any excuse for you to assume an attitude of hostility?" Still another possibility is suggested by Ozaki,

Kōchū, p. 188: In employing various people it is only natural that one of them should come to be more favored than another. According to this view, the Prince is presenting Izumi as merely a favorite servant (no doubt with the implied understanding that such a status involved receiving the lady's favors). This interpretation however involves an application of the honorific "on'oboe" by the Prince to himself—a weak point, as Ozaki admits. (For other examples of self-applied honorifics see notes 25, 42, 348.)

367. Evidently the nickname of a maid in the Prince's household (see note 91; for Chūjō see note 29).

368. The sixth year of Chōhō (1004). On the twentieth of the seventh month the year period was changed to Kankō, and the year became Kankō 1.

369. Reizei-in, Prince Atsumichi's father. His residence, the Reizei-in from which his appellation comes, was immediately outside the precincts of the Greater Imperial Palace (Daidairi), at the northeast corner of Nijō Ōji and Ōmiya Ōji. It is not clear whether the Prince's mansion was a part of this palace (cf. the Prince's remark to Izumi that his father's courtiers assemble outside every day, p. 187), or whether the courtiers have merely come to the Prince's residence as an escort (for a possible location of the Prince's mansion see Introduction, note 65). Yamagishi, *NKZ*, p. 259, note 7, takes the latter view. Ozaki, *Kōchū*, p. 192, says that it can be assumed that Izumi is installed in the "Southern Building" (Nan'in) of the Reizei-in. For a discussion of the problem of historical accuracy involved here see Introduction, note 243.

370. The original is simply "ana o ake" (They opened holes). I have assumed the presence of some kind of *shōji* (paper sliding-door). See Introduction, p. 87.

371. *Kandachime* 上達部 were the holders of the three highest court ranks; the Sangi, a group of advisors to the Emperor, were included in this category though they held only the Fourth Rank.

372. An expansion of "on'asobi ari" (There was [musical] entertainment).

373. The sister was Jōshi (see Introduction, p. 12). She was married to the Heir Apparent (Prince Okisada, future Emperor Sanjō) in 991 and became his Nyōgo on his accession in 1011. Nyōgo 女御 was one of the ranks of imperial consort, third in order after Kōgō 皇后 and Chūgū 中宮. An Emperor might have more than one Nyōgo, and Sanjō had another, Yoshiko [Kenshi] 姸子, the daughter of Michinaga. In 1012 Jōshi became Sanjō's Empress (Kōgō), and Yoshiko his Chūgū. Nyōgo was also used as a term for consorts of the Heir Apparent, and it is in that sense that I have here translated it "Senior Consort of the Heir Apparent" (*Nihon rekishi daijiten*, XVI, 99; *Yūsoku kojitsu jiten*, p. 635).

374. The *sato*, the home where she was brought up. Her father Naritoki (941–995) was already deceased. Tamai, *Shinchū*, p. 208, states that her grandmother, the daughter of Fujiwara no Sadakata 定方 (875–932), was then living there.

375. "Ware sae hitoge naku nan oboyuru" (Even I feel unhuman [i.e.,

294

despised]).

376. I have supplied this sentence.

377. I have supplied the adjective "dear." The children were Prince Atsuakira 敦明 (994–1051), Prince Atsunori 敦儀 (997–1054), Prince Atsuhira 敦平 (999–1049), Princess Tōshi 當子 (1001–1023), and Princess Shishi 禔子 (1003–1048). That same year Jōshi had another child, Prince Moroaki 師明 (1004–1085). None of these children ever succeeded to the throne.

378. "Kore yori mo mimi ni mo irehaberaji to omoitamaete" (For my part, too, I would not put [such things] even into my ears). An honorific would probably be needed if the ears were those of the sister.

379. "Chikō dani mikikoeji tote" (She would [rather?] not see, at least not close at hand). It could be either the Prince or the general situation that the Princess "would not see."

380. Her elder brothers were Tametō 爲任, Suketō 相任, and Michitō 通任.

381. "'Nyōgodono no ommukae ni' to kikoetamaeba, sa oboshitari" (When they said, "We have come as the Nyōgo's meeting [party]," [x] thought so). I have followed Tamai, *Shinchū*, p. 209; Ozaki, *Kōchū*, p. 198; and Shimizu, *Ōchō nikki*, p. 218, in interpreting "sa oboshitari." Endō, Iwanami text, p. 445, note 39, assigns these words to the Prince: "He realized his consort was going to the Nyōgo's residence."

382. "Ommenoto, zōshi naru mutsukashiki monodomo harawasuru o kikite, senji . . . to kikoesawagu" (Hearing the [Princess'] nurse having the distasteful things in her chamber swept away, the Senji became upset and said . . .). The nurse here apparently is that of the Prince's consort, not the one who lectured him about his nocturnal escapades (see pp. 142–143). Yamagishi, *NKZ*, p. 262, note 19, asserts that "zōshi naru" さうしなる ("the chamber's"; *zōshi* 曹司 were the sleeping quarters assigned to ladies-in-waiting in the palaces of the period) appears as "sō naru" さうなる in the *Sanjōnishibon*. The text as printed in "Ihon Izumi Shikibu nikki," *Bungaku* (Aug. 1933), p. 151, and Yoshida, *Zenshū*, p. 99, however, appears as さうしなる. The Musashino Shoin 1964 facsimile edition of the *Sanjōnishibon*, p. 109, shows う prolonged into し:

383. Izumi.

384. "Miya no Ue, onfumigaki, Nyōgodono no onkotoba, sa shimo araji, kakinashinameri to hon ni." Yamagishi, *NKZ*, p. 263, note 30, and Ozaki, *Kōchū*, p. 200, are of the opinion that this concluding sentence is a deliberate formal device of the original author. Endō, Iwanami text, p. 459, sup. note 143, also discusses this possibility, but points out as well that if it is regarded as an actual later addition, we have evidence here of the manuscript passing through three hands: those of the original author, who ended with the preceding sentence; those of the first copyist, who added the comment running through "kakinashinameri" (seems to have invented); and those of the second copyist, who added "to hon ni" (it says in the text).

I.   Editions and Studies of the *Izumi Shikibu nikki*, and Related Works

Azuma Setsuo 東節夫, Tsukahara Tetsuo 塚原鐵雄, and Maeda Kingo 前田欣吾. *Izumi Shikibu nikki sōsakuin* 和泉式部日記總索引. Tōkyō: Musashino Shoin, 1959.

Endō Yoshimoto 遠藤嘉基, ed. *Izumi Shikibu nikki*, in *Nihon koten bungaku taikei* 日本古典文學大系, vol. XX. Tōkyō: Iwanami Shoten, 1962.

—— *Shinkō Izumi Shikibu monogatari* 新講和泉式部物語. Tōkyō: Hanawa Shobō, 1962.

Enchi Fumiko 圓地文子, trans. *Izumi Shikibu nikki*, in *Koten Nihon bungaku zenshū* 古典日本文學全集, vol. VIII [*Ōchō nikki shū* 王朝日記集]. Tōkyō: Chikuma Shobō, 1960.

Fujioka Tadami 藤岡忠美, trans. *Izumi Shikibu nikki*, in *Gendaigoyaku Nihon koten bungaku zenshū* 現代語譯日本古典文學全集 [no vol. number]. Tōkyō: Kawade Shobō, 1954.

Ikeda Kikan 池田龜鑑. "Ihon 異本 *Izumi Shikibu nikki*," *Bungaku* 文學, I (Aug. 1933), 133–151; (Nov. 1933), 134–151.

Itō Hiroshi 伊藤博. "*Izumi Shikibu nikki* no seiritsu jiki o megutte の成立時期をめぐって," *Kokubungaku gengo to bungei* 國文學言語と文藝, 2 (May 1960), 29–37.

Izumi Shikibu nikki, in *Shinkō gunsho ruijū* 新校群書類從, ed. Kawamata Keiichi 川俁馨一, vol. XIV. Tōkyō: Naigai Shoseki Kabushiki Kaisha, 1938.

Kawase Kazuma 川瀬一馬. "*Izumi Shikibu nikki* wa Fujiwara Shunzei no saku は藤原俊成の作," *Aoyama Gakuin Joshi Tanki Daigaku kiyō* 青山學院女子短期大學紀要, 2 (Sept. 1953), 21–52.

Komuro Yoshizō 小室由三 and Tanaka Eizaburō 田中榮三郎. *Izumi Shikibu nikki shōkai* 詳解. Tōkyō: Hakuteisha, 1957.

Oda Hiroko 織田裕子. "*Izumi Shikibu nikki* no sakusha ni tsuite の作者について," *Kokugo-kokubun* 國語國文, 27 (Apr. 1958), 50–64.

Ogawa Juichi 小川壽一, ed. *Ōeibon eisha* 應永本影寫 *Izumi Shikibu nikki*. Vol. III of *Ryūkoku Daigaku Kokubun Gakkai shuppan sōsho* 龍谷大學國文學會出版叢書. Kyōto: Ryūkoku Daigaku Kokubun Gakkai, 1928.

Ōhashi Kiyohide 大橋清秀. *Izumi Shikibu nikki no kenkyū* の研究. Tōkyō: Hatsune Shobō, 1961.

Oka Kazuo 岡一男. "*Izumi Shikibu nikki* no kenkyū," in *Nihon bungaku kōza* 日本文學講座, ed. Yamamoto Sansei 山本三生, vol. V [*Zuihitsu-nikkihen* 隨筆日記篇]. Tōkyō: Kaizōsha, 1934.

Omori, Annie Shepley, and Kochi Doi, trans. *Diaries of Court Ladies of Old Japan*. Tōkyō: Kenkyūsha, 1961.

Ozaki Tomomitsu 尾崎知光. *Izumi Shikibu nikki kōchū* 考注. Tōkyō: Tōhō Shobō, 1957.

Shimizu Fumio 清水文雄, ed. *Izumi Shikibu nikki*. Vol. MMDCCL of *Iwanami bunko* 岩波文庫. Tōkyō: Iwanami Shoten, 1964.

——, ed. *Izumi Shikibu nikki*, in *Nihon koten kanshō kōza* 日本古典鑑賞講座, vol. VI [*Ōchō nikki* 王朝日記]. Tōkyō: Kadokawa Shoten, 1959.

—— "*Izumi Shikibu nikki kō* 考," *Kokubungaku shiron* 國文學試論, 3 (Dec. 1935), 31–126.

—— "*Izumi Shikibu nikki no issetsu: 'Hakanaki koto' ni furete* の一節「はかなきこと」にふれて," *Kokubungaku kō* 國文學攷, 20 (Nov. 1958), 79–82.

—— "*Izumi Shikibu nikki seiritsu ni kan-suru shōkō—iwayuru 'genkashū' o megutte* 成立に關する小考 — いはゆる「原歌集」をめぐって," *Kokubungaku kō*, 27 (May 1962), 84–94.

Suzuki Kazuo 鈴木一雄 and Enchi Fumiko. *Zenkō* 全講 *Izumi Shikibu nikki*. Tōkyō: Shibundō, 1965.

Suzuki Tomotarō 鈴木知太郎, ed. *Izumi Shikibu nikki*. Vol. XV of *Koten bunko* 古典文庫. Tōkyō: Koten Bunko, 1948.

——, ed. *Izumi Shikibu nikki: Kunaichō Toshoryō-zōbon, Sanjōnishi Sanetaka-kō hitsu* 宮内廳圖書寮藏本三條西實隆公筆 [facsimile]. Tōkyō: Musashino Shoin, 1964.

Tamai Kōsuke 玉井幸助. *Izumi Shikibu nikki shinchū* 新註. Tōkyō: Sekaisha, 1950.

—— "*Rōbyō no go kyōji ya* 老病の後狂事歟," in *Nihon koten zensho furoku* 日本古典全書附錄 (an insert supplement to the *Nihon koten zensho* edition of *Kenju Gozen nikki*).

Yamagishi Tokuhei 山岸德平, ed. *Izumi Shikibu nikki*, in *Nihon koten zensho* [no vol. number]. Tōkyō, Ōsaka: Asahi Shimbunsha, 1959.

Yanase Kazuo 簗瀬一雄. "Izumi Shikibu no nikki-uta to shū to no kankei ni tsuite の日記歌と集との關係について," *Shomotsu tembō* 書物展望, 13 (Apr. 1943), 15–22.

Yosano Akiko 與謝野晶子, trans. *Heianchō joryū nikki* 平安朝女流日記. Vol. IX of *Gendaigoyaku kokubungaku zenshū* 現代語譯國文學全集. Tōkyō: Hibonkaku, 1938.

Yosano Hiroshi 寬, Masamune Atsuo 正宗敦夫, and Yosano Akiko, eds. *Izumi Shikibu zenshū* 全集. Vol. LXXII of *Nihon koten zenshū* 日本古典全集, ser. 2. Tōkyō: Nihon Koten Zenshū Kankōkai, 1927.

Yoshida Kōichi 吉田幸一. *Izumi Shikibu kenkyū* 研究. Tōkyō: Koten Bunko, 1964. [Vol. I of a projected three-volume set.]

—— *Izumi Shikibu zenshū: hombunhen* 本文篇. Tōkyō: Koten Bunko, 1959.

—— *Izumi Shikibu zenshū: shiryōhen* 資料篇. Tōkyō: Koten Bunko, 1966.

II. Other Material Related to Izumi Shikibu and Her Poetry Collection

Fujioka Tadami. "*Izumi Shikibu shū no seiritsu* 集の成立," *Kokugo to kokubungaku* 國語と國文學, 28 (May 1951), 6–19.

Izumi Shikibu engi 緣起. A scroll in the possession of the Jōshin'in 誠心院, Kyōto. Printed in Ōhashi, *Izumi Shikibu nikki no kenkyū*, pp. 529–541.

Jōkyo 靜居. *Izumi Shikibu zenshū*. A set of thirteen block-printed volumes (two of which are missing) in the possession of the Jōshin'in, Kyōto, 1848.

Kubota Utsubo 窪田空穗, ed. *Izumi Shikibu shū*, in *Nihon koten zensho* [no vol. number]. 1958.

Okada Yoshio 岡田希雄. "Izumi Shikibu to Fujiwara no Yasumasa と藤原保昌," *Rekishi to chiri* 歷史と地理, 19 (Feb. 1927), 266–275; (Mar. 1927), 357–366; (May 1927), 570–577; (June 1927), 637–650.

Saeki Umetomo 佐伯梅友, Murakami Osamu 村上治, and Komatsu Tomi 小松登美. *Izumi Shikibu shū zenshaku* 全釋. Tōkyō: Tōhō Shobō, 1959.

Shimizu Fumio, ed. *Izumi Shikibu kashū* 歌集. Vol. 5542–5544 of *Iwanami bunko*. Tōkyō: Iwanami Shoten, 1936.

—— "Izumi Shikibu," in *Nihon kajin kōza* 日本歌人講座, ed. Hisamatsu Sen'ichi 久松潜一 and Sanekata Kiyoshi 實方清, vol. II [*Chūko no kajin* 中古の歌人]. Tōkyō: Kōbundō, 1960.

—— "*Izumi Shikibu seishū* no seiritsu 正集の成立," *Kokubungaku kō*, 1 (Oct. 1934), 61–100.

III. General Reference Works, Literary Histories

Ajia rekishi jiten アジア歴史事典, ed. Shimonaka Kunihiko 下中邦彦. 10 vols. Tōkyō: Heibonsha, 1960.

Bukkyō daijiten 佛教大辭典, ed. Mochizuki Shinkyō 望月信亨. 10 vols. Tōkyō: Bukkyō Daijiten Hakkōsho, 1931–1963.

Daihyakkajiten 大百科事典, ed. Shimonaka Yasaburō 彌三郎. 28 vols. Tōkyō: Heibonsha, 1935.

Daikanwa jiten 大漢和辭典, ed. Morohashi Tetsuji 諸橋轍次. 13 vols. Tōkyō: Daishūkan Shoten, 1955–1959.

Dai Nihon kokugo jiten 大日本國語辭典, ed. Matsui Kanji 松井簡治 and Ueda Mannen 上田萬年. 5 vols. Tōkyō: Fuzambō, 1928.

Dokushi biyō 讀史備要, ed. Tōkyō Teikoku Daigaku Shiryō Hensanjo 東京帝國大學史料編纂所. Tōkyō: Naigai Shoseki Kabushiki Kaisha, 1942.

Ema Tsutomu 江馬務. *Kokubun kojitsu fūzokugo shūshaku: yōgi fukushokuhen* 國文故實風俗語集釋容儀服飾篇. Tōkyō: Kyōritsusha, 1935.

Fujioka Sakutarō 藤岡作太郎. *Kokubungaku zenshi: Heianchōhen* 國文學全史平安朝篇. Tōkyō: Fuzambō, 1910.

Haikai jimmei jiten 俳諧人名辭典, ed. Takagi Sōgo 高木蒼梧. Tōkyō: Meiji Shoin, 1960.

Hisamatsu Sen'ichi, ed. *Nihon bungakushi* 日本文學史. 6 vols. Tōkyō: Shibundō, 1964.

Ikeda Kikan. *Heian jidai bungaku gaisetsu* 平安時代文學概說. Tōkyō: Yagumo Shoten, 1944.

—— *Kyūtei joryū nikki bungaku* 宮廷女流日記文學. Tōkyō: Shibundō, 1927.

—— "Monogatari bungaku 物語文學." Vol. VI of *Nihon bungaku kyōyō kōza* 日本文學教養講座. Tōkyō: Shibundō, 1951.

—— "Nikki bungaku to kikō bungaku 日記文學と紀行文學," in *Nihon bungaku kōza*, ed. Yamamoto Sansei, vol. V [*Zuihitsu-nikkihen*].

Imai Takuji 今井卓爾. *Heianchō nikki no kenkyū* 平安朝日記の研究. Tōkyō: Keibunsha, 1935.

Kokka taikan 國歌大觀, ed. Matsushita Daisaburō 松下大三郎 and Watanabe Fumio 渡邊文雄. 2 vols. Tōkyō: Kadokawa Shoten, 1963.

Kokon yōrankō 古今要覽稿, ed. Kokusho Kankōkai 國書刊行會. 6 vols. Tōkyō: Kokusho Kankōkai, 1905–1907.

Mikkyō daijiten 密教大辭典, ed. Matsunaga Shōdō 松永昇道. 3 vols. Kyōto: Mikkyō Jiten Hensankai, 1932.

Nihon rekishi daijiten 日本歷史大辭典, ed. Kawade Takao 河出孝雄. 22 vols. Tōkyō: Kawade Shobō, 1960.

Ogura Ken 小倉謙, ed. *Shokubutsu no jiten* 植物の事典. Tōkyō: Tōkyōdō, 1959.

Reischauer, Robert Karl. *Early Japanese History.* 2 vols. Princeton: Princeton University Press, 1937.

Sakai-shiyakusho 堺市役所, ed. *Sakai-shi shi* 史. 8 vols. Tōkyō: Sanshūsha, 1930.

Satō Aiko 佐藤靄子. *Nihon nōshokaden* 日本能書家伝. Tōkyō: Seiabō, 1962.

Seishi kakei daijiten 姓氏家系大辭典, ed. Ōta Ryō 太田亮. 3 vols. Tōkyō: Seishi Kakei Daijiten Kankōkai, 1934.

Sekine Masanao 關根正直 and Katō Sadajirō 加藤貞次郎, eds. *Kaitei yūsoku kojitsu jiten* 改訂有職故實辭典. Tōkyō: Rimpei Shoten, 1935.

Shinsen daijimmei jiten 新撰大人名辭典, ed. Shimonaka Yasaburō. 9 vols. Tōkyō: Heibonsha, 1938.

Tamai Kōsuke. *Nikki bungaku gaisetsu* 概説. Tōkyō: Meguro Shoten, 1945.

—— *Nikki bungaku no kenkyū.* Tōkyō: Hanawa Shobō, 1965.

Waka bungaku daijiten 和歌文學大辭典, ed. Itō Yoshio 伊藤嘉夫 *et al.* Tōkyō: Meiji Shoin, 1962.

Wamyōruijushō 倭名類聚鈔 ed. Masamune Atsuo. 3 vols. Tōkyō: Kazama Shobō, 1954.

Yanagita Kunio 柳田國男, ed. *Sōgō Nihon minzoku goi* 綜合日本民俗語彙. 5 vols. Tōkyō: Heibonsha, 1955-1956.

Zōho kaitei Nihon bungaku daijiten 増補改訂日本文學大辭典, ed. Fujimura Tsukuru 藤村作. 8 vols. Tōkyō: Shinchōsha, 1963.

IV. Poetry Collections

A. Imperial (*Chokusenshū*)

Gosenwakashū 後撰和歌集, in *Kōchū kokka taikei* 校註國歌大系, ed. Nakatsuka Eijirō 中塚榮次郎, vol. III. Tōkyō: Kokumin Tosho Kabushiki Kaisha, 1927.

Goshūiwakashū 後拾遺和歌集, in *Kōchū kokka taikei*, vol. III.

Kin'yōwakashū 金葉和歌集, in *Kōchū kokka taikei*, vol. IV. 1928.

Kokinwakashū 古今和歌集 in *Kōchū kokka taikei*, vol. III.

Kubota Utsubo. *Kokinwakashū hyōshaku* 評釋. 3 vols. Tōkyō: Tōkyōdō, 1960.

Senzaiwakashū 千載和歌集, in *Kōchū kokka taikei*, vol. IV.

Shikawakashū 詞花和歌集, in *Kōchū kokka taikei*, vol. IV.

Shinchokusenwakashū 新勅撰和歌集, in *Kōchū kokka taikei*, vol. V. 1928.

Shinkokinwakashū 新古今和歌集, in *Kōchū kokka taikei*, vol. IV.

Shinsenzaiwakashū 新千載和歌集, in *Kōchū kokka taikei*, vol. VII. 1928.

Shinzokukokinwakashū 新續古今和歌集, in *Kōchū kokka taikei*, vol. VIII. 1929.

Shokugosenwakashū 續後撰和歌集, in *Kōchū kokka taikei*, vol. V.

Shokukokinwakashū 續古今和歌集, in *Kōchū kokka taikei*, vol. V.

Shokusenzaiwakashū 續千載和歌集, in *Kōchū kokka taikei*, vol. VI. 1928.

Shūiwakashū 拾遺和歌集, in *Kōchū kokka taikei*, vol. III.

Yamagishi Tokuhei, ed. *Hachidaishū zenchū* 八代集全註. 3 vols. Tōkyō: Yūseidō, 1960.

B. Others

Akazome Emon shū 赤染衞門集, in *Kōchū kokka taikei*, vol. XIII. 1929.

Gonchūnagon Sadayori-kyō shū 權中納言定頼卿集, in *Shinkō gunsho ruijū*, vol. X. 1929.

Hisamatsu Sen'ichi, ed. *Kenreimon'in Ukyō no Daibu shū* 建禮門院右京大夫集, in *Nihon koten bungaku taikei*, vol. LXXX [*Heian Kamakura shikashū* 平安鎌倉私家集]. 1964.

Ichijima Kenkichi 市島謙吉, ed. *Fubokuwakashō* 夫木和歌抄. Tōkyō: Kokusho Kankōkai, 1906.

Ise shū 伊勢集, in *Kōchū kokka taikei*, vol. XII. 1929.

Juntoku-in gyoshū 順徳院御集, in *Kōchū kokka taikei*, vol. X. 1928.

Kakimura Shigematsu 柿村重松. *Wakan rōeishū kōshō* 倭漢朗詠集考證. Tōkyō: Meguro Shoten, 1926.

Kawaguchi Hisao 川口久雄, ed. *Wakan rōeishū* 和漢朗詠集, in *Nihon koten bungaku taikei*, vol. LXXIII. 1965.

Kokinwakarokujō 古今和歌六帖, in *Kōchū kokka taikei*, vol. IX. 1929.

Man'yōshū, The, trans. Nippon Gakujutsu Shinkōkai. Tokyo: Iwanami Shoten, 1940. Republished by Columbia University Press, 1965.

Murasaki Shikibu shū 紫式部集, in *Kōchū kokka taikei*, vol. XII.

Takagi Ichinosuke 高木市之助, Gomi Tomohide 五味智英, and Ōno Susumu 大野晋, eds. *Man'yōshū* 萬葉集. Vols. IV–VII of *Nihon koten bungaku taikei*. 1957–1962.

Takano Tatsuyuki 高野辰之, ed. *Nihon kayō shūsei* 日本歌謡集成. 12 vols. Tōkyō: Shunjūsha, 1928–1929.

Tsuchihashi Yutaka 土橋寛 and Konishi Jin'ichi 小西甚一, eds. *Kodai kayōshū* 古代歌謡集. Vol. III of *Nihon koten bungaku taikei*. 1957.

V.   Other Literary Works, Studies, Historical Sources

Abe Toshiko 阿部俊子 and Imai Gen'ei 今井源衞, eds. *Yamato monogatari* 大和物語, in *Nihon koten bungaku taikei*, vol. IX. 1957.

Baishōron 梅松論, in *Shinkō gunsho ruijū*, vol. XVI. 1938.

Brower, Robert H., and Earl Miner. *Japanese Court Poetry*. Stanford: Stanford University Press, 1961.

Chang Wen-ch'eng 張文成. *The Dwelling of Playful Goddesses*, trans. Howard Levy. Tōkyō: Dai Nippon Insatsu, 1965.

Chūko kasen sanjūrokuninden 中古歌仙三十六人傳, in *Shinkō gunsho ruijū*, vol. III. 1939.

Chū Yuimakitsu kyō 注維摩詰經, in *Taishō shinshū daizōkyō* 大正新脩大藏經, ed. Takakusu Junjirō 高楠順次郎, vol. XXXVIII. Tōkyō: Taishō Issaikyō Kankōkai, 1926.

Denreki 殿曆. 2 vols. In *Dai Nihon kokiroku* 大日本古記錄, ed. Tōkyō Daigaku Shiryō Hensanjo [no vol. numbers]. Tōkyō: Iwanami Shoten, 1960, 1963.

Forke, Alfred, trans. *Lun-Hêng*. 2 vols. Berlin: Georg Reimer, 1907–1911; 2nd edition, New York: Paragon Book Gallery, 1962.

Frank, Bernard. "*Kata-imi* et *kata-tagie*: Etude sur les interdits de direction à l'époque Heian," *Bulletin de la Maison Franco-Japonaise*, new ser., 5 (1958), 1–246.

Gonijō Moromichi ki 後二條師通記. 3 vols. In *Dai Nihon kokiroku* [no vol. numbers]. 1956–1958.

Gonki 權記. Vols. XXXV, XXXVI of *Shiryō taisei* 史料大成, ed. Kawamata Keiichi. Tōkyō: Naigai Shoseki Kabushiki Kaisha, 1939. Also vols. IV, V of *Zōho* 増補 *shiryō taisei*, ed. Zōho Shiryō Taisei Kankōkai 刊行會. Kyōto: Rinsen Shoten, 1965.

Hagitani Boku 萩谷朴. *Heichū zenkō* 平中全講. Tōkyō: Hagitani Boku, 1959.

—— and Taniyama Shigeru 谷山茂, eds. *Utaawaseshū* 歌合集. Vol. LXXIV of *Nihon koten bungaku taikei*. 1965.

Honchō seiki 本朝世紀. Vol. IX of *Shintei zōho kokushi taikei* 新訂増補國史大系, ed. Kuroita Katsumi 黒板勝美. Tōkyō: Yoshikawa Kōbunkan, 1936.

Honchō shojaku mokuroku 本朝書籍目錄, in *Shinkō gunsho ruijū*, vol. XXI. 1930.

Hsiao T'ung 蕭統. *Wen-hsüan* 文選. 2 vols. Hong Kong: Shang-wu Yin-shu-kuan, 1936–1960.

Huang Hui 黃暉. *Lun-heng chiao-shih* 論衡校釋. 2 vols. Ch'ang-sha: Shang-wu Yin-shu-kuan, 1938.

Ichiko Teiji 市古貞次, ed. *Otogizōshi* 御伽草子. Vol. XXXVIII of *Nihon koten bungaku taikei*. 1958.

Ikeda Kikan and Akiyama Ken 秋山虔, eds. *Murasaki Shikibu nikki* 紫式部日記, in *Nihon koten bungaku taikei*, vol. XIX. 1958.

—— and Kishigami Shinji 岸上愼二, eds. *Makura no sōshi* 枕草子, in *Nihon koten bungaku taikei*, vol. XIX. 1958.

Ishida Yoshisada 石田吉貞. *Fujiwara Teika no kenkyū* 藤原定家の研究. Tōkyō: Bungadō Shoten, 1957.

Kachō yosei 花鳥餘情, in *Kokubun chūshaku zensho* 國文註釋全書, ed. Muromatsu Iwao 室松岩雄, vol. III. Tōkyō: Kokugakuin Daigaku Shuppambu, 1908.

Kakaishō 河海抄, in *Kokubun chūshaku zensho*, vol. III.

Kamo Mabuchi zenshū 賀茂眞淵全集, ed. Kokugakuin Henshūbu 國學院編輯部. 5 vols. Tōkyō: Yoshikawa Kōbunkan, 1903–1906.

Kaneko Motoomi 金子元臣 and Emi Seifū 江見清風. *Wakanrōeishū shinshaku* 和漢朗詠集新釋. Tōkyō: Meiji Shoin, 1942.

Kawaguchi Hisao, ed. *Kagerō nikki* かげろふ日記, in *Nihon koten bungaku taikei*, vol. XX. 1962.

——, ed. *Kohon setsuwashū* 古本説話集. Vol. 5412–5413 of *Iwanami bunko*. 1960.

Kita Yoshio 喜多義勇. *Zenkō kagerō nikki* 全講蜻蛉日記. Tōkyō: Shibundō, 1961.

Kobayashi Tadao 小林忠雄. "*Yotsugi monogatari, Uji Dainagon monogatari no seiritsu ni tsuite* 世繼物語　宇治大納言物語の成立について," *Kokugo-kokubun*, 26 (June 1957), 32–47.

Kojima Yoshio 小島吉雄. *Shinkokinwakashū no kenkyū* 新古今和歌集の研究. Tōkyō: Hoshino Shoten, 1944.

Kōno Tama 河野多麻, ed. *Utsubo monogatari* 宇津保物語. Vols. X–XII of *Nihon koten bungaku taikei*. 1959–1962.

Koshigaya Gozan 越谷吾山. *Shokoku hōgen butsurui shōko* 諸國方言物類稱呼. Included in Yoshizawa Yoshinori. *Kōhon butsurui shōko shokoku hōgen sakuin*. (See below.)

Kosugi Hōan 小杉放庵. *Tōshi oyobi tōshijin* 唐詩及唐詩人. Tōkyō: Shomotsu Tembōsha, 1939.

Kugyō bunin 公卿補任. Vols. LIII–LVII of *Shintei zōho kokushi taikei*. 1934–1938.

Kurano Kenji 倉野憲司, ed. *Kojiki* 古事記, in *Nihon koten bungaku taikei*, vol. I. 1958.

Liu P'an-sui 劉盼遂. *Lun-heng chi-chieh* 論衡集解. Peking: Ku-chi Ch'u-pan-she, 1957.

Matsuo Satoshi 松尾聰, ed. *Ochikubo monogatari* 落窪物語, in *Nihon koten bungaku taikei*, vol. XIII. 1957.

Matsumura Hiroji 松村博司, ed. *Eiga monogatari* 榮花物語. 4 vols. In *Nihon koten zensho* [no vol. numbers]. 1956–1959.

—— and Yamanaka Yutaka 山中裕, eds. *Eiga monogatari*. Vols. LXXV, LXXVI of *Nihon koten bungaku taikei*. 1964, 1965.

——, ed. *Ōkagami* 大鏡, in *Nihon koten bungaku taikei*, vol. XXI. 1960.

Meigetsuki 明月記, ed. Kokusho Kankōkai. 3 vols. Tōkyō: Kokusho Kankōkai, 1911–1912.

Midō Kampaku ki 御堂關白記. 2 vols. In *Dai Nihon kokiroku* [no vol. numbers]. 1952, 1954.

Midō Kampaku ki (I). Vol. VI of *Nihon koten zenshū*, ser. 1. 1926.

Mitani Eiichi 三谷榮一 and Sekine Yoshiko 關根慶子, eds. *Sagoromo monogatari* 狹衣物語.

Vol. LXXIX of *Nihon koten bungaku taikei*. 1965.

Miyake Kiyoshi 三宅清. "'Sakizaki' no igi「さきざき」の意義," *Kokugo-kokubun*, 24 (Apr. 1955), 48–51.

Miyata Kazuichirō 宮田和一郎. *Ōchō san nikki shinshaku* 王朝三日記新釋. Tōkyō: Kembunsha, 1956.

Nakagawa Kiun 中川喜雲. *Kyō warabe* 京童, in *Kinsei bungei sōsho* 近世文藝叢書, ed. Kokusho Kankōkai, vol. I [*Meishoki* 名所記 (I)]. Tōkyō: Kokusho Kankōkai, 1910.

Nihon kiryaku 日本紀略. Vols. X, XI of *Shintei zōho kokushi taikei*. 1934.

Nishio Kōichi 西尾光一. "Chūsei setsuwa bungaku 中世說話文學," in *Iwanami kōza Nihon bungaku* 岩波講座日本文學, vol. VI. Tōkyō: Iwanami Shoten, 1959.

Nishishita Kyōichi 西下經一, ed. *Sarashina nikki* 更級日記, in *Nihon koten bungaku taikei*, vol. XX. 1962.

Niwa, Tamako, trans. *Nakatsukasa Naishi nikki*. Unpublished Dissertation. Harvard University, 1955.

Ōgishō 奥義抄, in *Nihon kagaku taikei* 日本歌學大系, ed. Sasaki Nobutsuna 佐佐木信綱, vol. I. Tōkyō: Bummeisha, 1940.

Ōtsu Yūichi 大津有一 and Tsukishima Hiroshi 築島裕, eds. *Ise monogatari* 伊勢物語, in *Nihon koten bungaku taikei*, vol. IX, 1957.

Ouki 小右記. Vols. I–III of *Shiryō taisei*. 1935–1936.

Reischauer, Edwin O., and Joseph K. Yamagiwa. *Translations from Early Japanese Literature*. Cambridge: Harvard University Press, 1951.

Ruijū fusenshō 類聚符宣抄, in *Shintei zōho kokushi taikei*, vol. XXVII. 1933.

Sakakura Atsuyoshi 阪倉篤義, ed. *Taketori monogatari* 竹取物語, in *Nihon koten bungaku taikei*, vol. IX. 1957.

Sakamoto Tarō 坂本太郎, Ienaga Saburō 家永三郎, Inoue Mitsusada 井上光貞, and Ōno Susumu, eds. *Nihon shoki* 日本書紀. Vols. LXVII, LXVIII of *Nihon koten bungaku taikei*. 1965–1967.

Seidensticker, Edward G., trans. *The Kagerō Nikki. Transactions of the Asiatic Society of Japan*, ser. 3, IV (June 1955); revised and republished as *The Gossamer Years: A Diary by a Noblewoman of Heian Japan*. Tokyo and Rutland, Vt.: Charles E. Tuttle Co., 1964.

Shūgaishō 拾芥抄, in *Shintei zōho kojitsu sōsho* 新訂增補故實叢書, ed. Kawabata Sanehide 川端實秀, vol. XXII. Tōkyō: Meiji Tosho Shuppan Kabushiki Kaisha, 1952.

Sompi bummyaku 尊卑分脈. Vols. LVIII, LIX, LX (parts 1 and 2)+index (*bekkan* 別卷 2) in *Shintei zōho kokushi taikei*. 1959–1964.

Sōshi yoku [Chuang-tzu-i] 莊子翼, in *Kambun taikei* 漢文大系, ed. Hattori Unokichi 服部宇之吉, vol. IX. Tōkyō: Fuzambō, 1911.

Sozawa Takichi 曾澤太吉. "'Nikki' wa hatashite Chūgoku kara no shakuyōgo ka「日記」は果して中國からの借用語か," *Kokugo-kokubun*, 27 (Oct. 1958), 96–105.

Suzuki Tomotarō, ed. *Tosa nikki* 土佐日記, in *Nihon koten bungaku taikei*, vol. XX. 1962.

Tachibana Shōichi 橘正一. *Hōgengaku gairon* 方言學概論. Tōkyō: Ikuei Shoin, 1941.

Tamai Kōsuke, ed. *Kenju Gozen nikki* 健壽御前日記, in *Nihon koten zensho* [no vol. number]. 1963.

—— *Tōnomine Shōshō monogatari: hombun hihan to kaishaku* 多武峯少将物語本文批判と解釋. Tōkyō: Hanawa Shobō, 1960.

Tsunoda Bun'ei 角田文衞. *Jōkyōden no nyōgo* 承香殿の女御. Tōkyō: Chūō Kōronsha, 1963.

Tsunoda, Ryusaku, Wm. Theodore de Bary, and Donald Keene. *Sources of the Japanese Tradition*. New York: Columbia University Press, 1958.

Umegaki Minoru 楳垣實. *Yome ga kimi* 嫁が君. Tōkyō: Tōkyōdō, 1961.

Vos, Frits. *A Study of the Ise Monogatari with the Text According to the Den-Teika-hippon, and an Annotated Translation.* 2 vols. The Hague: Mouton & Co., 1957.

Waley, Arthur, trans. *The Pillow-Book of Sei Shōnagon.* New York: Grove Press, Inc., 1960.

——, trans. *The Tale of Genji.* (Modern Library, G–38) New York: Random House, 1960.

Wang Ch'ung 王充. *Lun-heng* 論衡, in *Han-Wei ts'ung-shu* 漢魏叢書, ts'e 68.

Yamada Yoshio 山田孝雄, Yamada Tadao 忠雄, Yamada Hideo 英雄, and Yamada Toshio 俊雄, eds. *Konjaku monogatari* 今昔物語. Vols. XXII–XXVI of *Nihon koten bungaku taikei.* 1959–1963.

Yamagishi Tokuhei, ed. *Genji monogatari* 源氏物語. Vols. XIV–XVIII of *Nihon koten bungaku taikei.* 1958–1963.

——, ed. *Heichū monogatari* 平中物語, in *Nihon koten zensho* [no vol. number]. 1959.

——, ed. *Takamura monogatari* 篁物語, in *Nihon koten zensho* [no vol. number]. 1959.

Yanagita Kunio. "Josei to minkan denshō 女性と民間傳承," in *Teihon Yanagita Kunio shū* 定本柳田國男集, vol. VIII. Tōkyō: Chikuma Shobō, 1962.

Yokoyama, Masako. "The Inflections of 8th-century Japanese," *Language*, XXVI, Suppl.: Language Dissertation no. 45 (July-Sept. 1950).

Yoshizawa Yoshinori 吉澤義則. *Genji monogatari imakagami* 源氏物語今かがみ. Tōkyō: Shin Nihon Tosho Kabushiki Kaisha, 1948.

—— *Kōhon butsurui shōko shokoku hōgen sakuin* 校本物類稱呼諸國方言索引. Tōkyō, Kyōto: Ritsumeikan Shuppambu, 1933.

II. English Translations

General Index

Seng Chao, 264n178
Senior Secretary (Daishin), 5
Senji, 292n359
Senshi, *see* Akiko [Senshi]
Sen'yōden, 12, 13, 202n64. *See also* Jōshi
Senzaishū: and date of *Izumi Shikibu nikki*, 45, 46, 59, 60, 63, 69; *Senzaishū* poem *no. 968* and authorship of *Izumi Shikibu nikki*, 60, 61; *no. 843* and authorship of *Izumi Shikibu nikki*, 61; *no. 968*, 132; *no. 843*, 135
Sesonji Koreyuki, 225n299
Sesshō, 198n4, 251n96
Setsubun, 280n277
Setsuwa, 51, 209n151, 209n152, 210n153, 227n320
Settsu, Governor of: Fujiwara no Yasumasa, 15
Shakushin'a, 264n178
Shansi Province, 224n298
Shell-matching, 91
"Shell-Matching Held . . . in Honor of . . . Princess Ryōshi," 91
Shichikuan, *see* Koshigaya Gozan
Shigure, 263n176, 263n177
Shijōnomiya Shimotsuke, 112–113, 223n294
Shijōnomiya Shimotsuke shū, 112–113, 223n294
Shikashū (a *chokusenshū*): poem *no. 239*, 18; *no. 253*, 18; *no. 311*, 17
Shikashū (ie no shū), 102, 104–106, 112, 113, 114, 115, 116, 119; related to *nikki*, 102–116 *passim*; related to *utamonogatari*, 118–125 *passim*
Shikibu, a nickname, 6
Shikibushō (Ministry of Ceremonial), 6, 200n29
Shikimi, 24, 206n108
Shimabarabon, 40
Shimizu Fumio, 7, 8, 11, 52, 56, 212n176, 235ff n17, n18, n26, n42, n43, n53, n109, n110, n207, n212, n348, n354, n358, n363, n365, n381
Shimotsuke, Governor of: Minamoto no Masatada, 223n294
Shinchokusenshū, 62, 65, 225n300; poem *no. 643*, 132; *no. 644*, 133; *no. 825*, 135; *no. 826*, 135
Shinchūnagon, 8, 201n44
Shinden-zukuri, 236n19, 239n34, 249n87, 281n279
Shinkambon, 119
Shinkokinshū, 67, 214n193, 215n209, 226n306; poem *no. 1169* and authorship of *Izumi Shikibu nikki*, 52, 61, 62, 67, 68; and *Izumi Shikibu nikki*, 63, 65, 67, 68; *no. 1169*, translated, 157
Shinnō, 242n48
Shinobu, 96, 256n128
Shinobu no midare, 96
Shinobugusa. *see* "Grasses of longing"
Shinobuzuri, 96

Shinsenzaishū, 62; poem *no. 1739*, 132
Shinzokukokinshū, 62
Shirakawa-in, 219n243
Shirotae, 270n225
Shishi, Princess, 295n377
Shitōkan system, 239n29
Shitomi, 249n87, 256n122
Shō (Lesser), *see* Rank system
Shō (Senior), *see* Rank system
Shōbu, see *Ayame no sekku*
Shōgatsu kotoba, 204n83
Shōgen, 239n29
Shoi, *see* Rank system
Shōjin, see *Sōji*
Shōkōkan Bunko, 41
Shōkōkan text (ms. of *Izumi Shikibu seishū*), 200n27
Shokoku hōgen butsurui shōko, 204n83
Shōkū Shōnin, 6, 7, 21, 22, 23, 249n82
Shokugosenshū, 62; poem *no. 438*, 159
Shokujosei, *see* Tanabata
Shokukokinshū, 62; poem *no. 1182*, 160
Shokusenzaishū, 62; poem *no. 1423*, 159
Shōnin: title explained, 200n32
Shoshazan, 7, 21, 22
Shōshi, *see* Akiko [Shōshi]; Masako [Shōshi]
Shōshō, 233n7, 238n29, 257n135
Shōsō, 239n29
Shōyūki, see Ouki
Shū: a form of Heian literature, 98. *See also Akazome Emon shū; Chokusenshū; Fubokuwakashō; Fu no Dainagon no haha-ue no shū; Gonchūnagon Sadayori-kyō shū; Gosenshū; Goshūishū; Ise shū; Izumi Shikibu kashū; Juntoku-in gyoshū; Kenreimon'in Ukyō no Daibu shū; Kin'yōshū; Kokinrokujō; Kokinshū; Man'yōshū; Murasaki Shikibu shū; Seishū; Senzaishū; Shikashū (a chokusenshū); Shikashū (ie no shū); Shinchokusenshū; Shinkokinshū; Shinsenzaishū; Shinzokukokinshū; Shokugosenshū; Shokukokinshū; Shokusenzaishū; Shūishū; Shunzei-kyō no musume no shū; Wakan rōeishū; Zokushū*
Shūgaishō, 4, 199n16
Shūishū, 6; date and compiler, 4, 7, 200n28; quoted, 4; poem *no. 435*, 255n119; *no. 470*, 268n212; *no. 672*, 247n73; *no. 733*, 232n1; *no. 761*, 256n127; *no. 930*, 247n77; *no. 958*, 249n86; *no. 1104*, 260n152; *no. 1342*, 6 (*see also* "Kuraki yori" poem)
Shunkamon'in, 66
Shunzei, *see* Fujiwara Shunzei
Shunzei-kyō no musume, *see* "Shunzei's daughter"

Paul Schalow